The Complete Guide

TO WRITING SCIENCE FICTION: VOLUME ONE

FIRST CONTACT

EDITED BY DAVE A. LAW & DARIN PARK

WITH CHAPTERS BY: MICHELE ACKER, JEANNE ALLEN,
PIERS ANTHONY, MILENA BENINI, ORSON SCOTT CARD,
CAROL HIGHTSHOE, IAN IRVINE, DAVE A. LAW,
WIL MCCARTHY, MICHAEL MCRAE, TINA MORGAN,
BOB NAILOR, DARIN PARK, KIM RICHARDS,
SIMON ROSE, AND BUD SPARHAWK

DRAGON
MOON
PRESS

WWW.DRAGONMOONPRESS.COM

The Complete Guide to Writing Science Fiction:
Volume One ~ First Contact

Copyright © 2007 Dave A Law & Darin Park, Editors
Cover Art © 2007 Dragon Moon Press, with thanks to NASA
Interior Art © 2007 Janice Blaine

ISBN 10 1-896944-39-6 Print Edition
ISBN 13 978-1-896944-39-5

ISBN 10 1-896944-53-1 Electronic Edition
ISBN 13 978-1-896944-53-1

www.dragonmoonpress.com

Front Image: PIA8042 "Extreme Planets" is a shot from the Spitzer Space
Telescope. While we thankfully use the image from NASA, it should not be
interpreted as an endorsement for this book.

The Complete Guide

TO WRITING SCIENCE FICTION: VOLUME ONE

FIRST CONTACT

EDITED BY DAVE A. LAW & DARIN PARK

TABLE OF CONTENTS

PART I
DEFINING

CHAPTER ONE

TIME LINE: A HISTORY OF SCIENCE FICTION

Darin Park

"A handy short definition of almost all science fiction might read: realistic speculation about possible future events, based solidly on adequate knowledge of the real world, past and present, and on a thorough understanding of the nature and significance of the scientific method. To make this definition cover all science fiction (instead of 'almost all') it is necessary only to strike out the word 'future.'"
Robert A. Heinlein (1907 – 1988)

The title of this book is a bit of a misnomer: *The Complete Guide to Writing Science Fiction*. How is it possible to include everything about writing science fiction in just one book? The quick answer: it is not. What *is* possible is to include all the elements necessary to write a science fiction story or novel in order to complete the process of finalizing your work. Thus, *The Complete Guide to Writing Science Fiction* is a guide to aid writers in their quest to complete their work.

In order to create a science fiction story or novel, or for that matter, any fiction, a writer must indulge in the hard work of research. Every element in every story must ring true to the reader in order to maintain the suspension of disbelief. In science fiction (sci-fi, or more recently, SF) this is especially true, as the writer must create a believable context for stories as well as a solid foundation for the science inherent in the story. Which brings us to the next question: What is science fiction?

To explore the question and find our own answers, let's take a short trip through the history of SF starting with tales in ancient times to the modern styling of today's master writers.

PREHISTORY

Before written language, obviously, there was the spoken word. People communicated to each other in grunts, which later developed to a more sophisticated phonetically enhanced series of sounds. Although the written language has been present in most societies for thousands of years, it is within the oral language and the telling of tales where science fiction and fantasy most likely had its beginnings.

Possibly the oldest written story that can compare to workings of modern science fiction is written on 12 clay tablets in cuneiform script. *The Sumerian Epic of Gilgamesh* is about a historical King of Urek circa 2750 and 2500 B.C.E. *Gilgamesh* entails many elements of a modern day science fiction adventure: travel in exotic settings, the quest for immortality, alien life forms, and a hero with superhuman abilities. Another early tale is the Greek tale of Homer's epic, *The Odyssey*, written in 800 B.C.E. The story takes place after the fall of Troy and follows the Greek hero, Odysseus, through ten years of mystical adventures. Although it is a myth utilizing Gods of Greek culture, *The Odyssey* is a testament to the workings of imagination that can create a great story to entrance its audience and feed the ever-curious mind of the human being.

And human beings are indeed curious creatures. That curiosity creates in the mind suppositions for real world events. It is the formulation of the basic "what if" scenario that instills ideas to create stories, be it science fiction, fantasy, or any genre of writing. Travelers' tales, stories told by wanderers, were often well met in ancient times. The locals were entranced by tales of faraway lands they had never visited and most probably, the tellers of these tales embellished them to make their stories more exciting. Likely, the stories were based upon monsters or other such creatures and not what is considered "science fiction", but it is in the telling of the tales using imagination to embellish that creates the basic groundwork for science fiction. It is the idea of these possibilities that are non-existent in the real world but just may be able to occur with advancement in science that is the fundamental crux for science fiction.

SCIENCE IN EARLY SCIENCE FICTION

With an increase in scientific knowledge and technology, unrealistic tales slowly gave way to more credible versions of fantastic tales. As science supplanted myth, stories began to take on a more science-oriented direction. As early as 1634, Johannes Kepler's *Somnium* (The Dream) showed imaginary journeys to the moon. There was, as well, Cyrano de Bergerac's *Comical History of the States* and *Empires of the Moon* in 1656. Margaret Cavendish described an Arctic alternate world in the 1666 novel, *The Description of a New World, Called the Blazing-World*, which contained Spider-Men, Bear-Men, Lice-Men, and Ant-men. Space travel was described in *Micromegas* in 1752 by Voltaire. On a more socioeconomic basis, dealing with life in the future, Louis-

Sebastien Mercier wrote *L'An 2440* in 1752. Alien cultures are visited in the always popular *Gulliver's Travels* by Jonathan Swift in 1726 and *Niels Klim's Underground Travels* by Ludvig Holberg.

The 19th century saw science exposition tales grow in number through the workings of Edgar Allan Poe, Nathainel Hawthorne, and Fitz-James O'Brien. Alfred Lord Tennyson wrote *Locksley Hall* and talks about "the fairy tales of science and the long result of time." Voltaire called *Micromegas* a philosophical story rather than a fairy tale.

Perhaps the most famous novel of this early science fiction period is *Frankenstein* by Mary Shelley in 1818. This work is hailed as the first true science fiction story, although another of Shelley's works, *The Last Man*, published in 1826 could be cited as the first true science fiction tale.

EUROPE—SCIENCE FICTION

Although popularized in America, science fiction began most notably in Europe in the 19th century with the "scientific romances" of Jules Verne with inventor type fiction and the novels of H.G. Wells, who often used science based stories to vent social criticism. Other authors of the day rivaled the two major influencing authors with stories of their own. Samuel Butler published *Erewhon* in 1872, a startlingly prescient look at the idea that sentient machines could one day replace human beings. The creator of Sherlock Holmes, Sir Arthur Conan Doyle, dabbled in science fiction as well. One of his works, titled *The Lost World*, is a tale of an island, which features survivors of a shipwreck who have to deal with a plethora of dinosaurs.

Although known primarily for other great works such as *A Tale of Two Cities* and the supernatural thriller, *A Christmas Carol*, Charles Dickens ventured into the field of science fiction with his novel *Bleak House* in 1852 where one of his characters dies by spontaneous human combustion.

Another great British science fiction writer was Olaf Stapledon whose many works consisted of a recurring theme of trans-human condition and superminds composed of many individual consciousnesses. Many writers have since adopted the ideas he proposed in his major works, most notably, *Last and First Men* published in 1930, *Odd John*, 1935, *Star Maker*, 1937 and *Sirius* in 1940.

John Wyndham (1903 - 1969) is best known for his novel, *The Day of the Triffids*. His works generated a great deal of popularity and critical acclaim, although he used "logical fantasy" to describe his writings as opposed to "science fiction." He wrote almost exclusively for the American pulp magazine market, using many different pen names, but after the Second World War generated fame and fandom under his own name to a widening audience of science fiction fans and the general public.

AMERICA—EARLY SCIENCE FICTION

As the readership of the early pioneers of SF such as Wells and Verne reached international proportions, writers in America were also influenced by the genre embraced by the British and French authors. Even satirical writer, Mark Twain, wrote a science fiction story based on the "transmigration of souls" in his work, *A Connecticut Yankee In King Arthur's Court.* Jack London wrote an extraterrestrial story, *The Red One* and several others with a science fiction flavor including, *The Iron Heel* a futuristic story and *The Unparalleled Invasion* about germ warfare and ethnic cleansing. His stories included such ideas as invisibility and energy weapons. These kinds of ideas impacted science fiction and began a change in story format. More and more, science fiction became solidly grounded with the science required to enable the story to become a believable work with literary roots.

Edgar Rice Burroughs wrote science fiction for pulp magazines, publishing his first story, *Under the Moons of Mars* in 1912. He wrote many science fiction stories but his most famous story involved a man raised by apes, *Tarzan.* Before World War I, Edgar Rice Burroughs wrote mostly for pulp magazines and "pulp fiction" as it later became known had a dramatic impact on the readers of science fiction.

When Hugo Gernsback founded *Amazing Stories* magazine in 1926, this pulp magazine published as its mainstay "scientification" tales exclusively. Although such stories were viewed as sensationalism and not true literature, public awareness of the scientific speculation story grew dramatically because of this magazine. Other pulp magazines emulated this format and presented the genre to the general public. Hugo Gernsback became known as the "father of science fiction". The much-coveted Hugo Award given to writers for exemplary stories commemorates his contributions to the science fiction field.

SCIENCE FICTION—THE GOLDEN AGE

It was with the advent of pulp magazines that the Golden Age of science fiction began. In January 1930, the first issue of *Astounding* was published. The Golden Age of science fiction is roughly attributed to the summer of 1939 with the publication of the July issue of *Astounding* to the end of 1950. Not coincidentally, the start of this era began when an engineer, educated at the Massachusetts Institute of Technology and Duke University, took the helm of *Astounding* in

1938 at the age of 27. John W. Campbell Jr. essentially reworked and shaped science fiction as editor of *Astounding* and it was through his machinations that the Golden Age flourished. His theorems for good story telling were grounded in several ideologies: physics, chemistry, astronomy, and sciences in which laws are mathematically verifiable, biological sciences, disciplines which are in part descriptive or impure because they deal with living creatures and social sciences, such as anthropology, economics, political science, and experimental psychology, humanities such as theology, philosophy and clinical psychology.

As an intellectual, Campbell published stories in *Astounding* that had plenty of aliens in keeping with Campbell's faith that space travel was possible. He chose to publish fiction that dealt with the belief that the universe was not essentially hostile to man and that the decisions of human beings and their consequent actions counted in the universe. It as during Campbell's reign in the Golden Age of science fiction that prolific authors such as Isaac Asimov, Robert Heinlein, and Arthur C. Clarke began to contribute their stories. Science fiction rapidly developed into a genre that was fast becoming accepted as serious fiction.

Isaac Asimov, one of the most intellectual science fiction writers in the last century, divided science fiction into four distinct categories: from 1926 to 1938, adventure dominant; from 1938 to 1950, science dominant; from 1950 to 1965, sociology dominant and from 1966 to present, style dominant. Asimov survived through the last three of the four categories, writing a staggering number of books, over 500, before he died in 1992. Nightfall published in the September 1941 issue of *Astounding* has been voted the best science fiction story of all time and it is poetic that this story was created during the Golden Age of science fiction.

It was during this era of science fiction that Orson Welles produced a radio version of H.G. Wells' *The War of the Worlds*, which panicked radio listeners. They believed the program to be a real newscast and public mythology now allowed for the idea of invaders from outer space, which brought about by the popularization of science fiction.

Post World War II there was a great boom in the popularity of science fiction, although in the Soviet Union and European nations it was used as a vehicle for political commentary. Throughout the 1940s and 1950s, science fiction dealt mainly with atomic energy, flying saucers, and basic space opera. The continuance of the never-ending operatic stories involving mad scientists, robots turning on their masters and "Buck Rogers" type of stories eventually led to the downfall of Golden Age science fiction and virtual disappearance of pulp magazines. A new style of writing began to emerge as a result, beginning the "modern era" and the "New Wave."

MODERN SCIENCE FICTION

Modern science fiction is considered to have begun in the mid 1960s with the emergence of soft science fiction. Soft science fiction relied less on science for the grounding of stories and more on the concept of the mind and social implications of science as it impacted on human beings. In 1965, Frank Herbert published *Dune*, a highly complex detailed novel that intertwined political intrigue and religious beliefs in a future galaxy on the desert planet Arrakis. Not only did the novel explore the science in science fiction, it explored socioeconomic impact on the people in the story, language, and society.

Writers in Britain led the way with the New Wave, experimenting with surrealism, drama and using psychological and mainstream currents as the focal point for fiction. William Burroughs influenced this change in direction to a large degree and this new field of science fiction increased the breadth of subject matter, the depth of its treatment, political and literary consciousness of writing, more sophistication of language and technique and sexuality. The New Wave introduced for the first time more than a passing glance at sex in science fiction leading to a number of original works that investigated how sex could be an interesting source of material for the genre. The number of writers and readers increased exponentially as a result.

The New Wave is attributed to have started in England with Michael Moorcock who in 1964 became editor of the magazine, *New Worlds* (founded in 1946), while Harlan Ellison, a visionary in stylistic fiction, is heralded as the New Wave prophet. In an attempt to secure a place for science fiction in the literary mainstream, emphasis was placed on style and experimental writing with less attention to scientific accuracy. Also known as "soft" science fiction, many New Wave authors wrote themes concerning sociological and psychological impact. These included: general distrust of both science and technology, as well as mankind itself; shared conviction that things are getting worse, not better; belief that man's intelligence cannot save us from current predicaments; disbelief that man is inherently good; overall, that mankind is contemptible or of no consequence.

In the 1960s, almost every writer who made noteworthy contributions to science fiction became known as a New Wave writer. Predominantly, the New Wave authors included: Michael Moorcock, Jerry Cornelius, Brian Aldiss, J.G. Ballard, and Harlan Ellison. Philip K. Dick is included in this group but is described as an intellectual with roots in pulp fiction. Other New Wave authors included: Ursula K. LeGuin, Philip Jose Farmer, Samuel R. Delany, and Roger Zelazny.

As the New Wave took hold, science fiction began a flirtatious relationship with television. *Star Trek* brought realistic science fiction to a mass audience for the first time. Its appeal was such that even today there are books still written by authors predominantly interested in producing "fan fiction" (see the chapter on Fan Fiction) to keep the original premise of Gene Roddenberry's visionary series alive for a legion of fans.

Popular science fiction films were made, including most significantly *Doctor Strangelove, 2001: A Space Odyssey, THX 1138, The Andromeda Strain, A Clockwork Orange, Close Encounters of the Third Kind, Star Wars, Battlestar Galactica*, and a host of others. The most successful of these films, *Star Wars*, released in 1977, created an intense interest in science fiction for several years following its release, although the film itself can be best classed as a hybrid science fiction/fantasy story rather than pure science fiction.

The New Wave revolution in science fiction had now developed a literary foothold, which paved the way for writers to develop hard science fiction with style and character development, the precursor to the present-day modern science fiction. New technologies dominated the scene in the late 1970s and authors such as Frederik Pohl, enjoying heydays in the Golden Age, embraced modern science fiction and created works that excelled both in technology and character driven plots. Isaac Asimov flourished for several years into the modern era followed closely by Robert A. Heinlein. Orson Scott Card contributed to the genre with *Ender's Game* in 1985, which won the Hugo and the Nebula and went on to write its sequel, *Speaker for the Dead,* and the final two volumes in the series *Xenocide* and *Children of the Mind.*

SCIENCE FICTION—AT PRESENT AND BEYOND

Science fiction continues to grow in sophistication and intellectualization. With a wider emphasis on societal and psychological issues, its infancy has been shaken off and science fiction is now viewed as serious literature, which is studied in universities and colleges. The know-it-all-engineer who could immediately apply a fix to a problem has become a much rarer plot device. Modern science fiction has come to explore characters, their emotions and drives, plots concerning failures and limitations, and the human psyche as it relates to socioeconomic and psychological factors. In general, today's science fiction does not use or need violence or hard science as plot standards. There is tendency for some works to stray in the area of what is now called science fantasy, a trend exemplified by the Star Wars movies.

Included in modern science fiction is a subgenre called "Cyberpunk." "Cyber," of course, relates to computers and information systems, while "punk" refers to rebellious youth. *Neuromancer* published by William Gibson in 1984 and winner of both the Hugo and Nebula is considered the first cyberpunk novel. Definitively "New Wave", cyberpunk deals with the abstract world of virtual reality and artificial intelligence, usually set in the near future in a decaying technological society. The real world is a shadowy place for the characters in these stories and often they escape into cyberspace to relieve the tedium of pointless lives. Although finding a niche in science fiction for the short term, cyberpunk has not created much headway and its short life at this point appears to have ended.

Science fiction has come a long way since its birth throes and has gone through many changes. As of 2006, it seems that once more it is being edged out of popularity by an increasing interest in fantasy-related stories, such as *The Lord of the Rings* by J.R.R. Tolkien, (re-popularized by Peter Jackson's portrayal of the book on film). However, now that *Star Wars* has finally come full circle with Episodes 1, 2 and 3, there may be a re-awakening of the genre for a short burst of renewed interest.

This has been a short trip through the history of Science Fiction, and as such, there have been many leaps in this chapter, some of those jumps skipping over famous authors and periods in this genre's rich history. There is limited room in this volume to give you no more than a taste, but maybe that taste is enough to enhance the flavor and whet your appetite for a more detailed study. Indulge yourself. The more you learn about your chosen field, the better you will become at writing.

CHAPTER TWO

SEARCHING FOR THE DEFINITIVE DEFINITION OF SCIENCE FICTION

Jeanne Allen

INTRODUCTION

Type "definition of science fiction" into an internet search engine, and you're likely to find more entries than you can swing a laser sword at. In quotes from Asimov to Heinlein to names less familiar, definitions of science fiction often include words like science fact, scientific method, technology, rational, plausible, extrapolation, speculation, future, impact on society, modern myth, metaphor, and literature of change.

If your plan is to make money writing science fiction, it's important to know the market and the types of works science fiction publishers are searching for before submitting your stories. The intent of this chapter is to introduce you to various interpretations of the term science fiction by many who work in the field. It also aims to help you decide where your own stories fit within the spectrum of these definitions so you can better decide where to submit your works.

ACCENT ON SCIENCE

To understand what science fiction is, we'll begin with a review of the term science.

Science is a body of knowledge, and it's the process for obtaining that knowledge through the use of the scientific method, which involves taking systematic steps in the search for new facts. The scientific method requires recognition of a problem by asking a testable question, hypothesizing the answer to the question, collecting data through observation and experimentation, and then drawing conclusions from the data, which may support or disprove the hypothesis.

If much experimentation and evidence lead to the same conclusion, a scientific theory or law may result. Anyone performing the same experiment will arrive at the same result, no matter what his or her individual beliefs are.

But scientific theories are not set in stone. They may change over time as new evidence presents itself. For instance, it was long thought the Earth was the center of the universe until Copernicus proposed a sun-centered planetary system. Atoms were once thought to resemble tiny billiard balls until the electron, proton, and neutron were discovered. We now have an understanding of DNA's central role in determining the traits of living things.

Technology is the practical application of scientific discoveries. For example, not long after the electron was discovered, television was invented. And we've discovered the means to manipulate DNA. A gene from a fluorescent jellyfish can be used to make a mouse's skin glow.

SCIENCE FICTION

How does science relate to science fiction? In his book *Worlds of Wonder: How to Write Science Fiction & Fantasy*, David Gerrold writes: "Because science fiction is rooted in science...the writer has a responsibility to stay consistent within that body of knowledge."[1] Or, stated another way, those who write science fiction are not allowed to rewrite the laws of nature.

Ben Bova, in his book The Craft of Writing Science Fiction that Sells, makes this statement: "Science fiction stories are those in which some aspect of future science or high technology is so integral to the story that, if you take away the science or technology, the story collapses."[2]

Could *Jurassic Park* be the science fiction thriller it is without the idea of dinosaur DNA being extracted from mosquitoes preserved in amber? Absolutely not.

There are stories some refer to as "Mars Westerns," meaning, if you take away the ray guns and rocket ships and replace them with pistols and stagecoaches, the story line wouldn't be much different. The piece wouldn't collapse if the science was removed.

Robert Heinlein expressed it this way: "...The result can be extremely fantastic in content, but it is not fantasy; it is legitimate—and often very tightly reasoned—speculation about the possibilities of the real world...."[3]

Many consider science fiction a metaphor, its elements symbolic of the human condition. Futuristic societies are metaphors, as are alien life-forms and space travel. From this idea one could say, from a writer's imagination springs truth.

SCIENCE FICTION AS THE LITERATURE OF CHANGE

Science fiction is often called the "literature of change." In recent centuries, our world has gone through accelerating advancements in scientific discovery, in areas such as astronomy, evolution, relativity, computing, and how the body works. People have grown to believe the universe is knowable, and they hold the power to control their destinies, to accomplish virtually anything. We're able to send space probes beyond Pluto, develop smaller and faster computer chips, manipulate our genes, and aim warheads with surgical precision. We can change the world's ecology. Science fiction authors explore the consequences of such changes and make predictions based on what is happening now. Will new discoveries and technologies be used for good or bad? How will these changes continue to affect the individual and whole societies?

Frederik Pohl gives us this insightful passage about science fiction: "Does the story tell me something worth knowing, that I had not known before, about the relationship between man and technology? Does it enlighten me on some area of science where I had been in the dark?... Does it illuminate events and trends of today, by showing me where they may lead tomorrow? Does it give me a fresh and objective point of view on my own world and culture, perhaps by letting me see it through the eyes of a different kind of creature entirely, from a planet light-years away?"[4]

H. Bruce Franklin composed this definition: "Science fiction is the major non-realistic mode of imaginative creation of our epoch. It is the principal cultural way we locate ourselves imaginatively in time and space."[5] Continuing down this line of thought, the scope of science fiction is infinite. A science fiction story can project from our place in history to anywhere in the cosmos, during any time in the past, present, or future.

Deron Douglas, founder of Double Dragon Publishing, has this to say about how science fiction relates to change: "In most cases a good science fiction story will propose a situation that transcends and extends conventional insight much as old-time fables did in the past. While science fiction uses technology as its core device, it's about people and their reactions to their changing surroundings and each other."[6]

SCIENCE FICTION, HARD OR SOFT?

Science fiction can also be categorized as "hard" or "soft." At the core of hard science fiction is detail and accuracy in the "hard" sciences, such as physics, chemistry, and biology. The story's conclusion hinges on a scientific or technological development. Greg Bear's *Darwin's Radio*, for example, is known for its scientific details regarding molecular biology and evolution.

Soft science fiction focuses on human feelings over scientific detail and may be based on the "softer" sciences such as psychology and sociology. Ursula LeGuin tends to write social science fiction. For instance, her novel, *The Lathe of Heaven*, is a futuristic story about how a man's dreams alter world affairs and the ramifications of playing God.

SCIENCE FICTION, FANTASY, SPECULATIVE FICTION?

The NCF Guide to Canadian Science Fiction and Fandom website, edited by Robert Runté, takes the position that defining science fiction isn't so straightforward: "No one has ever managed to come up with a truly satisfactory definition of science fiction. Either the definition is too broad, including works which are clearly fantasy or horror, or else so narrow that it excludes much of the recognized field."[7]

Consider the following list of words: dragon, magic crystal, faery ring, wizard. What type of story do they bring to mind? Elements of magic or the supernatural are the basis for fantasy literature. A magic ring can bring unimaginable power to the one who wears it. Science isn't required to explain how it works.

Now consider this list: time machine, faster-than-light travel, wormhole gate to a parallel world. Are these the makings for a science fiction story? Some would agree, though others would place them in the genre of science fantasy because they don't obey known laws of physics. Many, however, regard these impossible technologies as acceptable conventions of science fiction if they're used in a realistic way. We can believe they may be developed in the future.

Orson Scott Card writes about the difference between science fiction and fantasy in his *How to Write Science Fiction and Fantasy*: "...science fiction is about what could be but isn't; fantasy is about what couldn't be." He goes on to say: "If you have people do some magic, impossible thing by stroking a talisman or praying to a tree, it's fantasy; if they do the same thing by pressing a button or climbing inside a machine, it's science fiction."[8]

James Gunn in *The Science of Writing Science Fiction* offers this view: "The basis of fantasy is psychological truth; nothing else matters. The basis of science fiction is the real world. Does the story respond to hard questions? Nothing else matters."[9]

In this light, if a special agent is given the job of hunting down the culprit who kidnapped a character from a classic work of literature, as in *The Eyre Affair*, we can't ask hard, real-world questions in a story like this. In contrast, in the novel *When Worlds Collide*, astronomers discover a rogue planet from outer space hurtling straight for Earth. The authors strove to make this collision of worlds true-to-life so the reader would think realistically about how such an event might affect the citizens of Earth.

In differentiating between science fiction and fantasy, author Darrell Bain returns us to Runté's comment about the difficulty in finding one satisfactory definition of science fiction. In his article, *"Fantasy vs. Science Fiction,"* Bain first defines both science fiction and fantasy traditionally, then speculates on the fantastic results that could stem from genetic engineering and reminds us of the counter intuitiveness of quantum mechanics. He concedes, "At best, the line between them blurs toward the middle, where the more fantastic the story, the more it resembles fantasy and the more realistic it is, the more it smacks of science fiction. A lot of it meets its other self in passing..."[10]

In bookstores today, it's common to find novels in the Science Fiction section all grouped together based on the very broadest definition of the genre. There are many who read and write both science fiction and fantasy, and, as we've determined, boundaries between the genres often overlap, so perhaps it makes sense to group them all into one section. But not all authors of science fiction desire to see their books blended into a mix, which places serious science fiction alongside science fantasies and tales of sword and sorcery. For this reason, some who write stories based on real science and technology classify their works as speculative fiction. They speculate how advancements in science will affect individuals and whole cultures. It should be noted, however, that others use "speculative fiction" as an all-encompassing term that includes the genres of science fiction, fantasy, horror, paranormal, and alternative history.

IN WHAT CATEGORY DOES YOUR STORY BELONG?

Many publishers are reluctant to define science fiction too narrowly for fear they might miss a worthwhile story among incoming submissions; others are more specific. On its website, Tor reports it publishes a very large and diverse line of science fiction and fantasy. For its science fiction series, Baen Books looks for story lines with "solid scientific and philosophical underpinnings." The independent press Double Dragon Publishing considers a broad range of science fiction stories, though preference is given to works with an "'after-the-holocaust milieu' with either environmental, extraterrestrial, or genocidal elements." *Analog Science Fiction and Fact* magazine searches for strong, realistic stories where the plot centers on some facet of science or technology, while *Asimov's Science Fiction* magazine stresses "character oriented" stories.

This section provides you with a process I used for assessing two of my own stories and is intended for you to use as a model for determining where your own story fits within the scope of science fiction.

In my novel, *Orphilion Dreams,* the planets (and their moons) are being exploited for raw materials. An authoritarian government rules the Solar System. People live and work under strict control and surveillance. The hero and heroine discover literature about past democracies, and it isn't long before they're no longer willing to blindly accept their subordinate status. Following a string of events, they become leaders of a dangerous revolt.

Futuristic? Definitely. Science fiction? Citing Dr. Bova's definition, will the story fall apart if the science is removed? It's a high-tech society in which they live. But could cars have replaced the spaceships? Could countries have replaced the planets? Could a present-day dictatorship have replaced the future government? The technology is such an integral part of the world in which they live, it wouldn't be the same story without it, and there are particular technologies that are important to the story's resolution. It fits in with science fiction being literature of change in the sense that the protagonists undergo a major shift in their worldview and respond to it in a way which significantly impacts their society.

In my novella, *Isadora*, a young woman lives in a post-apocalyptic Earth. She begins to rediscover scientific truths but quickly finds this type of innovative thinking isn't tolerated in her society. A mysterious man encourages her in her pursuit of scientific knowledge, but it must be done in secret. She's overheard to predict a solar eclipse. After the eclipse occurs, she's accused by leaders of her community of possessing evil powers and is sentenced to death.

Could the same story have been written without the science? Is there a change that people must deal with? The woman could have been discovering spiritual or magical truths, but essential to the story is the fact that she uses her skill of observation to learn new things about nature. Leaders become threatened by the philosophical implications brought on by her discoveries. They react in a way to preserve their way of life and Isadora must react rationally if she's to save her own.

- In evaluating your own stories, ask yourself the following questions:

- Is the work centered on real science, or can you take away the science and still have a viable story? Does it respond to hard, real-world questions?

- If the story uses science that is currently impossible, is it used in a realistic way, or is it employed as an element of fantasy?

- Does the story involve a social change because of a new technology or scientific discovery? How are the characters affected by this change? In what way does the change affect the society as a whole?

- How does the story reflect on the human condition today?

These questions aren't meant to set rigid limits on your stories, for where would science fiction literature be today if such boundaries had been set? Rather, the above questions are meant to be used as a guideline as you reflect on the nature of your story.

CONCLUSION

Even though no one definition of science fiction apparently exists, it's safe to assume that science fiction has some common elements. A science fiction story centers around a scientific concept that is essential to the plot, and the story goes on to depict how characters are affected by the change the concept has produced. The concept can be extrapolated from science that is currently known, and it may become so advanced that it borders on the fantastical. At any rate, if the science is removed, the story falls apart, otherwise it's more than likely a "Mars Western," which is not to say it can't be entertaining, but it's not true science fiction by the above standards.

To save a lot of time and misdirection, it's highly recommended that you study the submission guidelines of publishers and read science fiction they've published to see if what you've written is the type of story they seek. Hopefully, the checklist above will help you examine your own work to see where it fits under the umbrella of science fiction.

May you enjoy many successes in your writing!

CHAPTER THREE

SCIENCE FIRST, FICTION SECOND: THAT'S SCIENCE FICTION

Bob Nailor

Today's readers are more astute in their knowledge of scientific facts. A writer of science fiction who doesn't adhere to the basic laws of science will have irritated readers. The reader will find himself or herself constantly jarred out of the story due to obvious incongruities of the facts provided. Editors are just as knowledgeable of science and can quickly tell if the story is based on scientific facts or just a lot of unbelievable falsehoods, and are less likely to publish such a story in the first place.

A writer doesn't necessarily need to have 100% pure science facts in the story, there can be leeway given to expound and create elaborate designs on certain known facts. A good science fiction writer should be able to weave the falsehoods into the story so well that a reader accepts both the real and made up science as truths. There are three things that a writer can use to enhance the story using science to extend the truth:

1.TECHNOBABBLE

This is speaking with science also known as geekoid or geekese. An example would be:

> When the thrusters backfired, it caused an overload of the tyrsonia fields, which bled excessive neutrons out through the main shields.

In the previous sentence, the word 'tyrsonia' is technobabble while the rest of the sentence consists of common words used to describe a bad situation. When used as such, with the babble interweaved inside the conversation, the reader will move silently along accepting it. Of course, technobabble can work against the author if not properly executed, either by using it too much or creating words that sound childish and nonsensical.

2.NON-PHYSICAL POSSIBILITIES

The author creates the words that build the image within the reader's mind. The reader accepts the construction if what is being described is seemingly possible. For example in *Star Trek* the characters often set their guns to stun vs. kill. The reader accepts that a laser gun has settings just as they accept and know that a Colt .45 is only going to shoot a .45 bullet.

3.FLIM-FLAM

This is the art of dismissing certain facts, waving hands to make you ignore the truth. Example: 'Pay no attention to man behind the curtain' and FTL (Faster Than Light) travel. I don't believe that anyone has created a force field as described in so many science fiction novels. Whether we want to believe it or not, FTL has not been attained on any of our space missions although many teenagers may attempt this feat on Saturday nights.

Of course, one caveat a writer must know is that "today's scientific fact can be tomorrow's falsehood."

Let's examine a few facts and falsehoods to get a better understanding of what is stated. After all, anyone can say anything but it requires facts and figures to back it up.

THE EARTH'S FLAT. NO, IT'S ROUND.

Basically we all believe the earth to be round since Columbus discovered the Americas. Of course, until that time, the vocal majority believed the earth to be flat—this includes the scientists of the period. Remember, ancient sailors thought they'd fall off the edge of the world if they sailed beyond the sight of land. So, why did I sound so illusive? The earth can be said to be round but in reality, it is termed an oblate spheroid.[11] The diameter between poles is less than the diameter of the equator hence is has a slightly flattened shape. When writing science fiction, not all your distant planets must be round; using an oblate spheroid will add some interest to your written tale. To have a square planet, one would need to be able to explain how it can exist and spin on its axis. A hollow tubular planet might be easier to explain. Such a concept allows for exploring the differences between those living on the inside versus those on the outside, or even those on the opposite ends.

There is an atmosphere on the moon and life: It was once believed that there was air on the moon matching exactly what was on Earth. It was assumed that when man finally reached the moon they would be able to walk around just as they did on Earth. Jules Verne's novel, *From Earth To The Moon*, assumed that fact and planned for the travelers to walk about without special equipment and greet the inhabitants of the moon. *Apollo 11* proved that there was no atmosphere on the moon.[12] Also, not one alien has come forth to greet any of the astronauts that have visited the lunar surface.

VENUS, THE HOTHOUSE; MERCURY, THE ICEBOX

No, we can't live on Venus. Surprisingly, Venus is actually hotter than Mercury.[13] Although Mercury is closer to the sun, one would think it to be hotter, but since Mercury has virtually no atmosphere, there is nothing to hold the heat in. This means that on the dark side of the planet Mercury, the temperature can dip to a chilling -300 degrees F (-184 degrees C), yet when facing the sun it can get up to 800 degrees F (427 degrees C). Venus, on the other hand, has a very thick blanket consisting of carbon dioxide, water vapor, sulfur dioxide, and sulfuric acid particles. This swirling mish-mash traps all of the heat that Venus collects during the day and slowly releases that heat during the night. Venus' average surface temperature is somewhere around 850 degrees F (454 degrees C). This is definitely an extreme case of the "Greenhouse Effect" and any idea of rushing through a lush jungle of overgrowth to avoid Venusians has been pretty well eliminated by today's scientists.

WE ARE THE CENTER OF THE UNIVERSE. THE SUN REVOLVES THE EARTH

As far back as the 2nd century, Ptolemy decreed that the heavens revolved around Earth. In the 3rd century, the astronomer Aristarchus of Samos claimed that the earth revolved around the sun. It wasn't until the 16th century that Copernicus proved Aristarchus' point. Why did I go back so far? Simple. Storytelling and storytellers have existed since the beginning of time and an ancient Egyptian word weaver would use the knowledge of his time to tell his tale. What was considered scientific fact back then could have since changed or may change again tomorrow. Similarly, if you are writing about an alien planet, the scientific beliefs of that culture could be incorrect, which increases the dimension to your characters.

THE HOLLOW EARTH

For years rumors have surfaced that there is a whole unexplored world that exists in the center of the earth. The stories stretch from living dinosaurs and advanced cavemen to very esoteric, utopian civilizations. Some even believe that this is the source of flying saucers. Earth scientists now know quite a lot about the interior of our planet. By monitoring earthquake vibrations they have discovered the composition of our planet.[14] Earthquakes, especially the big ones, ring the whole planet like a bell. Seismologists, by carefully observing where the quake vibrations start and where they are detected, can tell the densities of the layers of the earth by the waves which they have traveled through.

WHEN A SPACESHIP EXPLODES IN SPACE THERE IS A FLASH

Perhaps there could be an explosion and there would be a sound, but the flash would be strictly momentary and the sound would expire even quicker.[15] Space is a vacuum and therefore sound can't travel through it. Sound travels via vibrations of matter. There are gases in space, which can aide in the explosion but probably not to the extent that we are familiar with from the movies since the only oxygen would be that found inside the spaceship. This oxygen would be so quickly exhausted that it actually would be useless or non-existent for the most part in the explosion. When you expound on a space war battle, remember that the explosion will be extremely short. Still, most readers of science fiction have accepted this aspect.

It is a known fact that in space an extremely small squirt of oxygen will move a body in the opposite direction. If a star cruiser is shooting missiles, there should be some sort of opposite reaction due to the gravitation and atmospheric conditions. Ask any astronaut that has performed a space walk about the intricacies of maneuvering in space and what a simple non-exertive push can do.

THE ATOM IS THE SMALLEST PARTICLE

Almost true. The atom is made up of three parts, which obviously must be smaller than the atom itself. At one time, the molecule was considered the smallest particle. Now take some time and check out hadrons[16] quarks, antiquarks, fermions, gluons, and bosons. That should get your head spinning and give you some great material to infuse your writing. As our technology continues to evolve, so will the depth of how small is small.

EARTH'S SOLAR SYSTEM CONSISTS OF NINE PLANETS

Up until 1930, Earth's solar system consisted on one sun and eight planets that rotated around it. Then Pluto was discovered. Years and decades have passed with schoolchildren learning about the nine planets of our solar system. Only the truly elders can remember back when there were eight planets. Then in August 2006, Pluto, the asteroid Ceres, and the trans-Neptunian object 2003 UB (now named Eris) were redefined as dwarf planets.[17]

A scientific fact as learned by so many over the years suddenly changed, and many stories, especially those dealing with our solar system, that have been written since 1930 will now be 'dated' due to this change.

There are many other scientific facts that have changed over the years since ours is not a stagnant existence as we continue to grow and learn. When you read older science fiction, you will happen upon certain facts that might catch your attention and make you pause to reflect on it.

SF CLASSICS

The older classics, filled with wonder and amazement for the readers of that era, stretched the imagination and goaded the scientists to create the marvels written about. Let's take a look at some of these classics, many written over one hundred years ago. It is amazing based on the science known of the time that the authors were able to create these futuristic marvels with such accuracy.

Twenty Thousand Leagues Under The Sea: Jules Verne wrote this in 1869, in which he described a very large submarine. This was not a fictional item of the time; in 1776, during the Civil War, David Busnell[18] built a one-man submarine, an extremely small egg-shaped contraption. Later, in 1801, American inventor Robert Fulton created a submarine; his was the first to have more than one mode of propulsion. More submarines followed but it was Jules Verne that created a submarine large enough to house not only many people, but also foodstuffs, and equipment. Imagine a cigar-shaped vehicle that was 230 feet (70 meters) long and 26 feet (8 meters) wide[19]—much larger than those in actual use during that period. Another remarkable item that he wrote of was the farming and harvesting of food from the sea. That in itself was not totally innovative since collecting salt from the sea was an age-old task. Still, the idea of collecting certain items from the ocean's floor was new. Today we harvest oysters, seaweed, kelp, and "farm" fish, which include breeding special species specifically for food. This concept of "farming" has been a mainstay for many science fiction writers where there is a colonization of a new planet or long-term travel between the stars. Captain Nemo only brought his submarine to the surface when they had to renew the oxygen tanks or attack some ship; otherwise, the crew existed in a solitary environment much like a crew would in space. The novel delved heavily into nautical terminology, oceanography, and general science as he wove his world for the reader.

From The Earth To The Moon: Jules Verne described a "hollow bullet" rocket that traveled to the moon in this novel. It was written in 1865 and it should be noted that he was not the first writer to describe a rocket as a bullet; Murtagh McDermott described a bullet style rocket in his novel *A Trip To The Moon*, which he wrote in 1728.[20] Today's rockets are elongated bullet shaped vehicles. In Verne's tale, three companions traveled for four days to reach moon. One hundred and four years later, in 1969, three U.S. astronauts spent 4 days reaching the moon.

The Time Machine: written by H. G. Wells in 1895, describes a future where social classes have been defined by two specific races that function without question to exist in a strange harmony. H. G. Wells maneuvers the science so well that it hardly seems to exist. He depicts future events and inventions through small segments and scenario flashes as our hero moves forward in time. The Eloi and the almost perfect environment of paradise that they exist in have been used many times over in later novels to depict mankind's future. The Morlocks are the given, depraved creatures of labor and the underworld representing the evils of mankind. However, it is the Morlocks that are the true rulers in the future and it is here that Wells is able to expand the science fiction of his story elaborating on the machinery and technology.

A Princess of Mars: Author Edgar Rice Burroughs created the character of John Carter in 1912 and transported him to Barsoom, Burroughs' name for Mars. Subtly using science, John Carter is given god-like qualities due to Mar's lighter gravity giving him extreme jumping capabilities, stronger muscles, and quicker reflexes. Edgar Rice Burroughs was the inspiration to later science fiction authors and scientists, including the likes of Ray Bradbury and Carl Sagan.[21]

The War of the Worlds: Written in 1898 by H. G. Wells, it details the invasion of Martians. Their science and machinery are beyond our expertise and it seems that the extinction of mankind is imminent until a germ foils them. This is probably one of the best known tales by H. G. Wells due to its broadcast by Orson Welles and the Mercury Theater on October 30, 1938 not to mention the two different takes by the film industry.

Written nearly one hundred years ago, the above stories helped to define the genre of science fiction by foretelling future events and inventions that might happen. When written they were cutting edge, mind boggling tales that took the reader to unbelievable areas of the mind. Those same stories are still great but many now consider them more tales of adventure rather than science fiction since much of the science is old hat.

Old science? An electric submarine with a crew might have been big news in 1869 but in the year 1969, we are already yawning when we read about a nuclear powered submarine with a crew of over one hundred men[22]. Still, there is science that won't change over the years and that is called scientific basics. What are some of these, you ask?

I'M LOOKING THROUGH ROSE-TINTED GLASSES

Even something as simple as the color of a flower can be distracting in a story if basic scientific laws aren't adhered to. Visualize yourself on a distant planet in some far off galaxy. You shield your eyes from the red sun. Is the grass green? The rose red? If the light spectrum were predominantly red, then the grass would be black, as well as the rose if it were indeed a red rose. If the rose were white, it would reflect back as pink to our eyes. If the shade of the atmosphere is different than then you must adjust what the eyes can see. As stated, simple scientific rules must be followed. Of course, if the character is color-blind, then different rules apply. Most humans can view the color spectrum from violet to red, with ultraviolet and infrared being invisible to our sight. Consider for a moment that your character can't see the color red, which should theoretically make anything that is red invisible as an extension of infrared. Your character would have a color range of violet to some shade of yellow and therefore a slight haze in the air, which he or she would consider normal.

THE GREAT SLINGSHOT EFFECT

It is amazing how many writers will use the "slingshot" theory in their composition when in reality they are actually committing the action to "gravity assist."[23] Think about it. Exactly where does the slingshot action occur? You pull back on a slingshot and when you release, the load will accelerate, but it's had no momentum prior to that. The slingshot hasn't given any extra speed to the load. The extra speed that normally is gained in the so-called slingshot comes from using gravity. You are already in motion and as the object pulls you with its gravity, you gain momentum. This then increases your speed which in turn gives it the momentum to shoot pass the gravitational object and into space. I guess "slingshot" sounds faster and better than "gravity assist" which seems to be a contradiction of terms.

ALIEN ANATOMY

Some say that we will find aliens that are humanoid in form. If you have watched the Star Wars movies, you will find that most of the aliens are indeed in the form of humans with a different head. Even the extra-terrestrial in Predator was human shaped except for the head. Many aspects must be taken into account when creating your alien characters. First and foremost is your planet's gravity; not every planet in the universe is going to be 1.0 Earth gravity—it just doesn't work that way. Mars' one third gravity was taken into account by Edgar Rice Burroughs and therefore allowed John Carter to jump great distances, which astounded the Martian inhabitants. Of course, as Burroughs continued the saga over ten novels, John's ability lessened as his muscles acclimated to Mars. If the planet's gravity is stronger, the alien should be stouter, possibly shorter, and lumbering. If the gravity were lighter than Earth's 1.0 base, then the alien would probably be thinner, taller, and more graceful. The humanoid factor allows the reader to connect with the alien. Zero gravity has been found to be possibly detrimental to humans and prolonged non-gravity might have a major impact on our makeup.[24] A French research team discovered that gravity plays a major role in the way that cells organize their structure. It was found that gravity was necessary for microtubules to form correctly in the cytoskeletons. With this small tidbit of information, you can now guide your story in another direction and use this scientific fact as the basis.

HELLO? HOUSTON?

Communication from some distant planet to Earth is a difficulty. We've watched characters in *Star Trek* send messages back to Star Fleet Command or other extremely distant locations and receive messages from these places almost instantaneously. Perhaps technology will change and it will become a reality. With our current technology, a message from Mars to Earth can take an agonizing 10 minutes[25], as that is the amount of time necessary for light to travel between the planets. If your characters are talking many light-years apart, the mode of communication incorporated should be part techno-babble (explained earlier) to bring an air of realism to your story.

ALIEN TECHNOLOGY

This falls into all three categories of technobabble, flim-flam and the non-physical. It is very easy to create imaginary items that perform fantastic feats: (flim-flam) a stone bed on Mars that when one dies it reconstructs the human body into that of a Martian; (technobabble) an alien power generator that extends 20 miles into the planet and gives more energy than can possibly be used; (technobabble) alien pods that land then extend legs to allow movement to carry the aliens; (technobabble and flim-flam) a crystal that can link two completely alien minds together for full understanding. All of those have been successfully used in one story or another to entertain us. Unfortunately, the most alien technology that we've been privy to so far is that of our own ancient civilizations; even there one can find curiosities to flame the seeds of a good story.

These issues are only a few of those that face a science fiction writer and gives the author an open reign to create the answer to his own question.

Let's review some of the above aspects from a writer's perspective:

THE WORLD IS FLAT

Take that scenario as a writer and how would you address the issues it brings to surface. No pun intended, but if the planet is flat, there is only the surface. Where would the water of the oceans go? Where does the water come from to support an ocean? Where and how would the sun work? What would happen to you when you finally found the edge of the world? Would you fall off? If so, where would you go? How would gravity work? Birds fly, fish swim, and how would a flat surfaced planet affect them? What would happen to the bird that flew beyond the edge? A fish slipping over the edge? Assuming that the land actually exists to the edge, what would the populace think? What would they see? Would the edge crumble and break off? If not, what keeps it from not crumbling? If so, how much longer will the planet exist?

ALIEN ANATOMY

If aliens appeared as humanoid as us, would we recognize an alien on the street if we met one? This scenario has been used to very good results in many different books and short stories. What if the alien is almost humanoid? Perhaps a human head on a strange body that resembles a cross between a pig and a peacock. Of course, maybe the head is alien and the body is human. Again, these ideas have been worked over immensely. Where some of the alien anatomy possibilities have been absent is in the size. Those that are very small in size—so small you can't even see them. So many stories relate that the explorers have on space suits and test the air for whatever. What if the air was alive with microscopic spores and or bacteria? In the novel *War of the Worlds*, a virus stops the invaders. Our own virus! What if these microscopic air-borne creatures could live in harmony within us as their hosts? Would we be aware of it? Would we care? Of course, size isn't the only thing to consider. Remember, there is skin texture, color, hair and scent that should be considered, not to mention any environmental influences, including gravity. The senses could be mixed so that the alien would have two noses, one of each side of the head to amplify and differentiate scents. Perhaps the whole body hears by harmonizing sound vibrations. For a writer, creating an alien can also be more exciting than the actual writing experience since the creation of these special characteristics that are the makeup of the alien can be instrumental in the plot or plot's outcome. I remember one short story that I read years ago where the alien planet was filled with insects that could camouflage themselves to appear as something else. One creature was able to get through the myriad of guards, remove a small segment of electrical wiring, and then stowed away on the rocket unnoticed in the electrical system. As the ship entered Earth's airspace, the creature was excited by the prospect of having made it to the new world. Of course, it was killed when the airlock was opened and that particular piece of electrical wiring that hadn't been used until that time was activated. Of course, the astronauts and technicians only saw it as a burned piece of shorted electrical wiring when they attempted to figure out what had caused the airlock not to open.

VENUS

Knowing now that Venus is not anything like Earth, or even a lush jungle as once thought, there is still the potential to create life on it. Bacteria was found to exist in the hot springs of Yellowstone Park.[26] If bacteria can exist in that heat, your imagination can create life that could exist on Venus' surface. Earthlings could perhaps exist in a dome or possibly even under the surface.

Science fiction authors don't necessarily need to be rocket scientists. However, being at least somewhat familiar with the finite details of specific science areas help when writing. Here are a few examples of writers, both new and old, that have scientific degrees.

ROBERT ANSON HEINLEIN

He was trained in physics and mathematics, his best known novel *A Stranger In A Strange Land* is a science fiction novel based on the classic Mowgli.[27] Even though "Stranger" was a satire of prevailing sexual, political, and religious attitudes, it still had science subliminally woven into it. Heinlein invented inter-universe travel and the concept of a fictional universe running in parallel with our real universe and our universe being fictional in theirs. Robert Heinlein, if nothing else, gave us the word "grok" which means to understand something so thoroughly that it becomes a part of the observer.

CATHERINE ASARO

She received a BS in chemistry, MA in physics, and PhD in chemical physics.[28] Taking the knowledge of her training she created a Skolian Empire weaving the details of her science into the eleven novels of the saga. Not only is there political intrigue but genetic engineering, physics, computer networks, bio-enhancements, and romance within the pages of her novels. It should be noted that most civilizations will continue to be directed by the science of their generation and the knowledge of life as they know it. Your skills in the nuances of science can make that science believable in your stories.

ISAAC ASIMOV

Received a PhD in chemistry and co-authored a college level textbook, *Biochemistry and Human Metabolism.*[29] Asimov is most noted for his creation of the three laws of robotics:

1) a robot may not injure a human being, or, through inaction, allow a human being to come to harm;

2) a robot must obey the orders given it by human beings except where such orders would conflict with the First Law;

3) a robot must protect its own existence as long as such protection does not conflict with the First or Second Law.

When writing SF, ground rules established by previous authors can give credence to your works but don't get caught in the rut of using what has been given. Take what is given to expand and expound, wrapping it in your imagination to give it reality.

ARTHUR C. CLARKE

Received honors in both mathematics and physics. Surprisingly, Clarke published a paper in 1945 laying down the principles of satellite communication with satellites in a geostationary orbit. *Extra-terrestrial Relays* was written twenty-five years before the reality of the principles were realized. The 1996 blockbuster movie *Independence Day* explained in detail how the aliens used this technology against us. Again, a point where science fiction became science fact. The orbit of today's satellites is named "The Clarke Orbit" in honor of Sir Clarke and is at geostationary level of 42,000 kilometers.[30] Arthur C. Clarke defined three laws stating that three were fine for the Isaacs, both Newton and Asimov:

1) When a distinguished but elderly scientist states that something is possible he is almost certainly right; when he states that something is impossible, he is very probably wrong.

2) The only way of discovering the limits of the possible is to venture a little way past them into the impossible.

3) Any sufficiently advanced technology is indistinguishable from magic.

Clarke went on to write more laws but he is most notably known for these three. As a SF writer, you need to be able to take the mundane and make it super-fantastic, move the realm of the impossible to reality and see beyond the constraints of our lives.

RONALD WAYNE JONES

Received a degree in industrial mechanical engineering and worked in the mining industry for many years. This knowledge is reflected in his novel *Black Breath of the Lutron*, where mining happens in the myriad of star systems. He feels that mining is the forerunner for pioneering, similar to the Gold Rush of 1849 in California. It brought the miners, then the pioneering families, and then finally the establishment of communities.

The above authors trained in scientific fields and used that knowledge to write their novels and weave the web of wonder for the reader. Not every science fiction writer has a scientific background and it doesn't mean that a scientific background will make you a science fiction writer.

EDGAR RICE BURROUGHS

He had no formal training in the science fields but graduated from a military school. Burroughs is most noted for his *Tarzan* novels and using pulp fiction as the basis for his, Martian, aka Barsoom, series with John Carter. He also created the *Pellucidar, Venus*, and *Caspak* series.[31] In 1912, he wrote *Under the Moons of Mars* which earned him $400. It was shortly after that when he became a full-time writer. One must consider that $400 was an extremely tidy sum of money in 1912, where a weekly big salary was $50.00 and the average annual income of a person working in manufacturing was $651.00[32]

RAY BRADBURY

With no desire to attend college, Ray Bradbury is another author that doesn't have a scientific background from which to draw. One of his most famous novels is actually a collection of short stories *The Martian Chronicles*. He is also well known for *Fahrenheit 451*, which is the only book that Ray Bradbury claims he has written as science fiction. The rest of his novels he claims are tales of fantasy or non-fiction, including *The Martian Chronicles* since what he wrote about can never happen, therefore making it a fantasy in his own words. Still, *The Martian Chronicles* is considered science fiction.

DENISE VITOLA

Author of the Ty Merrick series, prior to becoming a full-time writer, Denise Vitola was employed by the Department of Defense. As a civilian, she was able to glean both military and government auras for her novels. It was this insight that gives her stories a credible view of the future and how the civilian, military law, and government co-exist.

ROGER ZELAZNY

Although college learned, Roger Zelazny's BA is in English, not science. He helped to give a new direction to science fiction in the 1960s by adding literary aspects to his stories. He used mythic imagery and drew on the resources of varied ethnic legends: Native American, Greek, Hindu, Norse, Japanese, and Egyptian mythologies.[33] Roger Zelazny also used a "god" or "god-like" theme in some of his novels; this was new territory for science fiction authors.

FRANK HERBERT

Author of the *Dune* series, Frank Herbert went to college but never graduated. He studied what he enjoyed, then left. *Dune* was the first ecological science fiction novel,[34] and created a universe, religions, telling the tale of one family's struggle through multiple generations.

As detailed above, you don't have to be a science expert to write science fiction, but you have to know your science. Some of the best science fiction has been written by both those that are experts in scientific worlds and those that enjoy weaving an interesting tale. No matter where you take your reader in your story, to the farthest star of some distant nebula or perhaps inside Earth or just around the corner to Mars or Venus, the last verse of the poem by Robert Heinlein sums it up.

"We pray for one last landing
On the globe that gave us birth;
Let us rest our eyes on the friendly skies
And the cool, green hills of Earth."
~ Robert Heinlein ~

CHAPTER FOUR

THE MANY FACES OF SCIENCE FICTION: SUB-GENRES

Kim Richards

Genre writers often have to explain to the everyday person what a genre is. Science fiction is probably the most widely recognizable genre, next to romance. Therefore, what exactly is a sub-genre and why do we need them?

Turning to our friend, the dictionary, sub is a prefix when attached to another word means a division thereof. We define genre as a kind, sort, style, or gender. Style seems to fit nicely with writing. Therefore, a sub-genre is a division of style in this case.

Why do we need to divvy up science fiction? The reason is that it is useful to do so. Ever since God told Adam to name everything on his newly created Earth, man has within him, this need to name things, to classify them and to group them together. The common factor of each group allows us to identify members of that group and sometimes identify with them. We do it with everything from types of rocks to human lifestyles. As with anything man does, it comes with its positives and negatives.

There are four main reasons to create sub-genres in science fiction. They are ideas, style, submissions, and marketing. Let us take a closer look at each.

Where ideas come from vary from writer to writer. A common complaint of beginning authors is a scarcity of ideas but as you evolve, find your niche and style, you will find more ideas than physically possible to write in one lifetime.

Sub-genres can be jumping off places for story ideas. Just glancing through the various ones discussed here, particularly the newer ones, can inspire an idea. If you have never tried your hand at writing a military science fiction story, write one. You might be surprised with the results. The best way to grow and evolve in your writing is to simply write. Experiment with the different areas and have fun with it. Every word you write, whether it sees publication or not is beneficial to your writing skills.

Style is one of those proverbial two-edged swords. Few writers work solely in one sub-genre for their entire careers. Most will find their niche and garner some success in one or two. The trick is to not get lazy and trap yourself inside the walls of a single sub-genre. Just as actors can be typecast, authors can become associated with a style. It can make selling a different work more difficult.

Maybe you don't care if readers complain your latest story isn't about brain sucking aliens like the last five have been, but why box yourself in that way? Guaranteed at some point you will tire of the same old setting and want to do something else...say a time travel story. Give yourself the freedom and permission to write anything you want. After all, if you are not enjoying the process it will show in your work and you will be tempted to quit. Try them all. Grow. Expand. Surprise yourself.

Unless you use the sub-genre as an idea springboard, the best advice is to write your story and worry about what sub-genre it fits into later. Make use of human nature to categorize things. Ask others to read your work and tell you what kind of story they would label it. Joyce Saricks' *The Reader's Advisory Guide to Genre Fiction* and Catherine Cramer's *The Ascent of Wonder* remind us how science fiction is a genre that affirms the role of story in our lives. The story must come first. Classification will naturally follow.

The next useful aspect of sub-genres is for submissions. Heed the advice of publishers and editors by reading their submission guidelines. In those few paragraphs, they spell out for you exactly the style of story they want. Save yourself the waiting anguish, the postage, and the sting of rejection by not sending a space opera story to a publisher who states flat out they only want hard science fiction.

Let us take a closer look at each of the popular sub-genres. This is not an all-inclusive list since they evolve and grow. New ones come into play and old ones fall by the wayside (New Wave for example). It seems at first there are a lot of them. That is actually a plus because it means science fiction authors and readers have a wide selection of choices. It is a freedom unique to our favorite genre so try not to be intimidated by it.

There are authors who take great pride and pains to create a sub-genre for themselves. None of those are included here.

We need a good grasp of what is being done within the realm of science fiction, and use that knowledge to our advantage when pondering story ideas. This opens up your mind to available options, ideas never before attempted and helps avoid the overdone plot traps.

HARD SCIENCE FICTION

These are works driven by ideas more than characterization where the stories are based on real science and engineering. Character development is secondary to technology and plot resolution. Some folks see hard science fiction as "old school" or old fashioned. However, hard science fiction is more accepted as a literary form now than in previous years and is associated with intellectual content. A great many science fiction classics are hard science fiction. Look into the works of Isaac Asimov's *Foundation* and its sequels, Robert Heinlein's *Have Spacesuit, Will Travel, Space Cadet, Starship Troopers* and Poul Anderson's *Brainwave* and *Tau Zero*; all excellent hard science fiction examples.

To write good hard science fiction, you had better get the science right. It must be both plausible and the plot must center on it. It has been said no one reads science fiction for the science; however, fans of hard science fiction pay closer attention to those details. Whether something is purely futuristic or based on of our current knowledge of science and technology, it had better at least make sense in how it works and why.

Robot stories fall into the hard science fiction category. So do genetic manipulation and terraforming ideas.

One example of a hard science fiction plot would be a story about a super intelligent computer, which begins making decisions about humankind's fate. The focus would be on the computer, it's thinking processes and observations, how it evolved, and continues evolving with people being nothing but bodies in the way.

Hard science fiction stories are sometimes hard for readers to find. Perhaps the reluctance of writers to tackle these type stories comes from a fear of getting the technology wrong or viewing hard science fiction as "old school". However, it is a sub-genre that has retained a solid following across the years, and quality hard fiction stories are sought after by science fiction magazines such as *Analog*.

SPECULATIVE FICTION (AKA SLIPSTREAM)

There was a time when speculative fiction meant works focusing less on advances in technology and more on issues of social change, similarly to soft science fiction. It included modern day problems addressed in futuristic settings. Some also include fantasy within the parameters of speculative fiction.

In its earliest form, speculative fiction was made up of stories set in modern or near future times and could include magic or characters with superhero-like abilities. Urban fantasy fit in here neatly. It has since evolved and has become the new name encompassing all aspects and sub-genres of science fiction. While the words "science fiction" bring about a specific image to mind, "speculative fiction" is the newfangled word for any fiction addressing the questions associated with "What if?"

Strange Horizons, a web-based magazine of speculative fiction defines it as: "sci-fi" but which properly embraces science fiction, fantasy, magic realism, slipstream, and a host of sub-genres. "These stories make us think. They critique society. They offer alternatives. They give us a vision of the future—and warn us of the potential dangers therein. They help us understand our past. They are full of beauty, and terror, and delight."[35]

More in-depth information can be found at the Speculative Fiction Foundation <http://www.speclit.org>.

SOFT SCIENCE FICTION

This type of fiction is mainly character driven. It sometimes emphasizes social change, psychological aspects, romantic elements, religious stories, anthropology, and cultural based ideas.[36] One writer known for her soft science fiction is Catherine Asaro. Soft science fiction grew, beginning in the 1970s, as the number of women writers entered the genre, bringing with them the feminine examination of humanity and an interest in relationships.

An example of a soft science fiction plot might be a couple whose marriage is failing and so they take a trip on a space cruise liner, visiting various planets, in hopes of fixing the relationship. All of the things they love most and hate the worst in each other are brought out as outside forces such a shipboard disaster or the introduction of an alien lover turn their lives upside down.

SPACE OPERA

High adventure in space is most recognizable in *Star Wars* and Frank Herbert's *Dune*. Space opera involves large-scale worlds and governments. Plotlines cross stars and galaxies. Technology is less important and can seem magical or mystical.

With space opera, a sample plot might be the adventures of a band of mercenaries who take on odd jobs from various planets, sometimes hauling freight, sometimes fugitives, whatever, and whomever pays best. They take their business across a large section of a galaxy. We get to know the individual characters through their experiences.

MILITARY SCIENCE FICTION

A quick definition is armed forces in space. Along side the requisite armed forces tales, these also include detectives and police stories. Some best-known military fiction novels include Robert Heinlein's *Starship Troopers* and Joe Haldeman's *The Forever War.* These stories have technologies geared towards warfare. Sophisticated weaponry and genetically or cybernetically enhanced humans are common. The 2005 movie, *Ultraviolet* is another example.

Antagonists can be a warring world, another army, an alien species, futuristic drug lords, even a generally unruly local population works. Readers expect high casualties and warfare-like tactics worked into these types of tales.

One thing you need to consider is weapon choice. If a soldier has a laser pistol strapped to his leg, why would he choose to wield something more primitive like a sword or a whip? A coolness factor only goes so far before it destroys credibility.

Typical military science fiction plots are broad in their scope. An example plot involves following a particular Special Forces unit through their various assignments while stalked by a nemesis alien counterpart.

CYBERPUNK/SPLATTERPUNK

These "extreme theme" stories contain elements of fusion or conflict between man and machine: high tech, bleak, mechanistic, and futuristic universe of computers, hackers, and computer/human hybrids. Man has given up too much control to the machines in his world. There is a love/hate relationship underlying everything between them. This also includes cloning stories. A great example is *Neuromancer* by William Gibson published in 1984, often referred to as the story which set cyberpunk into motion. Movies such as *The Running Man, Robocop*, and *Terminator* fall into this sub-genre. Some authors, such as Marg Gilks and Moira Allen consider the recent *Matrix* movies cyberpunk.[37]

These stories have high body counts and often show technology gone wrong. The 1980s saw a trend in junkies being addicted to plugging into computers instead of street drugs. The focus is on man's struggle to survive in a terrible world of his own creation. There are always big guns and bold brave antiheroes ready to lead the charge.

FIRST CONTACT

These are stories where humans and beings, not indigenous to Earth, meet for the first time. This includes *X-files* intrigue stories. Aliens in human guise such as The WB's *Roswell* and *Invasion*. Novels such as Carl Sagan's *Contact*, John Wyndham's *The Day of the Triffids*, H. G. Well's *War of the Worlds* and movies such as *ET, Close Encounters of the Third Kind*, and *Independence Day* all fit into this category.

Lee Masterson suggests possibly the first novel about aliens coming to Earth was written in 1752, *Micromegas* by Voltaire.[38]

Most often, we encounter hostile beings in first contact stories but that is certainly not a requirement for the sub-genre. Typically, the focus is on human reaction to the contact and the survival/coping/acceptance to the resulting consequences. There is some speculation among science fiction enthusiasts that once mankind does make actual first contact that this sub-genre will no longer be necessary and, therefore, fall away. Until then, you are free to write them to your heart's content.

First contact plots can take place on Earth, during any time period, or away on other worlds where humans are the 'aliens'. They can be face-to-face, one on one encounters between a man and an alien, or larger scope ships vs. communities.

NEAR FUTURE

The future can be modern day or in the next few decades. This is what speculative fiction was in its earliest form. Near future works are often used for political and social statements of predictions and "what-if's" should society or technology continue as it is now.

An example plot of near future might be something say 100 years from now, in which entertainment involves the battle of giant robots (a kind of computer game of today brought to reality). An old movie titled *Robot Jox* plays along this style plot with the outcome of war being decided in the robot battle arena instead of costing human lives. Another example is the film, *The Running Man,* where criminals become contestants in a futuristic reality game show.

TIME TRAVEL

As its name implies, these stories are straightforward travels through time by mechanical or mental means. Time travel can be forward or backwards in time. Examples include *The Time Machine* by H.G. Wells, all three *Back to the Future* movies, and *Somewhere in Time.*

Always there are consequences. If you attempt a time travel tale, keep abreast with current time travel theories and watch your explanations of how the ability to move through time works. Once you define the rules for how it works and the consequences incurred, abide by them. A visual timeline for your work is vital for keeping the events and facts straight. One hint is to use different color pens/markers to indicate timelines used so you don't confuse intersecting events.

Another thing to be wary of is the repeated use of time travel to correct mistakes made by characters earlier on. After the second or third time, it gets silly and you lose believability. *Star Trek* and *Terminator* made use of this plot. You also have to deal with the possibilities of a character paradox: should a character meet himself, what happens? Do they cancel one another? Become best friends?

Time travel plots have to make sense. Whether the characters are lost and trying to find their way 'home' to their correct place, police chasing fugitives across centuries, lovers from different time periods falling in love or someone using time travel to research what really happened at some point in time, the time travel portion needs to be believable in how it works. We know that in the universe of *Back to the Future*, there is a specific speed that must be reached for the DeLorian time machine to cross the time continuum.

PARALLEL/ALTERNATE UNIVERSE

These are plot driven stories where the results created by decisions made or events occurring affects or creates another place where the decision or the event went differently. (Parallel histories, timelines, characters, events, dimensions.) These stories are sometimes paired with time travel stories. The one can be the means to reach the other. Somehow, the world has been "tampered with". The *Star Trek* and *Stargate* universes have made interesting uses of parallel dimensions and alternate histories. The Scifi Channel's *Stargate*: *Atlantis* has an episode where excess energy from a machine is siphoned off to another dimension where it is supposed to be harmless. Instead, it threatens to destroy an entire alternate world on the same time stream. One of the characters learns to travel between the parallel worlds in an attempt to fix things.

An example might be dimensional travelers who meet up with themselves in another reality to discover profound differences in personality and lifestyle due to different life experiences or world events.

STEAMPUNK

At first glance, the following movies have little in common since they all fit neatly into other sub-genre or genre styles. *Wild, Wild, Wild, West* is set firmly in the Western genre. *The League of Extraordinary Gentlemen* is a literary action/adventure. *20,000 Leagues Under the Sea*, the third installment of *Back to the Future* and *The Time Machine*, even the 1999 release of *Sleepy Hollow* all fit elsewhere but they all have in common a subtle sub-genre called SteamPunk.

What makes these stories similar is the use of inventions and gadgetry on a larger or more complicated scale than is the norm for the setting's time period. The time machine did indeed travel back and forth through time. The almost space-ship feel of Captain Nemo's submarine and gigantic sea life makes it very sci-fi. Also, the use of the locomotive to power the DeLorian time machine in *Back to the Future III* gives that story an element of SteamPunk.

A fun but seldom used sub-genre, this is the one time where it is acceptable to propel the storyline or save the day by an arbitrary and handy gadget. It is almost expected! Reverse that and you open up some great opportunities to expose your heroes to larger than their normal life threats.

An example might be that your good guy finds himself face-to-face with a mechanical robot, which is threatening total destruction of said hero's Victorian-era community. He must figure out a way to turn the machine upon its creator or destroy it but not without massive decimation in the town, plus several close calls for himself and his lady-love. Sounds fun does it not?

LOST WORLDS

What instantly comes to mind when the subject of lost world stories is brought up are tales of dinosaurs: self-contained valleys, secluded islands. This style also allows for ghost town style settings and unevolved areas of a planet (Earth or otherwise). Often the lost world is the catalyst to the rest of the story.

For an idea of a lost world plot, think back to some of the stories you have read.

Land of the Lost is an old TV show for kids in which a father and his two children find themselves back in prehistoric times. Other ideas have included hidden societies beneath the earth or as in *King Kong*, there is an island untouched by modern man complete with fruitful natives, dinosaurs, and giant gorillas.

You can place just about any of the other sub-genre plots within a lost world because it is more about setting than anything else. The one thing you must include is a way to get to this undiscovered place. Then tailor the events and threats to the type of lost world you have created, whether futuristic or ancient in nature. Take *Jurassic Park*, the "lost world" is created as a theme park accessible only by helicopter.

OTHER WORLDS

Relying heavily on setting, other world stories are set any place other than Earth. In science fiction's early days, before fantasy branched off into a full genre in its own right, other world stories were the means for some authors to write fantasy. The trick was to crash land on some alien world and go from there.

Other world fiction includes inner space, underwater cities, and self-contained space stations. This style of story does not necessarily have to feature humans either. Other worldly beings can make fascinating characters too.

World building for this type of story is worth the time and effort to create. The more detail you have on how and why this world works, and who the inhabitants are, the easier it will be for you to bring the entire thing to life.

Other world plots have a wide variety of choices. Your characters can be visiting these places, stumble upon them, crash land there or your story can simply take place *on* the different world with all the characters being indigenous life. Think the movie Enemy Mine, where the other world is foreign to both the human and alien characters.

FRONTIER

Frontier science fiction is often described as "old west in space". It includes works about colonization, people living in domes, mining etc... i.e.: television shows: *Firefly/Serenity*; original *Star Trek* series, and *Lost in Space*. There is always a hope for a better, brighter future but often these folks simply trade one set of problems for another. Typically, frontier stories have a human survival element with some characters taking on the role of protector and others the protected. There are strong elements of good vs. evil in frontier works. Antagonists can be other humans, alien life, weather conditions, or the world upon which the story takes place. Survival is once again the driving force.

A frontier plot might be one of an outpost struggling to survive on a remote planet after having been cutoff from the rest of the galaxy for whatever reason. Perhaps a vigilante group has taken control and become the very tyrants they were trying to rid their home of.

APOCALYPTIC-TYPE SCIENCE FICTION

The setting focus is on the end of the world or just after the end. This style includes disaster stories. Examples are *Mad Max, Night of the Comet*, and Stephen King's *The Stand*. These stories were popular in the 1980s. Again, this style usually contains plotlines about humanity's survival. Some zombie stories fall into this category. An example is the movie, *28 Days Later*.

The operating word for this style is aftermath. Though possible, most writers are hard pressed to write an apocalyptic tale without some decent explanation of what happened. At the very least, you-the writer-needs to know this part of the world's origins so that you can accurately portray your character's viewpoints and reactions to his world and its situations. One pitfall to watch out for is the sudden finding of a useful tool or weapon at just the right moment it is needed for a character to solve his problem. It sounds, and is, contrived so I recommend you don't use that ploy.

Suggested plot ideas might be along the lines of mankind's recovery after an alien invasion. What might need rebuilt? Does the threat of hostile beings remain? What resources are no longer available and how do people adjust?

DYSTOPIA/UTOPIA

These include Imaginative Fiction that depicts a world with different political structures, available technology, social and moral codes than we have on our own world today. Examples are Ray Bradbury's *Fahrenheit 451*, *Logan's Run*, and *The Island*. These works focus on setting more than anything else.

Dystopia is typically a depressing and stark view of fatalistic futures. One classic example is *Brave New World* by Aldous Huxley published in 1932. Also included are the *Planet of the Apes* stories. Dystopian views are often reflections of political or social statements of our current society and the direction is heading.

Utopian societies are nearly always too good to be true. They are perfect ideal futures but even those are not without their problems. Thomas Moore's *Utopia* and Francis Bacon's, *The New Atlantis* are early examples. What if a world is terraformed to a particular culture's specifications? Who gets crowded out or becomes extinct because of it? Who ends up doing all the behind the scenes work to make it all run?

SCIENCE FANTASY...CROSS GENRE FICTION

Amy Goldschlager of Avon Eos says,

"A hybrid and subset of speculative fiction in which either both science and magic work, science is so sophisticated it simulates magic, or characters posses psychic powers so strong they resemble magic."[39]

This sub-genre includes paranormal and extra sensory perception tales, called Pseudo-Scientific Fantasy by Heinlein.

Example plots might be a space station haunted by a ghost or a world where magic is required to power machinery. *The Death of Jabari* by Kim Bundy is a good example. Here magic and technology work hand in hand. In addition, there is a 80s cartoon called Visionaries where magic is needed to power character abilities or operate vehicles.

DARK SCIENCE FICTION

Dark means something evil abodes in space. *Event Horizon*, *Alien*, *Dracula 3000*, and *Lifeforce* are movie examples. A marriage of foreboding and futuristic, you want to keep the mood of the story dark and creepy. Horror in space comes to mind but it can be much more with gothic elements or sinister circumstances.

A normal plot for this kind of fiction must have some sort of evil either as villains or as the main viewpoint characters. There can be space traveling vampires or entire planets of them. How about a psychotic stowaway on a space station? Or an evil entity inhabiting a ship's computer?

NEW WEIRD

One new weird popular author is China Mielville who wrote *Perdito Street Station*. Mielville calls this sub-genre: "A freeing-up...Notions are sputtering and bleeding across internal and external boundaries...which cheerfully ignore the boundaries between SF, fantasy, and horror."[40]

New weird plots have a fantasy element to them. Seldom are human characters involved but strange invented beings for example: bug like, variations on sentient plants, trash heaps come to life. Mielville's story includes a race of cactus beings that live in a life-sized kind of terrarium city. Being a relatively new sub-genre, plot options are wide open. Your writer's imagination is the only limit.

BIZARRO

Another new sub-genre, Bizarro is also an "extreme theme" style. Just as with cyberpunk, it came about through the human need to group unclassifiable stories together. Bizarro is a blending of science fiction and horror. The emphasis of the story mood and plot can lean towards either. These stories are fast paced and often are short on description in favor of action.

Bizarro author and editor, Mike Philbin describes his genre thus: "...a normal protagonist is pitted against abnormal circumstance and has to thread his way through a more and more convoluted narrative to a conclusion...experiments in layout and sentence structure are aimed at setting the reader on edge...Sometimes the narrative of a bizarre book is the reader's enemy, not his salvation."[41]

It is hard to pin down a typical bizarro plot. These stories are in a league of their own and simply have to be experienced. If you have written something really strange and cannot find a home for it, look into bizarro. It just might be your thing. I highly recommend an anthology titled, *The Bizarro Starter Kit* published by Eraserhead Press, which features stories by ten leading authors of this sub-genre.

EROTIC FICTION

As implied, there must be strong elements of erotica and can include women's fiction. *The Huntress* (winner of the 2004 Dream Realm Award for Best SF Erotica) by Barbara Karmazin is a good example. Most often, these tales deal with human and alien sex or encounters onboard space ships. Ebook and online serial story formats seem to be most popular for finding erotic science fiction stories.

A sample plot might be a human female and an alien ambassador who fall in love and find ways to have sex.

HUMOR

Examples of humor are Douglas Adams *The Hitchhiker's Guide to the Galaxy* and movies like *Men in Black*. Does anyone remember the *Muppet Show* doing *Pigs in Space?* Let's face it, people love to laugh, and there's nothing more fun than science fiction/fantasy/horror humor. It feels like some kind of inside joke when you know you "get it" and someone else does too.

Humor includes parodies, spoofs, and situation comedies. Most often it is found in flash fiction or as skits on shows such as *Saturday Night Live*. When considering humor, don't overdo it. No one says you have to write an entire book of silliness and fun. You can if you want. However, small scenes and situations here and there can add depth to your characters and lighten up a heavy piece of work.

Consider humor the spice of science fiction. Add according to taste.

FLASH FICTION

Very short fiction typically anything under 1000 words. Check the individual publisher or magazine's guidelines because some of them want fiction of 500 words or less. It must be tightly written so that every single word counts for something.

A typical flash fiction story might have a twist ending where things are not what they seemed all along. A specific scene or slice of life bit works well. Jokes fit in this sub-genre also. Just remember to keep it short and make sure your plot includes the required beginning, middle, and end.

MEDIA/GAMING TIE-INS

These stories take place in common worlds and created for movies and games. Copyrights and world/character ownership can be tricky here. Most are not taken on unless assigned by a publisher who has the rights to publish within these worlds. Most have intricate guidelines with regards to what a write can and cannot do with the setting and characters. Everything from *Star Wars, Star Trek, Hellboy*, and *Buffy the Vampire Slayer,* along with games like *Doom, Resident Evil*, and comics such as *Spiderman, Superman, and Batman.*

Critics of these types of stories view the authors of having lesser skills or no new ideas of their own. The reality is these works are often held to a higher standard because of the preconceived notions regarding literature and common fan knowledge of the worlds and characters. There is some great writing out there among tie-ins, such as Michael Stackpole's *Star Wars* novels (*I Jedi*, and the *X-Wing* Series) and Yvonne Navarro's novelizations of *Hellboy* and *Ultraviolet*. Plus a ready-made fan base, and in some cases, convention circuits to meet these folks and show them what you have.

CHILDREN'S STORIES/YOUNG ADULT

The golden age of science fiction (SF, to those in the know), which spanned the 1940s and '50s, inspired generations of kids to become astronauts, physicists and engineers, to try to make at least some of the stories real. (And those kids remember their imaginative roots: NASA, for example, sometimes calls in SF writers as consultants.)—Gregory Mone[42]

The golden age for children and science fiction is twelve. However, more and more we are finding books for younger children. A children's alien abduction story, Ceto's New Friends, is written by a woman with an abduction tale of her own: Leah A. Haley. A great example in the young adult arena is the *Animorphs* series by K.A. Applegate with aliens and lycanthropic teens out to save the Earth. Also *Roswell High* by Melinda Metz, which the television show, *Roswell*, was based upon, in which teens are the direct descendants of the aliens who crashed in Roswell, New Mexico back in 1947.

Young adult works are considered perpetually in demand. There are specific restrictions that must be followed with regards to violence, foul language, and sex. Plots are open to any of the other sub-genres so long as they keep to those restrictions. The one exception is erotic fiction, which should be avoided.

By now you've noticed how many science fiction works fall into several categorical styles. No problem. That's part of that freedom we talked about earlier. If you have a piece, which fits in to, say, two sub-genres then consider it to have twice the markets to submit to and twice the potential audience. You can submit your story to publishers wanting either style. The worst they can do is reject it and you still have more places to submit to. Don't want stress over categorizing your work. Sure, it is important to consider but not worth making yourself sick over.

One very interesting use of sub-genres is the movie, *Pitch Black* and its sequel, *The Chronicles of Riddick*. The original *Pitch Black* is very much an other world/first contact story with rich characterization all around. The characters crash on a foreign world and must learn to cope and survive. Then they meet the inhabitants of this world and find themselves in grave danger. Every character in the story has positive aspects and flaws, making them interesting and memorable.

The Chronicles of Riddick however, ignored those sub-genres from before and took place firmly in a military science fiction/cyberpunk universe. This story contains warring peoples, an army of undead beings, a race of ghostlike elementals beings, and a bleak, dark future for all. There are giant ships with the ability to wipe out civilizations on a planetary scale. It is almost epic.

The reason I give this example to you is to illustrate how the same characters or worlds can be used in differing sub-genres. We are lucky because of how science fiction gives us a variety of choices. I again invite you to use sub-genres as a means to cultivate ideas and find markets for them. Use them as an excuse to write and not allow them to become stumbling blocks in your mind. Good luck and remember to have fun.

PART II
BUILDING

CHAPTER FIVE

TECHNOLOGY IN SCIENCE FICTION

Wil McCarthy

It's accepted by writers these days as an obvious truth that science fiction needs to be character-driven. As a result, fewer and fewer people are reading it. Here's an older truth: science fiction is about how technology affects people. Yes, you need characters and a plot and an interesting place for it all to happen. And yes, every element needs to be good; a thimble of sewage will ruin a gallon of soup.

But.

Science fiction exists to answer "what if" questions, and in a properly constructed story, all these elements emerge naturally from whatever you ask. Usually, these are technology questions. Think of Gibson's Internet, Sterling's rejuvenation industry, Vinge's bobbles and galactic zones or Catherine Asaro's star drives. The list goes on: Niven's ringworld, Herbert's stillsuits. On the softer side, what about McCaffrey's engineered dragons and medicinal super plants? What about George Lucas' light sabers?

"Start with a character," the experts advise. Pish. The giants of the field start with a gadget, and build their worlds and characters around it. That's oversimplifying, but only a little. My own fiction is often called "plot driven"—what a novel concept!—but in fact I don't write plots. I usually feel more like I'm deriving them, because the gadgets create a world, and the world creates characters, and the characters create problems, and there's really only one perfect way for it all to play out. In a real sense, the entire story is defined by its technology.

The same is true of mainstream fiction; we're just less aware of it. Could *The Three Musketeers* exist in a world without gunpowder and Damascus steel? Would *Network* or *Anchorman: The Legend of Ron Burgundy* make sense if TV news had never been invented? It's even true in real life; the *H.M.S Titanic* marked a new age of mass-casualty accidents, made possible when advances in the shipbuilding industry collided with old-fashioned greed, negligence, and hubris. It's a poignant story of technology gone wrong, and that's why we remember it when a thousand other shipwrecks lie forgotten. Their characters were every bit as real, but the stories just aren't as interesting.

That's what technology can do for your fiction: make it timeless, authentic, visceral, and true. Have I got your attention? Good, because this is nearly impossible to pull off if you don't understand the process. Here it is:

STEP ONE: PROSPECTING

Where do ideas come from? Well, honestly the world is full of them. Finding ideas is like sticking your hand out in a rainstorm; if it doesn't come back wet, you're not really trying. An easier, more seductive answer is to search the science magazines and documentary channels, which are always chock full of cool new concepts. In the short term it's fine to ingest these sporadically, but for optimum health I recommend them as a steady part of a balanced diet. There are ideas floating around out there that will immediately make sense to you, suggesting complex storylines that no other person would ever come up with. They start out as other people's ideas, or bits and pieces of ideas, but as they fall together they become firmly and uniquely your own.

You never know when this will happen, and you really don't want to miss it for the sake of *Scooby Doo* reruns, so if want to be a science fiction writer—a good one—you should make idea prospecting an integral part of your life. Heck, you probably already have; if you found that sort of thing boring, why would you want to write science fiction?

Something you may not have done, though, is to crawl back along the chain of scholarly references. Very few documentaries or popular articles are completely original work; they draw from multiple sources, including very technical science journals, conference proceedings, and patent publications. These can be a huge boon to a writer in almost any subject; they're a bit harder to sift through, but they put you closer to the raw feed. You'll get the ideas earlier, with less processing and commentary by other people. If you've never tried this, a trip to the nearest big library is definitely called for. You'll be amazed what you can find.

STEP TWO: KNOW IT WHEN YOU SEE IT

It's important to realize that "new" technology takes ten or twenty or even thirty years to reach ordinary people. For example, the transistor was invented twice in Germany during the 1920s and 30s, before a practical version was devised at Bell Labs in New Jersey in 1947. Even though transistors were an obvious replacement for vacuum tubes, the transistor radio wasn't introduced until 1954, and didn't really gain market traction until after 1960, when Japan and Hong Kong got involved and the prices came down.

A science fiction writer at the time could be forgiven for thinking the whole subject was dull, but look at its effects on our culture: the transistor radio brought music to the beach, to the woods, to cars and boats and bicycles. It brought music everywhere, with drugs and alcohol, and loose behavior following close behind. Given the Baby Boom—already in full swing by 1950—a savvy writer could have seen the transistor patent and predicted some of the counterculture of the mid-60s. This seemed very new and surprising when it happened, but in fact, it was the culmination of trends that had been building openly for decades. Imagine a 1950 story called "*1969: The Summer of Love*"—wouldn't that have made someone's career?

Today we can make a similar extrapolation by looking at nanoparticle coatings and demographic trends. In thirty years' time, we'll have a North America where white Europeans are less than 50% of the population, and where more people live in cities than in rural areas. We'll also have clear polymer coatings that can be applied to any surface to keep dirt or paint from sticking. We'll also have "gecko tape" that uses electrostatic forces between molecules—not glue!—to paste things together. Like the pads of a gecko's feet, this stuff is immensely strong and can be reused indefinitely.

Put all this together and you've got a *West Side Story 2040*, where Spanish and English-speaking gangs can climb the walls with "gecko gloves," unless the walls have been treated to prevent it. Graffiti takes on a new importance in this future, because a tagged wall is a climbable wall, and a potential escape route for some Juan on the run from a band of Bubbas. If the school-age taggers have done their job, the older gang members will find clearly marked highways to carry them through the city. Unless the tags have been tampered with by rival gangs, to lead poor Juan into a trap...

Maybe that's a bad example. Importantly, though, there are dozens of other trends like this going on right now, and they'll mean something different to you than they do to anyone else. So keep your eyes open; a firm understanding of the present lets you see into the future and bring back stories. But for all the same reasons, your futures will be shallow and unconvincing if your grip on the present is weak. Don't say I didn't warn you.

STEP THREE: RESEARCH

Having a great idea is only the first step to crafting a great story. If you want to be convincing—and you wouldn't be reading this book if you didn't!—you need to understand the technology, and/or the science behind it, well enough to fool your readers. While resisting the temptation to bore them with long info dumps, you need to say enough about your technology to convey a sense of what it looks like, how big or heavy or power-hungry it is, how people interact with it, etc.

Case in point: I recently wrote a humorous story that involved a homemade brain scanner. In my first draft, I called this a functional magnetic resonance imager, or fMRI, since that's a popular way to see inside the living brain. Unfortunately, real fMRI scanners are the size and weight of a Volkswagen, and produce powerful electric fields. The patient actually has to lie down on a table and be slid inside the mouth of the machine. This was clearly no good for my story, so I went instead with a technology called event-related positional electroencephalogram, or ERPEEG, which relies on a lightweight sensor cap. According to my research, this technique produces lower-resolution images than fMRI scanning, but with less of a time lag. It also requires the patient's head to be wetted down with saline gel, which turned out to be a great humorous detail for my story.

Did I drone on and on about the operational details? No. But I knew what the cap looked like, how the scanner's output would look on a computer screen, what the gel felt and smelled like, etc. A few brisk sentences conveyed the entire process, with enough realism to satisfy an actual neurologist.

This is an important point, because some of your readers will be neurologists, or astronomers, or cops or auto mechanics. If you get a detail wrong in their particular area of expertise, you'll throw them right out of the story and have a hard time winning them back. There's a school of thought that says, "So what? The other 99.9% of the audience will never know the difference." But in the first place, treating your readers with contempt is a bad idea, and in the second place, realism is never wasted. Honestly. Most readers won't know enough to spot an error, but almost anyone can tell the difference between a writer making stuff up and one speaking from a position of knowledge. The actual differences in the text may be minor—a few words here and there, a few sentences more or less—but the difference in perception can be huge. Realistic technology makes your world feel rich and sensuous, or gritty and wild, or jarringly silly in the way that real-life sometimes is.

So that's why you need to research technology. The next question is... how? As of this writing, the two answers I hear most often are *Google* and *Wikipedia*. Which is fine; both are excellent resources that would have been unimaginable in 1990, even to most science fiction writers. In this day and age, the whole world really is at our fingertips.

But only if you know what you're doing.

The problem with using *Wikipedia* as a crutch is that it's not authoritative; literally anyone can enter or modify the information there. All things considered, this works surprisingly well, but a 2005 study showed that *Wikipedia* was slightly less accurate than the *Encyclopaedia Britannica* on technical subjects, and a rash of news stories showed the whole system was subject to vandalism, slander, fraud, political spin, religious extremism, practical jokes, and assorted other abuses. In a global free speech environment, human error is the least of our worries.

The problem with using *Google* as a crutch is that you have to know which keywords to search on, what order to put them in, where to place the quote marks, parentheses, and Boolean operators (AND, OR, NOT, etc.). Keyword searching is such a complex subject that universities teach whole classes on it, especially in the library sciences. You can't expect to sit down with no prior experience and operate like an expert.

What's more, there are two problems shared by both *Wikipedia* and *Google*. First of all, both resources are in a constant state of flux. The article you put your faith in today may be gone tomorrow, or completely rewritten. This is particularly bad in journalism, but even in fiction, you may be called on from time to time to name your sources, cite your references, and otherwise defend your ideas. It happens to me all the time. The second and more serious problem is that keyword searching is in some ways the opposite of real research. It tells you exactly what you want to know—no more, no less. It undermines the serendipity of flipping through a book or magazine article and finding amazing details you would never have thought to look for.

To some extent, both problems can be alleviated by simply clicking around on as many different hyperlinks as you can get your cursor on. A datum from a random web site is nearly worthless, but the same information from multiple sources—especially university and government pages—can have quite a high credibility. Similarly, if you review not only the facts you're looking for but a goodly volume of the surrounding text, pictures, diagrams, related articles, etc., you'll be giving yourself a decent and very fast education.

To an even greater extent, you can step over these worries by adding a third crutch: *The Encyclopaedia Britannica Ultimate Reference Suite DVD*. This contains the entire *Britannica* in a handy searchable format, and while it's less complete and less convenient, and also surprisingly slower than the world of Wikis, it can be used to confirm key factoids and to provide authoritative background material. It costs around $30, so any working writer can afford to buy the latest edition every year. You'll be glad you did.

Still, even though three points make a tripod, I'm not recommending you rely on crutches. In fact, your research can and should be a natural outgrowth of your constant prospecting. For example, reading Science News every week can give you the rough outlines of a lot of different ideas. Later on, if you decide one or two of these are important for something you're working on, you can hop to the magazine's web site <http://www.sciencenews.org> to look up the articles, or even walk to your local library to search the stacks by hand. If you come across an idea that's truly interesting, it's also fun and informative to contact an expert. Many college professors, for example, are flattered and delighted to receive email from a science fiction writer. Doubly so if they've heard of you, which is more and more likely if you keep doing a good job on your research!

Finally and perhaps most obviously, you should read books on the subjects that interest you. This is pleasure, prospecting, and detailed research rolled into one, and the more you do of it, the more you'll amaze people with the depth, breadth, and wisdom of your writerly intellect. Books are the steroids of the mind, and you should take every opportunity to abuse them.

I know. Duh. Like every other writer in the world, you grasped this point by the age of ten. But it never hurts to hear it repeated.

STEP FOUR: SHAKE WELL BEFORE OPENING

One difficult point to grasp in science fiction is that technology is a means, not an end. Never mind how cool a gadget you've come up with, or how lame that other writer's technology may be. The point in both cases is: what effect will this have on people?

The best way to answer this question is to break it down into lots of little questions. What effect will this have on athletes? On cops and criminals? On butchers, bakers, candlers, and other tradesmen? Gibson's law reminds us that "the street finds its own uses for things," but little kids find their own uses, too, and so do artists. So do flaky New Age weirdos with no real grasp of how science and technology actually work. Everyone finds a use for everything, or else they push it away, and that pushing away can be a story in its own right. Think of the Amish, who pick and choose the technology they're willing to adopt based, quite simply, on whether it increases or decreases their freedom, community, and sense of personal empowerment. Believe it or not, 12 VDC solar energy is very Amish, where alternating current from a high-voltage power line is not.

Anyway, my point is that you don't want to rush straight into your storytelling the minute you have a great technology idea. Curry and spaghetti are both famous for tasting better as leftovers than as main dishes hot off the stove, and the reason is simple: after a day of sitting on the warmer, the ingredients are more thoroughly mixed at the molecular level. The same is true of science fiction; for best results, you need to let it cook for a while.

What do you do while it's cooking? Ideally, you write down some other stories that have been simmering in your back brain for a while, and you keep doing the prospecting and research that will generate new stories. But there's another outlet that too many writers overlook: nonfiction. If your idea makes for a gripping yarn, chances are the background information is interesting all by itself. The world is full of magazines looking for well written articles to fill their pages. Quite frankly, nonfiction writing is easier than making up stories, and in general, it pays a lot better and reaches a wider audience. So where's the downside?

Think of it as advertising. Think of it as a way to get double the pleasure out of your research, and to see the ideas and technologies from a different angle. Think of it as a lucrative side business, or as a day job to subsidize your fiction habit. Think of it as a way to use all those brilliant little details that just wouldn't fit in your story. But above all, just think about it.

STEP FIVE: CONTENTS UNDER PRESSURE

By the time you actually get around to writing your story, you should be a lay expert in the key technology, and the world expert in what it means for human beings in general, and your characters in particular. At some point, days or weeks or even years after you started, the story should suddenly come together in a sort of crystallization process. Or anyway it does for me, and all I can teach you here is what I personally know.

In any case, there'll come a day when the story is bursting from your fingertips. Best advice: clear your schedule and write it down. If you don't, it may fade. It may lose energy or detail, or your own personal interest may be drawn away to other shiny things, depriving the world of a story that might have been brilliant.

And when you write it, obviously, don't phone it in. Put your heart and soul into it, as you should into everything you do. *There's* a technology the world needs more of: dedication.

STEP SIX: REALITY CHECK

Let's say you did your prospecting right, and came up with a really good technology idea. Let's say you did your research right, exploring all the promises and pitfalls of this new magic. Let's say you simmered the mix for exactly the right amount of time, and uncovered exactly the right people and places and plot elements to show it all off to best effect. And let's say you were in top form when you wrote it all down.

Are you done? Not hardly.

The thing about technology writing—not just science fiction, but especially science fiction—is that it's difficult. First, you have to educate readers in all the basic science they need to know, in order for the technology to make sense. Some readers know a lot, and some know almost nothing, but you have to find a way to speak to all of them, without talking down, talking over their heads, or bogging down the story. Next you have to explain the technology itself: what it is, what it does, what it looks like, how it makes people feel. Next, you have to introduce your characters, get oriented in your world, set your plot in motion and hurtle the reader through crisis and climax and resolution. And you have to make it clear—if only implicitly—that this story could not have taken place without the technology you've described.

What's the chance of getting all this right on your first try? Basically zero. You're going to talk over some people's heads. You're going to confuse people. You're going to leave out crucial details, or drop in details that don't appear to make sense. You're going to choose the wrong word sometimes, and choose the wrong entire scene at others. It may sound like strange advice in a chapter on technology in science fiction, but once your story is written you should ask at least one nontechnical person to read it. You shouldn't necessarily expect them to enjoy it, but if they don't understand it, you've probably failed.

If possible, you should also get at least one technical person to read it, who's versed in the story's subject matter. Such folks can be really helpful in spotting errors, oversights, misunderstandings, and missed opportunities.

Finally, you should ask at least one professional writer to look over your text, to see if you're making optimal use of the language. There may be metaphors you're glossing over, or turns of phrase you're misusing. There may be sentences that are technically flawless and communicationally clear, but clunky. (For example, because they make up words like "communicationally", and then break for unnecessary parenthetical asides.) That's bad; your story should reel out as effortlessly as a dream, and as inexorably as the history of technology itself. If it doesn't, then all your hard work goes for naught.

More than any other branch of literature, science fiction is a demanding old hag. You have to tell a good story, wrapped around interesting characters in a setting people can relate to, but you have to do it on Mars, with brain scanners and quantum entanglement and androids dreaming of electric sheep. And God help you, you have to get every bit of it right or you'll never hear the end of it. Because more so than any other branch of literature, with the possible exception of Civil War fiction, you're writing for an audience that knows more about everything than you could ever hope to.

And yet with every story in a major SF magazine, with every novel that appears on somebody's Year's Best list, with every positive review or word-of-mouth bestseller, we find another writer pulling it all together, pulling the technology rabbit out of a hat as yet uninvented. And doing it brilliantly. These people are your competition; you have to write better than every single one of them, or you'll never get off the launch pad. Don't get me wrong; I'm sure you can do it, or you wouldn't be reading this book. Just don't kid yourself that the technology part is easy, or doesn't matter, or can be retrofitted onto a story you've already written. As in the field of technology itself, that kind of thinking leads straight to the poor house.

Good luck.

CHAPTER SIX

WORLD BUILDING

Kim Richards

World building is the single most important thing you do for your novel. The same principles apply on a smaller scale for short works but for the purposes of this discussion, we'll focus on book length projects.

WHY WORLD BUILD? THE BIG 'WHAT IF'

What's the big deal about world building? It sounds like a lot of unnecessary work, but is it? Writers sometimes get lazy when world building, usually when they are anxious to dive into the story. Sure, if that is your best style but to pull it off, you had better be an exceptional writer. No one enjoys writing himself or herself into a corner, which is the normal after-effect of being impatient with the underlying foundations for any novel.

Consider these words of modern day science fiction writers:

"World building is essential to anyone who writes." —Holly Lisle.[43]

This means everyone must world build, no matter what genre he or she writes in. Science fiction is simply the most obvious.

The scope of what is necessary depends upon where the story will take place. If you have a small town in mind, then a map of the town and surrounding counties may be enough. Large-scale projects spanning galaxies require less detail on individual planet specifics and more generic details about those worlds populating it, with zoom-in focus on those featured/visited in the story.

Sometimes world building is based upon historical evidence or on a real modern day town. Whether the world setting for a novel is based upon some truth, a creation of the writer's mind or a combination of both, the basics needed are still the same.

Victoria Strauss says, "When I first began writing, my solution was to wing it. I'd take an idea and plunge right in, letting the story take me where it would and allowing the world to develop spontaneously.

The problem was that I constantly wrote myself into corners... I realized I needed to find some discipline." [44]

Hers is a common experience of most writers in their early works. Why we have to learn these lessons the hard way is simply a part of learning the craft and finding our own individual styles. It is this discipline, which world building brings us. The process strengthens the story every step of the way and breathes life into it.

Good advice.

The most important thing you need to successfully world build is patience. That is the one word which can make or break your story starting with the world building phase. Take time to read, plan, mull it all over, and to search for solutions. Straight up, it is hard to do, this patience thing. You will not find it in instructional articles or books. You can only locate it deep inside of yourself. Yes, you can learn patience; it can be cultivated.

Every writer aches to dive into the meat of his or her story and get on with the fun part. One suggestion right off: have fun with the world building too. This part is as creative as the story writing process if you let it be.

Take time to read and research. Allow ideas to ferment as you plan. Give yourself permission to mull things over; mentally search for solutions. Take long walks in the park after a heavy research session and allow all that information to soak through.

Talk about it. Sometimes just vocalizing your ideas to someone else can bring important details to light and if they ask questions, you know you are on to something interesting. Brainstorm with them. They will become your cheerleader and, in some cases, hold you accountable for procrastination. It is okay to let yourself get excited about this.

The worst thing you can do for any story is rush through the world building phase, which is extremely tempting when you are anxious to get to the story. This chapter examines some of the reasons why and offers some suggestions. Just remember, no one can give you patience but yourself.

"Before I do anything else, I make sure that I have a firm grasp of my world's principles."—Victoria Strauss.[45]

Principles are the basic building blocks of any world. They include things like what type of atmosphere is there, what is the chemical composition of life, how does magic/technology work, and what are the physics rules which apply to them. Principals include the presence or lack of gender and their roles in the world, defining religious views or restrictions placed upon beings as a result. Do not forget specifics on physical limitations and exceptional abilities of the world and its life forms.

"One of the first things to be done before you write any story that steps out of the most severe, mundane reality is to set the limits on the rules by which your particular game is to be played..."—Marion Zimmer Bradley

Remember those two bits of advice. Heck, print them out and paste them where you can see them throughout the main world building stage. I say 'main world building' stage because the process never really stops until you type those two little words, "The End." Here we speak of the main body of creation where in space and time the story will take place is gathered together and linked in the way a suit of chain mail is constructed. Each link is a bit of necessary information which threads through other links. Any missing or weak links make the story armor vulnerable.

Steven Savage suggests a focus on:

> "origin, ecology, intelligent life and culture, economy, trade and limitations imposed, then technology."[46]

It is interesting to note the order in which he proposes these. They are in order of life importance. Origin affects ecology; both of those affect how life evolves and what cultures emerge, which in turn also affect economy, trade, laws, and the necessity for the creation of the last one: technology.

Let's look at each:

ORIGIN

This is the actual planetary creation and includes subsequent religious views on it. Is this world a product of some Big Bang theory? A former moon of a now destroyed world? Whether or not this information makes its way into your story is less important than you knowing it because this affects everything about the world: chemical composition, atmosphere composition and temperature, evolution of life, planet topography, gravity and more. These things, like the chain mail links, affect aspects such as weather and character dress, customs and technologies invented.

ECOLOGY

This includes planetary makeup, life basis (a common theory in the 1960s involved carbon versus silicon based life forms), chemical and mineralogical make up..., plus how those affect the world. What types of plant and animal life could plausibly spring up from the conditions you present? For example: if the atmosphere were acidic, what types of life would evolve? What would be their strengths for survival? Their weaknesses? Their prey and their enemies?

INTELLIGENT LIFE AND CULTURE

Keep in mind how the ecology will shape the biology of the life, their body types, modes of transportation, and customs.

ECONOMY, TRADE AND ANY LIMITATIONS IMPOSED

Again, the other points will affect this one and the other way around. If they have plundered necessary resources, it will shape their current law structures and basic needs (food, shelter, and clothing).

TECHNOLOGY IS DIRECTLY AFFECTED BY THE NEEDS AND DESIRES OF THE INTELLIGENT LIFE COMMUNITY

Let's face it, if a species has the ability to fly, why would they bother with the invention of motorized ground vehicles? If water is scarce, and necessary for survival, then tremendous resources will be dedicated to the collection, preservation of and protection of water.

There really is no specific way to begin. Some start with a premise, a plot, or even a scene. Some writers start with a character. This is where short stories are incredibly handy. Use them to try your hand at each. Don't worry about whether what you have there will grow into a novel or if you'll be able to publish the story somewhere. Those can be the perks for later. For now, learn about yourself and your story ideas to figure out what works best for you. I predict you'll discover different stories like different techniques. They're all at your disposal so use them.

Starting with the setting is often the most logical because the world around a character shapes his actions, his attitudes, and his physiology. If you prefer a 'reverse-engineering' way of doing things, that's okay too. As Steven Savage points out,

"Realistic settings and realistic characters go hand in hand, each improving the other and improving their story."[47]

Often they shape one another as you go along.

Heed this advice from the pros:

Orson Scott Card says,

"...no two stories are developed in exactly the same way. However, in my experience one thing is constant: good stories don't come from trying to write a story the moment I think of the first idea."[48]

"Every tale needs conflict between characters and each other and their environment... I developed a plot designed to dramatize the features of my invented world."—Stephen Baxter.[49]

According to Ben Bova,

"The background of a science fiction story is so important that it often shapes the path the story takes, just as the environment around us shapes our behavior."[50]

These writers are telling us the same thing: world building is important on various levels. Listen to them. They know what they are talking about.

I particularly like Ben Bova's seven tips[51] for making the background/setting work:

• Make every background detail work. It must be important to the story.

• Don't try to explain how machinery works; just show what it does

- Go ahead and invent new devices and bring on scientific discoveries. Just make sure they don't contradict known science today, or can be believably explained

- Know your background thoroughly

- Learn the basics of science

- Take care with names. They set the tone for the story. (And please make them pronounceable for all our sakes)

- The story must be consistent internally

Orson Scott Card reminds us,

"...because speculative fiction always differs from the knowable world, the reader is uncertain about what can and can't happen in the story until the writer has spelled out the rules."[52]

There is truth in the words of Steven Savage when he says,

"Nothing happens without a reason."[53]

It's your job to figure out what happens and what the reason for it happening is. He also recommends having a vision for your setting. "A feel for your world." Mr. Savage says,

"As you design your setting, the feel for it, the vision of it will evolve. Over time you'll start recalling things without looking at your notes, or finding connections that just pop into your mind."[54]

When you reach this stage, you are ready to write unabashedly.

"Do your research, learn how to craft a believable plot and realistic characters."—Tina Morgan.[55]

She has a lot to say about the necessity of thorough research.

"If you fail to follow through on your research, it will show in your writing. At the least, you may lose your reader's attention, and at the worst, their loyalty."[56]

Research is where you find many of the links to create your story chain mail. This is not the place to skimp on details, but where you want to concentrate a serious amount of time. You want to gather enough links to cover the entire story on all sides.

Morgan says it best here:

"Like any other genre, you will find readers from a variety of occupations but in science fiction you will find many readers who know science. Often their love for technology or space came from reading a science fiction or fantasy novel as a young child and they transferred that passion into a career in the technology or science industry. For this reason I say the most important aspect of creating your setting will be research."[57]

The research will make the world live; solidify it in your own mind and turn it into a place to walk into. Let it be real to in your own mind so that you can accurately show it to your reader.

Michael A. Banks says,

> "There's no doubt that science is a necessary element in science fiction—be it as a background or the source of conflict."[58]

He suggests three stages for getting the science in your science fiction. Stage one is to decide how technical you need to be. Stage two involves acquiring the necessary knowledge to create the setting. Stage three is figuring ways to work the science into the story without being obvious.

STAGE ONE

How technical do you need to be? As much as is necessary for you to comfortably work. Maybe you don't need to know the specifics of how an engine works but if at some point it fails as part of the storyline, you need to know why and how this happened. You need to know what the consequences of its failure are and the chances are for repairing it.

Do not be afraid to go back and figure out these details as you go along. There is no point in stressing over whether you've done enough research to begin a story. You have no way of predicting what may crop up and you certainly don't want to use world building research as an excuse for procrastination. If the physical world basics are there, and the cultures solid, then these situations will be minor details to work out.

Ask the hard questions: do any of your characters know about the science or technology, its problems and possible solutions to solving those problems? Why and how do they know? If they don't know, how can they find out?

STAGE TWO

Acquire the necessary knowledge. Look to the internet. Read. A lot. Ask experts. If you have a character who is colorblind, make an appointment with an optometrist to find out how this would affect their depth perception and distance. Call up a local geologist and schedule time to ask them questions about rock formations.

You don't need degrees in these areas when there are experts out there with the skills and knowledge to tell you. Introduce yourself and tell them about what you are writing. Most often, if they have the time, people are thrilled to talk about their area of expertise. Thank them and mention them in the book's credits. Send them a copy once it is published. They will become your best word of mouth advertisement.

STAGE THREE

Figure out how to work the science into the story without being obvious. This again goes back to showing the science at work, not necessarily going into long diatribes on how it works. If a character needs to know, let them ask but do not explain for the sake of explaining. Nothing is more boring than a character launching into a long explanation of how a laser rifle works when the other character just wants to know how to fire it. If the details fit into the conversation naturally, then by all means, include them. The trick is finding a balance between giving information and force-feeding it. That takes practice.

Marion Zimmer Bradley reminds us that every world has its own rules and you must have an understanding of these laws by which it exists. "...you don't simply throw the door open to unreason and abandon all the rules..."

"For the purpose of believability, however, you must adhere to the history you create."—Tina Morgan[59]

Both of these writers point out how important it is to listen to our own research and ideas. Filling up files or binders with information never used or blatantly discarded is a useless waste of time. Create your worlds, set up their technological/physical/ecological boundaries and then stick to them. Live within them. Let your world become real to you. Treat it as though it were as solid as the Earth you walk upon now. Only then can you accurately show it to your reader.

Have fun along the way. If the planet you're working on has a blue tint to everything, you'll need to know what would cause that... chemical composition? Think of how every day objects would look that way. Get a pair of blue lens sunglasses and walk around wearing them for a few days, inside and outdoors. How do things look? What happens to shadows and light? How does it affect the color of things? Take photos and run them through a program such as Adobe Photoshop or Paintshop Pro to give them a blue tinted filter. Print them out and put them around you. (If you don't feel comfortable with the computer work or don't want to spend money to have the local print shop do it for you, take a photo, and lay a piece of blue plastic over it. The colored plastic wrap works. This sounds silly at first but it does give you a real time experience and impression of your world as it looks.

Stephen Baxter says this about research,

"Building a world big enough to fill a hard SF novel involves a lot of heavy research. And I mean heavy: I'm talking about getting access to a university library or similar and going through undergraduate texts and research journals..."[60]

Michael A. Banks tells us there are two types of research: the kind you do yourself and the kind you have someone else do for you.[61] This involves making use of experts, university departments, and library services. There are ask-the-expert websites for nearly any subject, which are well worth the web-surfing time to locate.

Ben Bova, in his book, *The Craft of Writing Science Fiction that Sells*, categorizes research into three areas:[62]

- Your own life experiences

- Experiences you learn from others who have lived them

- Information found in books, on film and tape, or online

He also reminds us that research should include people, not just places and things. He says to read popular science books published each year. The one bit of his advice, which stands out, is this:

"Science is beautiful and anyone can understand the basics of scientific thought."

Keep this in mind if research intimidates you.

"...sometimes you can go overboard on details, or at the same time not have enough. The rule for how much detail one needs doesn't exits in my opinion," says Steven Savage, "You have to determine what you need to know. My advice is to have a little more than you think you'll need just to be sure you've got enough details straight and enough to have fun with."[63]

Don't let the research and planning become the reason for not writing the story. If you're writing along and have to stop to map out something or research a planetary phenomenon, it doesn't mean you've failed in your preparation. Just do what you need to and get back to the story.

Victoria Strauss says that she world builds in bits and pieces this way. It's her natural style. For her it prevents her from coming up with too much detail. She says,

"This is important since I've found that if I go to the trouble of making something up, it's incredibly hard to stop myself from including it, even if it doesn't really serve the plot."[64]

As with most creative endeavors, you must find what works for you and make it your own. Try different writer's suggestions. Toss the ones not working out but make good use of the ones, which do.

As Steven Savage points out, the main character in the story is the setting. He says,

"In writing original fiction, knowing, understanding, and creating your world is paramount."[65]

S.A. Swann has some good advice about understanding how your world is different. First, know what it's different from. Second, explain the difference, and third, follow your rules.

"Making your world different can be as simple as locating it in that vast unknown territory, 'the future'."[66]

Anne McCaffrey says this,

"Internal logic is essential in either SF or fantasy. You have to believe what you're writing, where you are so that it comes across to the reader."[67]

Writers commonly sit down and write detailed character sketches for their heroes, their villains, and sometimes minor characters. These 'scenes' help to cement the person in the writer's consciousness.

Why not a world building sketch? I suggest creating them as you go along through the planning stages for several reasons. First, sketches offer you a bit of writing time, which will temper impatient tendencies to skimp on world building.

Second, they give you solid images in your mind's eye of what this place you plan to spend months, perhaps years living in, is like. Whether these sketches end up in the manuscript is not important now.

The third use for world building sketches is as reminders. Throughout a novel's creation, real life throws things at us. Procrastination can widen the gaps between writing times. Sickness, family, and bill paying often pull us away from our writing time. Reading through the sketches can refresh your mental picture of the world and the story you're telling. Sketches also tweak your enthusiasm for a project.

TIPS FOR BEING ORGANIZED

It seems every writer has his or her own system for organization. Anne McCaffrey[68] and Dennis Jones make lists of names. Ben Bova[69] has a three ring binder with printouts of character sketches, maps, and world information. This is a good idea since it also serves as a back up in the case of a hard drive crash. Tabs inside make finding sections easy to spot at a glance. Some folks use sticky note software or create files in a cabinet on characters and setting.

Find whatever works best for your personal working space and style. If tacking maps and sketches up on a bulletin board works, then go for it. Just be consistent with whatever you choose to do. Take Steven Savages advice:

> "Choose a format that works, that is easy to use and that you can refer to easy. It also helps to imagine someone else may be reading it when you record your information—because what seems to make sense to you one day, may not the next."[70]

The plan is to learn your world so thoroughly that you no longer have to look something up but that the information is there, just as a safety net. With the lengthy publishing schedules today, the organization you do now may be your saving grace when a revision is requested more than a year after the initial writing of the novel. And consider the sequel. No one wants to have to recreate the original world.

WHAT NOT TO DO WHEN CREATING A WORLD OR SETTING:

USE OF COMPLICATED OR HARD TO PRONOUNCE NAMES

This is a common mistake often found in the early days of a writer's career and includes using special characters on the keyboard in the names. Yes, you want the characters to be memorable but their name is just as important as in real life. You don't want people to skim over them because the name is just too much work to figure out. Heaven forbid, you falter on your own pronunciation during a reading. Fans sometimes have alternate ways in pronouncing a name (a play on the word) which can be embarrassing, though a fun ploy for a villain to make use of when taunting the hero.

Think about the names a bit. They can portray a part of culture or social status in the way that Miss and Missus do in American English. The addition of 'son' (Richards versus Richardson) indicates place within a family. The history of our own names reveals this to us. Just look at how many last names came from ancestral occupations: Smith, Baker, Archer. The simple changing of a letter such as in the Spanish 'S' and 'Z' (Chaves versus Chavez) to indicate nobility can affect the way a character perceives himself or how others around him treat him.

The meaning of a name can be important to the story, if you so desire. Names often reflect the times, hopes, and attitudes of the parents. A name of Stormy brings up very different sets of expectations and mental images than one of Daisy. If there is a special reason a character has been given a name, its religious significance or reason for its choosing will affect his/her life. Upholding the 'family name' has been a long-standing human tradition across many cultures. Consider the negative outlooks on perceived 'crime' families' last names. How might this affect the way others treat a child born into such a family?

Silly names can ruin the character image you are trying to portray. The same goes for world names and what technology is referred to. Local story jargon and created languages can add flavor. Just as with spices in cooking, too much can spoil the whole dish. Create what you need but use it sparingly, intermixed with common words such that your reader identifies with their meaning without a need for a glossary.

Ben Bova warns us to be wary of science fiction jargon. The uses of it "usually show that the writer has not been very original. By using the standard jargon of science fiction you just might find yourself wallowing in the standard clichés as well."[71]

Take the recent fad of replacing cuss words with a made up word for the world. The idea was to make cussing unique to enrich the culture. It was neat when *Farscape* had its characters saying, "Frelling", and cool when the new *Battlestar Galactica* folks said, "Fracking." Then in *Firefly*... hey! Enough is enough. You don't want to simply follow the herd. When that goes out of style, so will your story.

PUTTING IN TOO MUCH DETAIL

You must know the world inside and out but that doesn't mean every minute detail must be told in the story. Only the relevant parts.

> "There are two reasons you must not tell the reader everything you know. The first is simply that no one reads science fiction for the science. The second is that the story is told from a character's viewpoint and that character is very unlikely to be thinking about scientific and technical details of his environment..."—Michael A. Banks.[72]

He also tells us to avoid contriving a scene to explain things to the reader and suggests narrative flashbacks, or better, to show science and technology in use rather than describing it.

> "There's no need to spend a lot of time explaining every element of your world but showing how your characters live can help bring a story to life... simple things that can be mentioned in passing will give a fictional world a third dimension in a reader's mind"—Tina Morgan.[73]

> "The details of the world should always be slipped in largely unnoticed..." — Juliet McKenna.[74]

Stephen Baxter says,

> "Show, don't tell: even though the point of the story is the new world, the story is actually about the characters, with their world as a backdrop; if I want to point out some neat feature of my world, it has to be relevant to—better, a significant contributor to—the story."[75]

Of the details you do reveal, Lee Masterson suggests,

> "These details do not play much a part of the unfolding events of your story but they will flesh out the world you are creating. Your readers will gain more insight into the times and places your characters must deal with and this in turn gives your story a more believable platform to spring from."[76]

THINGS TO CONSIDER WHEN WORLD BUILDING:

1) WHAT'S YOUR STYLE?

Author, Stephen Baxter said this about the influence of science fiction writers throughout his life: "I'm conscious I stand on the shoulders of Giants." He says,

> "Of course, when constructing a new hard SF tale, I don't consciously set out to build in references (to influential works)... my attention is on the development of an original science fiction idea and how it is to be embedded

in the structure of the story. But clearly my influences... do play a part in the shaping of the material."[77]

2) START SMALL, BUILD UP. BIG PICTURE, WORK IN DETAILS

Whichever will work better for your 'What If' idea. The scope or big picture you have in mind shapes your choices.

> "Of course every 'rule' is there to be broken. The story's the thing: I allow myself to do whatever I think needs to be done to make the story work."—Stephen Baxter.[78]

Consider the scope of your story. By "scope," we are talking about the big picture: whether this story deals with a small town on a small planet somewhere or spans an entire galaxy. Tailor the details to the story with regards to the depth and breadth of how much, or how little, world building is necessary.

The small town story certainly would need a good layout of the buildings and local landmarks. It calls for more specific details on the up-close descriptions of landscape and plant/animal life. Where a large scope, space opera style story, which covers vast areas of space, needs fewer of the microscopic details and more insight into how travel and communications work. The large scope story is more likely to deal with the governmental and social relationships between worlds and the need for space travel.

3) DOUBLE CHECK YOUR FACTS

Get them right or you will hear about it or lose your reader. It's worth the extra effort. Again, patience!

Take Anne McCaffrey's advice and find experts who will give you the specifics you need. As Ben Bova tells us,

> "Be certain that you have the factual information you need to make your story authentic; but don't let that stifle your imagination."[79]

With today's information rich society, there is little excuse for not making the science and technology plausible. Make use of libraries, the internet—particularly university and scientific company sites, magazines, blogs, podcasts, anything and everything you can find which pertains to your story subject. One note of caution: be wary of information websites, which are often fan-based. If you find some tidbit of information on one of these opinion-offering places, take the time and effort to check the truth of the facts before using them. This is not as important in fiction as it is in non-fiction but it serves you well to know where the ideas comes from, even if you go with the opinion viewpoint for a story.

4) LEVELS OF TECHNOLOGY

S.A. Swann, in his World building article, says to utilize unintended consequences,

"Every piece of technology will eventually find niches other than what their developers intended."[80]

This author gives six questions to ask when considering the technology for your world:

- For what purpose was it developed?
- Who developed it?
- Who opposes it and why?
- Name three uses other than the intended one. Take Sudafed for example. This drug was created to help those suffering from sinus and colds but it is just as commonly used today in the production of methamphetamines.
- Name three professions it will create or alter.
- In what three ways can it be abused?

Steven Savage would add one more: What cost is there?[81] All technology costs in terms of resources, time, training, discipline, and upkeep. It also can have social and ecological costs as well. Those are world-shaping considerations, which shouldn't be overlooked.

If you haven't noticed, world building involves many, many questions.

"If you're writing near future science fiction, you need to take into account the technology that's available today," says Tina Morgan.[82]

She recommends considering the rate of advances.

Along this line, S.A. Swann reminds us that change happens over time.[83] Technology evolves in decades and cultural changes in generations. Nothing changes instantly overnight.

5) UNUSUAL OR UNEXPLAINED SCIENCES OR TECHNOLOGY/ MAGIC

Dennis Jones says it best,

"Sorcery and hi-tech often function the same way... devices to advance plot."

Steven Savage defines it as,

"Magic and technology are to me the same thing... a way of interacting with one's environment to achieve results and to alter things."[84]

Enough said. Use them or don't. Just make sure the rules of how they work are clearly defined and that you stick to them.

6) RELIGION AND CULTURE

Author Steven Savage says about culture,

"Culture is not dull, static, or pointless—it's a living thing that enhances living, intelligent creatures. Like a person or like a population it has personality, ways of working and it adapts and grows."

"Culture exists for a reason—it's a way to pass on information."[85]

"(It's) what intelligent life creates and passes on—rules, ideas, language, ways of thought,"

and suggests the following considerations for yours:

- What traditions are necessary for and improve on survival?
- How are these traditions passed on?
- Which become corrupt over time, altered, misunderstood, or ritualized without meaning?
- Why has this happened?
- How does the culture go about controlling and enforcing traditions?

Steven Savage points out.

"When you deal with culture, you deal with religion. When you get down to it, religion is about how people think the universe works, how they interact with it, and what lessons they think they learn to apply to their lives. It's part of cultures, even if it may not look like religion initially.

In fact, embrace it, study it, theorize about and learn about it. It makes your cultures more real."[86]

7) ENVIRONMENTAL ISSUES AND HOW THEY AFFECT THE WORLD

Terraforming or lack thereof are issues to be considered. Are precious resources exploited or carefully managed. Ecology: Where does it come from and why?

"A good way to figure out the vital questions to help you think so high a level is, 'How does this universe differ from our own?'"—Steven Savage who defines ecology as, "organisms and their environment and their relationships. In other words... the contents/inhabitants of the world and their relations."[87]

Holly Lisle's great article on world building[88] gives us eleven rules for an ecosystem. Applying them to your world and its inhabitants will help keep what you've created realistic and making sense in relation to our own world or how it differs from modern-day Earth.

- Life feeds on waste
- Life grabs opportunities
- Life likes volatiles
- Redundancy matters
- There are at least five ways of doing anything
- Micro-climates demand micro-ecologies

- Big predators eat a lot
- Life's Big 3: Eat, Excrete, Reproduce
- Life is weapon's escalation
- Specialist life forms are more efficient
- Generalist life forms live longer

8) ATMOSPHERE AND GRAVITY, WEATHER AND LANDSCAPE

And how they shape the world and those living on it. How weather and landscape will affect the plant/animal and character evolutions.This is where a little reading on university astronomy websites or picking up used basic astronomy and physics textbooks can be extremely helpful. Depending upon the scope of your novel, a bit of biology helps as well.

Don't skimp on deciding how things work and how they affect one another... remember those chain mail links. For example: the mass and type of star a planetary system's sun is directly influences its gravitational effects upon the planets, their orbits size/speed/shape. Those determine weather factors, which in turn, tell what types of life would develop in that kind of environment; perhaps more importantly, what types of live would thrive there.

9) REFERENCES

If history is important to the story, make a time line of events for easy reference. Creating a map of your world for easy reference. Calendars too. Detailed maps make it easier to know where your characters are. They keep you oriented and prevent continuity mistakes with regards to placement. No one wants to be embarrassed by the docking bay suddenly being north of the city when last chapter it was east. It removes guesswork so you can concentrate on the writing of the story instead of wracking your brain to remember the layout of the main city. It's all about getting these things right the first time. Every writer could use fewer things to revise and edit in subsequent drafts of the manuscript.

This quote of Orson Scott Card gives us something to think over,

> "...when it comes to story telling... and making up maps of imaginary lands is a kind of storytelling—that mistakes are often the beginning of the best ideas."[89]

Ben Bova points out that real life maps are good places to find interesting names.[90] It's good to keep in mind how places are often named after famous persons or events and doing this in your created world fleshes it out just a little more.

He has a good point in that mistakes can be wonderful plot devices so don't despair if you find one in your work. You may not have to rework everything you've already created.

Steven Savage says to ask the following questions when you find an error. See if it can be turned into a part of the story.

- Is this an actual mistake? Perhaps you wrote something your subconscious mind remembers but your conscious mind forgot.
- Can it be explained?
- Can it be fixed by altering something?
- By adding something?
- Subtracting something?
- Can it be corrected by making it a part of the story and the continuity?

Mr. Savage reminds us

"a continuity error is not the end of the world. But be sure your solution isn't either."[91]

Along with maps, timelines can be anchoring points, places to show the history, which came before and the plot to come. They are excellent ways to have a visual reference of overlapping events.

"Every fictional universe has a past if only an implied one," says S.A. Swann, "When someone in a story has a different view of history than the reader does, the reader will gain some insight into that character's personality and culture."[92]

10) PAST, PRESENT, FUTURE

Just as the world shapes the plants, animal, and intelligent life present on it, the reverse is also true, particularly with regards to societies. Past actions of peoples can destroy or alter a planetary region. In terraforming cases, the entire world is changed for good or ill. War tactics and large-scale natural disasters affect the world rather quickly. How does this world recover from these abuses? Or does it?

Again, depending upon your vision of scope and the timeframe the story will span, how nature renews itself, or how a population sets out to rescue/resources, can bring about plot ideas and change the world make up.

World building is hard work, yet rewarding when all of the links connect and the story flows without any chinks. Nothing beats the thrill of a reader loving a world/setting you've created as much as you do. Be creative. Have fun. Do your research. Now, get to work!

CHAPTER SEVEN

ALIEN CREATION

Michael McRae

"What a splendid perspective contact with a different civilization might provide! In a cosmic setting vast and old beyond ordinary human understanding we are a little lonely, and we ponder the ultimate significance, if any, of our tiny but exquisite blue planet, the Earth... In the deepest sense the search for extraterrestrial intelligence is a search for ourselves."
Carl Sagan (1934—1996)

Science fiction imagines the possible, extrapolating ideas from the models supported by modern science to create scenarios of fantasy. For humans, there is arguably no bigger question in science than "Are we alone?"

Most of this chapter is aimed at the hard science writer who wishes to be as faithful as possible to present theories on non-terrestrial life forms. The first section explores how we might define life, how it may have developed, and the possibilities of finding it elsewhere in the universe. The second part is a rough guide to developing an alien entity for your story and explores where aliens fit into speculative fiction today.

Please note that this chapter is merely a suggestion on how one might want to approach the topic of alien development. Science fiction does exist on a spectrum, categorized by a rather hazy definition, so while I promote scientifically supported reasoning to found your creativity, I suggest that you be selective in the information you feel is relevant to your work.

PART 1: THE SCIENCE OF LIFE

"It's life, Captain, but not life as we know it."

This immortal, oft misquoted statement spoken by Commander Spock in *Star Trek: The Motion Picture* (1979) was made in reference to an newly-discovered entity that failed to fit certain preconceived concepts of life. It is a phrase that reflects perhaps one of the most important questions we face in modern science; how similar could extraterrestrial life be to our own?

WHAT IS LIFE?

In truth, when it comes to understanding what it takes for something to be considered 'alive', we have nowhere else to look but here on Earth. There is presently no concrete evidence of anything we could possibly describe as xenobiological, a word that literally means 'the study of foreign life'. Therefore life remains a purely terrestrial concept. To complicate matters further, the definitions we use are limited by critical weaknesses of human perception. Since we have a nasty habit of personifying nearly anything non-human, we end up with a rather anthropocentric view of things that are 'living'. Our morals, our social interactions, even our emotions are commonly imposed onto anything we define as 'alive'.

We talk to plants, describe animal relationships in terms of human emotion, and often use words that give an illusion of forethought or decision making to organisms too simple to be capable of such things.

Before we go anywhere near contemplating the relevance of aliens in science fiction, we need to agree on some way of defining what an alien might be. And to do that, we need to start from scratch in coming up with some agreeable idea on what it might mean to be 'alive'.

In school students often learn the acronym MRS GREN to make it easier to categorize 'biotic' from 'abiotic'. It is basic and inadequately addresses vague 'near living' entities, however does make for a good starting point. MRS GREN summarizes in seven simple words the essentials of what an object or system needs to be considered living.

MOVEMENT

Some form of mobility or transport is associated with all living things, even if it is limited to the simple movement of select chemicals across a membrane.

RESPIRATION

All life forms on Earth require energy to operate, taking in light energy to convert to chemical energy or simply taking in a high energy chemical substrate to manipulate. In many cases, oxygen and carbohydrate react to form products of carbon dioxide and water in addition to some surplus chemical energy. Organisms that don't require oxygen use a diverse array of other reactions that do similar jobs. While light is the dominant primary energy source for life here, any energy resource capable of being used for manipulating chemical reactions is feasible.

SENSES

All living things respond in some fashion to change in their environment. Even with a simple example such as phototaxis, where a bacterium might move towards or away from light, there is a common need for a physical response to an external stimulus.

GROWTH

Living things expand their dimensions, taking on nutrients to build up a solid structure. Subsequent loss of material through injury or reproduction also needs to be replaced.

REPRODUCTION

It could be argued that the core feature of what separates 'life' from 'non-life' is the ability living systems have to copy themselves *imperfectly*. This imperfect replication system is something I'll expand on later, but seems to be essential for our definition of life to exist.

EXCRETION

Absorbing nutrients in the form of complex molecules inevitably means certain chemicals are either not needed or will be changed into a form that is unnecessary or perhaps dangerous. Retaining them reduces essential storage space or, worse, could disrupt the functioning of the organism; the only answer is to remove them from the system.

NUTRITION

In order to grow, reproduce, repair, and maintain the functioning of the organism, essential chemicals are required to be taken into the system. These chemicals are subsequently changed in a system of reactions called 'metabolism'.

For something to be considered alive it must reflect all of these seven things. A crystal can grow and might even reproduce in some sense, but a crystal cannot take in nutrients in order to change them, hence cannot excrete. It might be argued that some crystals can respond to environmental change, yet they do not reproduce in an imperfect way and do not use energy to maintain a system of chemical changes. In no sense can we call them alive.

It should also be noted that all known living things are constructed from a common selection of chemicals. They are all organic, meaning that they based on a carbon structure. Common to all life is a group of nitrogenous organic structures called 'amino acids'. Replication is centered on another family of chemicals called 'nucleic acids'. All living things are cellular, being fully enclosed in a structure made from lipids, which keep an aqueous environment external to the chemicals making up the organism. The fact that these chemical groups are common to all life and are used in virtually identical capacities in all living things is evidence that helps support the model that all living things on Earth are distantly related. It therefore does little to help us understand how the biochemistry might operate in an unrelated life form, but it does offer us a few clues.

We can use all of this information to give us a basic idea of what universal law we can describe that might define unrelated living things. Life, as it stands for us presently, is a complicated system of chemical reactions that persists within a changing environment by some means of self-alteration. In other words, life could be described as any system that benefits by absorbing chemicals to use for energy, growth, and replication, and can subsequently evolve as a system so it can continue to exist regardless of limited environmental change.

THE DEVELOPMENT AND EVOLUTION OF LIFE

Already it's easy to see that this is a complicated definition and is far from black and white. For example: what constitutes a single living unit? Is it fair to think of all life forms as distinctive, separate from one another as individual entities, or as a single, interdependent system? Are we collections of living things, communities of chemical reactions cooperating in order to exist, and yet still competing with one another to remain viable? What of viruses, which don't fit all of the rules so neatly? Is there anything that is 'nearly alive'?

To investigate this further we should first explore the present model explaining how life might have formed on Earth. It will assist us in developing something of an appreciation for the development of life on other planets. About four and a half billion years ago, Earth looked very little like it does today. A cooling body of various metallic compounds, the infant planet was a rotating sphere of molten rock covered in a thin atmosphere. Just like a mixture of sand and gravel in water takes time to settle into layers, the heavy minerals were steadily sinking in towards the core as the lighter gases stratified in the atmosphere. All of this occurred amidst constant disruptions of meteorite impact as rocks descended in a relative stream from the cluttered heavens.

Unlike today, large amounts of ultra-violet radiation from the sun baked the planet's surface, unimpeded by the non-existent layer of ozone we now take for granted. Water vapor released from inside the Earth condensed into liquid as the planet radiated a large amount of its heat into space. The dominating gases in the slowly thickening atmosphere were carbon dioxide and nitrogen; pure oxygen was rare, most of it still locked away in various compounds such as carbon dioxide. With time, depressions in the crust filled with relatively fresh water in a constant stream of rain. We can hardly imagine life forming in this radiated, hot, oxygen-thin world.

Here lies our problem, though. Truth is we could not imagine modern life forming here. What we perceive as life are organisms that work well within this present environment. However, remember our definition for life? MRS GREN?

Life, at its most basic, is essentially nothing more than a relationship of rather involved chemical reactions. Chemicals react most efficiently in fluid media; in other words, gases and liquids. Of these, liquids are more energy efficient than gases as the particles are crowded closer together. Water is a superb medium to act as a solvent for chemicals due to its unique molecular properties. However, it is argued that water is not necessarily the only choice for a living chemical system to develop in. Liquid hydrocarbons, for instance, could possibly do just as nicely.

Therefore, we can reason that life developed on Earth in a body of water. Recall that modern life forms: a) are carbon-based, b) have amino acid structures, c) are enclosed in lipid membranes and d) rely on strings of nucleic acid to act as a 'template' for growth, repair and replication. As there are no life forms that do not follow this pattern, we can assume that that this system of chemistry was the most efficient (of perhaps several) in this developing world. The question remains, if modern life requires an interaction of all of these chemicals to exist, how could they possibly all have developed at the same time? In other words, I can't just have a bubble of fat membrane and call it 'alive' without amino acid structures and nucleic acid to make it work.

Or can I?

All living systems copy themselves, and do so imperfectly. Copies they make of themselves are not always exactly the same as the parent. Chains of nucleic acid molecules (Deoxyribonucleic Acid, or DNA, and Ribonucleic Acid, or RNA) have the special property of being able to make doubles of themselves through matching up to complementary pieces. This very 'double stranded' property, in the right environment (relying on subtle changes in temperature) can produce numerous copies of a single nucleic acid string. No, it's quite living, but basic forms of this process can technically exist independently of other reactions. Fluctuating temperature is essentially all it requires (we use enzymes in conjunction with this property in Polymerase Chain Reactions, PCR, to turn a small amount of DNA into more useful quantities).

A problem with this is the fact that ultra violet radiation breaks the bonds in chains of nucleic acid. Therefore, such reactions would have to occur in water beneath rock shelves or in deep water away from direct sunlight.

What does that leave us with, a rather general reaction of sequences of nucleic acid chemicals reproducing identical sequences? Actually, no. As I said, it's not perfect. These sequences are not identical; mistakes happen. Now, suppose in a select location some sequences of nucleic acid are better at making copies of themselves, or they physically do a better job of just existing than other sequences. These threads will become more common than other nucleic acid combinations; more individual nucleic acid chemicals in the pool will find themselves in these 'efficient' sequences than in any other 'less efficient' sequences. We know that some combinations of nucleic acid are more stable than others in varying acidities, temperatures, and salt concentrations.

Let's take this further. Forms of nucleic acid can interact with other chemicals, such as amino acid. Carbon is rather soluble in water and has bonds that are strong and yet have a degree of flexibility. Organic chemicals have been found inside chunks of meteorite, indicating that they are hardly limited to Earth. Amino acids can form in relatively diverse environments and have been demonstrated to be found in environments like that of early Earth. In other words, we don't need life to have simple biochemical building blocks.

Imagine that some nucleic acid sequences form which can associate with other groups of chemicals, occasionally ones that provide some small benefit. For instance, a select combination of nucleic acid might interact with an amino acid to provide some basic protection against ultra violet light. Again, these sequences will become more numerous. So far, the only real resource is bits of loose nucleic acid and perhaps an amino acid molecule. Pretty soon, we have basic competition in a chemical reaction that is beginning to become more complicated. More so, it is evolving due to the property of nucleic acid to be able to make imperfect copies of itself.

All life seems to rely on some form of distinctive boundary between it and its immediate environment. A membrane of lipids (fat molecules) is a perfect way of keeping a wall between the internal environment and the harsh aquatic world, with a hydrophobic tail pointing away from any water and the hydrophilic head forming the outer wall. We don't recognize any life forms as being 'acellular'. At some point, nucleic acid / protein structures became associated with biologically independent bubbles of fat called 'micelles'.

As the biochemical interactions became more complicated through simple chemical competition, those sequences that could access different forms of energy with greater efficiency gained an advantage. At some point a sequence developed that allowed it access to a chemical reaction between carbon dioxide and water, inspired by doses of solar radiation. Now able to trap light energy, this opened up the possibility for other reactions to occur that gave further advantages. Unfortunately, this ability to trap light energy and change it into useful chemical energy also released a rather destructive element called 'oxygen'.

And so the competition goes on. Countless sequences would be destroyed by oxidation, leaving only those that had combinations strong enough to cope. Life persisted, sequences recombined and eventually such a combination developed that led to a means of utilizing this oxidation as an energy resource in its own right. Enlisting oxygen to reverse the process, which it initially utilized to release it from carbon dioxide and water is called 'respiration': the main energy resource of a diverse array of modern organisms.

So, at which exact point can we call 'the beginning of life'? Where precisely did 'abiotic' turn 'biotic'? Was it when energy could be converted? Perhaps the first cells? The first successful sequences of nucleic acid?

Such is the spectrum of life; this question has no real answer.

Nucleic acid sequences are responsible for a single action we now call 'genes'. Humans have around 30,000 of them all contributing towards the creation of a single individual. Each performs some form of task, such as creating proteins, controlling the amount of work other genes do or protecting other more important genes. But they all work on that same principle as those first sequences did; if it means you can replicate yourself more efficiently than others can, you will make more copies. It reflects a simple facet of chemistry; imagine A and B react to make the product AB, and B and C react to make BC. Put A, B and C in the same environment—the reaction that is the most efficient will create the most products. If A and B react faster than B and C, there will be more AB than BC. A and C are competing for the resource of 'B'.

Initially, evolution was the result of a competition between individual gene sequences. This changes slightly when genes begin to associate with one another in a form of altruistic behavior, some sequences assisting others after finding it to be an advantage that they exist in the same vicinity. Those that could segregate themselves away from their environment into fat bubbles had another advantage. This arms race might have started over many times, occurred in many places, in many slightly different forms. Variants on these chemical interactions might have performed similar tasks and have commenced as their own protolife forms in competition with the one that ultimately led to our present version.

The common question asked is, 'So why don't we see this pre-life competition now'? Very simply, modern life is rather good at what it does. There is hardly a place on this planet which could be considered completely sterile. And of those places that are, most are rather inhospitable to even basic reactions. Simple nucleic acid sequences found in nature are often snapped up by bacteria that are efficient at searching for such things. So it is extremely doubtful that we could find such abiogenesis in nature.

This slow evolution of a chemical reaction based on pure chance would take time. It is hardly something that could be created in a test tube within a man's lifetime. It does, therefore, make it rather difficult to establish that this is indeed the way it happened. Science has to rely on clues rather than laboratory replication of the process.

Therefore, keep in mind that this is far from established truth. Like anything in science, it is a model that is supported by evidence. It's the best model we have. Questions still abound, and as this steady complication has taken literally billions of years, we can hardly hope to create a cat from a puddle of dirty water in the laboratory over a few lifetimes.

This model of life formation answers many questions about life today; the fact it is incomplete, has problems, and poses a multitude of questions does not discount it. It only demonstrates we need more information to fine tune it.

NEAR LIFE

Here's a good place to stop and ask, 'What, then, are viruses?'

Packets of nucleic acid wrapped in a protein shell, often lacking a lipid membrane and are incapable of self-replication without the assistance of a host organism's genetic machinery - they seem rather removed from our definitions.

Let's keep the idea in our minds that life is concentrated on the gene. The whole point of an individual gene is to replicate and it will cooperate with other genes to do this, something eminent biologist Richard Dawkins has described as 'selfish' in an effort to explain this notion of life. It is easier if we start by looking at this concept of a 'selfish gene'.

Transposons are genes that can remove themselves from one part of the nucleic acid sequence and insert themselves into another, thereby improving their chances at replicating. If this transposon can make proteins that help protect it when it moves around, we can call it a small virus, or 'vir'. If it is even more efficient, and can leave its immediate environment to find other genetic sequences in other cells, we could describe this as a 'virus'.

Again, it's all about replicating chemistry.

The role a particular trait takes can change with time and in association with other traits. It also relies on the nature of the environment. Our cartilaginous outer ears have developed from gill slits, for instance. As the environment changes, different genes, and gene combinations will be favored. Genes that replicate well in an acidic environment will suddenly struggle to dominate in an environment inundated by fresh water. However, if that same gene had a secondary trait that continued to offer an advantage—such as remaining viable under UV radiation—it would persist in spite of environmental change.

Changes in gene sequences abound; given a large amount of time and a large number of units, the number of different nucleic acid sequences is astronomical. Most don't work very well, if at all. However, every now and then an interaction will develop which will create a radically new sequence, which will out-compete all others to dominate.

For instance, the concept of different cellular units working together for the benefit of all is rather advanced. Taking this further, some of these sequences might find an advantage in exchanging genes to form a single 'super' sequence that can create those different types of cell—we're talking about multicellular life forms. Like ourselves.

Our own cells are actually a combination of two different life forms. Tiny units called 'mitochondria' assist in respiration. Mitochondria have their own genes, distinct from those in our cells' nucleuses. At one point in our ancestral past one cell engulfed another, the larger offering protection to the smaller one, the smaller in turn offering an advantage as it was efficient at converting energy. This partnership benefited both units, allowing this combination to persist. Plants have both mitochondria and a second organelle called a chloroplast. In other words, this event has happened more than once in Earth's biological history. It has possibly happened many times; the results of two such events have persisted where others have not.

To summarize so far, evolution has allowed simple sequences of a chemical called nucleic acid to develop into complex entities that can operate within a vast set of environments. Environmental change favors certain sequences, allowing some to proliferate more than others, something we now call 'natural selection' and was first described by Charles Darwin following his journey on the Beagle. While natural selection is not the only force determining which genetic sequences dominate, it is a rather important one.

This part of the chapter is far from complete. To do it full justice an entire book—maybe even a series of books—is needed. I'd recommend some decent research if you feel it makes a difference to your alien life form. But in the meantime, it will at least give us a place to argue what life might be like on planets other than Earth.

ALIEN BIOCHEMISTRY

To begin to develop your idea of what your alien life form might actually be like, we can only begin by looking at what we already know and asking 'How might it be different elsewhere?' Taking the basics, could we substitute any of the foundation stones of life? Do we have to be carbon based, lipid enclosed organisms reliant on nucleic-acid templates?

The short answer is; we can't see any good reason why not. Our definitions of life don't describe the need for particular physical components, after all.

It is often argued that carbon is not the only element capable of forming the necessary building blocks of life. For instance, silicon has similar properties to carbon, and could be a fine substitute. The problem with this is a rather fundamental one, however. Carbon's bonds are a little more flexible than silicon's, and carbon is far more soluble in water. It might seem trivial, but for higher life forms to evolve, we are looking at competition between chemical reactions. In other words, carbon would win out over silicon. And both being amongst the heavier of elements, it is likely that both would be present in some amounts in the same rocky body. Getting silicon to dissolve in decent amounts at pressures and temperatures that are amiable to a diverse range of other complex chemicals is nigh impossible.

So, carbon is the most likely starting element for life. Organic chemistry is probably universal to living things. Besides that? Well, the possibilities start to broaden.

We have already established that water may not necessarily be the only solvent option. Most forms of liquid hydrocarbon might provide an alternative, such as liquid methane or ethane. Required temperatures might be somewhat low, which might pose a problem in terms of energy, but this would simply slow reaction rates, not prevent them. However, as liquid water is by far a better solvent for living processes, there would need to be a plausible reason as to why it is not available.

What of nucleic acids? Since this is our 'seed' of life, if you like, we might find it difficult to imagine life developing without a basic form of polymer replication. In truth, any form of self-replicating sequence could work. Nucleic acid has some good properties but it is open to speculation on what other forms of complex chemical could fill this niche. It would probably need to be a polymer of repeating units that could replicate itself with minimal energy and interact with other chemicals in a controlled, predictable manner. However, these would be the only strict rules.

We have two types of nucleic acid chain; both have ribose (sugar) backbones linked together with phosphate, and five (adenine, guanine, cytosine, thymine and a thymine alternative: uracil) different 'bases' that in a variable sequence form the essence of the genetic 'coding'. The difference is that deoxyribonucleic acid has an oxygen atom missing in contrast with ribonucleic acid. It is possible to have variations on these two structures that could perform rather similar roles.

Is it necessary that all living things must be a form of 'cell'? I hesitate to say 'no' here, as I can't imagine how any higher form of life could develop without some form of segregation from its environment. Lipid membranes are good in aquatic habitats, however some other form of segregation would need to form in liquids which could dissolve fat, such as alcohol.

As we go beyond these basic physical necessities, the possibilities get broader and broader. For instance, oxygen is not the only way an organism can procure energy from the environment. Oxidation reactions are diverse and efficient, yet it might well be possible to have other chemicals produce similar exothermic reactions. A number of bacteria use other elements and compounds to do similar jobs to oxygen.

Variation in chemical structure can have drastic effects on the utilization of a given substrate. The 'chirality' or 'handedness' of a compound such as a carbohydrate or an amino acid makes a massive difference; the same compound arranged in a slightly different pattern could be unusable. Life on earth seems to be arbitrarily suited to left-handed chirality when it comes to amino acids. Subtle as this may well be, such differences could provide repercussions if considered in an alien species.

In the 1960s and 70s when the Apollo space missions returned from orbit, astronauts were quarantined for an amount of time. Though extremely remote, this was done on the off chance that they might have caught some form of biological contagion whilst in a new environment. In terms of risk, the possibilities of a human becoming infected with an alien pathogen are absurdly remote (not at all to disparage the action, which was nonetheless sensible). For a pathogen of any type to influence the biology of its host, it must have some biological property that is compatible with the system it is invading. Otherwise, it has no hope of reproducing itself. Viruses highjack their host's replication mechanisms. Bacteria interrupt the metabolism of their host, using the nutrients found in its environment. Parasites steal nutrients directly from their hosting organism.

Any alien life form we could possibly find would probably have little to no shared biological history with ourselves (I save the possibility of a very, very small shared history for the model of *Panspermia Theory*, which I will describe further later). Therefore, catching an alien's flu is not exactly hard science fiction. Consuming an alien's flesh (or them consuming our own) for nutrition again poses certain problems. Relative organisms would have no real use for incompatible biological building blocks, except for maybe some basic chemicals such as salts, water, and perhaps some simple carbohydrates.

Therefore, thinking about the basic sub-cellular construction of your alien might be advantageous if you wish to harden the science in your story. There is no reason you should sit and construct the biochemistry of your alien. However, being aware of some small facts such as these might inspire new pathways you could take in your story or add to the realism.

WHERE TO LOOK FOR LIFE

How rare would Earth-like environments be?

'Very', is the answer. However, in perspective, this doesn't mean a great deal.

Earth's orbit is situated in a region which astrobiologists (people who study Earth-origin life in space) call 'The Goldilocks Zone'. Not too hot, not too cold - just right! On average it is warm enough for liquid water to flow yet not so hot that it all evaporates into gas. It is also an orbit that remains a fairly consistent distance away from the sun throughout the year, maintaining a minimal variation to temperature on relatively small time scales.

Earth has a solid inner core which rotates at a different speed to the liquid outer core which surrounds it. The friction that arises from this contrast creates what is called the 'dynamo effect', a phenomenon that generates a large magnetic field extending away from the surface at the poles and enveloping the entire planet. This field prevents most of the sun's intense short-wavelength radiation from making it to the surface.

Ozone, a form of oxygen molecule, forms a gaseous layer that shields the less energetic (but still harmful) ultra-violet radiation. Without either our magnetic field or our ozone layer, it is unlikely that exposed-surface life could exist; as such, radiation would prevent many complex chemicals such as chains of nucleic acid from forming.

As a rocky planet, Earth has ample amounts of the heavier elements such as nitrogen, calcium, carbon, oxygen, phosphorus, sulphur, and iron. These are useful for making complex chemicals: consider Jupiter, which is mostly hydrogen, helium, and an extremely small percentage of the slightly larger elements. It is doubtful that anything too complicated could be found in the gas clouds of Jupiter simply because of the small selection of elements from which biological chemicals could be built.

Our sun is also a good size for supporting complex chemical reactions. A stable, mid-size star, it provides ample energy without bombarding the Earth with intermittent doses of intense radiation. Indeed, move elsewhere in our galaxy and we might find we have as a neighbor a dying star, which could regularly shower Earth with enough cosmic rays to give 90% of life a good roasting. This is a possibility we might yet face, given that our solar system takes billions of years to rotate around the centre of the Milky Way.

Lastly, Earth's single satellite body, the moon, has a calming effect on the weather patterns of Earth's atmosphere inadvertently through stabilizing the axial tilt of the planet. Without it, the weather patterns could vary to a much greater extent, possibly making it more difficult for life to diversify at the rate we've observed. Makes for rather dim prospects that life could exist elsewhere, doesn't it?

As far as our current observations have told us, all of the other planetary bodies in our solar system are barren. With its atmosphere long since stripped away by solar wind, Mercury's wild swings in temperature prevents any hope of complex chemical reactions taking place. Venus once inspired hope, its shy seclusion behind thick clouds of carbon dioxide inspiring many early space science-fiction stories. Once in its history it might have been somewhat Earth-like, however a run-away greenhouse effect, high atmospheric pressure, and acidic precipitation has made it incredibly unlikely that life could remain viable here.

Mars has been the planet of choice for early science-fiction authors, inspired by the observations of mid-19th century French astronomer Professor Percival Lowell who commented on the 'channels' running across the red planet's surface, interpreting them as intelligently crafted 'canals'. Seasonal fluctuations of the planet's shading were perceived as changes in vegetation. This was the dawn of the speculation of the 'Martian'. Unfortunately, we are yet to find evidence supporting the notion that even simple life might flourish on our close neighbor. Mars, like Earth, has elements that could give rise to life. Most tantalizingly, it has had a history of atmospheric temperatures that could allow liquid water to flow. The reality is, however, that Mars lacks that all-important dynamo effect Earth has. Being smaller than us, the Martian core cooled a long time ago, preventing any effect that could create a magnetic field. Without it, radiation sterilizes the surface. Most significantly, it also allows solar particles to strip slowly away the atmosphere, leaving it thin and cold.

If Mars ever did sustain life, which is indeed possible, it is unlikely that we'll find it on the surface. Sub-surface activity remains open to speculation.

What of other bodies?

The distant gas giants are too chemically simplistic to be of serious consideration. Large Kuiper belt objects such as comets (and I'll include Pluto here) might have the right materials, and be far enough away from the sun to escape damaging doses of radiation, but again they lack enough energy to provide a liquid medium or sustain chemical reactions.

However, surrounding the gas giants are numerous moons that are in their own right like miniature solar systems. Indeed, if Jupiter had ten times more mass, it might have enough gravity to start fusing hydrogen into helium. It would be a sun in its own right and its moons an internal solar system.

Europa, the ice-giant world, seems to be tormented enough by Jupiter's intense gravitational pull that the material beneath its outer skin has liquefied. Oceans of water up to 60 miles in depth could well lie beneath the vast sheet of ice that forms her surface. Recent calculations suggest that over its history a substantial amount of carbonaceous material might have crashed to its surface in the form of meteorites and comets to make it a serious contender for supporting life.

The recent Cassini mission to Saturn has provided us with a greater understanding of the moon Titan. Methane oceans and a rather complicated weather system, along with river channels and precipitation, might again be candidates for non-Earth based life forms.

However, until we find something that might fall in with our definition of a living system, we can do nothing but speculate. Earth, it seems, is pretty unique.

While we are a one in a million chance, we are also one of countless rocky bodies in the universe. There are approximately 10^8 sun-like stars in our galaxy alone. And there appears to be positively billions of galaxies. One in a million is actually not bad when there are so many possibilities. Even being stupidly generous and guessing that conditions similar to Earth's only occur one in every hundred million planets, we can still assume that there is an insane number of planets in our universe which are capable of supporting some form of life.

Nobody knows how common Earth's environment is. And nobody knows how likely it is that a series of life-inspiring chemical reactions could arise in a given environment. The temperature parameters, the chemical requirements, the time limits required—all are left up to educated guess-work. Which gives you, as a writer, plenty of opportunity to use your imagination, backed up by science.

A last matter for speculation is a theory that Earth's life arose elsewhere, on a planetary body other than our own. Panspermia Theory (also called 'Cosmic Ancestry') maintains that such 'living seeds' are spread across vast astronomical distances on extraplanetary objects, such as asteroids or perhaps even intelligently engineered artifacts. While it makes for a good story, scientifically it falls short of being taken seriously. There is little reason to think life could not generate on Earth. Shifting the creation point elsewhere does not help us understand abiogenesis (life forming from non-living components).

However, science fiction is the realm of such speculation. Panspermia could provide reason as to why Earth-formed life and extraterrestrial life might have certain similarities, should you so choose.

FERMI'S PARADOX

Let's assume that in a galaxy the size of the Milky Way there are numerous places where life can be sustained. *The Drake Equation*—developed by Dr. Frank Drake—implies that contact with an alien life form through advanced technology should be relatively common given the assumptions that, firstly, life of some type is a rather common phenomenon and, secondly, considering the age of the universe a significant number of these life forms should have evolved a form of intelligence capable of manipulating its environment to produce advanced technology recognizable to humans.

The question stands, therefore: why don't we have any concrete evidence of this? Even considering that we've only been capable of collecting meaningful information from space for less than a century, surely in that time we should have detected at least a modicum of alien whispering.

This is the paradox described by physicist Enrico Fermi. If intelligent life is so common, where is everybody? There are many things to consider in relation to this question. Absence of evidence, in this case, is far from evidence of absence. Intelligent life could indeed be rather common.

Before we take a detailed look at explanations for the paradox, let's ask the important question 'Is intelligence a common trait?' Life forms of some type might well be everywhere in the universe, but life forms recognizable to us as intelligent might be in the extreme minority.

As far as we are aware, human-like intelligence has only evolved once on this planet. Other organisms express various forms of intelligence, and many can create tools and manipulate their environment. But humans are the only ones who have ever possessed the means to translate one form of information into another through codes in order to be able to communicate across time and space. This is important when considering the prevalence of intelligent life on other planets.

For the purposes of this situation, we might define human-like intelligence by its key attribute: the ability to cognitively model the environment in order to be able to manipulate it in a predictable manner. Many organisms show similar abilities, and can adapt their environment within certain boundaries. However, intelligence that combines foresight with hindsight appears to rely on a rather energy-hungry process, one that involves a very complicated system of specialized cells called a nervous system. Advancing this outcome too far seems to be rather neglected by evolution.

Storing and manipulating information is central to this process. To do this requires a complicated system of sensing and communicating, one that would require energy that may not be immediately available. Human intelligence appears to have become as advanced as it is today due to numerous factors. Access to scavenged protein has allowed an increase in brain mass. In turn, a selection process has gradually seen that this brain mass has allowed more detailed communication in human social groups. This has had a knock-on effect which has allowed humans to access even more nutrients and energy-rich foods. We appear to have reached a limit of brain-mass due to a conflict between cranial dimensions and the fact humans are bipedal. To remain energy-efficient walkers, humans have rather narrow hips. Fitting a fat head through a rather constricted pelvic gap means humans have the most dangerous and most painful of childbirths in the entire animal kingdom. Therefore, it's unlikely that human heads could get bigger until hips widen (which is unlikely).

Intelligence in humans could develop further through other means; already we supplement it through recording information and processing it using alternative means such as computers. But, in short, human intelligence is the result of a rather specific set of circumstances.

Assuming that advanced intelligence seems to occur very rarely in the evolutionary development of a global ecosystem, it might contribute to the reason why we have no evidence of extraterrestrial life. In other words, alien intelligence of any remarkable level is non-existent. Humans are an abnormality.

Let's consider other reasons.

Perhaps alien technology exists, but is of yet at a stage unable to establish communication. Detecting intelligence from a remote location for us relies on intercepting information that cannot be attributed to a known, natural process, encoded in radar or possible laser transmissions. Humans have only been capable of this for about a century. That, in terms of universal history, is virtually nothing.

The Milky Way galaxy is a large galaxy, which means there are many stars that could harbor life. But there is also a vast amount of space in between those stars for information to cross. The nearest star to us next to the sun is four light years away. In other words, light takes four years to travel from it to us. Try to imagine crossing the entire galaxy, an astonishing 100,000 light years in diameter. For a civilization on the other side of the Milky Way to send a message to us at the speed of light, it would take just under 100,000 years.

Considering that the first 'meaningful' electromagnetic information sent from Earth is less than 100 light years away right now, it's easy to see why any alien information we receive now will be relatively ancient by any comparable means.

Extending this idea, perhaps such a life form existed once but either no longer does or no longer possesses the means to communicate. Extinctions happen, energy resources deplete, environments change, strangely it might even be a consideration that a life form evolves to no longer be intelligent in a way humans can relate to. Current information we have emitted has been technically accidental; it is the 'glow' of our transmissions intended only for our own earth-based receivers. As we become more efficient and less wasteful of these transmissions in coming years, we will reduce the transmissions that can be possibly picked up. In other words, unless we intentionally send out such information, we will fall silent to the universe.

This makes one think, could there be intelligence that simply has no wish to communicate? Having the intelligence is not the same as using it for a means we can understand. Given the ability we humans have to manipulate various energy resources and our seemingly boundless curiosity, isn't it strange that we have not yet colonized other planets? Intellectually we have long been capable of creating the technology. Politically and economically, we are not so driven. An alien species might not provide us with the means to detect their existence simply because as intelligent as they are, they just don't provide us with the means to know they are there.

Perhaps they are sending information, but not in a way we humans are capable of intercepting or interpreting. Modulation of electromagnetic radiation is the choice of human communication when it comes to sending information through the vast distances of space. However, there is the possibility that other means of communication exist that we are plainly missing, for example as-yet understood particle transmissions using neutrinos or maybe another sub-atomic particle that we simply cannot intercept.

SETI (Search for Extraterrestrial Intelligence) is a program dedicated to scanning our skies with radio telescopes for data that might be considered intelligent in origin. It is a mammoth task, considering the size of our heavens, and one that relies on being selective of where to look and what to look for simply to reduce the workload to manageable proportions. Outside a fifty light year radius, it becomes difficult to find 'accidental' radiation transmissions. A beacon intentionally aimed at us improves the chances again; however, we need to be looking at it to catch it. What if we are looking at the wrong things?

The reality of current political and economic restrictions unfortunately put a limit on what we are capable of receiving. Laser-based versus radar-based communication requires different resources to receive the transmissions; hence, investment needs are increased should one want to cover both possibilities. Time is perhaps the biggest resource and, arguably, the most expensive.

One last thing to consider is what people all over the world want to believe. Yes, the truth is out there. Isn't it? Have we already been contacted? Are we already in communication with alien intelligences? Are they already here?

It would be great to believe that. Unfortunately, we can only use speculation that is supported with concrete evidence, something that is strongly lacking with this speculation.

Space is a huge place. We can be fairly sure that life of some recognizable type is a universal law. Intelligence we can recognize is rare, but has probably developed to various extents on multiple occasions in the universe's fifteen billion year history. Obvious technology remains elusive for many reasons, such as distance between habitats and time of technological development.

We have explored only a small fraction of all possible wavelengths of electro-magnetic emission from only a small fraction of possible stars. Using our own civilization as an example, it may be likely that a given technology is only transmitting accidentally for a small time until it becomes efficient. From then on, only those intelligences intending on communication will be visible.

But for all of these limitations, there is a plethora of possibilities open for speculation. And speculation is what we are all about.

PART 2: ALIEN CREATION: BRIDGING THE GAP

I once wondered what it would be like to write a story about an alien species so bizarre, so absolutely alien, that everything about it was totally unique. For obvious reasons, I didn't even start it.

When we write a story—any style or genre—we need the reader to be able to comprehend what we are trying to tell them. The reader does this by associating what they read with what they already know. While spending thirty pages giving the reader some background knowledge might help, and make you seem rather intelligent, it will inevitably bore the reader and make them feel they are reading a journal or a textbook. This sort of association is one you, as a storyteller, can do without.

Therefore, it's necessary for you to create a strong bridge between your creation and the reader's imagination using what knowledge they already bring to the book. The more subtle you are in managing this, the more absorbed the reader will become in your world.

When creating an alien, this part is perhaps the most important thing to consider. What is it about this alien that your reader is going to associate with? There's a rather thin line to walk here. Aliens are supposed to be different to us, provoking our curiosity and our anxiety towards the unknown. Making them too similar to us raises questions and detracts from their extraterrestrial nature. Too different, and the reader will not be able to relate to their existence. Making that bridge between your alien world and the reader's own as strong as possible will ensure that the reader feels what you want them to feel.

SPECULATING ALIEN LIFE FORMS

Otherworldly beings have long been at the centre of human fantasizing. Gods, fairies, angels, demons, mermaids, the undead and the spectral—it is a common musing for man to wonder 'Is there something like me, but different?' As we become more scientifically aware, we start to underscore these questions with more evidence-inspired speculation. This has had a rather large impact on our social psyche. Myths and stories from other eras speak volumes of the fears and beliefs of the communities that embrace them. Just the same, our modern storytelling speaks of our present hopes, beliefs and deep-seated anxieties that confront us when dealing with the unknown.

Once, it was declared that victims of certain harmful nocturnal visits were being abused by demonic forces such as succubae or Satan himself. This same account evolved throughout the ages; today, alien experimenters are blamed in place of other malignant assailants. Interestingly, the descriptions of the alien abusers evolve as well. From beautiful Venetian figures resembling the Arian Ideal, to metallic robots to hairy ape-men, alien contacts have followed trends over the past century that seem to coincide with social expectations.

The latest in this time-line of alien evolution is the 'grey', a large-skulled, slight bodied humanoid with oversized black eyes, a slit for a mouth, hairless grey skin and the ability to communicate telepathically. So-called 'close encounters of the third kind' are almost exclusively dominated by this individual today.

This is significant because people have expectations of what aliens might look like. Space-traveling humanoids or lumbering slime-monsters from Alpha Centauri Prime, people recognize certain archetypes in depictions of alien life forms.

I call these 'template' aliens, much like high fantasy has 'template' races such as elves and dwarves. Templates have their uses. People expect space-faring aliens to be technologically advanced. They are often hostile, or in the very least unsympathetic to human emotions. Perhaps this expectation reflects a fear people have of our own advancing technology, science appearing rather cold and stoic in the face of human emotion.

The point is our expectations are a useful tool in creating an alien. Recognizing template aliens from movies, books, comics, and even stories in modern media is integral to playing with the established beliefs of your reader.

Alien races fulfil the same niche in science fiction writing as alternative races do in fantasy. They provide contrast to human themes, allowing the writer to explore questions without the influence of established bias and stereotyping.

STEP ONE: EMBODIMENT OF THEMES

Simple question: Why do you want to have aliens in your story?

Are they antagonists to your plot? Do they offer resolution through providing alternative information?

The point is; how necessary are they? Not all science fiction founded on space travel needs to have aliens. Simply having them exist for the sake of it can detract from an otherwise good plot. They can be an unnecessary complication that raises more questions than you are prepared to answer. Everybody has asked the timeless question of some poor piece of science fiction; if this alien can cross space in a faster-than-light spacecraft, how is it that they didn't understand some fundamental property of physics enough to be able to survive the plot twist? Sure, there might be reasons. But the question stands; why do you want an alien?

Nonetheless, for whatever reason, let's assume you've decided it is necessary.

Next, do you want them to perform a central role in your narrative, or do they support your themes by providing conflicting viewpoints?

Aliens can embody a number of themes. Typically, they will contrast human ones in some way purely because they are not human. In any event, to be able to relate to these themes they do need to reflect human understanding in some way. If it is intelligent and has a social history, how can we relate it to our own? For instance, slavery is hardly viewed as a positive social action by most of the modern western world. Alien behavior will influence your reader's expectations without you needing to say a thing. No matter what, your reader will categorize it in some way according to what they already know. Even non-intelligent entities must reflect something we can relate to, be it a particular animal, a plant, or even a pathogen of sorts. This will help you to define its traits much better.

How do you want to reader to relate to your alien? Sympathetically? Defensively? Offensively? Emotionally? Everything you describe about your alien will influence this relationship.

As you develop your basic plot outline, consider what role your alien will play in your story, and keep this in mind as you flesh it out.

STEP TWO: INTERACTIONS

It is likely that your reader will sympathize most easily with the human or human-like characters. Therefore, how these characters interact with the alien species will form the basis of the reader's association with the alien as well.

This is where you start to construct something of a description of your alien's behavior. Is it social? Is it intelligent? Does its behavior resemble our own? How easily can we associate and sympathize with it? Does it remind us of a particular life form on Earth? If so, what are its similarities and its differences?

Deciding on an Earth-analogue will help you to be able to describe the alien to your reader, and help define how your characters will interact with it, taking care to remain aware of all stereotypes and assumptions the reader and your characters might have. Sharks, for instance, are associated with a rather violent and bloodthirsty stereotype. It need not matter that in truth this belief might be misleading. A shark-like alien will be initially perceived as a cold-blooded, unintelligent killer.

Also, remain conscious of the fact that humans communicate through a very specific audible range with a very specific selection of vocalizations particular to our physiology. This is aided by non-verbal signs and visible movements. If your protagonists are going to communicate with your aliens, how might they go about this? How likely is it that a human protagonist could communicate in such a similar manner with your alien?

STEP THREE: MAJOR NON-PHYSICAL DESCRIPTORS

Filling in the blanks on function and behavior at this point will lead naturally from what you've already created. If your alien resembles a giant spider, are you going to have it act like a giant spider? What is its social hierarchy like? What is it going to do in your story when confronted by your plot?

This is also where you can begin to sketch out any technology your alien race might possess. How did they arrive at this? What is its history? Is it technology with foresight or more of a trial-and-error evolution? How involved is its social behavior?

It pays to remember that just as on Earth, aliens would not have evolved independent of other life forms. How does it associate with them? Is it a predator? What sort of ecosystem can we relate it with?

A lot of science should start to come in here. It makes little scientific sense to have an alien that produces energy from the sun to be also a predator, unless you can see a good reason in its behavior as to why this might be the case. Start with an Earth analogue and build up, diversifying it with reason rather than with pure creativity. Remember your high-school science classes and apply the basic rules of food-chain biology to your alien's behavior. For example, on Earth we can see food biomass pyramids where producers are represented by the largest amount of biomass, followed by first order consumers (herbivores), then second level consumers, all the way up to the smallest number of feeders, the apex consumers. At each step, energy is lost from the ecosystem as heat. Therefore, having a planet full of predators is not exactly efficient and would not last very long.

The amount of detail you create is up to you. You won't need to mention all of it, or even a small amount, but the important thing is that you can personally justify why your alien is the way it is. You control the questions you want the reader to ask, after all.

Step Four: Name

How will you refer to your alien? This is more important than it initially looks, as it will influence your reader's impressions from the moment they first read it.

Many authors use strange, exotic sounding names to enhance the foreign nature of their creation. But I always wonder; in terms of the back-story, how would such a name have come about in the first place?

Think of the first contact we might yet have with an alien species. I imagine it will be little different to historical encounters explorers would have had with novel species and societies. It is doubtful that we would possess a means to be able to communicate initially with the discovery, much as the first explorers would not have initially been able to speak with native populations. Therefore, many names would be invented using the language of the protagonists of a narrative.

Native Americans were 'Indians' from the western perspective, for instance, on account of Columbus' erroneous assumption that he had sailed to India. Only as communication developed did the names the natives used for themselves become part of the western vernacular.

In Australia, the many new types of flora and fauna were initially described with reference to western systems of biology. The word 'Aborigine' simply means 'indigenous', and it is a name that has stuck throughout Australia's commonwealth history. However, many animal names were adopted as colonials learned what the indigenous population called them. Kangaroo, koala, goanna...these are the names Australia's indigenous population used.

We might also have multiple ways of describing them, each promoting a different reaction. Scientifically (or, perhaps, formerly) they would be referred to using some official descriptor. It would be necessarily non-offensive and perhaps functional. Then you would have the colloquial forms; the slang terms invented by the masses that reflect their sentiments towards the new discovery. It would in all likelihood reflect existing stereotypes, and would definitely relate to the answers you came up with in step two.

Your aliens would have been encountered for the first by your protagonists' culture at some stage in their history. Is their present name personal to the alien species or is it protagonist nomenclature? Did your protagonists adopt it from another culture? Is it a code, something like Linnaean classification, or a catalogue reference?

If you choose to invent a novel word on account that it is adopted from an alien intelligence, it will be just as vital as if you gave a human description. Calling them 'Red Killers' might be kind of pointless for pacific fluffy bunny analogues. Likewise, crafting a rather innocuous sounding nonsense-word for a name, like 'Cuddlies' for a reptilian snake-analogue, will create conflicting sentiments towards your alien. As all words have an emotional content, be aware of how your name sounds in human terms. Perhaps this is a conflict you want; at least make decision after considering the consequences.

STEP FIVE: PHYSICAL DESCRIPTION

With steps one to four done, this step should pretty much write itself.

The physiology of the alien is perhaps the part most people will find the most interesting. We all remember expecting our first glimpse of the humanoids in *Close Encounters of the Third Kind*, their silhouettes grey against the blinding light of their ship. Or the ominous first sight of the robot Gort in *The Day the Earth Stood Still*. We are visual creatures, and the image you describe will be of great impact on your reader.

Indeed, perhaps you don't venture to describe anything, subtly insinuating what your alien might be like without providing a single snapshot. All the same, in your mind you should know the basic physiology of your creation in order to know its limitations. Size, appearance, physical capabilities...

Anatomically, one organism varies to the next in accordance with subtleties in its environment. 'Adaptations' are features that have been selected for in an organism's inheritance. An individual who is slightly darker than its siblings will fair better in an environment that has matching coloration. When the environment changes, that feature will no longer be as much of an advantage.

In addition to this, you must consider whether your alien could exist in the same environment as your protagonists. It is very, very unlikely that the percentage of different gases in an alien's atmosphere would be identical to Earth's. Even in our own history, it has varied greatly. Decrease the oxygen by as little as several percent and we will start to feel the effects of anoxia, which include nausea, giddiness, muscle fatigue, loss of concentration and eventually even death. Go climb a mountain to see how it might affect you.

Therefore, to sculpt your alien's morphology, you must have its native environment in mind. Again, look to Earth analogues to both a) form a bridge and b) to understand how form and function are related in reality. So it's again time to break out the textbooks and see how life on Earth varies in accordance with the environment.

Here, it also pays to keep Part 1 of this chapter in mind. The idea of an alien munching on an Earthling for breakfast might be appealing, but logically, is this feasible? How similar—on a biochemical level—is your alien to Earth life? Again, these are not answers that need to be provided, but knowing it yourself helps prevent embarrassing conflict or holes in your scientific logic.

ALIENS IN TRADITIONAL SCIENCE FICTION

Aliens in literature have occupied various themes in the past, often following trends in contemporary society. Fears of foreign antagonists, hopes of new discoveries, the anxiety over advances in technology, and even the role of spirituality in the future have all been addressed through alien themes.

It might not strictly apply to the 'alien' genre, but the three-legged killer plants in *The Day of the Triffids* by John Wyndham essentially fill the same niche. The back-story has these strange, ambulatory plants springing up all over the place in the 1951 novel, only to be cultivated for their oils. After a meteorite shower blinds much of the population, the plants escape their confines to wreak havoc. The protagonist is spared his sight through the fortune of having his eyes covered in hospital during the meteorite shower.

Written during the height of the cold war, Wyndham expresses the fears American people felt towards the Russians. The meteorite shower is attributed to a failed weapons system and the Triffids echo the sentiments of the west towards the biotechnological irresponsibility of the Reds.

In 1898, aliens were hardly commonplace in literature. In fact, speculative fiction followed the traditional themes as written by the likes of Victorian greats such as Mary and Percy Shelley, Lord Byron and Jules Verne. H.G. Wells introduced a novel element to fiction in *The War of the Worlds*, inspired by various social changes in *Fin de Siecle* Britain. England was the throne of a vast empire of colonies. Advances in technology offered a sense of security, something comparatively reciprocated in the novel when Wells contrasts Britain's own feeble artillery against the invading aliens at one point by having a soldier say, "It's bows and arrows against the lightning".

It is common today to dehumanize an enemy by portraying them as alien. We see it often. But this was probably the first time it had ever been done. Obscured within giant, three legged machines further reflected the 'fear of the unknown' factor.

The story ends with the aliens dying not because mankind defeated them, but because they encountered the common cold. The message is poignant; superior technology does not dominate nature.

A third example of an alien is the source of an extraterrestrial radio message detected on earth in the mid 1980s. Carl Sagan's *Contact* endeavors to be as hard in its science as possible, truly wondering what first contact might be like. It avoids speculating on alien physiology at all, focusing instead on the questioning of the process behind the contact. In this story, it's as if the actual nature of the aliens themselves is irrelevant, it's only the losing of our anthropocentric beliefs that's significant.

There are so many other examples of alien encounters in science fiction it could feed an entire encyclopedia.

Your alien species either can make your story something memorable and truly different, or can be the cliché that simply ruins an otherwise good plot. It can cleverly support themes that would be obvious and trite without an alternative perspective, or it can be the source of plot holes large enough for an interstellar battle cruiser to pass through.

It's up to you to decide how hard the science should be. The secret is, do your homework. Science fiction, unlike fantasy, places great value in logic and reason. Nobody is saying that your science need be flawless—it is, after all, fiction. However, good science fiction respects the conventions of scientific thinking. It means observing the basic tenets of critical thought and the methodology that describes the best models we can use to predict nature.

And, as Jules Verne said in *20,000 Leagues Under the Sea*, "We may brave human laws, but we cannot resist natural ones."

CHAPTER EIGHT

NAVIGATING YOUR WAY THROUGH OUTER SPACE: FACTS THEORIES AND CONJECTURE

Jeanne Allen

"Don't let your preoccupation with reality stifle your imagination."
—Motto of NASA Institute for Advanced Concepts[93]

INTRODUCTION

"Good to see you arrived safely on Cancri, Max. But you look a little peaked."

"I'll never get used to that wormhole drive. Felt like I was put on a stretcher."

"Need some time in the recovery room?"

"No thanks. Let's get down to the reason why I'm here...the little matter concerning the kidnapping of the Andromeda heiress..."

Characters in futuristic tales often zip around from galaxy to galaxy with relative ease, leaving the main focus of the story to be about them solving intergalactic crimes, exploring alien planets, or protecting their sector of the galaxy from alien invaders (though a tale about the journey of getting there can make a fine story in itself). In many instances, the means of travel is by way of faster-than-light propulsion, shortcuts through wormholes, or gates of some kind. Ships that travel through space are likely to generate gravitational fields that allow passengers to walk around as though their feet were firmly planted on terra firma. Other force fields are activated to protect the travelers from dangerous radiation, not to mention hostile enemy races.

The heroes and heroines in these stories usually aren't much different than you and I...well, they may be clones or have, to some extent, merged with technology by way of bionic parts, genetic engineering, or cerebral implants. By then, of course, science will have discovered a way for them to live for hundreds of years or withstand extended periods in suspended animation while they travel to their destinations. The characters may possess seemingly magical abilities akin to telekinesis or shapeshifting, all made possible by nanotechnology.

How far along is science toward making these concepts realities? NASA recently launched a spacecraft that passed by the Moon in 9 hours. (A trip to the Moon used to take days.) Biotechnology and computer chips can already enhance human characteristics to some degree. Scientists are working to solve problems of living in space for prolonged intervals of time.

This chapter highlights the strides science has made as well as obstacles yet to overcome if humans are to embark on odysseys into space. The following pages are chock-full of information pertaining to such topics as astronomical distances, the possibility of future generations reaching other star systems, the dangerous effects of space travel on the body, and how science might enhance anatomy and physiology so we can better survive the journey. To what extent will we merge with technology? Will our minds be uploaded into computers? Will we even need a body as we voyage through the vast distances of space? This chapter will also introduce you to various proposed propulsion technologies, as well as a few controversial ideas about how spacecraft might reach light speed—and faster! How would passengers traveling at such speeds be affected, according to Einstein? What would happen if their ship neared a black hole? I've also included sections on generation ships and on whether life "out there" exits.

I hope this chapter, whether addressing problems, solutions, or current speculations regarding space travel will ignite your imagination as you sit down to write your tales of space.

SPACE IS A MIGHTY BIG PLACE

That is quite the understatement. In trying to comprehend the scope of what this means, let's start close to home. The Space Shuttle orbits the Earth at a typical speed of 17,500 miles (28,000 km) per hour and circles the planet once every 90 minutes. Depending on the mission assignment, its altitude ranges from 155 to 600 miles (250 to 965 km). During the heyday of the Moon Missions, it took Apollo astronauts a little over 3 days to reach lunar orbit, a distance of 242,000 miles (390,000 km) from Earth.

In 2003, Mars was its closest to Earth, a rare event, at just within 35 million miles (56 million km). It would take a space shuttle 3 months to travel that distance. But interplanetary travel isn't as straightforward as that. Both Earth and Mars are in orbit around the Sun. Travel to other planets takes careful calculation. Scientists aim rockets from Earth to a position where the planet will be in the future. A more typical time for a craft carrying humans to reach Mars would be 7 months.

The Sun is 93 million miles (150 million km) from Earth. Light travels at a speed of 186,000 miles (300,000 km) per second. This is a speed roughly equivalent to 7.5 times around the Earth in one second. It takes light from the Sun 8.3 minutes to reach us. Expressed as a distance, we say the Sun is 8.3 light-minutes from Earth. This distance, between Earth and Sun, is one astronomical unit (AU).

Mars is an average 1.52 AUs from the Sun, Jupiter, 5.20 AUs. It took the *Voyager 1* spacecraft 1.5 years to arrive at Jupiter. In January 2006, the New Horizons probe left for Pluto, which is an average distance of 39 AUs from the Sun. The probe will travel more than 3 billion miles (5 billion km) at a velocity of 36,000 miles (58,000 km) per hour. With a gravity assist from Jupiter, it's due to arrive at Pluto in 2015. Radio signals from Earth will take 4.5 hours to cross this distance. After surveying the dwarf planet, New Horizons will zoom deeper into the Kuiper Belt, a region beyond Neptune teeming with Pluto-like bodies.

Extending our view of space to beyond the Kuiper Belt, *Voyager 1*, launched in 1977, has recently entered the heliosheath, a region at the edge of the solar system where solar wind and interstellar gas mix together. In July 2006, *Voyager 1* was 100 AUs, or 9.3 billion miles (15 billion km) from the Sun.

If these dimensions aren't mind-boggling enough, consider the star nearest ours. Proxima Centauri is 25 trillion miles (40 trillion km) from Earth. If *Voyager 1* were headed to this star, it would arrive there in about 73,000 years!

If our descendants are to travel to the stars, it's apparent they'll need a technology much more advanced than anything currently available.

Units in terms of light travel time are used to describe these enormous distances. A light-year (ly) is the distance a photon of light travels in 1 year, approximately 5.9 trillion miles (9.5 trillion km). Another unit of astronomical distance is the parsec (pc), which equals 3.26 light-years. Proxima Centauri is 4.2 light-years, or 1.3 parsecs, from the Sun.

Visible light, radio waves, and X-ray energy are a few of the forms of radiation within the electromagnetic spectrum. All electromagnetic radiation travels at the same speed, commonly called the speed of light. If a civilization existed near Proxima Centauri and we sent a radio signal to it, and they responded in kind, it would take 8.4 years (4.2 x 2) to receive their answer. The North Star, recently discovered to be a triple star system, is 430 light-years away. Polaris is one of its stars. Light from Polaris that's just now arriving on Earth left the star during the 16th century. This is why astronomers say that when we look at the stars, we see into the past. If Polaris went supernova, we wouldn't become aware of it for 430 years. It would take 860 years to send a radio signal and receive a reply from Polaris. You'd have to leave instructions for your descendants to listen for the return signal.

Our solar system resides near the edge of the Milky Way, a large spiral galaxy containing perhaps 200 billion stars. From Earth, the galaxy appears as a thick, hazy band of stars that arches across the night sky. The diameter of the Milky Way is 100,000 light-years, its thickness, 2000 light-years. The Sun, at about 26,000 light-years from its center, orbits the center at a rate of 135 miles (220 km) per second. It takes 225 million years for the Sun to revolve once around the galactic core.

Andromeda, the closest galaxy similar to our own, is 2.5 million light-years away. A cluster of galaxies called Abell 2218 is two billion light-years away.

Just how big is the universe, anyway?

The universe is all the matter and energy within space and time, observable or not. The observable part contains over 100 billion galaxies, or, by one estimate, 70 sextillion stars. (That's 70 followed by 21 zeros.) By analyzing the light of stars and galaxies, astronomers have concluded the universe is increasing in size. If we backtracked in time to about 13.7 billion years ago, we'd find the Universe condensed into a single point that suddenly expanded in a "Big Bang." Within the scientific community, the Big Bang theory is a widely accepted model for describing the origin of the universe.

Quasars are distant galaxies with tremendously brilliant cores. Light from the most distant quasars took 13 billion years to reach us. We see them as they existed when the universe was very young. And if that weren't amazing enough, some of these most distant quasars are receding from us at a rate of over 90% the speed of light!

Will humans ever reach other star systems? Considering the vast distances involved, not to mention the light speed limit, it seems an impossible task, but as you'll see later in this chapter, there are those who are keeping the dream alive by thinking outside the box, their sights set on the stars.

THE COLD, COLD VACUUM OF SPACE

Spacecraft and spacesuits protect today's astronauts from the extreme conditions of outer space. It's conceivable that dome constructions on the Moon and Mars will shelter cities of tomorrow.

TEMPERATURE

Because space contains very few atoms, it alone doesn't have much of a temperature to speak of. But the radiant heat of a nearby star can cause the temperature of an object to soar. In outer space near Earth, the Sun can heat an object to 250°F (121°C), and when eclipsed from the Sun, the object's temperature can plummet to -200°F (-129°C).

Absolute zero is the coldest temperature theoretically possible, which, on the Kelvin temperature scale, is expressed as zero kelvins (0 K). This is -459.67°F, or -273.15°C. In deep space, far from any heat-radiating body, the temperature is actually a few degrees above absolute zero, or to be more precise, 2.73 K. This few degrees is due to the cosmic microwave background radiation, a remnant energy of the Big Bang.

COMPARISON OF TEMPERATURE SCALES

A person exposed to outer space wouldn't freeze immediately, as there are no molecules to carry away heat from the body. But it's this lack of molecules that would get him anyway.

	Fahrenheit	Celsius	Kelvin
absolute zero	-459.67	-273.15	0
outer space	-454.49	-270.27	2.73
freezing point of water	32	02	73
comfortable room temperature	70	21	294
human body	98.6	37	310
boiling point of water (sea level)	212	100	373

EXPOSURE TO VACUUM

Our bodies are accustomed to the air pressure on the surface of Earth, which is 14.7 pounds per square inch, or one atmosphere. The boiling point of water at sea level is 212°F (100°C). Boiling point depends on the atmospheric pressure above the water. At 10,000 feet in altitude, there isn't as much air pressing on the surface of the water, and its boiling point is 194°F (90°C). This is why it takes longer to cook a hard-boiled egg at high altitude than it does at sea level. So, not only do liquids boil when heated but when exposed to lower pressures. Outer space contains a negligible amount of molecules (a vacuum) and the pressure is essentially zero. Water in a glass would vaporize away—even on the cold dark side of the Earth.

No one has entered space without a spacesuit. Conclusions reached as to what might happen if somebody did are based on observations of subjects that have been exposed to rapid decompression. If a shirt-sleeved person were suddenly thrust into outer space, death would not be immediate. Air would rush out of the lungs. (Holding one's breath, by the way, is not recommended as doing so would cause the lungs to rupture.) In the way soda pop fizzes after the can is opened, nitrogen gas dissolved in the blood and tissues would bubble into tissues and into spaces surrounding the joints, resulting in painful decompression sickness, also known as the "bends." (This is why scuba divers take precautions when rising from deep waters.)

A person caught unprotected in outer space would sense saliva boiling off the tongue. The skin and underlying tissues would swell. The body would cool due to the evaporation of water from the skin and at the same time, if exposed to the Sun, suffer severe sunburn. But contrary to depictions in movies, eyeballs would not bulge out; the body would not explode. Blood vessels maintain pressure and the skin has some strength, though lack of oxygen would quickly cause damage to tissues. The bends would occur, along with mental confusion. The person would lose consciousness in 10, maybe 15 seconds. Amazingly, if returned to normal pressure within 90 seconds, the individual could survive. If not, permanent brain damage would occur after about 4 minutes, if death hasn't occurred already. Shortly after that, the body becomes a freeze-dried corpse.

THANK GOODNESS FOR SPACESUITS!

Think of a spacesuit as a self-contained spacecraft with its own atmosphere, life support, and power pack. In today's Extravehicular Mobility Unit (EMU) suits, an inner garment contains fluid-filled tubes for heating and cooling. A gas bladder applies pressure against the body. A ventilation unit refreshes the air. Tough, reflective outer layers protect the astronaut against solar heat and from being pelted by micrometeoroids—tiny rock particles that can travel at 5 miles (8 km) per second. Radio transmitter and the requisite helmet, boots, and gloves complete the ensemble. (In case you're wondering, for going to the bathroom, spacewalkers wear maximum absorption diapers.)

EMU suits are bulky, weighing over 200 pounds (91 kg) on Earth. The gas bladder makes it hard to move. Astronauts on spacewalking missions report sore hands after working against the pressure of the suit for a number of hours. New suits are being designed that are lighter in weight, harder, and more flexible at the joints, though judging by pictures of this new design, a person wearing one of these suits will bear a striking resemblance to a giant marshmallow man. For a more streamlined suit, a new fabric is being developed which is elasticized to apply pressure on the body. Activating electrical signals would cause the suit to shrink around the astronaut. Embedded within the fabric would be sensors to monitor the body's vital signs and artificial muscles to help move loads.

Astronauts describe walking in space as a remarkable, even spiritual experience. There's a unique sense of freedom and the views are spectacular.

The day is as incredibly bright as the night is black. Cottony cloud tops, familiar landmasses, and brilliant blue oceans glide beneath their feet. During his first spacewalk, one astronaut reported the sensation that he'd float away if he became disconnected from the shuttle. Another astronaut described feeling a sense of dizziness during his first tethered moments. Though intellectually he knew better, on seeing Earth sweeping by at 18,000 mph, he thought he'd immediately be pulled to it by gravity. His reaction was to grab on harder to the handhold. In moments, he recovered and was able to enjoy the experience.

Not only can working on expensive equipment in space be stressful, but spacewalkers are highly aware of dangers that involve Newton's laws of motion. In the absence of gravity and air resistance, a mass in motion tends to keep moving (Newton's first law). A jet pack spews exhaust in a certain direction, allowing the astronaut to move in the opposite direction (Newton's third law.) The third law also applies when an astronaut pushes against an object she's working on. If she's repairing a satellite and pushes against it, the satellite pushes against her with an equal force. If she weren't held in place by a tether or foot restraints, she'd move off in the direction of the satellite's push without any means to get back to the ship, that is, if she were also unfortunate enough to be wearing a nonfunctioning jet pack.

GRAVITY, ANYONE?

As good as spacecraft and spacesuits are at protecting a person from the vacuum of space, they can't protect him from microgravity. (How could floating around in zero-g be dangerous? It looks like so much fun!)

MASS VS. WEIGHT

Matter is all the stuff made of atoms. Mass is a measure of the amount of this matter. Weight is a measure of the force of gravity acting on an object. The rate at which freely falling objects increase in speed, or accelerate, near Earth's surface is 32 feet (9.8 meters) per second for every second that elapses. This number also represents the gravitational field strength near Earth's surface and is often expressed as 1 g.

Sir Isaac Newton described gravity as being a force of attraction between any two masses in the universe. If the masses are large, so, too, is the gravitational force. If the distance between the two masses is large, the gravity is weak. Between you and Pluto, there is gravitational attraction, but because of the great distance, the amount of attraction is very, very small. There is gravitational attraction between you and the chair on which you sit, but the masses are very small, and so, too, is the gravitational pull. We notice our tendency to stay rooted to the ground because the Earth is a very massive object. The Earth and other planets stay in orbit around the Sun because of the force of gravity.

The mass of a person won't change whether he's on the Earth or on the Moon, but on the Moon his weight will be one-sixth of his weight on Earth. A person 82 kilograms in mass weighs 180 pounds on Earth. He'll weigh 30 pounds on the Moon. On Mars, at .38 g, he'll weigh 68 pounds. On Jupiter, at 2.54 g, if there was a suitable surface on which to land, he'd weigh almost 460 pounds! Many, many miles from a planet, at zero-g, a person would weigh essentially zero pounds. His mass, though, would remain a constant 82 kilograms at all locations.

MICROGRAVITY

An astronaut and the shuttle in which she inhabits both orbit the Earth, placing her in a constant state of free fall, in a never-ending skydive. She experiences apparent weightlessness and to maneuver must pull herself along by grasping cords and handles fastened inside the ship, but she's never truly weightless. In fact, her weight is still an appreciable fraction of her weight on the Earth's surface, but in this constant state of free fall, the effect is the same as being weightless. Because the apparent weightlessness isn't perfect, the term microgravity is used to describe the gravitational conditions around her.

On Earth, gravity is what shapes our bodies. Our muscles, bones, and heart have developed to the extent they have because we have to push against the Earth to get around. After an astronaut is thrust at 3 g's through our atmosphere and then into orbit around the Earth, her body tries to adjust to the sudden disappearance of g-forces.

EFFECTS OF MICROGRAVITY ON THE BODY

Located in the inner ear is a fluid-filled network of canals called the vestibular system. It helps us sense movement and keep our balance. Part of it depends on gravity to pull down tiny crystals called otoliths onto a jellylike mass that surrounds little hairs attached to nerve endings. It's how we tell up from down. Our sense of vision works with this system. However, in microgravity, the eyes receive conflicting messages. An astronaut will reach too soon for a falling object. On a space station, the arrangement of items in a room can be visually disorienting. According to one astronaut, it's as if you were to walk into your house on the ceiling; it would be hard to find the bathroom. Fifty percent of all astronauts experience space motion sickness. Though medication and mental exercises help, the body acclimates after a few days in space.

On Earth, blood pressure is higher in our feet than in our head, resulting in a blood pressure difference, or gradient. Without gravity, there's a loss of this gradient. The body's fluids equalize in pressure. An astronaut's face becomes puffy. His legs become thinner. He experiences a "cloudy head," not being able to think clearly for the first couple of days in space. The sense of taste is dulled and astronauts tend to crave spicy foods. The kidneys respond to this shift in blood pressure by eliminating fluid. Astronauts must drink plenty of water as a result. This loss of fluid results in red blood cells becoming more concentrated. Consequently, the brain signals the bone marrow to shut down red blood cell formation. In a few days, an astronaut typically loses 10 to 14% of his blood volume. If this wasn't alarming enough, the heart doesn't pump as hard and begins to decrease in size. Microgravity also triggers a reduction in lymphocyte function. Over time, the astronaut becomes more susceptible to diseases, including cancer.

In the absence of gravity, calf and thigh muscles are the first to weaken. Bones lose calcium and phosphorus in a manner similar to the onset of osteoporosis, except in space it occurs at an accelerated rate. The femur, hip, and lower part of the spine are affected the most. Yet as bones and muscles decay, the astronaut feels strong, superhuman. He could lift a major appliance with one finger. On a spacewalk, he easily stops a rotating satellite.

Vigorous exercise for over 2 hours a day can slow some of these effects. The regimen can include workouts against strong elastic bands or using a treadmill in a Low Body Negative Pressure chamber—a vacuum-cleaner-like device that simulates the effects of Earth gravity. The LBNP chamber works to restore the blood pressure gradient as well.

Once an astronaut is back on Earth, he's likely to suffer anemia. He feels thirsty and takes in a lot of fluid. It takes a few days for the blood volume to return to normal levels. For every day in space, that's about how many days it takes the muscles to recover when back on Earth. Depending on the amount of time spent in space, even with plenty of exercise, it could take months or years for the bones to recover.

There's obvious concern about space missions of long duration. Could an astronaut survive a two-year trip to Mars and back, most of the time spent in microgravity?

Studies show that even reproduction depends on gravity. Experiments conducted on sea urchin sperm show that sperm moves sooner and more rapidly in space, and after the introduction of certain egg chemicals, the process that halts sperm motility occurs at a slower rate. The timing and efficiency of egg fertilization could thus be affected. Other studies revealed that sperm production in rats stopped after six weeks of simulated microgravity. On the Russian space station, Mir, fertilized quail eggs failed to hatch.

Studies of frog and rat embryo development in microgravity revealed that embryonic cell differentiation is also gravity dependent. A leg might start growing from the neck region, an eye from somewhere else, resulting in a severely deformed animal, should it survive.

Young rat pups that develop on Earth, when placed upside-down in warm water, will turn upright in response to gravity. A study was done where pregnant rats were sent into space, then brought back to Earth to give birth. The space pups, when immersed in warm water, weren't able to turn themselves upright, though within a few days, they regained their ability to sense gravity's cues.

On Earth, gravity's a signal that tells the body how to function. Mechanical signals translate into biochemical signals that strengthen muscles and bones. In the future, when these signals are better understood, perhaps a drug will be designed to help astronauts survive long-term exposure to microgravity.

OFFSETTING THE EFFECTS OF MICROGRAVITY THROUGH SPACESHIP DESIGN

If a ship's velocity increased at a constant rate of 32 feet (9.8 meters) per second each second, it would feel like gravity on Earth to the crewmembers, but maintaining this rate of acceleration to a planet or star would require an inordinate amount of energy. The largest NASA spacecraft leaving our gravity field burns up its fuel in mere minutes, then moves at a constant speed on its own inertia—with minor adjustments in trajectory made by smaller rockets. There's essentially no acceleration, and therefore no artificial gravity.

A large, rotating space habitat in the shape of a cylinder, doughnut, or sphere can provide an artificial gravity. Two inhabitable spheres connected by a tether can be made to rotate around their center of gravity. In any of these systems, the resulting centripetal force acts toward the center of the rotation. The inside rim of the ship pushes against the feet of a person standing within. The person within the craft senses an outward force called centrifugal force. (A similar effect is felt on an amusement park ride where riders are pressed against the inside walls of a large cylinder.) Experiments have shown the human body would maintain health in this type of environment, though to build it will be no small feat of engineering.

In designing a rotating ship, not only will laws of physics need to be taken into account to determine the optimum radius and spin rate, but the internal environment must be designed for human comfort as well. Inherent in such a ship are forces that, when one moves about, distort the experience of living in simulated gravity, reminding one it really isn't gravity he's living in. Facing sideways may trigger motion sickness. Walking with or against the direction of rotation would cause one to feel a weight change. To offset these problems, visual cues, like certain colors or writing on certain walls can help people orient themselves to minimize or at least prepare themselves for the discomfort. If the craft is to be propelled toward a destination, there are still other distorting forces that must be taken into account.

For long-term voyages, a ship like this would have to be very large. It would have to be built in space, an expensive process by today's standards. Its symmetry would have to be perfect to prevent unwanted vibrations, not to mention it would take an enormous amount of energy to rotate and move the system along to its destination.

A more cost-effective answer to reducing physiological problems caused by microgravity might lie in using a more conventionally designed ship, by having on board a horizontal centrifuge that a person can operate with a bicycle-like attachment. A person could ride along the inside edge of this circle for an hour or so a day to keep the body in shape.

In the far future, perhaps science will discover a way to produce gravitons for maintaining a gravitational field on a starship. Gravitons are theoretical particles that are thought to transmit gravity in the way photons produce electrical and magnetic effects.

If humankind's survival depends on an exodus from our solar system, and if a suitable means of producing artificial gravity isn't developed, our descendants will have to accept the fact that during their journey through many generations, the human race will evolve into beings with large heads, withered muscles, bird-like bones, and nonfunctional legs. Their means of locomotion will be primarily with their hands as they pull themselves around in the weightless environment of their ship. The changes would be irreversible. Humans would never be able to return to Earth.

GRAVITY ACCORDING TO EINSTEIN

The general theory of relativity asserts that gravity isn't a force of attraction between masses but occurs because masses warp, or distort, space. Visualize a trampoline onto which you've rolled a bowling ball. The bowling ball has distorted the shape of the trampoline. Place a marble on the edge of the trampoline, and it will roll toward the bowling ball and then swing into orbit around it, similar to the way a planet orbits the Sun. Of course, in the four dimensions of spacetime, the picture is more complex, but this is Einstein's view, that gravity is a result of spacetime being curved by the masses contained within it. Even a beam of light takes a curved path near a gravity field, proved during a solar eclipse in 1919 when it was shown that a star's position seemed to change because the Sun's mass caused the path of its light to bend.

BLACK HOLES: GRAVITY GONE BERSERK!

An area of space so warped that not even light can escape from it is called a black hole. In this deep, dark, bottomless gravity pit, time comes to a standstill and information is lost to us. A black hole forms when a star 3 or more times the mass of our Sun runs out of nuclear fuel and collapses under its own gravity. It shrinks to a point of infinite density and zero volume, a singularity. Some distance from the singularity is an event horizon, a boundary from which nothing, not even light, can escape; the gravity of the black hole is that strong. Hapless space travelers who cross the event horizon are doomed. They'll be pulled toward the singularity, where space and time are squashed out of existence. Einstein's equations no longer compute.

There's evidence a black hole with a mass of over 3 million suns lies at the center of the Milky Way. Though a black hole can't be seen, its presence can be assumed by observing how it affects the movement of nearby stars. Stars are seen to orbit an unseen massive object. If a star is close enough, a black hole will pull in the star's material, causing the material to heat up and emit X-rays, which can be detected just outside the event horizon.

The radius of the event horizon varies with the mass of the black hole. A black hole the size of the one thought to be at the center of the Milky Way would have an event horizon radius of 5.5 million miles (9 million km). The black hole candidate, Cygnus X-1 is 10 solar masses with an event horizon of 18 miles (29 km) in radius. If the Sun were to collapse into a black hole, though its mass is too small for it to actually do so, its event horizon would be located almost 2 miles (3 km) from the singularity. If Earth became a black hole, the radius of its event horizon would be less than half an inch (.9 cm).

So intense is the gravity field of a black hole, the effects of entering one would be extreme. Imagine that Mary, a space traveler, nears a black hole a few times the mass of the Sun. Its gravity would pull her toward it slowly at first, then faster and faster the closer she got to it. If she approached the event horizon in a feet-first fall, the difference in gravitational pull between her feet and head would become so great it would stretch her out like spaghetti, or more probably, rip her apart before she even reached the event horizon. At any rate, friction would heat her to millions of degrees, and she would emit high energy X-rays. A super massive black hole would treat her kinder. Though the gravity is greater, the "tidal" forces wouldn't be as strong as she neared the event horizon—not that it would change her ultimate fate.

If somehow she could survive the entry into a black hole, she wouldn't know exactly when she crossed the event horizon. It's not a physical surface, but an information barrier, yet once inside it, she'd be unable to leave it, and she wouldn't be able to communicate with anyone on the outside. Yet in the moments it takes her to reach the event horizon, the universe behind her will have fast-forwarded to the end of time.

Max, on the other hand, watching her from a safe distance would never see her cross the event horizon. Time dilation would be so great; it would seem she's taking an infinite time to reach it, hovering at its edge for eternity. Struggling to escape the intense pull of gravity, light reflecting from her would lose energy and shift to the color red until she'd ever so slowly fade away. If Max monitored her heart rate, each beat would take longer than the last, until she'd seem to be forever frozen in time.

To Mary, however, time would pass by normally because gravity has stretched her whole existence. But as she's pulled toward the singularity, she'll be crushed into nothingness.

General relativity also predicts wormholes—black holes connected to other parts of spacetime. Mary may end up in some other universe. Of course, this might not be the most comfortable way to travel.

HAZARDS OF RADIATION

In current discussions about sending manned missions to Mars, the subject of exposure to radiation invariably arises. The longer an astronaut is in space, the greater is his risk of developing serious health problems.

On Earth, we're constantly exposed to radiation, be it from terrestrial sources or from outer space. Medical x-rays or certain occupations can add to our level of background radiation. If a dose becomes high enough, the likelihood of radiation sickness increases. A person experiences fever, gastrointestinal disorders, loss of hair, and possibly death. The effects of this radiation may occur later in life, or after one is subjected to a low level of exposure for a long period of time. Long-term consequences include cataracts, reduced fertility, cancer, chromosomal damage, and impaired functioning of the central nervous system. Usually the doses we receive are well below levels considered dangerous. In outer space, it's a different story.

SOLAR ENERGETIC PARTICLES

Solar eruptions can become powerful enough to send surges of x-rays and gamma rays toward Earth, with energetic charged particles—mostly high-speed protons and electrons—following close behind. On reaching Earth, these energetic particles trigger magnetic storms that produce shimmering curtains of auroras in the polar skies. They're also known for disrupting radio signals, disabling satellites, and causing massive power outages. They could kill an astronaut away from protective shielding within hours.

Solar energetic particles are most intense every 11 years or so, during the sunspot cycle. Thankfully, most that head for Earth are deflected by our magnetic field or trapped within the Van Allen belts—two doughnut-shaped regions of intense radiation found high above the Earth's surface—and the largest solar events don't happen very often. Depending on the intensity of the solar event, energetic particles from the Sun reach Earth in 30 minutes or in 1 to 3 days, so with Earth-based and satellite warning systems in place, scientists have time to advise astronauts and power companies of the oncoming barrage.

ELSEWHERE AROUND THE SOLAR SYSTEM

The four largest planets, Jupiter, Saturn, Uranus, and Neptune, also known as the gas giants, exhibit enormous magnetic fields. Jupiter's magnetic field is 20,000 times stronger than Earth's. Large, brilliant auroras hovering over Jupiter's poles have been recorded by the Hubble Telescope. One of Jupiter's inner moons, Io, known for its active sulfur volcanoes, spews materials into the magnetic field to produce a ring of charged particles around the planet. The tremendous radiation in the ring can damage an unmanned spacecraft and is lethal to humans.

But that's not all.

GALACTIC COSMIC RAYS

An astronaut must also be concerned about galactic cosmic rays (GCRs). Scientists can only speculate about the origin of these particles, knowing only that they come from beyond the solar system. Cosmic rays aren't really rays but high-energy protons and atomic nuclei that travel at nearly light speed. The atmosphere slows down the GCRs that penetrate Earth's magnetic field. Those that collide with atoms in our upper atmosphere cause showers of secondary particles to fall toward the ground. Thousands of these secondary particles go through our bodies every minute, though the level of this type of radiation makes up only a few percent of our yearly background radiation.

Astronauts beyond the Earth-Moon system would not benefit from the protection of Earth's atmosphere or magnetic field. Since the time of the *Apollo* Moon Missions, astronauts have reported seeing flashes of light inside their eyeballs. The cause—cosmic rays. More than three decades of data on astronaut health reveals a greater incidence of cataracts in astronauts who've been exposed to higher amounts of GCRs than in those who've been exposed to little or no cosmic rays.

PROTECTION FROM SPACE RADIATION

High-energy solar and galactic particles are known for barreling through cells and slicing through DNA and other biological molecules, damaging genes and otherwise causing cells to malfunction. With early warning systems in place, astronauts are given time to take cover within shielding, but if humans are to travel to Mars and beyond, they'll need shielding that will protect them for the long term.

Aluminum is good for absorbing radiation for a trip to the Moon and back. A thick layer of aluminum might surround the living quarters on an interplanetary craft. There are scientists who believe this won't be enough and propose tanks holding water 16 feet (5 meters) in thickness or large containers filled with liquid hydrogen to shelter the astronauts. A form of polyethylene plastic may work as shielding, since molecules of plastic contain carbon and hydrogen that would reduce the number of harmful particles reaching the crew. The plastic can be made stronger and lighter than aluminum and would also shield against micrometeoroids. But there's a major drawback to using any of the above methods. They'd add tons of weight to the craft.

Magnetic fields surrounding the craft might work, but this would require maintaining a field strength hundreds of thousands of times greater than Earth's magnetic field. In addition, it's uncertain what health effects these strong magnetic fields would have on the astronauts. Another option might come from an advanced propulsion system, which would speed the ship along and reduce the exposure time to cosmic rays.

A MORE RESISTANT ASTRONAUT?

Experiments indicate that long-term exposure to GCRs might also cause harm to brain tissue. Under normal conditions, repair enzymes in our cells are usually able to restore DNA that has been damaged. Studies are being conducted to develop enzymes that would repair or clean up cells damaged by radiation. Researchers envision molecular-sized nanoparticles injected into the body that would zero in on these cells, release enzymes to repair them, and destroy cells that are too badly damaged.

PSYCHOLOGICAL EFFECTS OF SPACE TRAVEL

Living in close quarters with the same few people for years and years on an extended space journey is likely to bring about special problems of its own. There's the high probability of a traveler becoming bored, irritable, homesick, or depressed. Lack of a 24-hour light cycle would disrupt sleep habits. Added to that, the traveler must cope with the fact that he can't leave the ship; if he does, he dies. There may be cultural diversity between him and the rest of the crew. Tolerating differences in language, behavior, and food choices could become taxing. Conflicts are bound to arise. All this emotional stress can impair judgment. Top it off with the fact that, depending on how far from Earth the ship is, it would take years to receive radio messages from loved ones at home.

Personalities must be taken into account before assigning people to long-term missions. The candidates must be observed and chosen to be part of a team based on how well they work together. Aware of the mental strain such a journey will likely place him under, an astronaut must make a conscious effort to behave respectfully and maintain self-control.

Spacecraft design might help alleviate some of these problems. Cabins can be personalized to suit an individual's tastes. Built into the schedule would be time for rest and recreation, exercise, and regular communications with home. Sunlamps and medications may help to regulate biological clocks. There might be a computer therapist programmed to read changes in facial expression that will head off problems before they become major issues.

If we consider the pioneers and immigrants of our past, we may find the ideal crew for an extended space mission will consist of young couples or families. There's a natural social structure among family members, and being around loved ones will make it easier to settle disputes. If it comes down to it, the survival of the human race may ultimately depend on 50 or so young couples who'll embark on a generation ship to repopulate a new planet.

REDESIGNING HUMANS TO WITHSTAND THE TRIP

If the science fiction story you're composing is set in a universe bound by current laws of physics, your characters must accept the reality that it'll take decades to centuries to millennia to reach other star systems—and that's only within the Milky Way galaxy. Even with an antimatter engine, it would take over 20 years to reach Proxima Centauri. How will a space traveler endure for this length of time and longer? Perhaps science will discover a breakthrough that will slow the aging process. The traveler might use the time to learn things on the way. He could master languages, musical instruments, or theoretical physics. Scientists may discover a way to place people into suspended animation, or the travelers may never live to see their destination but father the offspring of future generations who will, their ship a self-sustaining generation ship.

Or your space travelers might not have flesh and bone bodies to deal with at all.

BODY ENHANCEMENTS

While mining an asteroid, Max suffers a bad accident. His calf muscle has been mangled. The dispensary doctor replaces the muscle with a special plastic called electroactive polymer. When stimulated by chemicals in the body, the polymer expands and contracts like muscle. It's elastic and strong, fast-acting and silent. It'll do nicely for a replacement. Max is aware he's already made use of this polymer. It's woven into his spacesuit to assist him in his work.

While recovering from surgery, Max answers a call from the communicator embedded in one his molars. "Dad! Good to hear from you...I'm okay...I'll be back to work tomorrow. How are you doing?" Max listens as vibrations of his father's voice are transmitted through his jaw to his ear.

Max's father recently opted for the organ-replacement package. He tells Max his titanium heart, artificial kidneys, and gas-permeable lungs make him feel like a new man. They'll add decades to his life. The corneal and auditory implants enhance his vision and hearing to levels better than when he was Max's age. He's enjoying the drugs that are improving his memory, too.

Ten years later, in preparation for her mission to help build an outpost on Saturn's moon Titan, Mary has had her genome sequenced. By knowing which genes are defective, she can take advantage of a personalized health regimen. An army of tiny robots no larger than molecules has been injected into her bloodstream. These "nanobots" are programmed to deliver drugs to fight pain, treat disease, and control her mood. Some repair genetic defects. She's already received neural implants to improve her memory and learning. The details of her assignment on Titan are crystal clear. It's a lot easier to remember things than before the implants. Neural microchips have made her hearing sharp as a tack, too. And her vision has never been so good, now enhanced with infrared and ultraviolet capabilities. Mary's implants will give her the ability to record and remember every detail about her trip to Saturn, the enhanced colors, the famous rings and icy moons, the stories her crewmates will tell.

This will also be a mission to test a new procedure for long distance space flight. To reduce the amount of food, oxygen, and fuel that will have to be taken along, nanobots will chemically induce suspended animation in Mary and her crewmates. The ship's computer will warm the sleeping chambers periodically, and nanobots will release chemicals to awaken the crew so they can eliminate wastes. During these waking hours, through the implants in their brains, Mary and the rest of the crew will send commands to the food dispenser, and they'll dine together. She'll read some; it takes her a few minutes to complete a book. She'll upload a virtual reality interactive into her corneal implants. All the while, nanobots will be busy repairing any cells damaged by the suspended animation process, by cosmic radiation, and they'll work to keep her bones and muscles strong.

Another decade or two later, Max is headed to the Alpha Centauri star system, a momentous trip for the human race. Long ago, nanobots replaced his polymer-repaired calf muscle with new, living tissue. He had some plaque buildup in his arteries that was also treated through the use of nanotechnology.

Nanobots perform a new function: they regulate Max's "longevity" genes, allowing him to live actively for at least 500 years. Even with this advancement, during most of the time it'll take to travel to Alpha Centauri, Max will opt for nanobots to activate his hibernation gene. And speaking of genes, Max now has a gene that enables his body to withstand the effects of cosmic radiation. It came from the insect world. Bioengineered genes prevent his bones and muscles from withering away in microgravity. Max also received a gene that makes it possible for his lungs to work in low oxygen environments.

Neural microchips connect him to other members of the crew and to the ship's computer. Communication with others is usually accomplished by interpersonal signaling, or radiotelepathy. Even during suspended animation, Max can enjoy a virtual existence where he'll find recreation and companionship. He'll hike a mountain trail, meet others for dinner in this virtual environment, or he can shut down completely, and in a sense, bring time to a standstill, completely oblivious of the years it'll take to arrive at his destination.

FROZEN EMBRYOS

The solution to surviving long space journeys may depend on transporting frozen embryos. When a suitable destination is reached, the human population can resume, the first generation, at least, to be raised by the ship's computer— that is, if certain advancements in biotechnology and artificial intelligence can be achieved.

Scientists today have been unable to duplicate the network of blood vessels connecting a mouse fetus to an artificial womb. And they've yet to discover just the right amount of blood, proteins, and hormones required for proper fetal development. Should this research advance to humans, there'll be other aspects to consider as well. Without having to emerge through a birth canal, the heads of babies born in artificial wombs won't be so limited in size. During natural development, the fetus responds to the mother's emotions and moods, which leads us to another unknown. How would growth outside of the mother affect the child's emotional development?

Or by then, it's possible that today's idea of what it means to be human will have changed so much, we wouldn't even recognize ourselves. Evolution will play a part in this, but more likely, as some futurists predict, by our own doing, through the merging of genetic engineering and computer technology, our descendants may emerge from some form of human-silicon hybrid.

MELDING WITH COMPUTERS

At the rate computer chips are becoming smaller, faster, and more powerful, it isn't hard to imagine each of us connected to the internet by way of microchips implanted in our brains. We'd share a common consciousness, a "World Wide Brain," so to speak, yet retain our individual personalities.

Added to that, magnetic resonance imaging (MRI) scans of high bandwidth and high resolution might some day be able to map nerve cells of the brain, their connections, and neurotransmitters for the purpose of uploading our minds into neural computers. There'd even be back-up copies. Our living bodies will coexist along with our uploaded selves, or we may decide we've no need of bodies at all. As unbelievable as it sounds, futurists predict these things could happen by the end of this century, or further down the line.

What will these neural computer circuits be made of? One possibility is carbon nanotubes. Naturally found in soot, nanotubes are made of carbon atoms connected in a chicken-wire-like mesh rolled into microscopic tubes. They're excellent conductors of electricity when straight. They behave like transistors when twisted. They're strong and durable (the same stuff proposed to make elevators to the sky) and can be configured into three-dimensional arrays.

So versatile would nanotubes be, some envision they could be used to make swarms (trillions) of programmable nanotech robots. Each nanobot would have to be mobile, able to grip one another, and use available raw materials (carbon and other common elements) to self-replicate. They'd need to send and coordinate signals in a shared intelligence.

Swarms of nanobots could theoretically be used to construct about anything from diamonds to solar cells to food. They could become the bodies of software-based humans. An uploaded person might have one or more virtual bodies along with a nano-produced physical body that could be quickly reassembled by nanoswarms, thereby making shapeshifting possible. Nanoswarms could mimic any environment. A living room, for example, could transform into a park, complete with birds, flowers, and trees.

It should be noted, however, that many researchers doubt the possibility of nanotechnology being used in this way any time soon. Control of molecules is an extremely complex process, part of the reason being that atoms influence each other in three dimensions. To develop molecular robots that will act within nanoswarms to create or disassemble large objects would be a major technological breakthrough, indeed.

As to the idea of uploading our brains, should the astronaut of the future become an entity within a computer, will he lose his humanness, his personality? He'd still be a human thinker. But if the time comes when people merge with computer technology to this degree, it's likely the definition of what it means to be human will be hotly contested in courts of law.

As far as interstellar space travel, there'd be advantages if one were an entity in a machine. He'd survive a long-term shutdown mode. Instead of food, he'd subsist on nuclear or solar power. The ship would be very lightweight in return. His lifespan would become endless, at least in theory. His main purpose wouldn't be to sustain his body, but to seek out new knowledge.

It could be we've already been visited by aliens. Perhaps they aren't fleshy like us, but have joined their intelligence with technology and exist in the form of nanobots, smaller than sand grains, and rather than callously mine us for raw materials, as aliens are so often depicted, they're here only to collect information. We just haven't noticed them.

RELATIVISTIC EFFECTS AND TIME TRAVEL

Scientists may some day discover the means to propel a starship to nearly light speed. How would such speeds affect the crew within?

RELATIVISTIC SPEED

If Max were to travel in a vehicle that approached the speed of light, what effects would he notice on himself? Probably nothing special. He'd measure his ship and it would be the same length as when he'd left Earth. His activities and those of the people with him would slow down, but no one would notice because the clocks, too, have slowed. But if Mary, left on Earth, were able to measure conditions in Max's ship, she'd see things differently.

The ship's length would be significantly shorter, proving at least one of the predictions of the theory of relativity true—that length decreases as speed increases.

Mary would notice Max's clocks running slow, a phenomenon called time dilation. On Earth, this effect has been proven by comparing atomic clocks on jet planes with those left on the ground. The time dilation is very small, measured in only billionths of a second, because the jets traveled at speeds much less than the speed of light. Nevertheless, it's a measurable effect, and Einstein's theory is proved true again.

But traveling at relativistic speeds might not make a good diet plan. Here's why. As a spaceship moves sufficiently close to the speed of light, the magnitude of its mass and the masses of the people within it approach infinity.

GRAVITY

Relativistic consequences also occur around intense gravity fields. As mentioned earlier, gravity is the warping of space and time: space becomes curved and time slows down. Atomic clocks run a tiny bit slower on the surface of the Earth than they do on top of a skyscraper; gravity is weaker up there. This phenomenon becomes even more noticeable when the strength of the gravity field is gargantuan. Recall Mary's experience when she approached a black hole. The time dilation that occurs is similar to that which occurs while traveling at nearly light speed.

(Incidentally, relativistic time effects had to be taken into account during the development of Global Positioning Systems.)

TIME TRAVEL

Tremendous speed and gravity could conceivably result in a type of time travel. If Max travels for one year at 99.9% the speed of light, then turns around and heads back to Earth, two years will have passed for him, yet 45 years will have elapsed on Earth. He discovers his twin sister Mary is 43 years older than he is. Max has essentially traveled into Earth's future. Not only will he have to get caught up with family matters but with new technology, as well.

Making use of an immense gravity field might be another way to leap into the future. If it were possible for Mary to suspend herself very close to a black hole without crossing the event horizon, hang around for a year, and then return to Earth, thousands of years will have elapsed on Earth. There'd be no familiar faces to welcome her home.

Traveling through wormholes—those theoretical shortcuts connecting regions of warped space—might result in a person not only ending up somewhere else in the cosmos, but somewhen else. If the mouth of a wormhole were located near a massive star, time would dilate. Mary could jump through and end up in the future. If Max jumped through from the other direction, he'd end up in the past. But consider this. If Max hurries back through regular space to his original starting point, he could end up in a time before he left to begin with. This is a causality violation, a time travel paradox.

Debate goes on about time loops that result in such paradoxes. Some put a restriction on time travel, such as one can't return to a time before the time machine was built. Others would disallow a person going back in time to accidentally kill his grandmother when she was a child but would allow him to rescue her from life-threatening danger. Then the time traveler's father could be born and there's no longer a causality paradox.

Stephen Hawking proposed a "Chronology Protection Conjecture," which makes it highly improbable that spacetime can be warped enough to allow for time travel on a large scale.

FUTURE SPACECRAFT

THE TROUBLE WITH CHEMICAL ROCKETS

Let's assume that someday an interstellar ship will be designed to keep humans healthy and comfortable on a long space journey. What type of fuel will it use to propel itself? As the Space Shuttle roars into space, the fuel in those giant tanks lasts for about 10 minutes, just long enough to carry the shuttle into orbit. The problem, then, with using chemical rockets to reach the high speeds needed for interstellar travel is that the combined weight of the payload, engine, and propellant would be prohibitively high. And there are relativistic effects to consider. A craft that goes faster becomes more massive. It will need even more fuel to propel itself. Imagine the cost of this amount of fuel! Congress would never approve. Ingenious breakthroughs are needed if humans are to travel the galaxy. Even if such technologies are discovered, one still can't break the speed of light barrier...or can they?

GRAVITY ASSIST

Gravity assist depends on a craft "stealing" a bit of momentum from a moving planet. As a result, the craft's velocity increases or changes direction. Launches must be precisely timed so the planet is in the right place at the right time for gravity assist to work. The *Voyager 2* spacecraft flew by Jupiter and got a boost to Saturn. Saturn gave it a boost to Uranus.

Apollo astronaut Buzz Aldrin has drafted a proposal for sending multiple missions to Mars that takes advantage of the gravity assist provided by both Earth and Mars. The plan requires employing two reusable craft that would be in continual orbit between the two planets. Near Earth, a "taxi" carrying astronauts would dock with the Mars-bound craft and reach Mars in 5 months. On the return trip, the taxi would link to the second orbiting vehicle and arrive home in 8 months. This proposal calls for much less propellant than amounts required by chemical rockets.

NUCLEAR ENGINES

When the nuclei of atoms such as uranium or plutonium break apart, or fission, the resulting loss of mass releases a high amount of energy, as predicted by $E = mc^2$. A "compact nuclear rocket" would move liquid hydrogen through hot nuclear fuel. The resulting hydrogen gas would flow through a nozzle and provide thrust. Hydrogen could be replenished from planets like Jupiter for the trip home. A proposed method of using fission fragments as the propellant would enable spacecraft to reach appreciable fractions of light speed, thus setting the course for interstellar travel. But bear in mind, the radioactivity associated with the use of nuclear fuel might become an issue at the time of launch and during manned missions.

Fusion of hydrogen into helium is what powers the Sun. $E = mc^2$ applies here, too. During the reaction, some of the mass is converted into an abundant amount of energy. In searching for ways to harness fusion energy to power spacecraft, scientists predict one of the most promising fuel combinations would require the fusion of heavy hydrogen with helium-3, an isotope rare on Earth but plentiful on the Moon. The reaction would produce very little radioactive waste.

But the nuclei of atoms aren't so easily fused. During one method of initiating fusion, particles must be heated to temperatures found inside stars. What kind of container would hold such hot material? In laboratory settings, the reaction is confined within powerful magnetic or electrostatic fields.

Another method of fusing light elements together involves the use of lasers beams. Yet another proposal calls for the use of subatomic particles called muons. Using muons would reduce the repulsive force between atomic nuclei and ease fusion, eliminating the need for superheating. The proposed Project Daedalus would use electron beams to initiate fusion. It's predicted that such a craft would travel at ten percent the speed of light.

There'll be no easy methods for applying fusion to propel spacecraft. Both lasers and muon production require considerable amounts of energy. Devices for producing magnetic fields would add tonnage to the craft. If practical ways to initiate, contain, and control fusion reactions can be found, then we're on our way to exploring the stars.

THE BUSSARD RAMJET

Instead of carrying its fuel, an advancing ramjet would funnel in fuel from space. It's estimated that interstellar space contains one particle per cubic centimeter, most of these particles being hydrogen atoms. The ramjet would scoop up hydrogen with a powerful, forward-extending electromagnetic field. The collected atoms would be compressed and used for fusion energy.

Under optimal conditions, as the theory goes, the ramjet would accelerate at a rate of 1 g and reach very close to light speed within a year's time. The ship would arrive at the center of the Milky Way in 26,000 years, but with time dilation, only decades would pass for the ship's crew. If they ever returned to Earth, they'd find it a changed place, indeed.

ION THRUSTER

Deep Space 1, launched in October 1998 and retired in December of 2001, tested a new technology called the ion thruster. The spacecraft's solar panels generated electricity, which charged up a set of grids. The grids then expelled xenon ions from the engine at 19 miles (30 km) per second. The best chemical rockets produce an exhaust velocity of three to six miles (5 to 10 km) per second. *Deep Space 1* used very little propellant and produced a thrust so gentle that, according to the project's manager, it accelerated from zero to 60 miles per hour in four days. But good things come to those who wait. The craft eventually reached a cruising velocity two times faster than the orbital speed of the Space Shuttle while consuming less than one-tenth the fuel.

LIGHT SAILS

A way for a spacecraft to reach even greater speeds would be through the use of light sails. These would be exceedingly thin and lightweight, made of reflective Mylar-like material or strong carbon fibers that are able to withstand searing heat from the Sun and impacts from micrometeoroids.

A major advantage of traveling by light sail is that the craft wouldn't have to carry massive amounts of fuel. Photons of light from the Sun exert a very small force on Earth, that being 5.2 pounds per square mile (9 newtons per square kilometer). In using this force to produce acceleration, the object must have extremely little mass and a very large surface area. Once unfolded in space, a sail 0.3 miles (0.5 km) wide would accelerate very slowly, but the rate would be steady, because solar pressure is continuous. With time, the sail would reach a speed of 56 miles (90 km) per second, which is more than ten times the speed of the Space Shuttle. A trip from coast to coast across the U.S. would take less than a minute. It would take less than a decade for a light sail to overtake either of the *Voyager* crafts currently making their way to the outer edges of the solar system.

Since space is virtually empty, there'd be little drag on this craft. Greater accelerations could be achieved with boosts from large Earth- or satellite-based lasers aimed at the sail for days or weeks. With these boosts, the sail would accelerate to one-tenth the speed of light, then coast to its destination.

If it were only that simple.

Besides requiring a wispy mass, much less than the mass of a human, the Sun's rays are feeble beyond the solar system. If lasers are used, they'd have to be extremely intense and precisely aimed at a sail millions of miles away. If a problem is encountered, depending on how far the sail has traveled, it would take months or years for technicians to receive a radio message from the sail and an even longer time for a correction signal to reach the sail (because the sail will have moved farther along during that time). Some foresee the day when lasers or microwave generators are set up at space stations along the way that will push the sail down a type of interstellar freeway.

Robert Forward proposed aiming microwave energy (produced by a solar-powered orbiting transmitter) to push a fine wire mesh of 0.6 mile (1 km) radius. The sail would weigh a little over half an ounce (16 grams). Its wires would hold microscopic hardware to function as camera, sensors, brain, and transmitter. Two weeks of microwave blasting would accelerate the sail to one-fifth the speed of light. It would coast to Proxima Centauri in twenty-one years. Give it another burst of microwave energy, and it would send images home.

As for manned missions, scale this up a million times and the microwave transmitter would have to beam more energy than all the power stations on Earth currently generate. Besides that, at a million times larger, it would have to be an enormous sail.

ANTIMATTER

The answer to interstellar space travel might lie in matter/antimatter annihilation. A proton meets up with an antiproton and—KAPOW!—mass is converted into energy in a highly efficient reaction. Only 0.0015 ounce (42 milligrams) of antimatter contains an amount of energy equal to the fuel and oxidizer in the external tank of the Space Shuttle. With this type of energy, a manned spacecraft could reach Mars within a couple of weeks, as opposed to current plans of several months. The annihilation produces particles called pions that travel at nearly light speed. The pions would be the source of thrust, or they could be used to heat up a hydrogen propellant.

Why aren't we currently exploiting antimatter for our energy needs? At the present time, only a few nanograms (*billionths* of grams) of antimatter are produced by particle accelerators each year, and it's a very expensive process. Containment is also an issue. Because antimatter reacts immediately with matter, it must be handled with utmost care and stored within carefully controlled electric and magnetic fields. Perhaps a time will come when antimatter can be used on a smaller scale in combination with fission or fusion.

(While on the subject, the use of positron-emission tomography (PET) scanning for medical imaging relies on antimatter produced during radioactive decay. The radioisotope is released into the body. Its decay releases positrons, which meet up with electrons in the body tissue. The annihilation produces gamma rays that are detected by the PET scan.)

WILL WE EVER ATTAIN LIGHT SPEED?

Fusion, light sail, and/or antimatter propulsion systems may one day accelerate spacecraft to the high velocities needed to reach Proxima Centauri within a reasonable timeframe, but none of these methods will be able to push a craft to the speed of a photon. We may have to accept the fact that Einstein was right and neither radiation nor matter can travel faster than light speed, and humans may never venture to exotic locales like the Andromeda Galaxy at 2.5 million light-years away.

But hold on—what about space itself? Perhaps space can be altered to allow for faster-than-light, or superluminal, travel.

There's evidence that spacetime expanded at FTL speeds at the time of the Big Bang. Some groups of scientists are giving ideas in this realm of possibilities serious thought. They're researching theoretical sources of energy and ways in which a space drive could bring a craft to light-speed or faster while at the same time significantly decreasing or eliminating the need for propellant. From 1996 to 2002, NASA funded one such research group called the Breakthrough Propulsion Physics Project.

Many of the topics that follow are in the conjecture or speculation phase of development and are not without controversy in the physics community. Some have been discounted by scientific groups at this time (though it doesn't mean they can't be revisited in the future); others have been deemed worthy of further consideration. Should any of these concepts show promise, there'll likely be major technological hurdles before they reach stages of practical application. They are presented here as ideas for you to consider as you pen your stories of space travel.

GRAVITY CONTROL

We're already aware that gravity warps space, slows down time, and bends the path of electromagnetic waves. For years, we've been able to manipulate electromagnetic energy for many purposes—electric power, communications, medical X-rays, to name a few. By the same token, perhaps science will discover a way to manipulate electromagnetic waves to control gravity, inertia, and/or spacetime in a manner that would accelerate a starship through space. The technology could also be used to produce artificial gravity.

VACUUM ENERGY

It's theorized that even the vacuum of space contains energy, and a stupendous amount at that. This is called quantum vacuum energy, or zero-point energy. It's the random vibrations of electromagnetic energy left in empty space after all other energy is taken away. Calculations reveal that a thimbleful could boil away all the oceans on Earth. (Experiments, however, show the amount of this energy is closer to zero.)

Scientists are searching for ways to tap into this energy, that is, if usable amounts are actually found to exist. In quantum physics, minuscule "virtual" particles continually appear and disappear. These vacuum fluctuations add up to zero energy on average. If these fluctuations are constrained or "squeezed," negative energy results in areas, though greater positive energy ends up elsewhere because of energy conservation laws. One hint that negative energy exists is shown by the Casimir effect, where a vacuum energy gradient pushes two closely spaced uncharged metal plates together, the region between the plates being filled with a negative energy density. It's hoped that this asymmetry of vacuum energy could some day be used to propel a spacecraft.

It's thought by some that charged particles in matter interact with vacuum energy, and therefore gravity and inertia are linked to this energy. Inertia is that tendency of an object to stay in the original state of motion, that is, at rest or at constant velocity. There is speculation that inertia might stem from an electromagnetic drag force on the charged particles of the object as it moves through the vacuum energy. If there's a way to manipulate this vacuum energy, and therefore inertia, an object with less inertia would require less energy to accelerate.

WORMHOLES REVISITED

To produce a traversable wormhole, that is, if we only could, according to one scientist's calculations, all you need is some superdense matter on the order of neutron star material. Shape it into a ring a couple hundred million miles (a few million km) in diameter. You'd need another one of these rings placed where you want to travel to. Give them tremendous voltages, then whirl both rings at relativistic speeds. And presto! You've got yourself a way to travel the universe.

Ahem, yes...well, those hypothetical wormholes, whether produced naturally or artificially somehow—perhaps by revving up colossal space-based particle accelerators—might lead us through short cuts connecting distant regions of curved space. But wormholes would collapse under their own gravity, not to mention this gravity would destroy anything coming close to it. Negative energy is gravitationally repulsive and immense quantities of it would be required to hold open a wormhole.

ALCUBIERRE'S WARP DRIVE

According to this idea, matter with negative energy density could be used to warp space and thereby create a "bubble" where spacetime is contracted in front of a ship and expanded behind the ship. Reconfiguring space in this way would make FTL travel possible. What's more, time would not dilate, nor would mass increase. And unlike the g-forces space shuttle astronauts experience while charging into space, people inside the warp bubble craft wouldn't experience any acceleration effects.

But the use of negative energy to hold wormholes open or create space bubbles won't occur without incredible technological challenges. The energy required to produce such a bubble would be equivalent to that found in billions of stars, unless the devices are limited to microscopic size, but how could that be used to move a spacecraft along? And since the bubble would occur outside of the ship, how would one turn it on and off? To say nothing of the causality violations that would occur. In traveling through a wormhole or within a warp bubble and overtaking a ray of light, the traveler might return home before he left, and we know about the problem of a person going back in time and accidentally killing his grandmother. One other thing...no one has yet demonstrated how to collect even small quantities of negative energy.

QUANTUM TUNNELING

Nanoscale particles such as photons or electrons have been known to approach barriers and mysteriously appear on the other side of them, and at faster-than-light speeds, no less. There's a certain probability the particle will appear on the other side of the barrier, and sometimes they actually do. It's been shown the leading edge of a signal makes it through the barrier at superluminal speed, but the entire signal is bound by the speed of light. And whether a photon tunnels or not can't be controlled. It's random, so no usable information has crossed over the barrier. If it turns out there is usable information, how this could be applied to large FTL spaceships is the question of the hour.

(Note: Quantum tunneling has implications in the computer industry. As computer chips are made smaller and faster, there's the unwanted effect of electrons leaking across barriers. On the other hand, components in quantum computers will depend on these tunneling effects.)

TACHYONS

These theoretical particles travel faster than light. When they lose energy, their velocity increases. When they gain energy, their velocity decreases. The slowest attainable velocity for a tachyon is the speed of light. It's thought that one was discovered in a shower of cosmic ray particles but results have never been duplicated. Some hypothesize that a certain type of neutrino is a tachyon, but evidence is inconclusive. And with tachyons come those paradoxical implications for time travel.

In science fiction, the term tachyon has been expanded on as a mechanism for faster-than-light communication and transportation. It's also been used as a construct for time travel or as a means to communicate with someone living in the past.

USE OF HYPERSPACE

In theoretical physics, ten or so dimensions are predicted by string theory, though all but our familiar dimensions seem to be tightly curled up into loops of subatomic size. One scientific conundrum the theory hopes to answer is why gravity is so weak compared to the other known forces of nature. In 2007, the Large Hadron Collider at the CERN laboratory in Geneva will begin conducting experiments, which may reveal evidence of unseen dimensions. There are scientists who reason that some of these currently inaccessible dimensions may actually be quite large.

Interdimensional travel is an idea that comes in handy in the realm of science fiction. Since it's thought that other dimensions are folded into our familiar dimensions, a ship would somehow jump out of our space, into hyperdimensional space and exit at a desired point. Hyperspace might be given different properties than real space and allow for a spaceship to surpass the speed of light. Versions of how hyperspace has been applied in science fiction are covered extensively at the Astronomy Cafe and Wikipedia websites (see list of recommended reading in the reference section of this book).

TELEPORTATION

Perhaps a ship won't be needed at all to get us around the universe. The idea of teleportation usually centers on a device that scans an object to collect all its information. A transmitter sends the data to a receiver, and it's then used to make a replica of the original object. The replica may be reconstructed from the beamed matter or energy of the original, or it may be assembled from molecules at the receiver site. The phenomenon of quantum entanglement has made teleportation possible with quantum states (spins, for example) of photons and atoms. Onward to humans!

Maybe it will happen this way. Beings from an advanced civilization will arrive on Earth and bestow upon us a copy of their service manual that explains the mechanics of their FTL technology. Then we'll be all set.

MIGRATION FROM EARTH

In the future, whether due to natural disaster, nuclear war, or for political reasons, humans may be forced to leave Earth. An asteroid may approach and our descendants may fail to divert it. Pollution may have made Earth uninhabitable. Or having depleted ourselves of valuable resources, we will look to planets and asteroids for fresh supplies. We may discover a new resource we can't live without. The Moon, for example, holds in its dust helium-3, a potential fuel for fusion energy.

Ethical dilemmas are bound to arise. If forced to leave, who should go? Women and children? Scientists? Many young and few old? Will some on board become malcontents and force their way into power? Will there be laws and policies that will give direction on how to interact with alien cultures?

Even if we manage to remain on Earth for eons, in five billion years, the Sun will expand to a red giant and engulf the Earth, scorching it to a lifeless cinder. We'll be forced to leave the solar system entirely. But some believe our departure will occur long before then.

It might be that our migration won't be for reasons of species survival but because of our adventurous spirit, our desire to explore, to search for alien civilizations, to better understand the universe, to pursue our dreams. Already entrepreneurs are banking on space tourism. In a few years, $200,000 will get you a ride into space to experience a few hours of weightlessness as you watch the sun rise and set every 90 minutes while you orbit the Earth. There'll come a day when tourism will extend to the planets and stars. The Moon could be used as a launch station for travel to more distant places. One futurist predicts that in 100,000 years, urban sprawl will have spread across the galaxy.

The survival of the human race may depend on generation ships. Energy and resources to build and propel them will be costly, and the ships will have to be constructed in space. What means of propulsion will a generation ship have? It will use solar power when it can, but it will also have to carry a considerable amount of fuel. The ship may be cylindrical, doughnut, or sphere shaped, and, unless someone has discovered a way to use energy fields to produce a suitable gravity field, it will have to rotate. Will it hold hundreds of people or tens of thousands? Will it be a colony orbiting a planet, or will it carry the remains of humanity to a faraway star system?

A generation ship will require a stable environment and life-support mechanisms. It will need protective shields for radiation. Two back-up systems (redundancies) will have to be in place in the event something goes wrong. On board will be robots, nanobots, and human engineers to ensure smooth operation of the ship's systems. It will be a regular city, albeit circular in shape, with housing, government offices, and research laboratories. Some of the inhabitants will work at the power plant; others will work in the hospital or school. Farmers will grow crops for food and oxygen. There'll be forests and parks for recreation. The ship will be self-sustaining with a means of recycling waste, a regular Biosphere III.

How will this play out socially? Will the people accept their fate as ambassadors of humanity or will the social structure break down? Will the culture be a peaceful one, or will crime and violence break out? Will leaders be elected democratically or will a dictatorship form? Over a thousand years, once they arrive at their destination, will future generations remember their humanitarian purpose, or will memories dim, leaving planet Earth to be remembered only in myths and legends?

SEARCHING FOR ALIENS

At the time of this writing, astronomers have discovered over 200 extrasolar planets, those planets that circle stars other than our Sun, with more being discovered all the time. There's bound to be some that are hospitable to life. In 2004, Dr. Frank Drake, of SETI, the Search for Extraterrestrial Intelligence, estimated there are well over 10,000 advanced civilizations in the Milky Way with which we could communicate. If this is so, why haven't any been detected?

Researchers at SETI have found it a monumental task to comb through space in search of alien signals. SETI has explored only a tiny portion of the entire "parameter space" of sky, frequency range, and power levels. In other words, the size of space is so great and the range of frequencies so broad it's easy to miss a signal. Besides that, incoming frequencies can get absorbed by interstellar dust. An alien civilization may have sent us a message while we were swimming around in primordial soup. The age of the galaxy is estimated to be over 13 billion years, so the chances of our existence coinciding with an alien civilization's are slim. Maybe they've observed us from afar and decided we aren't capable of communicating with them at their more highly evolved level, or it's their policy not to interfere with alien life-forms in their natural environment. It's quite possible that extraterrestrials are out there and haven't contacted us because they don't live in technological societies, or if they do, they don't use radio waves for communication, which is why SETI recently began searching for optical signals.

Perhaps aliens haven't visited because FTL travel isn't widely in use. Or we live off the main route of interstellar travel. Or perhaps they're here now but we haven't noticed them, because they're smaller than grains of sand.

CONCLUSION

The intelligent interstellar probe that could...

Imagine a softball-sized probe programmed with artificial intelligence that would land on a moon or asteroid to gather resources like carbon and iron. It would be able to evolve and adapt and grow more complex in its thinking. It would set up radio transmitters and make copies of itself, and the copies would head off in different directions throughout the galaxy, and they'd in turn make more copies. They may even carry seeds to ready suitable extrasolar planets for humans to colonize. In terms of energy required, these self-replicating, self-repairing Von Neumann machines would be exceedingly easier to send out to the stars than manned spacecraft. They'd be inconspicuous as they gathered information about distant civilizations. They'd upload this information onto an Galactic Internet, for all of us to peruse at our leisure. The greatest effort on our part would be in constructing the first one. After that, they're on their own. Or it just might happen that our own intelligence, uploaded into these softball-sized probes or into nanobot swarms, will some day permeate the universe.

The possibilities for story ideas are as varied as the topics throughout this chapter. I hope it has given you exciting ideas for further exploration as you create stories full of wonder. As you can already imagine, the scope of science fiction is as boundless as the universe!

CHAPTER NINE

I DON'T KNOW THAT BUG-EYED MONSTER FROM ADAM: CLICHÉS IN SF

Milena Benini

PUBLIC ENEMY NO. 1

There are many definitions of SF. But, whichever definition you look at, odds are that somewhere in it, there will be words like "what if," "extrapolation," or, at the very least, "imagination"[94]. This means that clichés are particularly dangerous for SF-writers, as they take the reader's attention away from the idea, and can make even the freshest idea seem stale. Furthermore, SF readers read looking for the ideas behind the text, and will therefore spot the clichés more easily. Clichés will jar the readers, disappoint them, and generally destroy the reader's trust. And once the reader's trust is lost, it's very difficult to win it back.

However, it should also be stated that, very occasionally, clichés can be used deliberately, either to achieve a certain effect—most often in humor—or sometimes as a sort of shorthand. This can be useful, particularly in short stories: when you're writing within a specific genre—such as science fiction— you can rely on your readers to be aware of certain clichés and accept them. This can save space: if, for example, you write that a spaceship travels through space through a wormhole, the existence of cliché will allow the readers to recognize it and accept it, and you can then both move on with the story without wasting any more time on explanations. But, be careful: too much of this and your story will start to look like an old *Star Trek* script.

Of course, it isn't always easy to distinguish between the "good" (or at least acceptable) clichés and the "bad" ones, the ones that will throw your reader out of your story. But this chapter will look at both situations, and try to help you distinguish between the two. And to make orientation easier, we'll first split the clichés into two groups: "large" and "small" ones. So, let us look at these public enemies, neatly classified, like specimens in a jar...of Tang.

BIG-TIME CROOKS: THE STORIES WE ALL KNOW AND HATE

These are the "big" clichés. They include things such as stock plots, settings, or characters. Due to the specific history of SF, they are sometimes even expected, and can be incorporated into narratives or used to construct stories without the readers (or editors) getting upset about it. In a sense, they are the godfathers of SF, stemming as they do from the times when SF was primarily pulp-fiction.

However, always bear in mind that godfathers are like Don Corleone. They can seem very helpful but, like all mobsters, sooner or later the clichés you use in constructing your story are going to ask for payment, and, usually, that payment will also be large and can have painful consequences. This is particularly true of clichéd plots: although most SF readers will not mind seeing a plot they're already familiar with, you had better give it a completely original twist or else the readers will feel disappointed and cheated.

All writers were readers first. However, it is often possible to miss entire portions of SF history, or a single, but seminal, short story. Because of this, writers, particularly novice writers, sometimes come up with an idea that seems fresh to them, but to most others it's something that they've read a gazillion times before, or—and this is equally damaging—only once, but in a version so good that the attempt they have before them seems like merely a poor copy. This also sometimes happens with mainstream writers who take a side-trip to the genre without knowing enough about it. The result usually makes SF readers angry. But they will be a whole lot angrier at a writer who wants to be part of the genre and still doesn't know enough about it.

As is so often the case, prevention is the best cure: if you intend to write in genre—any genre—you should read just about everything in the genre that you can find, so you will know what's been done before you and how it's been done. It's also a good idea to look at different sources, such as anthologies and bibliographies, and make sure you haven't missed anything important. Even though SF is not taught systematically in most schools, there is a rich body of theoretical work pertaining to it, and you should not be afraid to make use of it. But in case you missed something, here's a short list of stories you should not attempt to write unless you have an incredibly new twist on them. There are much longer lists available on the Internet, but this is a short overview of the most important ones. We'll start from storyline and setting clichés, because—particularly in SF—they are often connected.

THE ADAM AND EVE STORY

Any story where, at the end, there are only two survivors on a life-friendly planet and their names just happen to be Adam and Eve. Do not go there. Ever. Or Adamer.

ALIEN LOVE

Stories in which an alien is stranded on Earth and falls in love with a human, but eventually goes back home or stays on Earth forever, never revealing his true identity to anyone but his loved one. A variation on this was used in *E.T.*, with friendship taking the place of romantic involvement. In either case—and particularly if your plot involves bad government officials and ways in which your alien and his Earthling partner defeat them—it's better to avoid this plot. Also, the idea of aliens who are physically very similar to humans (and sometimes can even procreate with humans) is another cliché. It is mostly due to old TV shows, where it was cheaper and simpler to have human actors with a few bits and pieces added on than to create completely non-human aliens. With the development of Computer Graphic Imaging (CGI), we may have hoped that this would change, but the idea that aliens look just like humans except for the pointy ears or frowning foreheads has, unfortunately, already taken too strong a root in many minds. In writing, though, you don't have to worry about CGI expenses, so feel free to have your aliens look... well, *alien*.

APOCALYPSE TOMORROW

This is a story where, in a post-apocalyptic world, disheveled armies struggle to overcome threats such as biker gangs or mutants. They used to include attempts to throw the Enemy (usually Russians) from the U.S., but this variation died out with the end of the Cold War. They also include stories of a post-plague world where most men or most women have been wiped out and/or made sterile. Do not write these stories unless you have something very new to say—or, at the very least, unless your way of telling the story is so new that you think your readers will forgive you the travel through well-known territory.

ARNOLD VS. JESUS

Time-travel stories in which the bad guys travel back in time in order to prevent the hero from being born or reaching maturity. A variation on this is the story in which the hero travels back in time and winds up becoming a historical figure. This was done to great effect by Michael Moorcock in his *Behold the Man*.

BUBBLE WORLDS

Any story or setting which depends entirely on the fact that society has been closed down as if in a bubble (sometimes literally), and yet the world outside the bubble turns out to be perfectly inhabitable. Such settings usually have some very important limits, such as all citizens being required to die once they reach a certain age, and the hero discovers that this is not necessary because their resources are not limited after all and there is a better, free world outside. Watch *Logan's Run* for details... and then forget about this story.

BUG-EYED MONSTERS

Any story in which the aliens are all bug-eyed monsters and are trying to take over the Earth. This sub-genre, although one of the oldest in SF (see *The War of the Worlds*), has been dormant for a long time, but the last ten years or so have seen its revival, particularly through Hollywood movies. It remains a bad idea, especially if you intend to defeat the BEM's, who are technologically superior, through human ingenuity and/or sheer chutzpah.

GENDER BENDER

Any story or setting based on simple reversal of traditional gender roles: males are gentle and considered "soft", while females are aggressive, leaders in society etc. If you intend to use this as part of your story, make sure to have good reasons for this. Traditional human gender roles were based on a large number of physical and historical factors. Do not, under any circumstances, have your Earthling heroes come to this kind of society and show them the error of their ways.

A variation on the gender bender is the "plain bender", where beings at first perceived as pets or slaves among the aliens are in fact the masters, while those whom humans considered the masters are really pets or slaves.

JAR OF TANG

Any kind of plot where the whole point of the story is to allow the author to cry "Gotcha!". This kind of plot was used in at least two thirds of the *Twilight Zone* scripts. The name comes from the ending "...for, you see, we're all living in a jar of Tang!". Similar endings can be "...for, you see, I am a dog!" or "...for, you see, I am a robot!" or "...for, you see, I am only three inches tall!" etc. Douglas Adams used jar of Tang stories several times in his Hitchhiker books, but, remember, he used them to comic effect! A particularly bad variation of the jar of Tang story is the "it was all just a dream/virtual reality/computer game" ending: almost guaranteed to make the readers throw your book over the room, causing potential damage to cats, dogs, and houseplants on the way.

KILLING HITLER

Time-travel stories in which the good guy travels back in time in order to prevent something bad from happening, for example to kill Hitler. They usually have one of three possible endings: a) the good guy succeeds, but what happens instead is even worse, or b) the good guy thinks he's succeeded, but, upon returning to his home-time, discovers that some previously overlooked detail has caused his efforts to fail, and c) the good guy discovers that it was his attempt to stop the bad thing that actually caused the bad thing to happen. All three are well known, and should not be attempted unless you are a trained professional.

KING-KONG HAL

Stories in which computers go crazy and do monstrous things, only to be defeated in the end by the hero's ingeniously giving them a riddle they cannot solve, and/or falling in love with a human character. In case you're wondering where to look for the ultimate takes on these things, look at Isaac Asimov. There are really good reasons why he is counted among the greats.

PLANET OF THE HUMANS

Any story in which the hero(es) end up on an unknown planet with a society significantly different from the Earth they know (medieval/feudal, with apes as the ruling race etc.) but it turns out in the end that it's in fact the Earth in the distant future.

PLANETARY SOCIETIES

This cliché pertains to settings and not plots, but it is nevertheless a very important one. Remember that Earth is neither very big nor very old—but it still has numerous variations in cultures, attitudes, physical appearances etc. If you have alien planets—or even entire galactic empires/federations/unions—remember that it's highly unlikely they will all have the same appearance, mores, and beliefs. Also, remember that differences in cultures, political systems, and geography do not prevent nations on Earth from forming alliances, but they do create problems. Work from that—and do not have all aliens look and think the same, even if they are from the same planet.

ROBEO AND JULIET

A human falls in love with a robot, or a robot falls in love with a human. Generally, humanoid robots are best left alone, unless you think you can beat Isaac Asimov. Other than for amusement purposes, it is in fact very unlikely that humanoid robots will actually be mass-produced—we humans have a very poor construction from the point of view of engineering, you know.

THIS IS NOT STAR WARS

A whole group of plots and settings which take their ideas from well-known (usually media) series and merely file off the serial numbers: a group of rebels is fighting to overthrow the evil intergalactic Empire, a lost ship traveling millions of light years to get home, etc.

Of course, not only stories and settings are prone to clichés. There are several stock-characters of whom everyone has already seen too much and are thus best avoided. Here are the most common ones.

Heroic Hero

Yes, heroes are supposed to be heroic, but their heroism should stem from what they do, not who they are. Nobody is all good: if your hero is a perfect creature who never swears, has no weaknesses, and is always in the right, he is not a human. More importantly, he quickly becomes boring to the readers. A fearless hero in a dangerous situation is much less interesting than a fearful one who has to overcome the fear in order to act.

A particular variation on this is the Mary Sue kind of hero—a perfect, wonderful character whom everybody adores, usually found in a story where s/he saves the day to much admiration from everybody. This is usually just a wish-fulfilling alter ego of the author and, much as it can be entertaining for the person whom such a character embodies, it is utterly uninteresting for anybody else. Often found in fan-fiction in the form of "ensign Brown", who saves the main characters due to a unique ability or characteristic and is then lauded for it. Sometimes also gets to turn the head of a main character in the process. See also the Villainous Villain.

Reluctant Hero

Stories in which the hero, usually a scientist, is seen at the beginning as having retired from government service, probably due to moral differences with his bosses. Government representatives arrive to his home trying to talk him into coming back to solve just this one problem and, although he refuses at first, we all know he'll agree to it in the end. Best skipped as part of the story setting. In general, if you picture Roy Scheider as your scientist hero, it's a sign that his character is well known. If you don't know who Roy Scheider is, on the other hand, it's a sign that you need to work on your knowledge of SF movies.

Also includes former heroes (scientists, warriors, pilots, etc.) who are now washed-out drunks but snap out of it because of the looming crisis, and inexperienced boys (or girls) who have super-powers (are strong in the Force, are telepathic) but are afraid to use those powers because they don't know how.

MAD SCIENTIST

This is one of the oldest clichés in SF. Like most clichés, it began its life as an original idea, but that was around the time of H.G. Wells. Ever since, the mad scientist trying to destroy the world and/or the human race has been an instant sign that the story is actually a parody. So, unless you're writing one, make sure that all of your scientists are reasonably sane.

KIND ARNOLD

A bad guy, often an alien or a robot, who turns to the side of good once he gets to know humans/people from the past or future/colonists or any other group he's been sent to destroy. Although a character changing sides is not a bad idea in and of itself, this kind of twist has to be worked very carefully to succeed, particularly if the character is initially presented as programmed, either literally (being a robot) or psychologically.

THE TALKATIVE VILLAIN

Villains who explain their machinations in detail while gloating over the hero about to be executed in a complicated way that will allow the hero to escape at the last moment belong only in parodies, and even there, they're a little old by now.

THE VILLAINOUS VILLAIN

If your villain wears a goatee, has a tendency to cackle, shoots his minions for spilling his tea or speaks with a British accent, forget about him. The greatest villains are those who believe that they are doing the right thing. It's not enough just to give him a pet in order to make him human (particularly if the pet is a white or hairless cat): you have to know why he does what he does—and no, wishing to take over the world is not good enough, especially if that means destroying most of it in the process. People may be selfish, ambitious, ruthless, and even plain evil but they never perceive themselves as the bad guys. So if you're going to have a bad guy, make sure he has reasons for what he's doing—and make sure that your readers can understand those reasons. See also the Heroic Hero.

Once again: if you have an incredibly new twist on any of these plots, characters or settings, feel free to use them and write your story. But even then, it's going to be very tough to sell those stories unless you make it perfectly clear from the start that your take is new, so it's usually better to avoid them all together, or at least to wait until you've built a reputation for yourself so that readers (and editors) will give you a little more credit. It may not seem fair, but it's true.

SMALL TIME CROOKS

And now let's turn to the "small" clichés. They affect writing but can be even more damaging than the big guys in their own way. Some are applicable to any kind of writing, and some are specific or at least more often encountered in SF, but all of them will have the same effect on your readers, leaving them with an impression of a lazy, sloppy writer. Unlike the "Don Corleones", these small-time criminals can only damage your writing and should always be avoided unless you're going for a very broad comic effect. At the same time, they are insidious and often find a way to wriggle into writing, so all writers should be careful of them. Over time, most writers will discover that they are prone to one or two of the clichés listed below. The good news is, once you identify the ones that plague your writing the most often, it's relatively simple to either avoid them or get rid of them in the revision. But to be able to do so, you must know your enemy.

ALMOST JUST

This problem pertains to all those "little" words that create unnecessary clutter in your prose. They are modifiers and half-modifiers, such as 'almost', 'similar to' and 'half-', or false groupers such as "a kind of" and "a sort of". If you use them too much, you will end up with a lot of vague, ridiculous statements, such as "He was half-afraid" and "She wore an almost yellow dress". In most cases, it seems simply as if you were unable to think of the right word: half-afraid is better stated as 'anxious' or 'worried', and 'almost yellow' is ochre, light brown, the color of sand, or off-white.

As always, no rule is absolute. Sometimes, using half-modifiers and false groupers can be the best way of putting things; just make sure you're aware you're using them and be careful not to use them as an excuse not to have to think of the right words.

Another group of almost just symptoms are apparent modifiers, words with no real meaning, such as "just", "really", or "only". The easiest way to get rid of this plague is to run a search-replace routine on your text and see how many hits you get. Words such as these often wriggle into your writing from your spoken-language patterns. Remember, in spoken communication, we all use some words as mere indicators that we're thinking about something, placeholders which tell other people we haven't given up our turn in the conversation yet. In writing, however, there's no need for such placeholders, and they should be eradicated ruthlessly.

Obviously, this rule does not apply to dialogue, where you want to reproduce speech patterns. However, remember that written dialogue not only need not, but must not be exactly the same as real-life speech; you need to make it more coherent and condensed, or you'll end up sounding like some sort of a highbrow literary experiment.

AS YOU KNOW BOBS

One of the main problems in science fiction is that it usually takes the readers to a world different from our own. Obviously, the author has to inform the reader in which ways the world is different but it should not be done through long, boring information chunks, known as info dumps. One of the particularly bad ways of dealing with this is the "as you know Bob" technique, sometimes also known as "AWAK" (As We All Know), where two characters tell each other things they obviously both know already, solely for the benefit of the reader. This is the result:

> "As you know, Bob, we are stranded on this planet 736 light years from Earth, and only have enough air in the ship for three days! We have to do something!"

> "I know, but we cannot go outside the ship because the planet is inhabited by horrible bug-eyed monsters, as we found out on the first day! And we cannot call for help because our superluminal e-mailer broke in the fall!"

While to the novice writer this may seem like a good way to deal with the setting information, almost every reader will recognize it as the info dump it is and laugh at it. Another info-dumping technique is to include in the text chunks of quotes from a "neutral" source such as *The Encyclopaedia Galactica*. Yes, it worked for Douglas Adams—but, remember, he was writing a parody!

So, you wonder, how does one deal with the necessary information? Or, more to the point, how does one deal it out? The answer is, basically, a little at a time. You are writing science fiction. Trust your readers to have the patience and the will to work things out gradually. Give them just enough information to get them oriented and incorporate it in the storytelling (or dialogue) so that they do not stand out. Look:

> "Are we still incommunicado, Bob?"

> "Yup. The fall broke the power circuitry in the superluminal; I'll have to scavenge some other system to replace it. How's it going with the air recycling?"

> "Not so good, either. We're still limited to emergency reserves."

See? True, we didn't pack as much information in the above dialogue as we did in the first one, but here the characters are actually exchanging information instead of just giving it out to the reader. After all, your purpose is to get the readers to want to find out more. They know that the characters are in trouble, that they can't reach anyone and that they're limited to emergency air reserves. How much those reserves actually hold, as well as the bug-eyed monsters, and the exact distance from Earth, can wait. Particularly since, now, you have characters who seem to have at least average intelligence, and the readers will want to know about them. In the first case, they behave like dying tenors—and, outside opera, nobody's interested in such characters.

Another form of the info-dump problem is a stapledon. This is a name commonly given to situations where a character, often suddenly and unprovoked, takes center stage and explains things at great length or sometimes even solves the problem for the characters. It's really just another form of the "as you know Bob", except Bob is now talking to himself—or, actually, to the reader.

A specific problem with dealing out information is the description of the hero or heroine, especially if they are also the point of view characters. Newbie writers often try to solve it by having their POV character stop before a mirror (pool, polished ship hulk) and contemplate their blond hair and green eyes. This is one of those things that you should not do. Unless, of course, there's a good reason for it, such as your character being a self-obsessed slicker or going out to receive her first medal won in intergalactic action. Even then, however, it's more likely they would contemplate their clothes and hairdo, not their features as such.

Generally, it is always better to avoid solid chunks of description. Instead, you should try inserting little bits of description into the action. Be careful to avoid nonsensical false tricks, such as "She pushed her curly blond hair out of her eyes." This is sometimes tempting, but it's also very irritating to read: how often do people actually think like that? You push hair out of your eyes, not your curly blond hair.

You can, on the other hand, do something like this: on her way to the medal ceremony have your character meet someone. If it's a friend, she can comment on the fact that "that dress uniform really brings out your hair". (And then your POV character can consider her blond hair.) Or it can be an enemy and she can offer a biting comment, such as "you know, if I had such light coloring, I'd use makeup. Your eyebrows are almost invisible; the dress uniform makes you look like a rag doll." This technique is additionally useful as it helps you flesh out the situation. We see that the character has enemies, or at the very least that she's either attractive or capable enough to produce jealousy. From there on, it's your call whether you want to make her self-possessed and disdain the biting comment or create a self-doubting ninny who will continue on her way on the verge of tears. But none of these additional elements can be presented nearly as effectively if you just have her stop before a mirror and admire herself.

Generally, remember this: action is better than mere description and interaction is better than mere action. Conflict is usually the best kind of interaction.

BOOKISMS

For some reason, people often think that they have to use big words in writing fiction. Some authors blame it on the school-writing style but, whatever the reason, the problem is there, and the way to avoid it is really very simple: do not use complicated ways of expression where simple ones will do.

There are three groups of bookisms that one should be particularly wary of. The first are the so-called "said-bookisms". These are situations where writers replace the standard dialogue tag "said" (or "asked") with complex and more "literary" expressions such as "he exhorted", "she inquired"—and, of course, the most (in)famous "he ejaculated". An experienced editor once told me that the best dialogue doesn't need tags anyway, because the readers can work out for themselves who's saying what. While this is something of an exaggeration, particularly if there are more than two people involved in the conversation, the rule of thumb for dialogue tags should be that "said" (and "asked") tags are so invisible they almost cannot be overused.

A similar mistake often encountered with newbie writers is the way of referring to the hero by multiple constructions. A relative of the false-action description mentioned earlier, this happens when inexperienced writers try to emulate Gustave Flaubert, who was famous for making sure that, in his manuscripts, no word was repeated twice on the same page. The hero is thus first referred to by his name, but transformed into "the dashing Englishman" in the next sentence, only to become "the daring engineer" in the next. Usually called "the burly detective" syndrome, this problem carries the double pitfall of confusing the reader (Is John both the dashing Englishman and the daring engineer?) and throwing the reader out of the story.

In general, it is best to stick to one name of the character when referring to him or her. If your hero is called John, than John he should stay throughout the story—he can only become the dashing Englishman when perceived from the point of view of a slightly smitten teenager who doesn't yet know his name.

Finally, there is the "pontification of expostulation" problem. New writers sometimes use long, complicated words and structures simply to indicate to themselves and the world that they are writing *literature*. When this problem attacks, characters ambulate instead of walk and get golden orbs for eyes. The principle here is still the same: keep it simple. Yes, a little metaphor can add to the color of the story, but the accent should be on "a little", not on "metaphor".

Particularly in science fiction, metaphors can take readers down wrong paths. While in "realistic" fiction the phrase "her eyes followed him around the room" may pass unnoticed, science fiction readers will mostly hear the "boing boing" sound the eyes make on their way. Again, unless you're writing comedy, this is definitely not the effect you want.

FUZZY LOGIC

This is a problem that attacks the construction of the story rather than style, but it still needs to be avoided. The situation arises when the author has not worked out the inner logic of the story beforehand and forces the readers to follow her own thought process on the page.

There are three basic ways in which fuzzy logic becomes apparent, although the way to deal with them is similar and boils down to this: always know your story beforehand. To start writing without knowing exactly where you're going is a bad idea. Although some people prefer to "think on paper," that first stage should remain hidden from the readers. Make notes and explore if it makes you feel better but do not just copy/paste those notes into your story.

The first example of this problem is the "white room" syndrome, a situation when the main character wakes up in a white room and spends the first third of the story wondering about it. The white room is actually the white paper the author faces at the beginning of the story and will bore the reader silly even before the story starts. The general rule that will help you avoid such a situation is this: start the story as late as possible. Choose the latest point where you can start the story without resorting to flashbacks and work your way from there.

The other form of fuzzy logic is the, "You can't fire me, I quit!" trick. This is a false trick: the author presents the readers with an unconvincing, unbelievable situation, but thinks that the readers' suspicions will be put to rest if only the main character says something like "if I hadn't seen it with my own eyes, I wouldn't have believed it". Always remember, science fiction is a literature of ideas—but those ideas have to be based on facts or at least extrapolated from them. So, if you have a scene like this in your story, be very sure that you offer a completely plausible explanation for it—preferably beforehand. Even though your main character may still remain in the dark as to the real situation behind the incredible incident, your readers have to have enough information to work out what's really going on. However, be careful not to make your heroine an idiot: if she has all the data at her disposal, she should be able to work it out, too.

Finally, the third form of "paper thinking" is the presentation of bogus alternatives. Again born out of insufficient preparation, this is the situation where the main character is forced by the author to do something simply to serve the plot. The author tries to disguise the truth by having the character list off alternate actions and discard them: "I could have stayed in the ship but then I wouldn't have enough air. I could have tried to spend the night high in a tree, but I had no way to secure myself to it and if I fell during the night, I would have attracted the bug-eyed monsters. So I had to keep on walking, even though I knew that the trail will be littered by bug-eyed monsters' smeerp traps." Etc.

This is irritating for several reasons: one, if you lead the action well, we will know why the character couldn't stay in the ship or spend the night in a tree, so this is just rehashing of information we already know and, two, if you force your character to a stupid decision, the readers will perceive it as such, no matter how many arguments you throw at them. So, what we see here is simply the author working out her plot problems in the story instead of in preparation notes. In short, when you find such a scene, cut it out.

GIBSONIANA

This particular cliché has come to science fiction relatively recently, following the explosion of cyberpunk. It is recognizable by "brand-name fever", the habit of inserting masses of (invented or real) brand names into the text in the hope of making it livelier. So the character drives around in a Toyota and drinks Evian, with a Heckler in his glove compartment and a Nokia in the pocket of his Hilfigers. A few pages of this and the readers feel as if they've mistakenly picked up a mail order catalogue instead of a piece of fiction. Furthermore, a brand name is not a replacement for a description: Toyota produces many different cars, and who knows what their cars may look like in the future? Nokia phones made only two or three years ago were very different from the ones they produce today, and it's up to you, the author, to let us know what they will be like a hundred years from now.

This procedure did work for William Gibson but that was for two reasons: one, he used brand names to achieve a very specific effect, and two, when he started doing it, it was a procedure normally encountered almost exclusively in crime stories, so it gave a different flavor to his writing. Nowadays it's stale, and will only make your story a faux-Gibson. Unless that is your intention, use brand names sparingly and only when you think it contributes something to the story.

And while we're talking about emulation of known writers: this is good as an exercise, but should not be used for the final draft. Of course, we are all products of our past experiences, and if a particular writer has been your favorite for years, you will probably show the influence in your own writing. However, as a writer, you should try to find your own voice as well. Copying somebody else's style can help you analyze the process but if you intend to sign a story with your own name, it should be your story, not somebody else's.

Generally speaking, in science fiction, the easiest thing to do is to follow Isaac Asimov's advice and go for the so-called "invisible" style, i.e. simple and clear. Usually it's the idea that powers the story and you don't want anything to take the readers' attention away from it. However, occasionally, a more "visible" style may be called for—this was the case with cyberpunk, for example—but, as with all other writing decisions, it has to be a consciously made decision and you have to be able to stick to it consistently throughout the story or novel.

In short stories, experimentation can be given a little more room, exactly because they're short stories. But whether you are writing a 100-word piece of flash fiction or a 150,000-word epic, always be aware that you have to remain consistent; otherwise, the readers will wonder what's going on. So, unless you have a good reason, stick to simple style and, once you find a perfect word for something, use it from start to finish. There are, hopefully, plenty of other things in your story that will keep the readers guessing.

REDUNDANCY

Another problem that stems from misplaced wordiness, redundancy is a situation where you use two or more words when just one would do. Most often, redundancy is found in noun-adjective combinations, where a giant is described as "large", or a statue as "monumental". The easiest way to get rid of redundancy is to follow Heinlein's advice and try to use an adjective of opposite meaning. If you get a ridiculous result—for example, a "small giant"—then you're giving redundant description and should simply get rid of it. This is particularly important in science fiction, where you are taking your readers through unknown worlds. If the first inhabitant of an alien planet that they meet is a large giant, most readers will spend the rest of the story wondering when the smaller variation is going to pop up.

REVERSING THE POLARITY— TECHNOBABBLE

Unlike most other problems we've discussed so far, the issue of technobabble is limited almost exclusively to science fiction. The scientific foundation of SF stories usually demands a certain amount of technical terms. Here, the principle is simple: if technology is relevant to the story, give it room; otherwise feel free to gloss over it. Do not fall into the trap of some writers, who feel that they have to provide engineering details for every single device they introduce. Unless it's important for the story, your readers will be perfectly happy to know that there are nanobots in your world; you don't have to tell us how they function unless we need to know it.

When you do use technobabble, make sure it's convincing. Avoid the overused quasi-technical expressions known from TV series: in other words, do not reverse polarities as the solution to all technical problems. If you have no background in the field of science you need, find someone who does and ask them to help you.

Also, bear in mind that engineers and technicians will use simple words when talking to laymen ("your hard drive is busted"), and will talk differently when communicating with each other ("the head is all right, but the FAT portion is scratched"). And remember that your audience consists, by definition, of non-experts—in other words, keep the purely technical portions of dialogue short and, unless you're deliberately trying to confuse the readers, make sure it's easy to follow.

On the other hand, many writers fall in the reversed polarity field in a totally different way: they forget to think through all the consequences of their invented technologies. For example, they introduce practically instant travel through wormholes, but describe space communities as equivalents of Wild West towns. In the days of the Wild West, traveling from one place to another wasn't easy and wasn't safe. If you have almost instant transport, the lawlessness of the Wild West will, quite simply, not happen—unless, that is, you introduce reasons why traveling through wormholes is reserved for adventurers and people so desperate they won't care for the danger.

TAKE US TO YOUR LEADER: THE SMEERP SYNDROME

Science fiction often includes alien cultures. This, of course, means that those alien cultures will have alien characteristics. After all, even the Earth in a distant future will have certain elements that are alien to us. Because of this, authors feel obliged to provide the readers with a glimpse of those alien elements through their basic tool: language.

The creation of languages is full of dangers. First of all, there is the English-speaker syndrome. This problem is particularly apparent with writers who do not speak another language: all of their made-up words and names sound as if they were derived from English. It's only natural, of course, to lean on your mother tongue when working with words but if you want to create something that will sound original and different, you have to go further. It's usually also a good idea to know where you are going. Do you have a friend who speaks another language or maybe know someone from another country? Ask for their help. (Linguist friends are best, of course, but not always available.)

Also, always bear in mind that aliens are alien and will therefore probably have different non-linguistic elements as well: body language and facial expressions have different meanings even in different parts of the Earth. When you create beings from a planet 567 light years away, don't automatically make them frown when they're thinking and smile to show friendship. As we have already mentioned when talking about "alien love" plots, this kind of "faux human" aliens is largely due to the constraints of old TV-shows. Again, do not be afraid to go where no CGI has gone before. Make your aliens different—and perhaps incorporate communication problems in your plot.

Poul Anderson was particularly good in using this kind of thing. In his *Rebel Worlds*, for instance, a member of a carnivorous species used the expression "I scent" instead of our "I see". With this one tiny departure from the ordinary, the readers were instantly reminded that this character was not the same as humans and were given a glimpse of a totally different worldview—and all of it without a single exotic word. This is, needless to say, a *good thing*. But make sure you don't overdo it. Here, as always, the general rule is that very little goes a long way.

Be particularly wary of the smeerp syndrome, named thus by the great late Damon Knight. This is the situation where novice writers, in an attempt to make their alien or futuristic worlds more alien or more futuristic, use invented words for already known things—and so call their small, long-eared, furry mammals "smeerps", when "rabbit" would have done just as well. For some reason, there are two areas that are particularly struck by this syndrome.

The first one is measurements. Distance and time are particularly often the victims, and wind up measured in invented words or else unusual variations of the existing ones. True, if you're talking about a non-Earth culture, it will most probably have its own measures of both time and distance. However, in communication with Earth cultures, these will have to be re-calculated. Any translator will tell you that when translating from English to French you are expected to transpose miles into kilometers. The same will apply for interplanetary or intergalactic contact. After all, what you're presenting to your reader is also a sort of translation, from the language of Sirius Beta to one of our Earth languages. So be a good translator, not a bad one.

The other smeerp-infested area is, strangely, coffee. I don't know why this is so, but it is. How many times have you seen SF characters who drink "klaav", "jav", "kaff" or something like that? There is absolutely no basis for this. Coffee has been around for a long time, and it's always been called coffee. Even cross-culturally different coffees, if they are drinks based on coffee beans, are still called coffee. (A mother of a friend of mine once visited France and spent two weeks drinking only hot chocolate, because she couldn't stomach the strong, short variation that is normally served in France. But both that and the long American versions that seem soupy to Frenchmen are called coffee.) So, unless there is something importantly different in your dark-bean-based beverage, call it coffee. Calling it something else does not make it cool—and who likes cool coffee, anyway?

Finally, we have to mention another stereotype that has become almost a convention in badly written SF—but it's really a cliché. Credits. Many writers substitute this word for currencies. Again, this has to be based on something. Maybe economy has changed enough in your world that currencies no longer exist. It's possible—after all, we're witnessing significant changes in economy today, and may even live to see the death of currencies—but it hasn't happened yet. And if it does, it will have consequences far more reaching than just a mere change of name. (Look at what happened in Europe with the introduction of the euro.) So make sure you show that those consequences exist as well. If that's not an important part of your story, if your only reason for calling Dollars or Pounds (or euros) "credits" is because it's usual in SF, I have only one advice for you: *don't*.

TOM SWIFTLY

This name describes the situation where writers are either too lazy or too inexperienced to find the right words, so they feel they have to "strengthen" their choices with too many modifiers, usually adverbs: "Let's go," said Tom swiftly. Although in some occasions adverbs are necessary, usually it's best to try and find a more precise word or trust the reader to work it out. If you have bug-eyed monsters getting into the ship, most readers will assume Tom is speaking swiftly even without being told.

USING THE CROOKS

At the end, there's only one more thing to be said: no rule should ever be followed off a cliff. Writing isn't an exact science where only one solution will work. Clichés can have their uses. What's important is to be aware of them and to use them sparingly. If you absolutely have to provide the readers with an info dump, be ironic about it: write down "And now for the info dump" and tell the readers everything they need to know. Use redundancy in speech patterns for characters who are pompous and supposed to look ridiculous and provide your cyberpunk hero with Leica eyes. But always, always bear in mind that clichés are crooks and must never be allowed to take over.

PART III
CRAFTING

CHAPTER TEN

BRINGING CHARACTERS TO LIFE

Tina Morgan

Think about your all time favorite books, regardless of genre. What common factors do they all share? Vivid settings? Intriguing conflict? Artistic language? While all of these aspects are important to a story, could the part of the story that truly makes it a favorite be the characters? Without a character to care about, setting is merely a pretty picture, conflict is sensationalism, and words are just bits of poetry. Maintaining a reader's interest for more than a few sentences requires an emotional investment in the story: characters that pull at our heartstrings or make us revile them.

Creating evocative characters isn't accomplished by blatant emotionalism, but by careful, well developed characters. There are many ways of making your characters feel as three-dimensional to your readers as they do to you.

Your characters do feel "real" to you, don't they? After all, if you don't care about them, why should your readers? If you know this to be true but are having problems conveying that depth to your readers, then let's explore the many aspects of character development, from the basic to the complex.

CHARACTER TYPES

PROTAGONIST VS. MAIN CHARACTER

Starting with the basics, every story needs a main character and a protagonist. These are not always the same person, though they typically are. The protagonist is the character that creates change throughout the novel, the person who can alter the outcome.

The main character shows the reader the story. This can be the narrator or the main POV character. She can be an observer who is affected by the protagonist and the conflict, but does not need to be the hero.

ANTAGONIST

Every story needs a challenge; this does not have to be a villain. It can be a force of nature, an internal conflict within the protagonist, a government or embattled societies. The most common antagonist is the evil person whom the protagonist needs to defeat. Care must be taken not to make this a stereotypical, one-dimensional villain.

Villains should have a background as complex as your protagonist. A believable motive for their actions will intrigue your reader and help them relate to the story. This does not mean that the reader has to agree with the villain's purpose or reasoning.

While these are the characters that drive the main plot, they often need a little assistance along the way. Subplots are a crucial part of any novel and can be built around lesser characters. Short stories require a smaller cast, thus subplots and minor characters should be limited but let's explore the potential types of characters you may wish to include in your story.

LOGIC

This is a character often seen in science fiction and great vigilance should be taken in his creation and use. Like Mr. Spock, this character is often the one who clarifies the plot and explains the situation to the less enlightened reader. He shows up at emotional times to focus his human allies on the facts of the situation. If careful thought isn't given to the role he plays, the Logic character can come across like a textbook or dictionary.

The writer must trust his readers to understand and follow the storyline and technical information well enough to comprehend the story. Hard science fiction often includes detailed scientific theories, but the writer should resist the desire to allow her passion for the science to outweigh the narrative of the story. Take care not to allow your logic character to become an information dump.

WILDCARD

Many science fiction stories are based on wars and violent conflicts and most of these stories contain at least one emotional wildcard; such as the soldier who's suffering from post-traumatic shock who becomes unhinged during stressful situations. However, it could also be the impulsive child who darts out into traffic and forces the mutant mother to show her talents to save him or the reckless teen that places the rest of the characters in peril. These wildcards can add conflict but they must be used with restraint or they become obvious plot devices.

COMPLICATION

Novels require more than a straightforward storyline. They need "complications" along the way. This can be in the form of a seemingly friendly character that none-the-less complicates matters by making your protagonist question his beliefs. It can be the character that somehow always finds herself in danger and needs rescuing.

SIDEKICK

Or to quote from *Sky High* "Hero Support":

> Every main character or protagonist needs a little help somewhere along the way. In every hopeless situation, there's a sidekick waiting for a chance to help or inadvertently hinder (making her become the Obstacle). The sidekick's loyalty is unquestionable and unshakeable, even when he/she knows the hero is making the biggest mistake of his life.[95]

SECONDARY CHARACTERS

These characters move the plot forward, sometimes merely by showing up on the page. They may have a significant presence or a minor one, but they play a crucial role in how the plot unfolds. They can fall into any of the other categories: sidekick, complication, wildcard or logic, but they often fill more than one role. They are the companions that keep your hero on track, the villain's henchmen (or women). They can be the love interest or the unrequited love.

BACKGROUND

Once you've determined the literary role your character will play in your story, you need to decide who your character is. In simplest terms, this is gender, age, body type, personality, and place in society/family. However, science fiction has a rich history of bending or even breaking gender rules and it gives us free reign to challenge, change, or rearrange gender roles as we know them. By creating alternative histories, we can apply these changes to our own world, but unless we alter the genetic makeup of our genders, some stereotypes will hold true, such as: women give birth to babies and the average man is stronger than the average woman.

Every major character that walks onto the set of your book needs a background. This background does not have to be included in the text of your story, but if you're familiar with your characters' histories, then you will be better equipped to tell their tales.

Avoiding stereotypes is crucial in developing your characters' backgrounds. For example, while it is true that abused children often grow up to be abusers, many also grow up to break that cycle of abuse. Not all rich kids are spoiled and not all poor kids are thieves.

Remember, the *strength* of a character is not the same as *character strength*.

One refers to the literary portrayal of the character while the later refers to the quality of the person being portrayed.

Give even your weakest characters the power to touch the reader. Know what makes them tick.

Who a character is will determine how she reacts to the situation you've fashioned. You can't take an uneducated, inexperienced adult and turn them into a techno geek who saves the space station from a reactor core meltdown. Unlikely heroes make good stories but impossible heroes make implausible plots.

EDUCATION: FORMAL AND INFORMAL

Never underestimate the power and value of an informal education. Hobbies teach us a great deal and the time spent on them should be considered when creating your characters. Think about how your own education has impacted your life. Are you reading this book because writing is a serious pastime or educational pursuit? What would your protagonist spend his spare time doing?

Most writers can think of at least one teacher or supervisor who, despite years of higher education, was less than effective. Sometimes formal education can take a passion and turn it into a brilliant career. Other times even the best teachers can't produce an adequate employee or performer.

INTELLIGENCE

Despite the fact that you may be writing about a world far advanced from ours, you should evaluate the need to have a race of super humans before you make everyone a genius. Like the temptation to create only beautiful protagonists, there tends to be a desire to make our characters smart and witty, but not everyone fits those descriptions and the world would become a very monochromatic place if they did.

What your characters do with their education will depend a great deal on their intelligence. Many people complete college yet can't find a job once they graduate. This isn't always because of the job market. There are many aspects to intelligence other than academic understanding. Some characters lack common sense. They feel that because they've graduated from a university that they should start out with a very high paying job and not have to work their way up. Their expectations don't match the reality of the job market, nor are they willing to compromise those expectations.

Other characters may be very intelligent but severely lacking in social skills—but consider making your "geek" character one of the exceptions rather than the stereotype. Also avoid the common trend of making your intelligent character an autistic savant—unless you research the disorder carefully.

FAMILY/FRIENDS

Those who surround us early in life have a profound impact on our development. This may be negative or positive but regardless, it is not something we are able to leave completely behind. Our role in our family often determines our social and financial situation in later life. If we are the peacemaker, we may find ourselves constantly trying to placate our friends or family, when we should be standing our ground. If we are the leader, we may become the head of organizations or political parties.

Friends and family are a crucial part of our lives. Friends come and go and the type of friend a character has can change as she grows and develops. Villains can have loving families despite their acts of cruelty. Take a look at the history of serial killers in our own world and you'll discover that many are sociopaths who weren't typically abused as children.

MEMORIES

Memories can be full of holes and the truth is what we bring to the situation. Playing with memories can add detail and depth to your story. Two characters can have radically different memories of the same situation. How your character perceives their upbringing can have a profound affect on how they handle conflict later in their lives. Memories can trigger violent reactions in otherwise non-violent characters. Think about the events that have had the greatest impact on your life. If you asked a close friend or family member to describe the event, would they tell the same story as you?

CHARACTER TRAITS

PHYSICAL APPEARANCE AND ABILITIES

Lois McMaster Bujold's, Miles Vorkosigan is an interesting example of an anti-hero. His childhood of pain, surgery, and broken bones would have forced most kids to resort to a sedentary life of chess and word puzzles. While Miles spent a lot of time recuperating and learning written lessons, adversity was a motivator instead of a deterrent.

Because we are visual creatures, we tend to create characters we would find physically attractive. Our good characters tend to be beautiful and our bad characters are ugly and/or scarred. To a degree, this is understandable. Many of us read or write to escape the stress of day-to-day life. We enjoy imagining ourselves as being more alluring and our love interests as beautiful as models or actors. We want to step outside our mundane world while we're immersed in the pages of our favorite stories.

Take a look around. How many truly (naturally) beautiful people do you see every day? We use a lot of different techniques to alter our appearances and abilities: braces, contacts, steroids, plastic surgery, makeup, the list is extensive. If your story is taking place in a post apocalyptic world, how realistic is it to populate that world with only beautiful people? In a face-to-face meeting where pheromones can play a role, your reader might be distracted purely by looks, but on the written page, your characters need more than a pretty surface.

While some stories are going to demand more exotic characters than other, it isn't necessary (or always believable) to make your protagonist not only strong and an expert fighter as well as beautiful. Don't forget also that beauty is in the eye of the beholder and may be seen for a variety of reasons. Jet Li or Mikhail Baryshnikov may not be particularly handsome yet watching them dance or fight is a very graceful, beautiful thing. One can appreciate the time, energy, work, and talent that go into their performances.

Your character's past athletic experiences can be valuable background information about who your character is. Team sports can teach a child to work with others or to be a "prima-donna". Not all of your characters will take part in sports, some won't be physically able to and, for some, the act of squeezing a friend's hand is an achievement. Take the time to determine who your character is physically and don't assume that he must be the epitome of physical fitness to be attractive to your readers.

SCARS: EMOTIONAL AND PHYSICAL

Scars come in all sizes. Some are worn as badges of honor, like the old "football" injury that the fading athlete talks about in his later years. Or they can be hidden deep within the character's psyche. A bully never has to touch another child to make the child fear for his safety. An abusive parent can wound a child for life by telling them how worthless they are. These scars have the potential of affecting your plot far deeper than the worst physical injury. However, you need to consider these wounds carefully and decide how they should be integrated into your story. Like all plot devices, the possibilities should be foreshadowed and not dumped on the reader during a crucial climax.

MANNERISMS

Mannerisms are those unique little gestures and movements we make that set us apart from those around us. They are ingrained into our subconscious and we rarely realize we're doing them. Often we learn these traits from a beloved caregiver or other influential people in our lives.

Giving our characters these little idiosyncrasies can add depth and human appeal. They can also add detail to our stories: a villain who bites her nails in tense situations can leave behind DNA clues, or alphabetized CDs or cereal boxes can be a poignant reminder to a surviving spouse.

Characters are more than just their conscious actions. What they do when they're nervous, happy, scared, bored, or angry adds layers to your story. There are a wide variety of mannerisms. A trip to your favorite restaurant or store, a day at work or your place of worship can yield a wealth of options for your characters.

The following are just a few examples:

- tapping a foot
- chewing nails, a lip or the inside of a cheek
- greeting everyone with a hug or handshake (even people she knows well and sees on a regular basis)
- a toss of the head
- running fingers through hair when thinking or nervous
- an inability to meet another's eyes, walking with head down
- snapping fingers or cracking knuckles
- blowing breath out through the nostrils or mouth in exasperation
- walking on tip toes because of nervous energy
- laughing the exact same number of times, every time

There are so many more options but each one can give your reader clues about your character's personality or mood without blatantly saying, *"Eogan's scared"*.

> Eogan's eyebrows rose and he bit his lower lip. The scattering of freckles over his nose was the only color on his face.
>
> "We need help," he said.

Mannerisms help your reader visualize your characters with greater clarity. A few well-placed nervous ticks can help define who your character is, but like any good thing, they should not be used to excess.

HABITS

Like mannerisms, habits are those little eccentricities that can make one character stand out from the other. This can include habitual mannerisms, like chewing on a lower lip or twirling hair when thinking or they can be actions that require planning and conscious thought. Habits are those good and bad things that we do: remembering to lower the toilet seat so your wife doesn't get angry, driving too fast while talking on a cell phone.

Anyone who has tried to give up smoking, drinking alcohol or caffeine can tell you just how difficult breaking a habit can be especially when it includes a physically addictive aspect. Some people will make excuses for why they should be allowed to continue their bad habit, even when they know that they should stop.

RELAXATION

What a character does to relax can say a lot about that character. Many people enjoy watching TV because it's typically mindless entertainment. It doesn't require a great deal of thought to sit back and watch a story unfold in front of your eyes. Writing is an intellectually stimulating activity that many people would not consider relaxing in the least, yet if you're reading this book, you would probably disagree.

Inventing new forms of entertainment can be a challenge and a thrill. What will your characters do for fun? Will they space walk for excitement or has that become a mundane activity? Will they hunt? Maybe human prey? With a little imagination, something as simple as what your character does in her free time can be developed into a subplot or a full-blown storyline.

EMPLOYMENT

Whether your character is the CEO of a major tech company or captain of a starship, your reader will have certain expectations of your characters simply because of the jobs you give them. Most readers would expect a starship captain to be able to make clear decisive choices unless the world/society you create is one that allows nepotism and favoritism to the point of promoting incompetent officers. A CEO of a powerful corporation doesn't get there by being weak. These stereotypes will be hard to shatter unless you take the time to explain (in small, easily read snippets) to your reader just how your world is different from ours.

Because most science fiction stories deal with advanced science, it's imperative that you do the necessary research to back up the things your characters say and do in the course of their high tech jobs. Don't rely on what you've seen in movies or read in other books. Take the time to do some research in scientific journals before you make the critical mistake of not portraying the science properly. Unfortunately this mistake happens all too often, sometimes even in major NY published works. If your reader catches these mistakes, they may be unwilling to buy another novel or magazine containing your work. Credibility can influence sales.

Don't forget to take your plot into consideration before you decide what job your character is going to do. Will it have more impact on the story if your character is a struggling ensign? If she's the president of one of the most powerful countries (planets) in your world, will she have the ability to move about without an entourage? Will the restrictions of her responsibilities make it impossible for her to fulfill the requirements of the plot? If you start out writing about a politically or financially powerful character but find that the story would be better told by someone farther down the ladder, don't be afraid to make that change. The worst thing you can do is force your character into an unsuitable role.

EMOTIONS

Have you ever noticed that characters that aren't supposed to have emotions either do have them, or they desire them? Consider the infamous Mr. Spock or Lt. Data from the Star Trek series. Mr. Spock didn't want the emotions he had and Lt. Data wanted what he didn't have. While Brent Spiner did an excellent job of playing the emotionless android, his desire for human emotion is a human emotion in and of itself. Regardless of whether you're working with an entirely human or non-human cast or a combination of the two, your characters have to possess qualities that your readers can relate to or they're not going to keep reading.

How your character handles the emotions they have will make a difference in how they respond to conflict. Some people shut down emotionally when exposed to stressful situations. They bottle their emotions so tightly inside, that those around them think they're not feeling anything. Others become hysterical or overwrought. People who appear calm and collected in stressful situations can fall apart in what you may feel is a trivial matter. Tempers can flare at the most inopportune times and insecurities can lead even the strongest person to say or do things they normally wouldn't.

Does your character behave in a manner consistent with their age and experiences or do they behave younger? Older? The state of your character's emotions and his ability to control them should be taken into consideration when writing about your character's personal and/or professional relationships. Using mannerisms to show your characters emotions can help set the tone and mood of your story, but don't forget that dialogue is another key element.

DIALOGUE

One of the most difficult things for many writers to master is dialogue. It's easy to fall into the habit of writing our characters' speech in the same manner as our own and if we're not careful, every character ends up sounding the same.

Dialogue is not a conversation between characters despite the fact that they're talking. If we wrote our characters dialogue the same way two people have a conversation in real life, the reader would probably become confused or bored. Next time you're in a busy restaurant, subway station, or shopping mall, listen in on a few conversations taking place around you.

What you'll notice is the verbal shorthand most speakers employ. They know the person they're talking to and both people share a common knowledge. They'll speak in half sentences, use gestures, and leave out details that are necessary for a stranger to know exactly whom or what they're discussing. If the people don't know each other or lack the common background, they're more likely to spend a lot of time explaining the details of the situation. Dialogue must be clearer and more to the point. Typing all the sounds, grunts, sighs, and other non-verbal communication is awkward at best.

Dialogue needs to be more than inane chatter. It should contribute to the plot, show your characters' personalities, and/or reveal something about how your character is feeling or what she is thinking. Reading a conversation between two characters that contributes nothing to the story is about as much fun as listening to static on the radio.

Each character's speech patterns should fit their unique background, education, and temperament. By altering the way individual characters speak, it becomes possible for the reader to know exactly who is speaking simply by the words they use. Choosing your characters' words carefully makes it possible to show how your character is feeling instead of resorting to obvious dialogue tags such as: Sue said angrily, John hissed, Mel stammered, etc. (see the character interviews and bios at the end of this chapter as an example).

There is the risk of allowing your logic character to use dialogue as an info dump. Instead of conveying the information through the actions and narrative, the author has the logic character give the other characters a long lesson in his area of expertise. This is a flaw that often comes up in science fiction stories where the writer wishes to expound upon his favorite scientific theory or to explain something he is passionate about. Not only does this disrupt the flow of the story, but it can also be risky if you're not as much of an expert as you might wish to be.

One stereotypical flaw is having your villain take the time out of his dastardly plans to explain to your protagonist exactly why she is tied up and about to be killed or tortured. This is a major risk if your villain has had very little page presence in your novel or short story.

DESCRIPTIONS: WHEN/WHERE

Before writing this chapter, I looked for writing articles about character description and while I found several that talked about physical traits; I didn't find any that covered character description from the point of timing.

What I did find reaffirmed the idea that we need to read and research the genre we're writing to develop a good feel for what works with fans of that genre. Science Fiction tends to be more straightforward and less flowery than fantasy. There is a difference in style and tone.

One way many new writers try to hook their reader is to describe their character so the reader can "see" them. In order to take a look at how professional authors handle this, I chose several books off my bookshelf and examined when and how the author described their protagonist.

In Liz Williams' *Nine Layers of Sky*, the first hint of description we find is on page six when Elena is standing outside at a police checkpoint. *"Ice crackled in her hair; she could see a frosty blonde fringe just above her eyes."* The next snippet comes on page 33 when Atyrom is scolding her for not eating and he says, *"You're already as thin as a crack."*

On the first page, of Orson Scott Card's *Enders Game*, we learn that two people are discussing a child and that one of those people is a man. No description, no idea of age or physical abilities. On page ten, Ender gives us a description of his brother, Peter, but we still don't know what Ender looks like. By page seventeen we finally learn that Ender is six years old, but we still don't know what color his hair or eyes are.

Both books rely on the character's situation and not the character's description to capture the reader's interest. While descriptions did help me "see" characters better, they weren't as important to the stories as I'd expected them to be. They were secondary information compared to how the characters were feeling, how they interacted with other characters, and how they were going to behave in the next paragraph. It was the exceptional story that needed a detailed character description.

In contrast, the opening paragraph of Anne McCaffrey's, *The Ship Who Sang* is completely about Helva's description and condition. The very first line throws the reader directly into Helva's world, *"She was born a thing and as such would be condemned if she failed to pass the encephalograph test required of all newborn babies."*[96]

Lois McMaster Bujold's, Miles Vorkosigan is such an oddity in his own world that his physical appearance and health plays a major role in how he interacts with those around him. So she describes him fairly quickly (by page six in *Cetaganda)* but Bujold is quick to bring the story back to Mile's personality. After comparing himself to his handsome, strong cousin, Ivan, Miles thinks that perhaps his supervisor ordered Ivan to accompany him because: "*On the other hand, maybe Ivan had been sent along to stand next to Miles and make him sound good. Miles brightened slightly at the thought.*"[97]

DREAMS

Do you remember what you wanted to be when you were five years old? Sometimes as we mature, we lose sight of how intensely we wanted those childhood dreams to come true. Dreams come in all sizes and shapes; many kids dream of making it through the day without being bullied. For others, it's to have enough to eat or to survive suicide bombers, while others fantasize about winning the video game they've been playing, or to getting a new car for their sixteenth birthday. There are as many dreams as there are kids. While adults may not be as willing to admit their dreams, even to themselves, most still have hopes that tomorrow will be better than today. Giving thought to your characters dreams can lend insight into your character's motivations.

MOTIVATIONS

Perhaps the most crucial aspect of character development is in understanding what motivates our characters. What do they want, need, and/or wish for? Their desires are what propel your plot forward. If their needs don't mesh with your intended conflict resolution then the story won't work.

When asked about writer's block in an interview with *Fiction Factor's* e-zine, Orson Scott Card said, "Writer's block is my unconscious mind telling me that something I've just written is either unbelievable or unimportant to me, and I solve it by going back and reinventing some part of what I've already written so that when I write it again, it is believable and interesting to me."[98]

What a character wants or even needs isn't always what the character consciously views as important, but if your character is going to have an epiphany, that sudden change of realization must match where your plot is going or the story will feel disjointed. This epiphany can came at a crucial moment in the story, but should be foreshadowed so that the reader isn't left feeling like the writer reached the same conclusion and simply threw the ending together. If you don't outline your story in advance (and sometimes even when you do), it may happen you and your characters come to the same realization simultaneously, but this is where editing becomes crucial. Once you've finished the story, reread it with foreshadowing and motivation in mind. Make certain your character's motives are believable for the character you've created and for the story you've developed.

Motives don't have to transform at the last moment. Change can come earlier in the story and become the driving force behind your character's actions. If this change is dramatic then you need a strong reason for it to happen. Science fiction is often plot driven, but if the characters don't live up to the complex storyline you've developed, then you're not writing a strong story.

GROWTH

Throughout the course of your story, your characters should grow, evolve, or even possibly devolve. They have to change or the story becomes stagnant and boring. Growth does not always equal positive change.

There are 'slice of life' stories but these typically sell to literary, not genre publications. Science fiction is a genre that requires a defined and solid plot. If you neglect to affect or change your characters by the plot then you've lost the impact of your story. Change can come in many forms, emotional growth, physical victory or defeat, political revolution and shift of power, or cultural change. Science fiction often explores cultural issues in a way that makes the story a parable to our own world. This can be a very effective and thought provoking story but only if your characters are affected by the cultural mores and values you're discussing. They can't be bystanders to the conflict; they must be involved. Think of it this way, would you rather attend a sporting event, musical concert or movie yourself, or have someone tell you what another friend said about it? Bring your reader into the story by having your character experience loss, grief, pain, joy, love, happiness and all the other emotions that come with living a full life.

MARY SUE AND GARY STU

There is an insidious character that shows up quite often in fan fiction and spills over into other fiction writing as well. The infamous Mary Sue (or the male version: Gary Stu). This character is the author inserting himself or herself into the story as the hero. Often the character is someone very typical and normal whom the other characters overlook, but when it comes time to save the world/ship/universe, this character miraculously steps in and saves the day. Underdogs can be heroes, the millions of dollars the Lord of the Rings trilogy has earned is proof positive that a seemingly inconsequential character can win and be believable. However, Frodo wasn't acting alone. He had a full fellowship at first and to the very end; he had Sam's support. Nor was Frodo a minor character.

The other purpose of the Mary Sue character is wish fulfillment and one of the first ways she can spill over into our own novels without even realizing it. Are you creating the perfect parent, lover, child, or friend? If you've written several stories or novels, take a look at your characters. Do you consistently have one type of character that appears in all of your stories? Is this character like you? Is this character someone you would like to be or want a loved one to be?

Mary Sues can also come out of the writer's obsession or love for his characters. He (or she) is so besotted with them that they give them every desirable attribute and everyone loves them—except unfortunately, the reader.

For more information about Mary Sue characters turn to Carol Hightshoe's chapter on fan fiction.

OUTLINING A CHARACTER

While secondary characters don't require the intense, in-depth creation that your protagonist and villain require, there may be aspects of their lives that you'll want to spend more time on, especially if you're using a secondary character as a catalyst. Research and develop these characters carefully.

The following writing exercises can help pull together all of the information and thoughts in this chapter. Exercises like these can help you fill in the missing aspects of your characters. A character interview will allow you to explore your character's personality and dialogue style. By writing the interview as if you're watching his/her response, you can include physical movements and facial expressions as well.

Doing a character bio will give you the basics. I've placed the bio at the end of each interview so you can determine if I've given each character enough of his own voice that you can surmise much of his bio before you read it. I've chosen to use two characters I'm developing for my latest novel.

NAME: KELLACH MOLAN

1. *Do you like your job? Why or why not?*

Kellach arches his eyebrows and regards me as if I have two heads. "Oh sure, it's a great job. Who wouldn't want to keep a sadistic spell stable so that a bunch of asexual women can continue to live their pointless lives throughout eternity? I'm wondering what they think they're going to do when I die and there's no one left to hold onto their souls while they complete the transfer?"

2. *Transfer?*

He smiles, but it's not a convincing expression. He places one pale finger on his lips, "Shh! Top secret."

3. *Do you have any friends? Significant others?*

"Lady, what universe are you from? What part of tortured prisoner aren't you understanding?"

4. *What is your idea of success?*

His eyelids drop and the fine white lashes stand out against the dark circles under his eyes. "Freeing mother."

Nothing less?

"No."

5. *What did you have for breakfast?*

"You should have been there! It was fabulous! I had a liter of recycled air with a kilo of imagination."

You're not getting fed regularly?

He stands and poses like a body builder but his clothes hang on his emaciated frame, "Too much food would ruin this marvelous physic."

NAME: KELLACH MOLAN

Gender: male

Species: human

Age: 29

Education: equivalent to our masters of science

Employment: former government scientist, currently imprisoned

Political affiliation: none, strong anti-authority feelings

Hobbies: keeping a video journal, practicing his sarcastic wit and reading prophecies

Likes/dislikes: freedom and his secret talent/himself, his captors and other people

Temperament: currently very depressed, typically pessimistic

Moral/ethical/religious beliefs: strong ethical code, agnostic

Quirks/eccentricities: Talks to himself as himself, visits people in their dreams

Fears/phobias: fear of dying before he frees his mother's soul

Short term/ long-term goals: keeping the Modir spell stable/freeing his mother's soul

NAME: SIMARION MOLAN

1. *Do you like your job? Why or why not?*

Simarion leans back in his chair. His office is immaculate and opulent. He steeples his fingers and smiles but the smile doesn't reach his eyes. "My job is quite satisfying, but you understand that I cannot discuss it with you."

2. *So you've made peace with your failure to be accepted into the Elite Guard?*

Simarion's face turns pink but he doesn't show any outward signs of anger. I decide to push the subject to see if I can break his composure.

I understand your psyche evaluation did not come back favorably?

"That is no longer an issue. It has been dealt with. Next question?

3. *Are the Emissaries operating in an ethical manner?*

"Ethics are never as clearly defined as the media would portray them. During the height of the Gorian atrocities, ethical, moral Ithkai were forced to steal for food, kill for survival. Ethics are more than a simple set of values. They are determined by the needs of the time."

4. *So you're saying there isn't a clear cut set of rules we should follow? Life isn't sacred or of value?*

"But of course life has worth. How much worth depends on the situation and whom you ask." He smirks and arches an eyebrow. He seems to be laughing at a joke only he understands.

5. *Do you believe in luck?*

"Luck is for those who are too weak to make their own fortune."

6. *You don't seem to have a lot of respect for other humans.*

"Respect is earned, not given simply because you breath." At that he stands and walks toward the door. He gestures graciously for me to exit. "Thank you for your time," he says but his smile still doesn't reach his eyes.

NAME: SIMARION MOLAN
Gender: male

Species: human

Age: 62

Education: political science major (wanted to be soldier but his psyche test revealed sociopathic tendencies)

Employment: High-level government official in covert ops.

Political affiliation: loyal to himself

Hobbies: military strategy, obtaining immortality and creating super soldiers

Likes/dislikes: power, control/weakness

Temperament: contained emotions but contemptuous of those he perceives as less than him.

Moral/ethical/religious beliefs: he believes it's for the greater good to use and destroy people, the lives of those lesser people hold no value.

Quirks/eccentricities: OCD traits, obsessively neat and organized

Fears/phobias: fear of dying, losing at anything

Short term/ long-term goals: Stabilizing the Modir spell and gaining access to the Gallda technology/killing Zuria, becoming a demi-god

Writing exercises can help you discover your character's quirks and emotional weaknesses. If your characters are developed fully, you won't need a lot of dialogue tags to explain their tone of voice or attitude.

CONCLUSION

Lois McMaster Bujold's, Miles Vorkosigan books have a loyal fan base because Miles jumps off the page. He's bigger than life and a lot of fun to read, though in real life, he would probably be exhausting to work for or with. Fortunately, Miles is a character in an entertaining story, even when he's facing death, danger, and dismemberment.

Anne McCaffrey's, Helva is a physically imperfect hero who captures the reader's attention from the first page even though she lacks arms and legs. Helva has such strength of personality that despite never being able to touch her human brawns; her love, contempt and compassion for them is believable and compelling.

Characters come in all shapes, sizes, personality traits, and genders. Explore the different options. One of the great things about writing science fiction is the tremendous range of choices you have. You're not limited by today's morals or technology, so long as you keep your world consistent, and your science believable, you can write about characters, creatures, and worlds most other genres can't utilize.

Creating characters that leave your readers wanting to read more is the mark of a good story. You want your readers to buy your next book or the magazine that contains your next short story. Take the time to learn how to craft realistic characters that "live" for your readers. Once you do, your readers will become fans who anxiously await your next novel or short story.

CHAPTER ELEVEN

ATTACK OF THE MONSTER PLOT: IDEAS, SETTINGS, AND PLOTS

Milena Benini

WHERE TO START

Any writer will tell you that the question they are asked the most often is "where do you get your ideas?" The answer is usually—"everywhere". If you are a writer at heart, you will probably have the problem of too many ideas, rather than the one of finding an idea to write about. But many writers, even if they work in science fiction, start from ideas that are not SF as such: characters, a scene, things that as yet lack a setting or a plot. If you are such a writer, you may find yourself with an idea that needs fleshing out.

How to get ideas for science fiction stories? Basically, they are always the consequence of the writer asking herself, "What if?" and then going on from there. In three words:

EXTRAPOLATION, EXTRAPOLATION, EXTRAPOLATION

The best way to find science fiction ideas is to extrapolate on current science. Follow the science news. Think about fast-developing fields such as communication technology, and try to think of the possible next breakthrough. It always comes down to the, "What if?" process: what if communication technology developed to the point that messages could be projected directly into your cortex? What if we developed nanobots that could be programmed to battle cancer? What if we found a way to break the speed of light limit?

Some writers worry that extrapolation will be difficult if they're not experts in their chosen field of extrapolation. Not true. As long as your basis in fact is strong—or at least looks that way to the average reader—your extrapolation will be accepted. There is no obligation to guess accurately. You are not prophesizing the future; merely playing with it.

In the golden age of SF, space travel was the logical extrapolation area: it was the period when large sums of money were getting poured into space programs.

Things have changed in the meantime, and the most exciting developments have happened in completely different areas. In Isaac Asimov's David Starr series, for instance, mankind had colonized the Solar System, but computers still communicated through punch cards. (Yes, that was really how computers communicated once.) The first, extrapolation, did not come true; the second, a sort of a "non-extrapolation", went forward with unexpected speed. Does this make us think less of Asimov today? Not in the least. We recognize that he worked within the rules he knew then, and played with them in acceptable ways. This is all the obligation he had—and he met it.

There are two ways to extrapolate. One is something I'd like to call "careful extrapolation", the kind that Arthur C. Clarke used in his *Space Odyssey*. It means that you take a bit of the current science, and then carefully work out exactly what may happen with it in the future. This kind of extrapolation takes a lot of scientific knowledge, and produces what is usually called "hard SF". It's not for everyone, though: Clarke had a strong scientific background, and used this kind of extrapolation deliberately, making what he and Stanley Kubrick called "a classic SF film".[99]

The other way of extrapolating could be called "extrapolation rampant". This is the kind that does not stick so carefully to immediately possible developments, but takes current knowledge and goes with it as far as possible. In this extrapolation, you can get far more outlandish results—but the basis in fact still has to be there. So, no magic, please—although it's always a good idea to remember Arthur C. Clarke's famous Third Law: *Any sufficiently advanced technology is indistinguishable from magic.*[100]

Finally, when you're thinking about ideas to use in your SF plots, there is one more thing to consider, and that is to avoid using ideas that have been used a gazillion times before. (If you're not certain whether your idea is one of those, take a look at the chapter dealing with clichés in SF.) But if you're certain you've got a novel twist on those old stories, be careful to avoid the mistake most commonly found in mainstream writers who pop into SF without having read anything in the genre before:

RE-INVENTING THE WHEEL

Science fiction is much older than the naming of the genre. Because of this, there are certain conventions that are already accepted in the field, and, when breaking them, you need to be even more careful than you would be when charting completely unknown territory.

Such conventions include, for example, faster than light spaceflight. This idea has been around for a long time, and has become a convention. If you need FTL spaceflight for your story, feel free to use it, and don't feel particularly pressed to actually explain how it works (unless the principle is important for your story). The tradition of SF already has several solutions to this. Whichever one you pick, if it's within the convention, your readers will accept this piece of extrapolation rampant, and will play along. Just make sure that your FTL ships do not screech in turns and otherwise do not behave like racecars. Unless, of course, you're writing a parody.

Other such borderline-science conventions include apocalyptic events of global proportions (meteor strikes, atomic wars, diseases that decimate the population), time-travel, or first contact. All of them have been done before, so if your idea includes one of them, you have to make sure that your interpretation of the idea is new and original. But if you absolutely need one of them for your story to work, feel free to use them—just don't bore your readers with explanations they have already seen a million times before.

TO YOUR READER ALWAYS BE TRUE

Whatever your extrapolation or convention, there are two things that you always have to bear in mind: the first one—and I cannot stress how important this is—is to *think your world through*. If you have a piece of technology, no matter what it is, it will probably not influence just one part of people's lives. This is particularly true for areas such as power, transport, and communications. Think about their implications in our own world: when the price of gas goes up, this brings up the prices of transport, and that, in turn, brings up all the retail prices, because all the goods need to be transported to their sales points. So, if you have instant transport—say, teleportation—which is cheap and reliable, it will probably influence all areas of life. If you keep the society the same as it is today, except for the fact that you can whiz around using your personal teleportation device, this will leave the readers wondering why the technology did not have wider impact. In other words, it will seem like magic instead of technology—and, although this is also a legitimate way of writing, it's not what you're trying to achieve in SF.

The other important thing is to *always be consistent*. This rule, by the way, applies to everything, from ideas to execution. In science fiction, you get to invent a part of the rules. But once you do invent them, you have to stick to them. Do you have computers with a high level of artificial intelligence? Then don't try to destroy them by telling them to work out a paradox. Do you have a planet with half the Earth's gravity? Then don't have people born on it come to Earth and walk around with no problems—their bones would break in twice the gravity they're used to. And so on. Think about your world, and make sure you follow its rules. After all, if something doesn't fit, you can always go back and change it so it does. But the end result has to have internal consistency; otherwise your readers (not to mention editors) will feel cheated. And readers who feel cheated will not return to the author who cheated them.

WHERE NO WRITER HAS GONE BEFORE

Now that you know the basic rules, and you have an idea, you have to start filling in the background. Every story takes place *somewhere*, and *somewhen*. These somewheres and somewhens are called settings. In science fiction, settings are especially important, because they are usually different from the world that surrounds us. Not always, of course: some SF stories take place in everyday world. But even those stories do not accurately reflect every single element of our entire world. You, the author, choose the region, the group of people, the social milieu in which the story takes place. This is your setting. And the setting has to be very convincing, because it's what anchors the story. If the readers don't believe in your setting, they won't buy the plot, either. Here are some of the ways to create settings in SF.

USED FURNITURE

One of the simplest ways to create a setting is to use an already existing universe. If it's Earth today, let the readers know from the beginning. This is science fiction: unlike "realistic" fiction, your readers won't start from the assumption that they know where your story is taking place. You have to tell them. You can do this by putting an X-files style header, saying: "New York, 2007", or you can incorporate the time in the opening paragraphs—or you can simply start your story realistically, with traffic jams and newspapers and a well-known piece of music blaring through someone's radio.

Remember, though: *always know your setting.* If you place your story into a country you've never been to, make sure that you find someone from that country and check your information. Especially nowadays, with global communications so developed, there is no place exotic enough that someone who knows it well won't see your story. SF readers will readily play along with you in any extrapolation—but only if they believe the bits that are anchored in reality.

Alternatively, you may choose to use a setting that already exists in fiction. This is called fan fiction, and is usually connected with copyright issues. If you're serious about your writing, you may do this as a sort of an exercise, the same way as you may consciously try to emulate a particular writer's style in order to learn something about it, but you should never try to sell this kind of fiction. It's against the law.

Some writers try to "file off the serial numbers", and use an existing universe in disguise. They create a group of Runaways battling the evil galactic Kingdom, led by a King who is strong in the Black Side of the Power. Needless to say, this is not a good idea. Readers are not stupid, and neither are editors: they will recognize the origin, and will mark you down as someone who isn't imaginative enough to come up with their own ideas. Even when writing a parody, you should be careful to avoid being too direct. Unless you're very good at it, painting your point in large red letters will ruin the comic effect instead of creating it.

However, occasionally, used furniture can, indeed, be re-used. You can, for example, have space cowboys or space pirates. Use a well-known setting of old adventure stories, and give them a new twist. Beware, though: notice, first, that these settings are much wider than the ones in fan-fiction (the Wild West, the old-fashioned pirate novel) and do not come under copyright. No less important is the fact that such used furniture settings also have to be used with a very new twist in order to be acceptable. Otherwise, they'll seem over-familiar to the readers even if the story itself is completely new. All in all, it's better to try to come up with a world of your own. How to do that?

OFF-WORLD SETTINGS

If you go off to another planet, the first thing to do is to make sure you know what kind of planet it is. The universe is a vast and varied place. Is your planet very Earth-like? Even then, you have to take into account the laws of physics and their consequences. Is gravity exactly the same as on Earth? That's hardly likely. A much more believable situation is a planet with gravity close to that on Earth. It may be a little less—this will make humans slightly stronger—or a little more—in which case Earthlings will be a little weaker than the natives. What's the atmosphere like? Can humans breathe it, and for how long? All those questions need to be answered before you start. You may choose not to incorporate all that exact information into your story—in fact, usually most of it will remain off-stage—but you, the author, must know those things, so that you can remain consistent throughout and follow your own rules.[88]

The same thing pertains to the creation of alien cultures. Social behavior isn't something that just happens in a vacuum. It is influenced by technology, history, and environment. Remember that whatever culture you create will also have its own history, level of technology, and environmental elements that have made it what it is. Make sure that your readers can see that. It doesn't mean that you have to provide them with a history book on your bug-eyed monsters. But don't have beings from a very fertile, warm area be barbaric tribes, and don't have bug-eyed monsters from a cold, harsh region develop the equivalent of Greek tragedy. This defies the logic that we know from Earth: if you just reverse the situation, your readers will wonder how that happened, and you had better provide them with an explanation for it. Otherwise, they'll feel cheated, and you know what happens when readers feel cheated.

A common mistake found in the construction of alien societies is oversimplification. All aliens from the planet Goombal speak Goombalian, have recognizable green tan, share mores, and beliefs. Look at our own planet, which is neither very big nor very old by space standards. Despite this, we have numerous different cultures, races, languages. What makes you think that the planet Goombal would not have such variety? Yes, in many ways, the Earth is uniting, but, despite this, we also work on preserving our cultural differences. There are at least three major ways of counting time and celebrating New Year's—and the celebrations for all of them remain widespread. So don't make your Goombalians all be alike unless they all come from the same cultural, historical, and environmental background. It will ruin their believability.

There is another thing to bear in mind when creating off-world settings. No matter how alien your aliens are—they can be sentient vapors that create spontaneously in the depths of the Universe—your readers are humans. And they need a way to connect with your characters. So, unless your story revolves about the inability of the human race to understand an alien one—like in Arthur C. Clarke's *Rama*—you had better make sure that your aliens are, at least in some ways, also human.

EARTH SETTINGS

We've already talked about "current Earth" settings—but what if your chosen setting is the future or the past? Obviously, some things are going to be easy—the geography, for example, and most physical elements—but some are going to be very difficult. The trick to creating a convincing future Earth setting is by knowing a lot of history. In that way, you will be able to work out what kind of future development looks convincing. Again, the same thing applies that we mentioned with extrapolation: don't worry about being 100% accurate. Your goal isn't to create a completely accurate image of the future. Your goal is to create an image of the future that will convince your readers. To achieve that, the most important thing is to know your world well. If you do, you will be able to put it on the page convincingly. Again, think through all the consequences of your inventions, and work them into your story.

Knowledge is doubly important for Earth settings in the past—for instance, in time-travel or alternate history stories. In both these cases, you will be working with an actual period in history, and you have to convince your readers that you know what you're talking about. This means that you have to know your chosen period very well. And it doesn't pertain just to technology levels.

Of even more importance is the knowledge of the "inner working" of the period, the *Zeitgeist* (spirit of the times). This is the area where most writers slip up when dealing with Earth past. Our 21st century sensibilities are a product of all the centuries of our past. If you move to other times, you will find different beliefs underlying everyday life. Let's look at an obvious example, ancient Greece.

Usually, we feel that we have a good idea on how ancient Greece functioned: there were many city-states, Athens was democratic, and Sparta was the polis with warrior obsessions. But, careful. In ancient Athens, you could participate in political life provided you were old enough (initially, you had to be over 30), a free citizen, of Athenian ancestry (everyone born outside of Athens was a "barbarian" for Athenians), and if you could pass the property census. The fact that you had to be a male didn't even have to be mentioned—women were really just another form of property. At the same time, in Sparta, money was forbidden. Spartan women who died in childbirth were the only Spartan citizens who had the right to have their name on their headstones, because they have given up their lives for the future of Sparta. So if you write a story with a Spartan mercenary and an Athenian woman that influences her husband, you had better have a way to explain how they got to their extraordinary positions.

That said, there is another factor to be taken into account. If you happen to know a little-known historical or physical fact—especially one that people are often mistaken about—and use it in your story without spelling it out, the majority of your readers will assume you are simply mistaken, and will feel just as cheated as if you were wrong about your facts. So make sure you don't perform your card tricks in the dark.

IS THAT AIR YOU'RE BREATHING?

Finally, once you decide on your setting, remember that one of the most important ways to achieve believability is *atmosphere*. Atmosphere is created through many different elements: style, plot, character names, and dialogue. If we're reading a humorous work, we'll be playing by different rules than in a dramatic work, and an adventure story will require a third kind of suspension of disbelief. This is part of the contract between the author and the reader, and it's always a good idea to let the readers know early on what kind of a contract they're getting into. Look:

> "Bzoing!" went the megablaster as Jimmy Banana dived behind the bar. He knew that selling faulty water containers to Goombalians was a bad idea, but, hey, he had to make a living, and, anyway, who would have thought they'd have the intelligence to actually check the goods?

From the first sentence, we can see that we are about to get into a humorous adventure story. And now look at this:

> Jimmy dived behind the bar even before the alien fired. He knew that selling faulty water containers was a bad idea, but he had to make a living. And he hadn't thought that big G's would actually have the intelligence to check the cargo.

Still an adventure story, but not announcing humor. Or look at this:

> The alien creature extended one of its upper limbs and let out a sharp trill. Jimmy bit his lip. Selling faulty water containers was a bad idea, even on this god-forsaken low-tech planet. In the confines of his life-suit, he heard the echo of his own breathing. Don't check it, he thought, please don't check it.

We're still starting the same storyline, but here the emphasis is different, so we know there won't be that much action as in the first two examples. So, remember: every word you choose contributes to the atmosphere of your story. And, as with everything else, consistency is important. If you start your story humorously and then forget about the humor halfway through, the readers will feel cheated. You can combine more than one element effectively, of course, but the overall atmosphere of your work has to be consistent.

FROM POINT A TO POINT B: HOW TO PLOT

Plots are the first thing that makes the readers want to read the story. But few writers begin with the plot, particularly in longer works. Some people even fear plots: they feel that their ideas are too vague. However, plotting is really an easy part of the process, if only you know how. It helps if you think about the start of your story as point A, and your ending as point B. All the plot has to do is get you from point A to point B, preferably in an interesting, logical manner. There are several ways to achieve this, and we'll look at some of the most important ones.

GET THINGS GOING

Plot can be anything. It's simply "what happens in your story". However, if you're stuck for a plot, the easiest way to create it is to use a conflict. Conflicts are always interesting.

One of the best-known traditional interpretations of plots divides plots into seven different kinds of conflict:

- man vs. man
- man vs. nature
- man vs. his surroundings
- man vs. technology
- man vs. the supernatural
- man vs. himself
- man vs. gods/religion

This is by no means the only division of plots. However, it's useful because it's not too long (there are divisions with 20 and more different plots), nor too short (the shortest one being "love" and "death"). So, if you're looking for inspiration, it's a good place to start.

Think about the elements that you do have. What is your story going to be about? Is it about Jimmy Banana, a small-time crook who becomes a better person through contact with an alien race? In that case, you're dealing with man vs. himself conflict, and all the elements of your story should reflect that. In one of the scenes, for instance, you can have your big G's run after Jimmy into an Earth-style amusement park, where Jimmy fights reflections of himself.

Or is it about Jimmy Banana's attempts to get away from Goombalian mobsters? Then it's man vs. man (even though, in our case, one of the men is a six-limbed bug-eyed monster). The scene in the amusement park will not work well in this case—but a final wrestling duel between Jimmy and Don Goombaglione will.

Whatever you decide, it's important to know what the central conflict of your story is. If you aren't sure, feel free to explore your story a bit. Usually, our subconscious knows what we're really trying to say, so after you've written a bit of the story, you will realize where its heart lies. But then, in revision, bear that in mind and make sure you align other elements of your story to reflect its central conflict. The story will be a lot stronger that way.

CAUGHT IN THE MIDDLE

Now that you know where you're going with your story, it's time to start developing our point-A-to-point-B map. There are many ways to give structure to your plot. The simplest one is the traditional three-act plot. Each story has a beginning, a middle, and an end.

The beginning is the place where things start. It has to establish the setting, and introduce your main characters. If you have a protagonist and an antagonist, we should meet both of them in Act One. Act One should also provide the readers with the outline of the conflict, and should end with the crisis leading to Act Two. In a short story, the beginning can be as short as a paragraph, or even a sentence. A very rough rule of thumb is that the beginning should not be longer than one quarter of your story. Go on longer than that, and you'll lose your readers.

Now it's time to go on to the middle, or Act Two. This should take up at least two and a half quarters of your story (more than half, for the unmathematically minded), and should be the most interesting part. This is where all the action takes place. If you think about plot as a character with a problem, this is the place where you have the character trying—and failing—to resolve the problem.

The failure is of great importance: if your character solves the problem the first time around, you'll end up with a very short, rather uninteresting story. Look:

> Jimmy bit his lip while the alien examined the water container. Just don't check the safety valve, thought Jimmy.
>
> Goombal etiquette did not allow to check bought goods in detail. The Goombalian paid Jimmy and left. Jimmy instantly went to the spaceport, paid for his ticket, and returned to Earth safe and sound.
>
> The end.

Now, that wasn't much of a story, was it? Of course, if you like Jimmy very much and want him to succeed, you may prefer this to the shootout, and it's your right—but no one except you will be interested in reading about Jimmy in this case. The general rule that some novice writers sometimes forget is this: Suffering builds characters. Unless your characters have problems, they won't really become characters in our eyes. Make us root for Jimmy through his failures to return to Earth—and then, when he succeeds in the end, we'll be happy for him. Otherwise, sadly, we just won't care.

A good way to create Act Two is by repeating failures and increasing the stakes every time. Some writers use the "two failures and a success" principle, with the two failures representing Act Two. This is a good principle to use, because it makes up the total of three attempts, and three is a number that works well on humans. (Think of all the jokes that have three people in them, or one person doing things three times.) However, if you feel more comfortable with more attempts, don't worry. The main thing is to up the stakes each time. If, at first, Jimmy is trying to get back to Earth just because he is homesick, then, after the first failed attempt, he should get additionally pursued by intergalactic mobsters to whom he sold the faulty water containers. Then introduce the second attempt, when he tries to get aboard a Smargolian freighter going to Earth—but accidentally catches a glimpse of a Smargolian harem, for which the sentence is death. Now both Goombalians and Smargolians are after him, and Jimmy is in danger of losing his life. This is the moment where you end Act Two—the lowest point for the hero.

You will find other explanations for the three-act structure. Some sources will tell you that the end of Act Two is the moment when the antagonist possesses the chief interest of the protagonist (be it the love-interest or something else, like a ticket for a flight to Earth). Go with that kind of structure if you feel more comfortable with it. But always remember that the middle has to be the place where the majority of your plot happens, and always remember to make it varied.

Of course, there are more ways to twist a story. In some places, you will find a four-act structure, which divides Act Two into two acts, and there is, of course, the ancient Greek structure, probably the oldest, with five acts. Those five acts consist of an introduction, a complication, a development, a reversal, and an ending. What we do in three-act structure is simply putting the middle three bits—complication, development, and reversal—into one act. However, some people are more comfortable working with this structure, particularly since it allows them to work in roughly equal portions of the story. There is also the nine-act structure, more present in screenwriting[101], which details the reversal plot. It's interesting to note, however, that the "beginning" and "end" bits will almost always be the same—it's really all about the middle.

Even in three-act structure, there is one more thing to note—it becomes even more obvious in more detailed structures—and that's the point of reversal.

Reversal has to do with goals. When you begin your story, your central character should have a goal. That goal can be external—a ticket to Earth—or internal—finding home. It can be expressed consciously, or it can lurk somewhere in your heroine's unconscious. But it's important to give your protagonist something to wish for. Without a goal, your characters will just meander around the story wondering what they're doing there. Pretty soon, the readers will start wondering the same thing—and give up on the story.

If your main character is an actor (no, not in the George Clooney sense), he or she will decide what they want and go for it. If your character is a reactor, he or she will react to events around them. Jimmy's desire to get to Earth because he's homesick makes him an actor: he has a goal of his own. If, on the other hand, you decide to have Jimmy live happily on Goombal and only think about returning to Earth once the local mobsters are on his tail, he will be a reactor. In either case, however, he will have a goal, and will be working throughout the story to achieve that goal.

We talk about reversal when your protagonist's goal changes. This may seem like simple sloppiness, and sometimes it is. The reversal only works when it's set up well—i.e., when we can foresee the reversal happening, and can understand the reasons for the change. That change can come from new information that the character has not previously had, or a new understanding of previous information. But, be careful: if you're going to introduce new information about two thirds into your story, it has to be foreshadowed from the beginning, or else—you guessed it—your readers will feel cheated.

Let's say that Jimmy finds out that one of the mobsters is really an undercover agent from Earth trying to bring down Goombalian gangsters. If you just spring that information on everybody when Jimmy needs help the most, it will seem like a deus-ex-machina solution, and readers will feel cheated. So you have to find ways to make the readers suspect something is unusual about that particular Goombalian from the start. In that way, when Jimmy finally realizes he can turn to the agent for help, instead of crying "cheat", the readers will go "aha!"—and your reversal will work. Then the agent and Jimmy can work together to get the necessary documentation and bring down the Cosa Goomba.

Alternatively, you can have Jimmy change his goal through a new understanding of already present information. He can, for example, realize that he doesn't want what he thought he wanted—to go back to Earth—but rather to find a home for himself, a place where he will feel he belongs. While hiding with Rastafastans, a nomadic Goombalian tribe, he realizes that he feels at home with them, and so the real problem isn't how to get away, but rather how to face those chasing him and protect his new home.

Again, you have to make sure that your reversal is foreshadowed. If you just have Jimmy whiz through the story and suddenly fall under the rustic charm of Rastafastans, that won't work. Show us from the beginning that Jimmy doesn't feel at home at *Goombal*, but indicate that he didn't feel at home on Earth, either. It was that feeling of being an outcast that pushed him to the life of petty crime and brought him halfway around the galaxy. In that way, when he suddenly finds himself accepted, it will be easy for the readers to believe that he feels more at home tiptoeing his way through the Rastafasta desert in company of six-limbed pink nomads and their goats than he would back on Earth.

So, to recap: a plot is, basically, a character with a problem. It has to have a beginning, where we meet the character and the problem, a middle, and an end. The middle is the hardest thing to solve, because it takes longest and it's where most of the action takes place. Remember to up the stakes, give your character at least two failures in his attempts, and/or change their goal, taking care to warn the readers beforehand not everything is what it seems.

Oh, and, of course, don't forget Act Three, the end, where everything is resolved and your character solves the problem. (If you're writing a tragic kind of story, the character can also fail one final time, but we have to understand why there will be no more attempts after that failure.) Make it brief and clear and, if you've done everything else well, the ending will be the easiest thing to write.

STEALING PLOTS

Still stuck for a plot? You have the general idea, but lack substance? Well, then, steal a plot. No, I'm not joking. Many famous writers in history used this technique. It's not the plot itself; it's the telling that makes things interesting. Shakespeare never invented a single one of his plots. But his sources are forgotten today, and Shakespeare is remembered. Because what mattered was what he did with those plots.

So, how to steal a plot. First, you have to reduce it to structure. This is a good exercise in itself, because it will help you notice the structure and teach you how to work with it. Take a look at a well-known story. It doesn't even have to be a science-fiction story. Take, for example, a story everybody knows: *Jack and the Beanstalk*. What happens in it? A protagonist driven by curiosity explores something he should have left alone. That exploration takes him to a great danger, in a place where the rules are completely different from those in his own world. By cleverness, he manages to overcome the obstacles and gains a reward.

Now you take a science fictional setting. Make Jack a scientist exploring a new development in communication technology—the direct cortex communication. He tries the communication equipment on himself, and finds himself trapped in the world of his own brain, where rules are completely different from the ones in the outside world. Once he realizes those nightmares are his own, he thinks of a way to defeat them and get "out". Along the way, he has gained new insight in himself and worked out a technical problem in the communication device—that's his reward. Voilà, your story.

Or you can make Jack an astronaut participating in the exploration of a newly discovered planet prior to colonization. His curiosity drives him to follow a native animal, a giant blue rabbit. The rabbit leads him to its lair. There, Jack realizes that the animal is in fact an intelligent inhabitant of the planet, and the rabbits take Jack as their prisoner. He manages to think up a way to communicate with the species, and thus free himself and prevent a possibly deadly conflict between humans and blue rabbits. Same plot, different story.

As you can see, this technique is really very simple, and can be used over and over again. Take your favorite story and try to analyze it in this manner. Who is the protagonist? What is the driving force of the story? Where's the complication? How is it resolved? Is the outcome positive or negative for the protagonist? Try not to let yourself be fooled by superficial elements, such as names and settings. It doesn't matter whether you're dealing with lions or Danes—the plot with the king killed by his brother and avenged by his son is always the same. But it's the telling that will make your story unique.

CONSTRUCTING PLOTS

Of course, even if you've come this far, you may still find yourself stuck somewhere in your plot. Here are some general tricks to smooth your path from point A to point B.

One of the techniques is building the plot from the bottom up. Some also call it the snowflake method. The principle here is to start from a very short description of your story, preferably one sentence. This is your foundation. Remember Jimmy? We could sum up his story like this: "A small-time crook making ends meet on a faraway planet gets into trouble with the local gangsters and, while trying to escape, realizes the faraway planet has become home for him." Notice how we didn't name any of the characters or places? At this stage, we're going for structural elements: Jimmy is defined by who he is (a small-time crook), not what he's called. Perhaps later we'll find a different name for him, maybe one better reflecting the overall tone of the story. For now, all we need is a way to define him.

Some people even like to reduce the story to an even shorter, more abstract motto. In Jimmy's case, the motto would be something like "Home is where the heart is." Of course, sometimes it's hard to know from the beginning what your story is about. We start from odd bits and pieces, and it's only while constructing a story around those bits that we realize what's really going on. So if you can't summarize your story or give it a motto from the start, don't worry: there's always time to do that in revision.

The next step will be to construct a more detailed storyline. There are several ways to do this and each one is as good as the other—decide what works best for you. You can start with an "objective" storyline—i.e., outlining what happens in the story from start to finish. Alternatively, you can start with a character-related storyline. In that case, you'll concentrate on what happens to Jimmy. If, for example, you plan to include a scene between Don Goombaglione and the undercover agent, this will belong to the objective storyline. The moment when Jimmy realizes he just wanted a place to call home will be part of his "subjective" storyline. Either way, it's a good idea to have at least three storylines: a protagonist storyline—what happens to Jimmy—an antagonist storyline—

from the perspective of Don Goombaglione—and an objective one, putting events together. In a simple short story, much of the storylines will overlap. In a novel, differences will probably be greater. But taking a look at your story from more than one perspective will always help you flesh it out. Inexperienced authors tend to stay in their hero's head for too long, and thus overlook inconsistencies or get stuck. If you make sure you take more than one look at your story, this will be less likely.

The next step in this manner of plot construction is to sketch out the rhythm. Remember the three-act structure? Decide which parts of the storyline should go into Act One, and flesh them out. Then do the same for Act Two, and Act Three. Or if you prefer the five-act structure, go with that.[102] The important thing to achieve here is a detailed sequence of events. You can do this in a spreadsheet, or using charts, flashcards, or ordinary notebooks. Colored pencils can be of help as well. But, whatever technique you use, your goal in this step should be to construct your story step by step.

If you want to make sure the plot flows smoothly, this is also the moment to check that your so's and your but's are in place. Write out the whole storyline on a piece of paper, but write SO on the left side of it and BUT on the right. Now, start writing, like this:

SOBUT

Jimmy is a small-time crook living on Goombal, making his living selling stolen equipment:

SO:	BUT:
he tries to sell a bunch of faulty water containers,	but the mobsters find out and want revenge.
Jimmy has to run from his cheap apartment and go into hiding.	He tries getting back to Earth, but he cannot afford the ticket, so he tries to stow away on a ship from Smargol.
He hides in what he thinks is the cargo space,	but it turns out to be a Smargolian harem, a place forbidden to all males.
So, Jimmy tries to disguise himself as a female	but one of the harem females realizes he's lying and alerts the guards.
So, Jimmy runs away from the ship,	and tries to get lost in the spaceport, but he is seen by Bango "Five Arms",
a member of the Don Goombaglione gang,	who runs after him.
So, Jimmy hides in a cargo of warm blankets bound for the Rastafasta desert...	

Etc. If your storyline is about equal on both sides, you're doing well. If there is a lot more text on one side, this probably means that your story is uneven and could do with a little more complication (if the SO's have it), or a little more action (if the BUT's are much longer). If you have something that doesn't seem to fit into either category, you should probably check whether you need it at all.

If you're one of those people who start with a few key scenes in mind but don't know what exactly to do with them to make them into a story, this is also a good way of working with them: try inserting your scenes into place in a so-but chart, and then filling in the blanks until you have a whole story. You can also do this without the chart, using flashcards or a spreadsheet, and simply shuffling the scenes around like a sort of narrative quanta and fleshing out the plot until you're satisfied with it. As long as you end up with a plot that has a beginning, a middle, and an end, it doesn't really matter how you got there. And there's always the revision to make sure it all works.

GET THAT MACGUFFIN!

Sometimes, though, you have a pretty good idea of all three key elements, but there are still smaller things that trouble you, such as how to get from one place in the plot to another, or how to get things going more quickly. Such problems are solved with plot devices.

Probably the best-known plot device is the MacGuffin. The name is attributed to Alfred Hitchcock, and designates a focal point for the plot. A MacGuffin has no actual importance itself. If both your protagonist and your antagonist want secret documents, it doesn't matter whether those documents are a plan for a new weapon, the key to an ancient instant-transport device, or the PIN for a bank account with an enormous sum of money. The documents are a MacGuffin, something that's just in there so that everybody would have a reason to work against each other. A famous example of a MacGuffin is the One Ring in Tolkien's *The Lord of the Rings*: the ring itself is not important, it hardly gets used at all—but the fact that everybody wants it makes it an important element of the plot.

We could have used a MacGuffin in Jimmy's story as well: instead of just giving him faulty water containers, we could have had him accidentally pick up the wrong disk—not the one with the key to his payment, but rather one containing orders from Don Goombaglione, a crucial piece of evidence against him. Then everyone could go after Jimmy and the disk. Jimmy could still run from them, and still realize that Rastafasta desert is more of a home for him than Earth ever was.

Another good trick for getting a bit more life into a plot is the running joke. This is the joke repeated throughout a story. It can work even in an otherwise serious story, as comic relief or a way to make the dramatic events of the story stand out more. For a running joke to work, however, you have to remember never to have less than three instances of, and to provide a payoff. The payoff is the situation where the readers, who have already started expecting the same joke again, are surprised and rewarded by a novel twist.[3]

You could, for example, give Jimmy a nervous habit of whistling when he thinks. This repeatedly gets him into trouble: he whistles while waiting for the Goombalian mobster to pay, and tips him off as to the valve problem; he whistles in the hold of the Smargolian ship, giving himself away; he whistles when he first gets to the Rastafasta tribe, which attracts all the tribe's desert goats, smelly creatures that bleat annoyingly. Then, at the end of the story, it's time for the payoff: Jimmy goes towards the desert, thoughtful, and then consciously whistles for the desert goats, knowing that the whistle will make him the best desert-goat-shepherd that ever walked the Rastafasta. In this way, the running joke provides us with a neat way of closing the story, and reflects once again its main theme: here, at last, is the place where whistling won't get Jimmy into trouble.

Other useful plot devices are cuts—moments where you go from one point of the story to another. Cuts can be straightforward storyline cuts[103]—where you go from one place in the plot to another that follows logically—or storyteller cuts, where you follow a non-linear logic in order to achieve a certain effect. A plot cut can be, for example, ending a scene with Jimmy first joining the Rastafastans, then beginning the next with "Three days later, they were deep in the desert." You have cut out those three days because nothing particularly interesting happened in them. We would be using a storyteller cut if we were to go from a scene where Jimmy runs away from the bar to a scene with Dom Goombaglione raging at his underlings for having lost the disk with his orders.

Storyteller cuts are particularly useful for special effects: introducing a flashback, or creating additional effects by skipping part of the action. You show the setup and the end result, letting the audience work out what happened in the middle. Jimmy could be talking to the Rastafastans about desert goats. (Remember, we've already established his habit of whistling while he thinks.)

"What is that smell?" asked Jimmy.

"Our goats", said Yamarla. "They're very useful. And they like sharp tones—hence our flutes."

But Jimmy wasn't listening any more, trying to think of a way to get Don

Goombaglione off his back.

By the third day, Jimmy had his thinking whistle almost completely under control. Herds of over-friendly goats will do that.

Using a storyteller cut, we've skipped the actual scene where Jimmy is mobbed by the goats: it's a good scene, but an equally funny effect is achieved with skipping to the end result, and we've moved the story on faster. Notice, also, that in this manner we achieved the same goal as we did with the storyline cut—fast-forwarded to three days later—but with an added element, making the story livelier. This is, after all, the whole point of plot devices. Although, from the point of view of characters, the best stories are just "one damn thing after another", it's your job as the storyteller to make that journey interesting and amusing for your readers.

You can think of plot devices as spices for your story. And, as with all spices, be careful not to overuse them. No matter which devices and plot construction you use, at the end, the reader has to know exactly what the story was about: where it started, where it ended, and how it got there.

ALL SYSTEMS STUCK

Sometimes, despite all the plotting techniques, you'll find yourself stuck, either someplace in the story, or even at an earlier stage, with the idea or a bit of character but no story as yet. How to resolve this? There are many ways.

The first thing to do is to identify the source of the problem. If you're normally happy and prolific when writing, there's probably a reason why you can't make any progress right now. The first thing to do is to wonder whether real life is interfering. If you've just got a new job or a new child, don't expect yourself to be able to keep writing as you previously did. However, if nothing in your circumstances has changed and you still can't make any progress on a story, there's probably a reason within the story.

Perhaps the story is not yet ripe. Some stories take years to mature. If you have a character, and force her into a plot neither of you is comfortable with, it won't work. Or perhaps your story is not about what you thought it was—so, while you're trying to write a humorous story about intergalactic mobsters, the story is really about finding one's place in the universe. If that's the case, the scenes you're trying to write are not right for the story, they sound wrong, and you just can't decide why that is so. In such cases, the step-by-step procedure described earlier will be of great help. Try to find out what your story's focus is. Give it a motto. Once you know that, it will be a whole lot easier to work out which plot elements will make up a story, and which are just things that happen but don't add up to a powerful whole.

It's also a good idea to check that your structural elements are sound. Is your character an actor or a reactor? (Of course, we're all a bit of both, but if there's too much jumping around from one to another, the character will come out uneven.) Think of Hamlet: he's a reactor. Everything he does is caused by outside stimuli. He doesn't trust his own judgment. He doesn't believe that he's right in suspecting his uncle, he doesn't believe that Ophelia really loves him, and he doesn't take action until he's forced to it by outside events. His antagonist, the uncle, is the opposite—a true actor. He wants to become king, so he kills his brother. He wants to get rid of Hamlet, so he spends the five acts scheming and working to achieve that goal, while Hamlet spends the same time agonizing over his suspicions and taking only indirect steps towards confirming them. This is part of why *Hamlet* works so well: the central character is a reactor, and he's confronted by an actor. The opposition moves the plot forward smoothly.

If you have an antagonist, make sure that he's the opposite of the protagonist: having both of them be reactors will stop the story cold, with both the hero and his opponent waiting for the other to make his move. Having them both be actors will fill the story with unrelated actions and confuse the readers.

Take a look at your stakes. Do they become higher with every attempt-failure round? If the answer is yes, and your story still feels flat, perhaps you should try changing the goal.

When all else fails, follow Jim Macdonald's advice and insert naked women screaming. No, seriously. Adding a totally unrelated, spectacular element into your story will definitely get it moving. Then you'll start working out who those naked women are and why they are screaming, and this will put the whole story into a new perspective. You may decide to get rid of your screaming women later, but they will have helped you solve the immediate problem, and get the story going.

You can pick any random cliché—a mad scientist, a cowboy-style shootout— and add it to your story. Usually, your subconscious will know where it wants to go, so the cliché you choose will help you see what's really happening, and, again, you can always get rid of it in revision. If you want an even more dadaistic technique, try writing down several plot ideas, tossing them into a hat, then pulling one out and working your way from there.[104] But kick that story into gear—there's always revision for fixing problems later.

ALL SYSTEMS CLEAR

So now you have your idea, setting, and plot, and you've written the story out. Is it time to do what Salinger suggests, make your story a sandwich and put it on a train? No, not yet. It's time for revision.

Some people love the revision process. Some hate it. But everybody needs it. If you're very good and very experienced, you may luck out once or twice in your life and write a perfect short story the first time around. (Nobody writes a perfect novel that way.) But if you are a mere mortal like the rest of us, your first draft will be exactly that —a first draft, and will need more work before it's ready to face the world.

There are two ways to go about revision. One is to write out the whole story in one attempt, leave it for a while (this is important!) then go back to it and revise. The other way is to start writing your story, get a little way into it, go back to the beginning, revise, return to where you stopped, keep writing, go back, revise, keep writing... etc. This is usually called "rolling draft" writing. But whether you use rolling or clearly separate drafts, you will need to revise. And no, revision is not just making sure there are no typos.

It's always a good idea to let a story cool off a little after the first draft. (If you use rolling drafts, let it cool off once you reach the end.) This will allow you to get a fresh perspective on your story. While you're writing, you will be immersed in the story world: you'll know everything there is to know about Jimmy and Don Goombaglione, you'll see the green sky of Goombal and the Rastafasta desert instead of your own sky and streets. But when a little time passes, you'll have forgotten at least some of it, and when you go back to the story, you will see that, in the story text, you forgot to mention that Goombal skies are green.

Here's what you need to do in the revision process:

Establish that your story is structurally sound. Even if all that talk about structure didn't help you in the first draft of your story, now is the time to get your structural tables out and make sure everything works and fits together. Check that the beginning is short and informative; check that the middle flows smoothly and logically; check that the ending is even shorter than the beginning, and that it springs naturally from everything that went on before. If your ending seems too abrupt or unconnected to the rest of the story, go back and foreshadow it: insert little hints that the reader will pick up on, even if your character will overlook them.

Be careful, however, not to make your character seem like a complete idiot. If you provide him with all the elements he needs to solve the problem in the first third of the story and then drag it out for twenty more pages, your readers will feel they're reading about an imbecile and will give up on the story. There are two good ways to avoid this.

Introduce important elements early on, before we can figure out their importance. If Jimmy saves himself by giving the data disk to the Earth agent, let us know the disk is missing early on. (Jimmy doesn't have to know that; readers do.)

Another way to make sure your foreshadows are all in place but your character doesn't come up looking like an idiot is to introduce something even more important or urgent at the moment when he makes the discovery. If Jimmy finds out that his disk contains incriminating material on Don Goombaglione at the moment when Don's thugs are breaking down his door, it's fine for him to jump through the window first, and think about what to do with the disk later.

This is also a good moment to introduce another concept: character and story arcs. A character arc describes the status of the character within the story. In our example, Jimmy's arc would be going from a drifting, cowardly small-time crook to a person who has a home and is willing and able to fight to protect it. Story arc, on the other hand, is a story-related unit, describing a sequence of interconnected events. We have the "lost disk" story arc, the "Smargolian revenge" story arc, and the "bring down Cosa Goomba" story arc. If you want, you can think of both character and story arcs as small stories-within-stories.

What's important, however, is how all those arcs act in relation to one another. If you look at our example above, you'll see that Jimmy's arc, his transformation, serves as an umbrella for the story arcs. This is a good thing, because that's what we set out to do—tell the story of Jimmy's finding a home. If our goal had been to show how criminal minds are all alike regardless of race or species, this structure would be wrong: we would need to move the "bring down Cosa Goomba" arc in the umbrella position, and reduce Jimmy's arc to one of the "lower" places. We could still use the same plot, but we would need to change the emphasis and the rhythm. We'd probably add a Don Goombaglione arc, etc.

This is why it's important to notice and use your arcs. Depending on their mutual position, they will change the overall effect of your story. If aligned well, the arcs will take your point across to the readers in a satisfying manner; if in disarray, they can ruin the effect.

After you check that your story is structurally sound, it's time to check the small fish—are all your words well chosen, can your prose be tightened, etc. And then... well, then, it really is time for the Salinger recipe: make your story a sandwich and put it on a train. That's all a writer can ever do. Put your story in an envelope and start sending it out. Sometimes that, too, can be difficult and even scary, but, don't worry: if you've got this far, you'll be able to take that final step.

CHAPTER TWELVE

SCIENCE FICTION AS WESTERN UNION

Orson Scott Card

Samuel Goldwyn has been quoted as saying, "Pictures are for entertainment, messages should be delivered by Western Union." Of course, a similar quote ("If you want to send a message, use Western Union") has been attributed to Darryl Zanuck, Louis B. Mayer, and Jack L. Warner.

What is the message here for writers? If you come up with a good line, people will think somebody more famous than you said it first.

More than any other genre of writing, science fiction demands that writers trade in ideas.

In the Campbell era, the ideas were generally scientific or technological ones. In order to set up the problem that the hero had to solve, the reader had to be informed of the scientific issues at stake.

For that matter, any story structured as a mystery has ideas at its very heart. The whole story is about trying to find out the unknown, to solve for *x*. There's a dead body —that's the fact; the rest of the search is for an idea, the why of the death.

But those are ideas that are part of the flow of the story. Often when we talk about "ideas" in science fiction, we're thinking of something else.

We're thinking of those poor high school students whose English teachers have assigned them to find the "theme" of a story, as if the only thing that mattered about a story were an Aesopian moral. What is the theme of Asimov's *Foundation*? Um ... let's see...don't let missionaries from a high-tech religion come to your planet? Well, no, that's only part of it; um, human history is completely predictable in mathematical terms once you understand the great social forces at play?

No, dear child, that's not the theme, that's the *premise*. It's the interesting scientific idea that may or may not be true, but upon which the rest of the story is predicated.

Them maybe the theme is that when you have accurate prophecies, it gives your nation more confidence and makes you bolder!

Well...that's certainly one effect of Hari Seldon's prophecies, if that's what you want to call them. But the prophecies also make the people of *Foundation* too confident.

That's the theme!

No. It's an idea. There are ideas all over the place in stories. But how absurd, to try to reduce them all to a single theme.

The ideas that are intrinsic to a story cannot be extracted from it and still carry their meaning with them. After all, *the facts of Foundation* were made up—which is true of all fiction, ultimately, but certainly is true of science fiction. That is, the events which distinguish *this* story from all other stories are precisely the ones that were imagined by the author. What is provably true is that which can be shared by all stories set in that milieu; what is unique to this particular story is that which cannot be demonstrated convincingly in the real world.

The Mississippi does indeed flow toward the New Orleans and the Gulf of Mexico—that is "true" in *Huckleberry Finn* and in all other works of fiction that choose to use that real-world setting. But that is hardly the "theme" of *Huckleberry Finn*. And any of the proposed themes for the novel—ideas about friendship and loyalty, about courage or faith or slavery itself, or equality of the races or honor or nobility—even ideas about lying itself, in a book of lies—are candidates for themehood only because they cannot possibly be proven in the real world, for there never was a Huckleberry Finn or a runaway slave named Jim or any of the other colorful characters that people the book.

The ideas that matter, as morals or themes, are made up.

Because there *are* books and stories that have clear themes, and they are especially common in science fiction. One might argue that the ability to tell stories that clarify a theme is one of the prime reasons for having science fiction in the first place.

Let me offer one brilliant example: Ursula K. LeGuin's *The Left Hand of Darkness*. Her premise was a world where the human species has evolved so that during estrus, an individual might change sexes, or might not. That is a powerful intrinsic idea, but it is also a theme, because LeGuin wished it to be understood as commenting on the real world. Our society would certainly treat genders differently if we knew that any individual might be of either sex at some time in his/her life.

She wanted us to think: Would we regard men as "entitled" to leadership if we knew that any man might be a woman next month? Would we tolerate having women treated as second-class citizens if we knew that we might spend much of our lives in that class?

As a premise—an idea intrinsic to the story, on which the causal system of the story is based—this one is enormously productive of more ideas, the kind we call extrapolation. If the premise were true, then how would we handle pronouns? Would they be gender-specific? How would we handle marriage? Could it persist beyond the next estral cycle in which a partner changed sex? Who would be the soldiers, and who the secretaries?

But as a theme—an idea extrinsic to the story, commenting on the real world—it does not prove anything, it merely raises questions. If you already believed, before reading *Left Hand of Darkness*, that there was no important physical difference between the sexes (something it was still somewhat possible to do when the book was written), and therefore complete equality of the sexes was desirable and achievable, then you might applaud the book for its support of your belief.

On the other hand, if you believed that gender is more than a superficial difference between organisms, that there are differences in mental function and other physical characteristics that result from gender, which cannot be denied and which shape the preferences and abilities and biological imperatives of each gender, then this theme of *Left Hand* might seem naive to you.

You might even make a case that the book really demonstrates the opposite of its apparent theme. For the only way LeGuin could make a case for complete gender equality was to create a situation contrary to fact: An estral cycle for humans and the seemingly random change of an individual's physical sex. Since we don't have those, then by the logic of *Left Hand,* shouldn't we assume that we should not assume the complete equivalence of the sexes?

If this discussion seems silly, that's because it is: It depends, not on what is in the text of the novel, but on what we bring to it—our conception of the way the real world works. Fiction cannot prove ideas, it can only demonstrate them. And if you disbelieve in the idea a novel is demonstrating, it is hard to take the book seriously, for the suspension of disbelief on which our experience of the novel depends is already compromised. The pretense that the story is true is harder for the reader to maintain; at some point, strained enough, disbelief can no longer be suspended.

That is why "themes" and other extrinsic meanings are perilous. They are the shoals on which many a fiction crashes. And yet it is precisely the desire to demonstrate extrinsic ideas that drew Dante to write *The Divine Comedy*, More to write *Utopia*, Butler to write *Erewhon*, Swift to write *Gulliver's Travels*, Voltaire to write *Candide*, and LeGuin to write *The Left Hand of Darkness*.

Which of those would we willingly do without?

EXTRINSIC VS. INTRINSIC IDEAS

If there's one thing I've learned about writing, it is this: There are no unbreakable rules in storytelling. There are merely tools and costs. If the use of a particular tool costs you more than its value, then you would be wise to decline to use it in this case. But no technique is without cost. Using a dangerous, expensive tool may cost you many readers who are offended by the result; but if, in order to avoid offending those readers, you make your story safer and more predictable, you may lose another, entirely different set of readers, who are bored because your story breaks no ground that is new to them.

Every choice you make costs you some readers, or weakens their experience; but making a different choice will probably cost you other readers. How many? Does it matter? Do you make your artistic decisions based on imaginary polls of future readers?

It is a fool of a writer who deforms her work in order to try to increase the number of readers (or buyers); but the writer who deforms his work to try to please an elite, deliberately casting away otherwise eager readers is just as big a fool.

So as we look at the "rules" of idea-handling, keep this in mind: You must do in your story what feels important and true to you. You can show your story to trusted readers to help you find *inadvertent* flaws—places where, without meaning to, you have been unclear or your story has become boring or unbelievable.

You can also do your best to *compensate* for decisions that you know will cost you readers, to minimize the damage. Why not? You don't write your stories on wind, you write them on paper, in the hope of finding an audience that will receive the story you intended to help them create in their memory. Therefore you must give them every help you can—as long as the story that you believe in and care about is still there.

Which brings us back to the ideas that appear in and often drive science fiction.

Let's take one of the great examples: Arthur C. Clarke's "*The Star.*" The core idea is this: When the star appeared over Bethlehem, it was really a supernova, the explosion of a star. However, future human startravelers discover that the explosion that marked the birth of Jesus also wiped out a beautiful civilization, which only had warning enough to leave a record of their existence on the outermost planet of their solar system, where someone—we—might find it.

Is this an extrinsic or an intrinsic idea?

It is certainly Clarke's purpose in writing the story to convey this idea—the story exists solely for that purpose. It is the premise.

His point of view character is a Christian so that this revelation will come to him with particular irony: to him, it is the greatest event in human history, but now he discovers that God, in order to create a "special effect" to mark the birth of his son, slaughtered a marvelous race of beings.

Without this idea, there is no story. It is definitely intrinsic. But notice that because it is intrinsic, nobody expects the reader to receive it as *true*. Clarke is not trying to convince you that there really was a civilization that was destroyed. He is not saying anything about God at all.

It happens that (as I have been told, anyway) Clarke is not a believer in God, or at least in the Christian God, so he can hardly have intended this story to be a comment on the nature of a God he doesn't believe in. He is not making a theological point. So the premise is definitely intrinsic. You believe it only for the duration of the story.

Which is why the identical story could have been written by a believing Christian. It is neither an attack on God nor a defense of God—it's a story about the experience of a believer who finds out a terrible irony about a God that he believes to be merciful and/or just, but who has a sense of values that is baffling to him.

But the fact that the premise is intrinsic does not change the fact that Clarke wrote this story in an era, and to an audience, that was very familiar with the Christian God. Clarke, being British, grew up in a nation with a state-established church. He could reasonably expect that everyone knew the basics about the Christian God. So he does rely on the expectation that his audience will include many Christians and many more who are at least familiar with Christian belief. To that degree, the idea is extrinsic—he does not need to explain to his audience who Jesus was and what the star signifies to Christians.

So we could still wonder: Would the story mean anything like the same thing to an audience for whom the Christian God and the story of Bethlehem simply didn't exist? He would have to have written it very differently, explaining many points that are simply assumed in the text that we have. But such explanations would be rather like explaining a joke—once the explanation was done, what would be left?

Would the achristian audience, even after the explanations, even care about the story? If you grew up believing, say, in Zeus and the whole Greek pantheon, and somebody confronted you with "*The Star*," then would it do any good to explain to you all about Jesus and the wise men and the star of Bethlehem? I believe that the story gets all of its emotional power from the extrinsic aspects of the premise: the reader must have a sense of living within a Christian community, even if he personally is an unbeliever, for the story to be anything other than a puzzlement: What's the excitement about?

Indeed, to Zeus-believers, the real question might be, "Why should anyone worship a god who wouldn't feel free to wipe out a civilization that got in the way of something he wanted to do? What wimpy, useless sort of god would it be, who refused to do his own will just because a bunch of mortals would die?"

So even though the premise of "*The Star*" is intrinsic to the story, it still depends on extrinsic effects—only a certain subset of the human race will receive the story with anything like the intended effects.

DATING THE TALE

This effect applies to many stories from the Campbellian era of science fiction (late 1930s to late 1950s, perhaps): Many stories existed only to inform the readers of a lovely new scientific idea by telling a story that depended on knowing that idea. Thus part of the exposition of the story involved letting the readers know the cool new scientific idea, either before or after the solution to the puzzle was revealed.

All these ideas, because they were the premise of the story, were intrinsic; but they had extrinsic aspects that ultimately damaged the stories. The most obvious one is this: Ideas that were new and exciting in 1938 were likely to be old hat by 1958, questionable by 1978, and absurdly wrong by 1998.

The story then becomes an artifact of a more ignorant age. The original audience read the story and learned the cool idea along with its characters. The modern audience reads the story and sees the idea as a curiosity—look what people used to believe. The result is that the story is no longer readable. You can read the words, but you cannot join the audience for which it was intended. You know too much. That audience has ceased to exist, and therefore the story is effectively dead, killed by the passage of time and the progress of science.

Of course, science fiction is hardly unique in having this effect. I've always been uncomfortable with Shakespeare's *Richard III* because his Richard is so self-consciously vile. It still worked, more or less, as a play, even though I had no desire to direct it or play the title role.

But in the last twenty years I've read enough history and seen enough of how history was created to serve the political purposes of the winners of wars that I no longer have any grounds for believing that the Richard depicted in *Richard III* is anything other than a vile political slander created by the Tudors to justify their raw usurpation of power from what was, in fact, a very good man and a pretty good king.

For instance, the best evidence points to the idea that it was *Henry VII* whose agents murdered the two princes in the tower; all the available evidence indicates that they were alive right to the end of Richard's reign. It is even doubtful that

Richard was a hunchback. But in an era when few people saw the king in person, and when people knew to keep their mouths shut when an official story violated their direct knowledge, it is quite possible to create a political slander that, within a generation, is received as unquestioned truth.

This was hardly Shakespeare's fault: He lived several generations into the Tudor era and had no access to any information that would challenge the official story.

Someday I may write my own *Richard III*, just to set the record straight.

Think of the statement I just made. What am I saying? How can a fictional play set any record straight?

Here's how: The only reason most people who know of *Richard III* as a villain have their picture of him from Shakespeare's play. The dramatization is now the primary carrier of the political story from a distant age; the best counter to it is to write a comparable dramatization (or narration) that carries a very different character.

That may sound ridiculously ambitious—Card would pit his play or novel against Shakespeare? But I'm not a complete fool or egomaniac: *Richard III* is far from being Shakespeare's best play, and because Shakespeare is always performed in Elizabethan English, which fewer and fewer people understand, and my version would be in contemporary English, easily understood by anyone, I will have a fighting chance.

What matters for this discussion, though, is that "setting the record straight" is my declared motive. That is an extrinsic motive. I intend to write a fiction in order to transform the public conception of the life and times of a maligned historical figure. I want to change people's minds.

Can it be done? Of course.

POLEMICAL FICTION

When you want to persuade people, your writing is called "polemic." It is often treated as a "bad" word—but in fact being "polemical" in your writing is only "bad" when you're caught at it.

In recent years, because the hatred of President Bush has become so pervasive among the American academic-literary community (like the hatred of Margaret Thatcher among the Brits a generation before), I have been disappointed to see a lot of writers put words into the mouths of their characters that referred to particular bugbears in the current political scene. In many cases the opinions expressed were ones that were almost laughably wrong for the character that the writer had established. It was as if a character that we had come to believe in as flesh and blood was suddenly revealed to be a marionette—because the author's political comments were forced onto the character, we could see the strings.

There is nothing morally wrong with writers inserting their heartfelt passions into their work. If you believe something, why not say it? Writers have no obligation to be even-handed or fair. But, as with all decisions, there are costs.

When you have your character speak political opinions that seem irrelevant to the immediate situation—or, worse, that seem not to be like the attitudes the character has shown before—the reader will feel that something false is going on. The reader will see the strings.

Here is the law that cannot be broken: The idea that is consciously received can be consciously rejected.

So when you put forth your ideas in a way that calls attention to them, you increase the likelihood that your readers will notice them in a way that distracts them from the story.

It also makes your work less effective as polemic. In other words, it is a law of diminishing returns—the more blatant your polemic, the less persuasive it will be!

When a character who has always been a tough, violent cop suddenly delivers a diatribe on the evils of fighting a war in Iraq, or when a character who has himself used torture to extract information he needed in order to save someone's life gives a rant on the subject of the torture of detainees in Guantanamo, the reader who agrees with these sentiments will notice them and, perhaps, be relieved. This character might be a violent torturer, but he agrees with *me*.

Those who disagree with the political opinions the character has suddenly acquired, however, will hardly be persuaded. On the contrary, they will feel rejected by the author. They will feel, consciously or not, that the author no longer is writing to them; they may continue reading the story, but will no longer be as caught up in it as before. They have become wary readers.

And some who might agree with the sentiments will also be put off, and wary, because they will perceive—correctly — that the writer is now putting his stories and his characters at the service of his opinions. What once was seen as fiction is now seen as partly or entirely essay. And we don't take essays and swallow them whole the way we do fiction.

Twenty years from now, when readers no longer remember or care about some or all of the particular political issues these writers have inserted into their stories, such moments will simply be baffling. What in the world are they talking about? Does this have something to do with the story? Did I miss something? Such political insertions become instant anachronisms.

Even the great science fiction-like satires that we call "utopias" after Thomas More's original *Utopia* (perhaps the only science fictionish story written by a Catholic Saint) are interesting only to the degree that the issues they address transcend the political moment.

We still enjoy Jonathan Swift's "*A Modest Proposal*" because it is not fiction, but rather an ironic document. We don't read it because we care about the fate of starving Irish children, because children in Ireland aren't starving any more. Swift's essay runs no risk of making us angry, because none of us are on the opposite side of the political issue from him—we all agree with him now, and so we don't think his writing is grossly unfair in taking the stand it does on a most specific political issue.

Gulliver's Travels, however, is not a satire on a particular political issue. It's a satire, but it mocks general human traits that still persist today. Most of the things that Gulliver learns are still applicable. So as we read *Gulliver,* the setting may seem old-fashioned, but the situation of being a giant among lilliputians or a toy-sized person among the giants is still intriguing to us. When, at the end, we see that Gulliver prefers horses ("houyhnhnm") to humans ("yahoos"), we know we're being mocked, but we have rather come to agree with him.

Still, we know that the story is making a point. It does so cleverly and we are delighted (partly because we think of ourselves as being superior to the sort of human who deserves to be called a "yahoo"), but we are not responding to the story emotionally, we are responding intellectually. We laugh because we get the author's joke, not because we are lost inside a character's life and point of view.

So we may or may not come away from *Gulliver's Travels* persuaded to see the world as Swift does.

As polemic, it is not terribly effective, because it is obvious.

Take another work of literature—a Pulitzer-prize-winning historical novel that was the single most dominant work of fiction in the 1930s and 1940s: *Gone with the Wind.* This magnum opus of an extraordinarily talented writer, Margaret Mitchell, seems even upon close examination to be entirely about its characters, most particularly the morally complicated Scarlett O'Hara.

Readers have been known to get quite heated, arguing about just how bad a person Scarlett was. "Look what she did to her sisters, stealing their beaux away and leaving them old maids." "But she had to marry Frank Kennedy to save Tara!" "What's so important about Tara, except to her? And she didn't marry Charlie to save anybody, it was just to make Ashley jealous, and it didn't even work!" Etc.

In other words, the arguments are still within the terms of the story, about particular choices that the author means us to receive as morally questionable.

Meanwhile, the story had a strange yet powerful moral effect on its audience without anyone noticing at all. *GWTW* portrays plantation slave owners as members of a gracious culture, and the destruction of that society as a tragedy. Scarlett's choices are morally questionable in the terms of that society, and we watch the other main character, Rhett Butler, become converted to that old nobility even as Scarlett rejects it more and more.

It was a romanticized version of the Old South, in which slaves rather liked their masters and were loyal to them, and no plantation owner who was worth anything would mistreat his slaves. What it does not suggest is that slaves were in fact human beings fully capable of living their own lives without the "guidance" of a master, however beneficent he might have meant to be.

The readers of *GWTW* were thus given several hundred pages of living in a world in which owning slaves was OK, as long as you were nice. Not that it persuaded anybody to agitate for the restoration of slavery—but it made the Old South morally acceptable throughout a nation that had, less than a century before, fought a civil war to destroy the evil of slavery. It was the rehabilitation of the South. It was the anti-*Uncle Tom's Cabin*.

(So it is doubly ironic that blacks viewed as disloyal to their own race are called Uncle Toms—even though Tom in fact resisted slavery as best he could. They should have been called *Pharaohs* or *Porks* or *Big Sams*, after characters in *GWTW*!)

Yet it's more complicated than that—for to many (perhaps most) white readers of *GWTW*, the black characters in the book were the only black people they had actually met. Outside the South, most whites could live their whole lives without ever meeting a black person who was not in a servant's uniform. So *Gone with the Wind* might well have helped move America just a little closer to the belief that segregation was wrong and should be abolished—after all, it is only when you believe in a subjugated race as individual human beings with names and distinguishable characteristics that you start to feel urgency about removing them from permanent servitude.

Which of these moral effects of *Gone with the Wind* were intended? I have no idea, but my guess is that what we received was not Margaret Mitchell's political agenda; rather, while reading the novel we lived within a world that she truly believed in and cared about. She did not create the society of *GWTW* in order to persuade us to a political course of action; she created it because she believed in it and was nostalgic for it (even though it probably never existed, at least not the way she portrayed it).

WHAT YOU BELIEVE IN AND CARE ABOUT

As a storyteller, you make a thousand unconscious decisions for every dozen conscious ones. Most of them consist of decisions not to show things you could have shown, simply because they aren't interesting to you. For the first moral statement your fiction makes is: This event is important enough to show.

Think about that: Every single thing you show (or tell about) in your story is thus declared to be more important than all the things you chose not to show. This is why it is impossible to tell a story of any kind without moral judgments.

But your readers aren't sitting there thinking, "Ah, we're being given a moral lesson." Their response is much more visceral. If you show your characters thinking long and hard about which outfit to wear for a particular occasion, they may reject it, but not because they consciously disagree with the author—rather, they reject it by feeling bored. By starting to skim; eventually, by putting down the book and never picking it up again.

So you can't necessarily force your story on people. But those who are persuaded that most of your decisions about what is important are right do not see you as persuasive, they see your work as fascinating.

If you are depicting a society in which costume choice has great ramifications, then you will persuade most of your readers to become as costume-conscious as the characters you depict. This may translate, at least slightly, at least for some readers, into a greater awareness of the meaning of costume choice in the real world.

But this will only work if (a) you are not conscious of trying to make people more costume-aware and (b) if you make the costume-choice issues so important within the story that the reader also quickly comes to care about costume choice within the world of the story. You and the reader will see this as an issue of interesting vs. boring; thus to the degree you make your work entertaining, you have changed the perceptions of your readers.

The same issue arises with believability. You can make anything believable in fiction—if you take the time to show, step by step, how the people of your fictional world got to where they are from a condition that is more obviously believable in the real world.

Science fiction, by definition, takes place in an unbelievable world—it is different from the reality that sane people think they live in, and therefore we sci-fi writers must invest a considerable amount of time in not just informing the readers about the world (exposition) but also persuading them that it could really be this way.

Again, nobody—neither you nor your readers—will consciously think of it as "polemic." Rather you'll think of it as explaining and clarifying, and your readers will see it the same way (except the ones who found it so outrageously unbelievable that they rejected it before you were able to win them over).

But the result is far more persuasive than any obvious theme or other extrinsic idea. The world you create is intrinsic to the story and is not experienced in isolation, as something separate from the tale. So you can take readers who did not see the world as you do and persuade them by giving them many pages of entertaining fiction set in a world that you have made them believe in.

When readers are done with your story, you have put into their memory a series of causally connected events that create a picture of how the world works, of why people do the things they do, and of which human actions are important and which too trivial to notice. There is an enormous persuasive effect.

Moreover, most of the persuasion is not even visible to you, the author. Because along with the world-creation that you are aware of—the aspects of the world that you know are contrary to the received version of reality—you will make thousands of decisions about how the world works that are based on your true, unconscious beliefs about how the real world works. In other words, wherever you aren't deliberately creating a sci-fi world, you are revealing the secret inner world that serves as the lens through which you view all of reality. You are not aware of that lens, by and large; it is simply there, filtering and deciding things for you in your life and in your fictions.

TRUST YOURSELF TO TELL THE TRUTH

That is why I believe writers are usually making a serious mistake when they try to use their fiction to persuade readers of a particular idea. What you consciously put into your story will be consciously received, and you will end up preaching to the choir, as all who disagree with you see what you're doing and turn away.

Besides, it is often true that what you think you believe—the opinions you know you hold—are contradictory to what you really believe, at the deepest level of your soul. Often the ideas you defend or proclaim most fervently seem so important to you precisely because you unconsciously doubt them.

If you tell your story as plainly as possible, concentrating on making the story believable and interesting and clear to your readers, your fiction will end up being far more effective at persuading readers to come to see the world the way you do.

Mark Twain thought he was an atheist, sophisticated, unsuperstitious. In *Tom Sawyer* he openly mocks Sunday school stories and folk beliefs.

Yet there's something odd here—because every superstition (except the use of stump water to cure warts) turns out to be true. Not in an obvious way, but in ways subtle enough that Twain himself might not have realized what he was doing. The more I studied Twain's life and work in grad school, the more I realized that he argued against religion because he could not escape it in his personal worldview; the more he mocked superstition, the more strongly he relied on it in the unconscious choices he made in his fiction.

Thus the more Twain denied the Calvinist God of his upbringing, the more he felt himself to be damned in the eyes of that unforgiving deity. And it shows up over and over again in his fiction, in the subtle movements of stories in which the obvious statements reflect his conscious beliefs.

Since you can't keep your fiction from revealing what you really believe about humanity and morality and causality, why not trust that? You might be revealed not to really believe in some of the things you want everybody to think you believe in, but what of that? Those secrets are going to be exposed in your stories anyway, at least to those few readers who understand how morality works in fiction.

So to the degree that your unconscious beliefs are consonant with your conscious ones, your fiction will be more effective at persuading others if you try not to make your characters speak your opinions. It's worth remembering Polonius, who makes a speech filled with some of Shakespeare's best advice and most-quoted lines: "To thine own self be true" (which is what I'm saying here, isn't it?), "Neither a borrower nor a lender be."

But Polonius is something of a buffoon. We receive that speech as the tedious advice of a father to his departing son; we even laugh as the aphorisms pile one upon another.

It is because we are laughing that we do not notice that these are the lines that stick in our mind. We don't think Shakespeare is preaching; because he put these bits of wisdom into the mouth of a buffoon, we aren't put off.

Unfortunately, some readers will insist on thinking that your characters are all speaking for you—particularly when you have a character advocate a point of view that they hate. It happens to me all the time—naive or malicious readers think they've caught my "meaning" when in fact they've only seen what my characters believe. I've had people attack me and my work quite savagely as if I were espousing ideas that I don't believe in. But my characters believe them. I have characters who are atheists, and characters who are Christians, and characters who subscribe to religions I invented myself; I have characters who pretend to be religious but are frauds, and characters who are faithful to beliefs I personally find absurd or offensive. Yet there are always readers who think that my character's words are my own.

You can't stop people from wilful misreading of your text. Most readers, however, receive a story as no more than itself—without a chip on their shoulder, they are not looking for opportunities to be angry with the writer.

So my rule for myself is: When a character starts preaching, I make sure he's either preaching ideas that I don't believe in, or his preaching is treated as a joke within the story. What I can't afford to do is let my readers catch me preaching, because the moment they do, they'll stop listening to me. Instead of using my characters to preach for me, I trust that my stories will reflect my truest, deepest beliefs. Because I am letting this happen unconsciously, I run the risk of persuading people to believe in things I don't believe that I believe in. But since I really do believe in them, then the worst thing that can happen is that they'll experience being as dumb—or as wise—as I am.

We writers can hardly persuade people to be smarter than we are, can we?

JUGGLING IDEAS

We have to be aware of the intrinsic ideas in our fiction. Wherever we know our readers will be unfamiliar with ideas that our story depends on, we find clever expository strategies to help them come to understand how our sci-fi world differs from the world they are familiar with.

We are juggling, hoping to keep all the balls in the air until the readers reach the end of our tale. The readers will think they see flying balls; we know where we are catching and tossing to make the whole thing work.

What we don't see are all the balls that are chained to our feet—the ideas that we don't realize we're putting into the story. We drag them along quite unconsciously; we have always had them, so we don't even notice that they're there.

Our readers might come away trying to juggle some of the balls we juggled. But they know they're juggling.

Meanwhile, they also come away dragging some of our balls-and-chains, in place of the ones they used to have. They didn't even notice the switch. They will drag those balls around with them long after they've dropped the balls we gave them to juggle. What happens in front of our face has far less effect (though it might be quite dazzling) than what we unknowingly drag along behind us.

And if you hate that metaphor, well, it was the best I could do at the moment. Pretend that some idiotic character said it.

You can be sure, when I write my *Richard III*, that I will not have any obvious preaching of the "truth." I'll just have people do things for believable, understandable motives; by the end, if I do my work well, I'll have readers (or audience members) who carry around in their memory my version of that story, not because I persuaded them, but because I let them live through it.

Do I really mean, six thousand words after beginning this chapter, that what you do with extrinsic ideas is "leave them alone and they'll come home, dragging their tails behind them"?

Yes indeed, that's what I mean. Concentrate on the sci-fi world creation, on the motives of your characters, on the rules of the society they live in; and don't waste a moment trying to teach your readers how to translate your fiction into beliefs about the real world. Because they're already doing it without any interference from you; and the more you preach, the less persuasive you are.

When I want to preach, I write essays, put them up on a website, and let people scream at me (which they do).

When I want to tell stories, I lock the doors to keep the preacher out.

(And if you think it's a mixed metaphor to have a juggler suddenly become a preacher, well, you must not know much about preaching ... or juggling.)

CHAPTER THIRTEEN

SLASH & BURN: WHEN TO MAKE YOUR MANUSCRIPT BLEED

Tina Morgan

One of the best feelings in the world is typing two little words, "The End" after the last sentence of your manuscript. The sense of satisfaction and accomplishment is justifiably quite strong. Take a few moments, days, possibly weeks to bask in this feeling because once it's faded a bit, it's time to start editing and rewriting your work. This isn't a sarcastic comment, but a very real suggestion. The longer the work, the more time you should allow to pass before picking up that red pencil.

Editing can be the hardest aspect of writing especially if you've become too attached to the characters and world you've created, but the perfect story doesn't exist and you have to take a serious, critical look at your work if you want to polish it to a publishable level. Once you've given yourself a little time away from the work, go back over it with this checklist in mind:

Read it out loud

- Get a second opinion
- Mechanics: plot, setting, characterization, pacing, dialogue, point of view
- Check for consistencies
- Remove unnecessary words and subplots
- Read for active vs. passive voice
- Show don't tell
- Simplify
- Look for the obvious: spelling, grammar, and typographical mistakes
- Double check your formatting - both computer and manual
- Print it out
- Re-edit

READ IT ALOUD

This can be very difficult, especially if you don't like the sound of your own voice, but reading your words out loud can reveal a lot of flaws and even show you some of your work's strengths.

If you don't feel comfortable reading yourself, have a trusted friend or family member do it. Recording the reading is also helpful as you can listen and read the words at the same time. Reading aloud is a great way to study your sentence structure. Your pacing and rhythm becomes clearer. When I read out loud, I usually discover too many short sentences. My work sounds choppy. Rather like portions of this paragraph. After I read this to myself, it was difficult not to combine a few of the sentences. I left them to illustrate a point. Read the prior paragraph aloud to yourself and see if you come to the same conclusion.

GET A SECOND OPINION

Like any relationship in our lives, the one we build with our characters and worlds can be difficult for us to analyze. What we see as the problem may not actually be an issue to the reader. Unless you're working with a co-author, writing is a very solitary craft. If you're only writing for yourself, then the opinions of others aren't going to matter, but if you wish to improve your skills and/or seek publication, then asking someone else to read over your work is beneficial.

Having a friend or family member read for you can be risky in two ways. Many loved ones mistake the desire not to offend with being supportive. They'll tell us that they enjoyed the story even when they saw serious flaws. Depending on their level of education and reading experience, they may not understand how to offer a helpful critique, because they don't see the flaws. The other side of this problem is the person who has negative feelings about the writer's passion. Instead of offering a sincere opinion, they condemn the work for real and imagined flaws. What writers really need is a balanced view of our work. Someone who will be honest about the flaws they see and supportive enough to couch their critiques in diplomatic terms.

Workshops can be a great source of help. Finding a workshop/critique group that matches your current level of writing is crucial. Be realistic, if you're just starting to write fiction, then look for a group with other new writers. If you find that the group isn't as advanced as you need, look elsewhere and politely say your good-byes.

Workshops can be online or in person. You will need to try a few to find which method works best for you. If the workshop requires a certain number of critiques before you can submit, do those without complaint; critiquing other writers' work will help you learn to spot to flaws in your own writing. When you receive critiques on your work, remember that they're intended to help, not hinder. Be prepared for criticism (it's why you're there) and remember that if the workshop isn't working or if you're receiving flames instead of critiques, you don't have to stay... just don't trash the other members while you're there or while you're leaving. The science fiction industry is very small and close knit. Don't burn yourself in the heat of the moment.

Another alternative is to hire an editor. This can be a very costly alternative to workshops but if you feel your needs are not being met by the critique groups you've joined, then a professional editor may be beneficial. There are lots of editorial services advertised in the writing magazines and on the web. Be sure you check for credentials and experience. Has the editor actually been paid to edit science fiction in the past? If you're paying for services, then you want someone who actually knows the genre you're writing.

While taking a writing class doesn't always offer critique services, they are valuable to a new writer. You do not need a college degree in creative writing to get published, but creative writing courses can teach you a lot about the basics. Some courses will offer class critiques of shorter works and can help you understand where your weaknesses and strengths lie. As with editors, make certain the instructor is qualified to teach the class.

Attending workshops and classes for other genres can be interesting, but they won't always address the needs of a specific genre.

THE MECHANICS:

You can write the most beautiful prose in the world, but if the mechanics of your story are weak, then you've only done part of the job. However, whatever flaws you're dealing with, they can be fixed during this stage. This may take a serious amount of time, but it is well worth the effort. Let's break down the different areas into a more manageable size.

PLOT

Plotting problems can run one of two ways: not enough or too much. Have you ever seen an expanse of snow after children have played in it? The myriad of footprints is impossible to follow. If you have too many subplots in your story, it will read much like those tracks in the snow. Your plot can take a few twist and turns but when you reach the end of the story, the reader should be able to look back and see the path.

Subplots should advance the plot and add to your character development. Too often subplots are an excuse for the writer to go off on a tangent and spend time on a fantasy or exploring their favorite character. If during the course of your writing, you discover a character you like better than your protagonist or antagonist, that's fine... but save them for a story of their own. Also, make certain that your subplots are neatly wrapped up by the end of the story, with the exception of the subplot that will become the plot of your next novel in a series.

If you're writing a short story then you will need to limit your subplots to one, maybe two. A novella may be able to hold three if they're uncomplicated. There simply isn't time for a lot of subplots in a short work. Your plot must be clearer and more defined than a novel. A novel has a bit of time to roam; short stories must be concise.

Another plot issue is resolution. Is there a clear resolution? This can be trickier to determine if the issue you feel is the main conflict isn't the same as your reader would have chosen. If you've been focusing on Zana's growth from a scared young girl into a strong leader of her people, then the reader needs to understand that. If they think that the conflict was Zana's attempt to overthrow the government and you end the story with that conflict unresolved, then the reader is going to be very disappointed. This is one of those areas where a second opinion can tell you more than rereading the story yourself.

Make certain that your characters are facing real consequences. If the plot seems to have little effect on them and they're simply there for the ride, then the story isn't compelling enough.

SETTING

If you're creating a unique world and/or universe then how you handle your setting is going to be critical to your story's success. You have to balance what your reader needs to know with how much you would like to share. The description should transport your reader to that new world without becoming a scientific journal of the flora and fauna you've created.

Descriptions should be interspersed throughout the story. Much like your characters' background, descriptions should not come in large unpalatable chunks, but in easy to read and enjoyable snippets. Remember, the focus of your story is on either your characters or your plot.

Too little description is also a weakness. Did you use all five senses when describing your world? You don't have to use all of them in one paragraph, but using a variety will make your story more entertaining and interesting.

Your characters, their actions, and the time period should all agree. Science fiction is not restricted to near or distant future. It can be set in times past or in an alternative historical setting but if you do so, you will need to be even more cautious about how your characters and setting work together. Using current slang in an 1800s setting isn't going to work, nor will giving a Chinese woman in the Ming dynasty a 2006 attitude and view on life.

The order of events should remain consistent throughout the story. Technology must be developed in order (guns after gunpowder) and if your main character dyes her hair blue in chapter 7, it had better be blue in chapter 8 unless she's had time to change back.

CHARACTERIZATION

While my previous chapter highlighted how to create realistic characters, it never hurts to go over the basics and look for trouble spots when you're editing.

Your characters should feel "real" to you, but have you portrayed them that way throughout the story? Are they complex? Do they have a wide range of emotions, unique mannerisms, and speech patterns? Do they feel like stereotypes of other books you've read?

Are your characters consistent? Remember that blue hair dye? What about eye color? If you're going to describe your characters in detail, then those details shouldn't change unless you tell your reader why they've changed. A character with a disability on page one had better have that disability on every other page unless they're miraculously cured through intentional divine intervention or medical technology.

Here is an example of inconsistency: imagine an autistic character as a strong secondary character that later becomes the hero of the story. Unfortunately, at the end of the story, the young girl is doing things that weren't possible given her degree of disability and level of intelligence. She suddenly knows and understands things that there is no logical reason for her to comprehend. It is possible and even desirable to have a character change, but subtle improvements foreshadow the actions the character takes at the end of the story. Had this been done, then during the climax—if she did something she couldn't do before—the stage would have been set for that change. The reader would find it believable.

Change is crucial for your protagonist. If nothing truly happens to your character over the course of the story, then the reader is going to be wondering why he just spent several minutes, hours, or even days on your novel. If there's no change, then what is the purpose of the story? This change does not have to be a positive one. It can be bittersweet or even devastating. Many readers like a happy ending, but that's not crucial to a good story. A strong narrative progresses through a beginning, middle, and end, and that means that a conflict was resolved somewhere along the way (note: conflict does not equal violence or physical battle).

Did you give the characters' backgrounds in large lumps or small manageable pieces? Because we are setting up new worlds and societies, there is a risk amongst science fiction (and fantasy) writers to give long drawn out descriptions of our characters, societies, and worlds. These are often done in prologues that are nothing more than a history lesson and lend very little to the story. Slowly revealing your characters' background over the course of the story gives your reader time to become attached to them, to care about what happens. It becomes a journey of discovery for the reader.

Your antagonist should be more than a cardboard cutout or cartoon villain. Though for all the bad comments made about cartoon villains, many have a great deal of depth, if you take the time to read the original comics. Your antagonist shouldn't be defeated simply because your hero is the fair-haired boy (or girl) wonder. Thought and planning should go into their downfall.

PACING

Have you ever read a book that moved so slowly, you thought it would be more interesting to watch grass grow? Some storylines are not detailed enough to support a novel length work, no matter how hard the author tries to stretch it out. Throwing a bunch of subplots into a story that lacks a strong central narrative isn't going to solve the problem. It then becomes a jumbled mess that no one can figure out or wants to read. If your book is moving at the speed of the answer to your last submission to a major NY publisher, then you need to look at the storyline. Is there a way to increase the conflict and add tension so your reader actually wants to turn that next page?

What about the book that leaves you gasping for breath and wondering what the heck just happened? This is a serious risk for many writers, especially if they're like me and they enjoy big budget Hollywood movies. Many of these movies sacrifice plot and characterization for visual effects that leave us breathless. Keep it firmly in mind that books and movies are two vastly different mediums. This is why some books don't translate well to the big screen and some movies simply can't be written into an enjoyable novel. Compare any movie to the book it was based on. The book will have subplots that slow the story down. Characterizations that you can see within a few seconds on the screen will take a page or two to explain, especially if they're done well and spread throughout the text.

Many writers enjoy writing the action scenes, the ones where a major conflict is being resolved, but in a novel, chapters that develop subplots and characterization must divide these scenes. A story is more than just an adrenaline ride and subtle scenes need time to allow the reader to understand the nuances.

Pacing should also match the genre you're writing. Typically, science fiction will move faster than literary works. It can have elements of a melodrama, literary novel or even a love story, but it's not going to read like *Wuthering Heights*. You can write it that way if you wish, but odds are, fans of the genre aren't going to enjoy it.

Take a close look at your action (or other intense and crucial scenes). They should not read like "Space Wars for Dummies" or any other type of technical manual. Did you remember to throw in a little character development along the way? Is your hero wiping sweat out of his eyes or worried that his space suit's systems can't keep up with the perspiration and his visor may become fogged? Are her hands shaking over the weapons button or is she coolly focused? Don't forget to use all five senses during these scenes and if you have used them, do you need to remove a few observations to keep the action moving at the desired pace?

DIALOGUE

A common flaw you'll find in workshops is dialogue that's been bundled together with a paragraph that describes the actions of a different character. For example:

> John stopped to check the air quality on his suit before entering the airlock. "I'm worried about our air supply," Tim said. "Do you think we have enough?" John nodded as he shut the door behind them.

Who's Tim? Even though you might know who he is from the previous paragraph, you're reading about John and his thoughts, and all the sudden Tim interrupts? It confuses the reader and makes it difficult to follow the story. Make certain your dialogue placement, tags, and punctuation are correct.

Your dialogue should match your time frame and it must be consistent. Don't switch between two centuries of slang unless your characters are time traveling. Also, try to avoid clichés or heavy dialects. Dialect is difficult to write and rarely comes across the way you intend, especially if your reader isn't familiar with the dialect you're using.

If you analyze conversations you hear in real life, you'll notice that most people use a lot of sentence fragments. This isn't as effective in written dialogue. Use sentence fragments judiciously and get a second opinion on whether or not your dialogue is working for your readers.

Along with those fragments, watch for characters that ramble on to the point of boring your reader. You may have modeled your character after someone you know who has this trait but you don't need to go on for pages to illustrate your point. Having the characters around them react negatively to their rambling will say more than excessive dialogue. Avoid allowing your educated or knowledgeable character to give long-winded explanations on how the technology in your world works. Your reader really does not want a lesson in quantum physics. They want to know what's going to happen to the ship, the crew, and the world.

Does your dialogue match the conflict that's taking place between the characters? While it's true that sex sells, it adds nothing to your story to force your characters to have a sexually laden conversation if you're not including a love and/or sexual relationship between the two.

During the middle of a violent physical altercation is not the time to have your characters launch into an extensive philosophical debate. It's also not very believable that they're going to be talking excessively when they're fighting for their lives unless the conflict is primarily verbal and the physical fight is limited. After all, when you go to the gym are you talking while you're exercising strenuously? Most conversations are saved for before or after the work out.

Each character should have his or her own manner of speaking, just as you or I do. Some characters are going to have a limited vocabulary; others will use more complex and elaborate words. Some will speak very formally while others use more slang or profanity. Limiting the amount of profanity in your work is always a good idea. It's an easy thing to do and it's better not to offend your readers. Remember, the editor you submit your work to has to read it before he or she can decide if it should be accepted.

POINT OF VIEW

If you've finished your short story or novel and you find that it's too long for the word limit set by the publisher you wish to submit to, then one of the best ways to cut excessive wording is to check your point of view. If the story is told from more than one point of view then it is going to take more words to switch from one character to another. If your story is told from one POV then make certain to delete any information your POV character does not have access to. When my co-author and I finished our first novel, it was over 220,000 words. It rambled. Excessively. We rewrote the entire novel and while we used a multiple, limited, third-person POV, we made certain that each scene was in one character's POV all the way through. By ascertaining that all scenes with our protagonist were told through his eyes, we were able to shorten the novel to just over 150,000 words.

Much like my previous example of unwieldy dialogue structure, having a story jump from limited third to omniscient to first person or the rarely used second person makes it almost impossible to read. Make certain you're consistent throughout. While these errors are harmful to a long work, they're death to a short story. Mistakes made in POV in the last chapter of a 400-page novel will be forgiven more quickly than those made on page five of a seven page short story.

For those not familiar with the technical terminology, here is a quick definition of the different types of POV:

First person: The story is told from the POV of the storyteller: "I grabbed for my plasma rifle."

Second person: "You grab for your plasma rifle." This style is rarely used, though it is prevalent in "create your own adventure" type stories.

Third person omniscient: This is told from the viewpoint of many characters and is very difficult to do well. It's often referred to as 'head-hopping' if you move from character to character quickly: "Mary grabbed for her plasma rifle, hoping she would be in time to save her crew. John followed behind, his thoughts more on saving his own skin." (A rough example, but it illustrates how both characters' thoughts are written).

Third person limited: This is probably the most used in the genre. This style may use more than one character's POV but should be limited to one character per scene or chapter. When using a limited POV, you should not be showing what the other characters are thinking, though you can relay this to your reader through the characters' actions and dialogue: "Mary grabbed her plasma rifle, hoping she would be in time to save her crew. John followed behind at a slower speed. Mary glanced over her shoulder at his pale face. "Put the safety on that gun before you shoot me by accident!" she commanded."

When changing between character POVs in a shorter work, a scene break is often used instead of a chapter format. This gives the reader an indication that either a large amount of time has passed or that you're switching POVs. When you do this, you should identify the lead character quickly so the reader isn't thinking that they're still reading from the previous character's viewpoint.

CONSISTENCY AND REDUNDANCIES

Just as the mantra for valuing real estate is "location, location, location" the mantra for editing should be "consistency, consistency, consistency".

Whether it's in your technical details, descriptions, POV, or characterization, consistency is a must. If you've written yourself into a corner with your plot and the only way to resolve the problem is to bend the rules of your physical universe then you need to back up and rethink the situation. You can't change the rules mid-story. Your reader isn't going to accept it.

Characters shouldn't change eye or hair color unless they've put in colored contacts or dyed their hair. The gender of the animals used should remain the same; this is a common mistake in stories that include real animals such as horses. If you're not familiar with the correct terminology, learn it: ex: geldings are castrated males, stallions are not. You must maintain the same type of POV throughout and your space ship shouldn't change from a destroyer to a freighter midway through the story... unless you've docked at a spaceport for some extensive rebuilding.

Redundancies come in many forms. I have a bad habit of reusing the same word over and over again. Take this example that I edited out of my characterization chapter: *Despite the fact that you may be writing about a world far advanced from ours, you need to evaluate the need to have a race of super humans before you make everyone a genius.* My first reader made one comment about the sentence "I'm feeling needy." I changed the sentence.

Another way to shorten your word count is to pay careful attention to how many times you relay the same information to your reader. Only one character needs to point out that the ship is about to explode, it does not need to be restated by several characters. Saying it repeatedly will not add to the tension. Nor do you need to emphasis your conflict by having separate scenes with different characters point out the same problem. Make certain you're only telling the story once.

Each time you introduce a new character, you must take time developing him/her for your reader. This adds to your word count and complicates your story. Take a careful look at the minor characters in your work. Can you remove some of them? Can you combine some of their roles? Would the scene be stronger if one of your more important characters filled the role of some of the minor ones?

Subplots should move the story forward, not slow it down, or take it off in a new direction. If you have a subplot that you find interesting but it does nothing for the story you're telling, remove and save it. You may be able to work it into a novel or short story of its own.

By double-checking for redundancies, that 150,000k novel I mentioned at the start of the POV section became an 119,000k novel.

ACTIVE VS. PASSIVE VOICE

There are times when a sentence will have more impact if told through passive voice, but for the most part, your story will be stronger and more concise if you rephrase your work into active voice. Strunk & White's, *The Elements of Style* has some excellent examples of active vs. passive voice.

Which is stronger?

"The spaceship was buffeted by asteroids." or

"Asteroids buffeted the spaceship."

Using a more active style gives your voice power and typically makes your prose more direct and succinct.

SHOW DON'T TELL

Have you trusted your reader to understand your characters' emotions or are you leading them by the hand? Did you tell them? "John was scared." Or did you show them? "John followed behind at a slower pace. The muzzle of his rifle quivered in his shaking, sweating hands."

Did you tell them about your setting or did you allow them to experience it? "The land was arid and empty." "Sgt. Rabin shielded his eyes against the sun's glare. Sweat soaked his hair and the only sound he heard were the drops splattering against his leather vest."

If you do tell the reader something, make certain it's to the point. Don't tell us that "Mary started to pick up her plasma rifle", just have her do it. "Mary picked up her plasma rifle." Wishy-washy prose is annoying. If the sky is blue, then say so. Use a specific shade of blue if you wish, "The sky was a brilliant azure" not "the sky was a bright, shade of darker blue." Be specific.

SIMPLIFY

Keeping your plot clear and concise is critical to writing a short story. Avoiding plot twists that only confuse your reader and add nothing to the story is imperative. Just because you have 100,000 words for your novel doesn't mean you should fill that space with prose that doesn't propel your story forward.

Do you really need that flashback? Can you rearrange the order of the story so it takes place in chronological order?

Did you keep your descriptions strong and to the point? Did you use positives to describe your world? Using the word 'no' or 'not' makes your prose more convoluted. Look for these words and see if you can rewrite the sentence to tell us what 'is' instead of what 'isn't'.

Did you strip the extraneous sentences out of your dialogue? By keeping your dialogue on target, your story will be sharper and have a stronger, tighter feel.

SPELLING, GRAMMAR, & TYPOGRAPHICAL MISTAKES

One of the quickest ways to make certain your submission is rejected is to have a lot of spelling, grammatical or typographical errors. USE YOUR SPELLING AND GRAMMAR CHECKER. These programs are far from perfect but they do help. Too often I see poorly written submissions sent through workshops with the writer's warning before the story, "I'm not a good speller" as if that is supposed to make the participants want to sludge through 5 or 50 pages of spelling errors that make the prose difficult to read. Why would anyone want to decipher poor spelling when a spell checker can catch many of these mistakes?

Grammar styles vary so investing in a style manual can help you write a quality story. I mentioned *Elements of Style* because it's a short, simple, and easy to follow book, but there are others: *The Chicago Manual of Style* by the University of Chicago Press Staff, and *A Pocket Style Manual* by Diana Hacker are two.

As mentioned, spell checkers won't catch everything, especially if you've typed the wrong word. Homophones are a particular problem as they are pronounced the same but spelled differently: meet/meat, pear/pare/pair, here/hear, etc. If you know you have problems with words like these, then have someone read over your work with this in mind. Common typos also include incorrect words such as 'he' instead of 'she' or 'the'. While the word is missing letters, it's still a proper word so the spell checker won't catch it. Sometimes these mistakes will be caught by the grammar checker but not always.

It's easy to anticipate the words you intended to write. You know how you wanted the story to read, so your mind sees what should be there instead of what really is there. Taking time away from the story or switching to another format (writing long hand, computer screen, hard copy) can help you spot these errors.

FORMATTING

Again, consistency is an issue. If you use three asterisks as a scene break on the first page of your short story, don't switch to a pound sign or line on page three. Make certain your margins are the same throughout the story. Line spacing should not vary. If you start out single spacing with double spaces between paragraphs then maintain that style. Double-check the guidelines for the magazine or novel publisher you wish to submit to and format your story to meet their requirements. If you were taught to double space at the end of a sentence, make certain that this won't cause a serious formatting problem with your emailed or electronic format submission.

Are your page numbers correct? Did you use the proper heading on each page? Did you set a hard page break between chapters?

Don't trust your computer screen to show you how your story will look when you print it.

PRINT IT OUT

While your story or article may look perfect on your monitor, when you print it out, some of the formatting may fall apart. If you forget to set a hard page break at the end of your chapters then there's a good chance that your spacing will be messed up when you print. Simply tabbing down to the next page won't guarantee the proper spacing, the same with soft tabs. Format your work with hard indents so your paragraphs are consistent.

It is often easier to catch mistakes such as these on hard copy than it is on a glowing computer screen. Computer screens cause eyestrain quicker than paper so most readers will scan through a story faster on the computer than they will on hard copy.

RE-EDIT

When you think you've finished your rewrite, put the story away for a few days. Then read it again and be prepared to fix problems you may have missed the first time around. While you're doing this, take time to notice the improvements you've made. Doesn't the story read better this time? Are there sections you like more than others? Places where the story flows better than others? Can you find a way to make the rest of the story read as well?

CONCLUSION

Don't be afraid to cut sections out of your novel or short story. It's easy to become attached to the characters and world we've spent so much time creating, but a story doesn't always need the number of characters we've included. Taking these extras out doesn't mean you have to lose them. You can place the deleted prose in a file for later use. Characters, settings, and dialogue can be recycled, rewritten, and reused in other stories.

Keep in mind that some writers are easily influenced by other authors. Be honest as you reread your story. Are you trying to mimic another writer's style? Wouldn't your story be more distinctly yours if it were written in your voice?

Editing and rewriting may not be as fun as the initial creative process but when you're finished and you've had a chance to read the edited work again, the results may surprise and delight you.

PART IV
SPECIALIZING

CHAPTER FOURTEEN

LAUGH LINES

Bud Sparhawk

Of all the difficulties facing the writer, perhaps deliberately writing something to amuse or at least bring a laugh to the reader presents the most daunting challenge. Everyone's sense of humor differs and, as many of us learn the hard way, not everyone can successfully tell a joke.

But writing something humorous shouldn't be as difficult as being a stand-up comic. This is not to say that humor shouldn't be approached as a serious business for the writer, regardless of how difficult it seems to be. Most often, such difficulty comes either from a lack of understanding of the structure of humor or an appreciation of the rules governing it.

As a matter of fact, by following a few simple rules, you can significantly increase the chance that the amusing parts of that last submission have some chance of tickling a reader's, or more importantly, an editor's, funny bone.

Before we talk about the rules, let's examine where humor fits into the greater scheme of writing. Humor occupies a strange place within genre writing. By and large, it is terribly unappreciated, considering the amount of writing effort it takes to produce it. Humor is hard to conceive, tougher to write, and an absolute dogs-mother to edit.

Too many readers, and nearly all critics, think of anything humorous that appears in fiction is lightweight, done without thought, and of little or no consequence. Nobody's gotten serious literary awards for their humor (awards for humor are another matter entirely.) As Esther Friesner, a winner of two Nebula awards once said:

> "One of the hardest rows to hoe in the SF/Fantasy fields...is that of the humorist. No one takes funny stuff seriously, or at least seriously enough to award a piece of humorous SF/F the kudo of a Nebula or Hugo... When it comes to humor we read, we laugh, [but] we don't give it a second thought."[105]

Despite this perception, professional writers often write humor into their work, even when the entire piece is far from being humorous.

Humor is sometimes difficult to write because, in addition to requiring an understanding of human behavior, it also requires that you be able to twist a situation to simultaneously make a point, highlight a characteristic, or change a setting while eliciting laughter, or at least a smile, from the reader.

Any hack writer can make a reader cry by scribbling about a dying dog, starving child, or some other tragedy, but it takes an outstanding effort to write about these and make everyone laugh.

Let's start this article with a little background. Humor can arise from any situation, be a play on words, or result from some contrived mechanism. Most often, the way the writer gets a humorous point across is through a *joke*.

RULE: EVERY JOKE HAS A BASIC STRUCTURE CONSISTING OF A SET-UP OR PREMISE, AN EXPOSITION, AND A PUNCH LINE

The premise is the humorous foundation of the joke. It can be a natural part of the story line or simply be a situation, character, or plot device introduced to highlight some aspect of the story. The premise itself need not be humorous.

> A man walks into a bar and orders a pint of beer. He takes his first sip and sets it down. While he is looking around the bar, a monkey swings down and steals the pint of beer before he is able to stop it.

The next part of a joke's structure is the exposition. This usually expands on the premise and develops it for the reader, often introducing more complexity, to establish the context of the joke.

> The man asks the bartender who owns the monkey. The bartender replies that it belongs to the piano player.

Once the concept of the premise has become thoroughly developed for the reader, the writer has to create an epiphany where the various parts of the premise and the exposition are brought together to prepare the reader for some resolution.

> So, the man walks over to the piano player and says, "Do you know your monkey stole my beer."

Usually, but not always, the resolution of the exposition should be unexpected—perhaps offering the reader a different understanding than they were led to expect.

The punch line is the point of the entire effort and is most effective when it is short, on target, and, if the writer writes it to be sufficiently mind-altering, ensures that whatever the reader was drinking comes out through their nose.

> The pianist replies "No, but hum a few bars and I'll fake it.

The humor in the above well-structured example arises from simply making a connection among the exposition's elements, all of which were present from the outset, but twisting them in an unexpected way on the punch line.

A reader sometimes laughs when they can intellectually sneer at the poor protagonist who has gotten his butt in the wringer in ways that maybe could never happen to them. Perhaps this is one reason that humor is treated so lightly—the readers are never quite certain of when the joke is going to turn on them.

Stories where the joke's premise itself tickles the funny bone are usually the most memorable and funniest. These stories read even better when they also make a nice point - preferably one sharp enough to pierce some pretension.

RULE: DISCOVER A SOURCE FOR YOUR HUMOR

Each writer must find for themselves a source for their humor and a method of reaching that source. This could be a mood, certain music, or, since there has never been a *new* joke, simply borrowing another humorist's material.

You may find that your personal outlook affects how you deal with humor. You may find that writing humor comes easier when you are depressed, perhaps because only then do you fully appreciate the futility of taking anything you write too seriously.- More frequently, the humor of a situation simply bubbles up from the unconscious as you merrily go along writing the narrative or dialogue. Sometimes the resulting humor is pertinent to the story, but often, it is not. Occasionally, and too infrequently, a bit of improvisation seizes the piece and, despite your original intention, twists it to something more amusing than you intended.

Aside from mood, another important aspect of humor for most writers is to discover something at which or with which to poke fun. Fortunately, the science fiction and fantasy genre contains sufficient fodder for an endless stream, nay, a virtual river of sources for humor. The genre is replete with tropes, clichés, and settings beyond imagining. Over the last century, the field has accumulated warehouses overflowing with concepts, conceits, and situations strange, fantastic, and oft-times patently ridiculous.

But beyond the settings and ideas, the science fiction and fantasy genres have also salted their stories with a rich vein of bizarre characters and creatures. These stories are replete with virtual stockyards of unique and stereotypical beasts, armies of aliens in every size, configuration, and color, mutants horrid and sympathetic, animals appendage-rich, strong and weak, and capable of every act imaginable. Then there are the characters themselves. In fact, our genre has generated far more than its fair share of bizarre personalities, both fictional and live.

There are no limits to the places from which humor can be harvested. From our genre's fictional multiverse of worlds, those fields of endless novelty, it would be difficult not to harvest the grain that could be grist for the writer's mill.

But sources and mood by themselves are not sufficient for introducing funny material into your writing. The manner through which you inject humor into your work is equally as important as the way you use your sources. In other words, we need to talk about how to jog the reader's brain in a way that will simultaneously surprise them while relating it to the story.

To illustrate some of the rules, let's quote from Sam Boone:

"Front to Back to show how the rules can be employed."[106]

RULE: THE HUMOR SHOULD BE RELEVANT TO THE STORY

Humor can't exist in a vacuum. It must arise from the story in a natural way and become integral to development of the larger story and therefore acceptable to the reader.

In general, you cannot get by with simply reeling off an endless run of jokes unless you are writing a joke book. The only writer who has successfully pulled this off is Spider Robinson in his series on Callahan's bar.

The best humor grows naturally out of the characters and situation that you have so skillfully (or not so skillfully) created. It need not even be a large part of the story. It could be a mere decoration to the plot, an ornament to the piece rather than essential to the story's architecture.

Descriptive adjectives or analogies interspersed in the narrative flow can be used to bring out the precise mental image you want to create in the reader's mind.[107]

> As the door slid shut behind him, he took a deep breath of relatively fresh air to clear his nasal passages of the alien's stench. As soon as he had his respiration under control he reflected on the situation. There was no way he could tolerate sharing a cabin with a creature that was more offensive than a campsite full of bean-fed boy scouts.

On the other hand, a reader might laugh when something completely incongruous is introduced, a surprise element that pulls their mind out of its comfortable rut. In the following example, the reader is expecting a rather straightforward description of bizarre alien shopping only to realize at the end that that alien appears all too human:[108]

> Most of the other aliens he had taken on tour appeared puzzled by nearly everything human—'part of the charm,' a fifteen-segmented worm in a fuchsia environment suit had remarked casually as it purchased a ceramic urinal in a hardware store and perched it rakishly on its head with one of its antennae sticking through the drain hole.
>
> "Isn't it just me!" it preened.

RULE: HUMOR MUST BE GROUNDED IN SOMETHING FAMILIAR TO BOTH THE READER AND THE WRITER

One of the worse sins a writer can commit is forcing humor into a situation where it does not belong or bringing up something about which the reader has no knowledge. Doing either of these painfully wrenches the reader's mind out of their state of shared belief in the story itself.

At the same time, introducing something that might not be familiar to all readers is quite acceptable, providing that it is otherwise amusing as well. There is a well-followed tradition in SF/F of Tucker-ising, which is (mis)using the names of well-known individuals in stories.

My Sam Boone stories in *Analog*, in addition to being rife with Tuckerisms, were all grounded on the shared, hard SF conceit that there may very well be a vastly superior galactic civilization in the universe that will some day discover us (or vice versa if they are unlucky.)

> Aliens came from throughout the galaxy to see the wondrous sights that Earth had to offer, places incomparable to any other in the civilized Universe: Disneyland, Hoboken, and Kawasaki's Sushi n Ribs were the most sought after sights, although, it was reported by some of Earth's returning traders, many of the Galactics were not keen on their young being exposed to such bad art, gross pornography, and wasteful pleasures as the three attractions. Which of the three had which attribute was still being argued extensively throughout the globe as most of the visitors were unwilling to discuss the matter.
>
> Some even blushed.

RULE: HUMOR MUST BE INTEGRAL TO THE NARRATIVE STREAM OF THE STORY IF IT IS TO BE EFFECTIVE

It is important to thread the humor through the narrative so that it is integral to the narrative and relevant to the theme or plot. Sometimes relating something amusing about an interesting event occurring off stage is sufficient to add humor to the story. Humorous development of a facet of a protagonist's personality, or any of the other characters, can be used to good effect as humor.

In the following example, Sam is dealing with some creatures that inhabit a planet orbiting incredibly close to a star.

> He tried to picture Lattice 512 and his buddies going to the edge of a sea of boiling iron, spreading out their plasmoid blankets and getting a nice rosy glow to their plasma shell when the temperatures were right. Could be a great market for sunscreen, he guessed. But, of course, it would have to have an SPF of forty billion or more, he mused.[109]

RULE: DON'T TRY TO EXPLAIN WHY SOMETHING IS FUNNY

As anyone who has ever attempted to talk about humor or explain a joke will attest, explaining takes all the fun out of it. For anyone not acquainted with science, the humor of the aforementioned extract would be completely lost if you had to explain what many of the terms, or even SPF, meant. It is far, far better (and more rewarding) when the readers figure out the jokes for themselves.

RULE: USE THE HUMOR OF THE SITUATION TO HIGHLIGHT A DRAMATIC TURNING POINT

Humor can be used to highlight an emotional high point in the story. Hollywood frequently uses this device to set the audience up for an emotional belly punch by having them laugh just a few seconds before something significant or tragic occurs.

The clumsy, acrobatic, frantic, and fumbling antics of a drunk of a ledge might be amusing to watch, but only up to the point that he plunges a hundred feet to the ground and certain death. It is the disparity between these conflicting emotions that gives the latter more "punch" than it otherwise would convey.

Conversely, humor can be applied to soften a dramatic situation, helping the reader gain a measure of emotional distance. The best examples of this can be seen most obviously in the spate of "jokes" that immediately follow every disaster.

RULE: DON'T RESTRICT YOUR HUMOR TO NARRATIVE

Using dialogue to develop a joke can work equally as well as contriving a situation. A colorful combination of the two might work even better, such that this adds more color to the humorous palette used to paint the picture in the reader's mind.[110]

"What is the problem with you," Sam asked.

"It's the change," Town [a two-foot high, tree-like alien] replied, "I'm in the early stages of what you would call adolescence. I will soon be mature."

"So you'll be able to vote?" Sam suggested nervously, not sure of what rights and privileges an adult alien enjoyed.

"Much more than that," Town replied with an azure dribble of spit. "I'll be allowed to breed." "And that is why I need your help," she said shyly

Sam was unsure of how he could help her. Although he liked her well enough, their physical incompatibilities alone would—

"I need some of father's money," Town went on, ignoring Sam's squirming discomfiture.

RULE: DON'T LET HUMOR STAND ALONE— BUILD ON WHAT HAS GONE BEFORE

Sometimes a joke can be nothing more than the simple repetition of some otherwise slightly amusing action or statement. Humor builds on itself, each joke making the reader more receptive to laughing at the next. As anyone who has attended a joke-telling session can attest, the standard for eliciting laughter drops lower with each successive joke. A joke that would ordinarily fall flat can seem outrageously funny when it follows a series of other, more humorous ones. It is as if with each laugh we set ourselves up to be amused further, jiggling those endorphins a little more each time.

> A musician was practicing his hot licks on the saxophone when there was a knock at his door.
>
> "Do you know it's three o'clock in the morning," his irate neighbor asks.
>
> "No," replies the musician as he lifts his instrument to his lips, "but hum a few bars and I'll improvise."

For the writer this means to put your weakest jokes after the better ones and thereby intensify the humor.

Keep in mind that you should always try to find new ways to express the thought each time it appears; a joke quickly loses its flavor with successive, unvarying retelling.

RULE: USE HUMOR AS AN AMUSING INTERRUPTION TO THE NARRATIVE AND MOMENTARILY DISTRACT THE READER OR PUT THEM AT EASE

In all cases, the funny bits should derive from something already a part of the narrative or dialogue. Even though an incongruous introduction might amuse the reader, you should not abandon logic and simply throw something in as a surprise. Instead, you should include something more true to the story, such as having a character momentarily out of character and becoming embarrassed, or a comedic misunderstanding between the protagonists. Better yet, let the reader think they are going in one direction, but suddenly take them to a far different place.

> One of Earth's big mysteries was why the Galactics chose to establish their base in Trenton when the capitals of the world –London, Washington, Paris, Moscow, Beijing, Capetown, et al—had offered their very souls for the opportunity. Brill, Mardnn's daughter, had confided in an embarrassed hush that Sam was not to reveal it if he treasured his job. "We put it in Trenton," she said, "because it is so convenient to Hoboken."

RULE: USE AMUSING, EVEN INAPPROPRIATE WORDS

As an old vaudevillian once said "Cabbage is dull, but rutabaga is funny." Why is that statement itself amusing? Is it the sound of the words themselves that impart humor to the statement or the ridiculousness of the statement itself? Had the old vaudevillian said the same about apples and oranges it would have neither the humor nor could we make the sense of the statement. Why is Hoboken funny and New York is not? It is the words themselves, their sound, that makes it amusing.

In the quote below, the names of the aliens and their races were deliberately chosen to both to sound funny and to relate to their ordinary meanings.[111]

> Offal/taint of mustard, as leader of the Scrofulousans, would always wait until

Fluthth was finished before clicking her mandibles and squirting the haze of chemical mist that explained the Scofulousan point of view. The windy flatulence of the Mephitisite delegation, combined with the odors produced by the Scrofulousans, usually left the negotiation room smelling like an explosion in a fart factory.

If that type of foolish word play doesn't work for you, perhaps using an apt metaphor or simile, but dissonant to the reader might give rise to amusement. Liking a man's nose to a rutabaga might cause the reader to reflect and then laugh at the image it engenders. Or perhaps if your alien creature acts in a too familiar manner might work better.

Word play is the writer's curse and it is difficult to remove puns and alliterative elements from a story once they begin to appear. It is almost as if the writing mind seizes on this form of mild compulsion and cannot, or will not, relinquish its hold. Pratchett's *Discworld* and Aspirin's *Myth* series of books illustrate where this compulsion has taken firm hold, much to the amusement of their fans and the benefit of their popularity.

Another relative in the humorist's family is satire, the accepted child of humor, parody, its embarrassing uncle, irony, the bittersweet nephew, and lampoon, the cousin we try to hide in the basement whenever company comes to call. The role of all these is to poke fun at a significant issue without mentioning the issue itself.

The key to using these tools is to leave enough truth and clues to insure that the jibe will be missed. As an example, a description of pigs feeding at the trough might be ordinarily descriptive, but, if you write that the pigs are named for various states, it is perhaps an observation on the behavior of certain politicians.

Satire, parody, irony, and even the broad humor of a lampoon need to be written with great care, especially where the reader is likely to be the brunt of the joke. If this is done clumsily, it will certainly anger or alienate the reader enough to make them stop reading, or at least turn a deaf ear to whatever point you are trying to make. However, when written well, any of these can be used to convey some observation or truth the reader has not been aware of (or, at least, keep their attention long enough for you to make your point.)

RULE: THE MORE COMPLEX THE SETUP, THE MORE REWARDING IS THE PUNCH LINE

A joke's structure by itself is not sufficient to convey something humorous; it must be developed to heighten the impact of the punch line. You have to craft an effective piece of work by ensuring that you use the appropriate words and employs them in the service of the story as well as the joke.

P.G. Wodehouse was a past master of the complex set-up. This allowed the reader to feel superior as he watched Bertie Wooster, or one of the other myriad characters that populated his universe, squirm through some highly contrived situation. It was the sheer inappropriateness of each character's reaction that delivered the humor, even though the description was quite straightforward.

An interesting corollary is that the more complex you build the comedic situation, the more complex the humor becomes, and, the more amusing the punch line.

RULE: LET THE SITUATION EVOLVE FROM THE VIEWPOINTS OF THE CHARACTERS

Situational humor is always effective, especially where the protagonist misunderstands or fails to appreciate the situation. While everything is completely rational, the result for the reader becomes comical. The following is what happens after Sam's agent has put a number of schemes over on him. Sam thinks that he has gotten the better of her this time when she gives him a new assignment.[112]

> In the distance he heard the [spaceship's] great hatches close to signal their departure. But Sam didn't care. He had finally gotten the best of [his agent] Ahbbbb. There was no way she was going to screw him this time. This was one fine suite, indeed.
>
> Now, he wondered as he turned the pages of the [intergalactic] guide, where the hell was this Andromeda place, anyway?

RULE: USE MISDIRECTION

You shouldn't be too obvious about any single part of what you are trying to do. In fact, the best humor works when the reader doesn't realize where the setup, exposition, and epiphany are leading until you deliver the coup de grace in a brilliant and effortless statement (effortless on the reader's part, that is—as stated earlier, writing humor is hard work!)

RULE: BUT DON'T BE OBVIOUS.

Sometimes the reader should be led to expect a joke, but not necessarily the one they expected. This technique allows anticipation to build and suddenly spring the punch line from ambush. In this way, the reader is not disappointed, since he has anticipated a joke, but is nevertheless surprised at the novelty twist.

If you are too clever by half, you can slip the joke in so subtly that the reader initially passes it by, pauses, and then re-reads the passage slowly to see if that really was what they thought it said.[113]

> Sam tried to imagine the effect of the teacups tossing the diminutive [aliens] over the heads of the merry crowd, and maybe splattering a few against the walls of the nearby Capt'n Cook's Samoan Restaurant. "I doubt it," he answered.

Of course, in the above sample about Sam's adventures in a place like Disneyland, I had to assume that the reader knew something about the ill-fated captain and the carbohydrate-free dietary habits of the Samoans.

RULE: DON'T RUSH, NOR HOLD BACK, A JOKE'S DEVELOPMENT

Pacing is an important aspect. Moving from premise to the punch line too quickly can seriously reduce a joke's impact. On the other hand, taking too long and drawing the situation out can spoil the fun. Going from premise to punch line logically often appears more humorous than it otherwise would be. Then, too, the more the punch line deviates from the obvious reality or logic it follows the funnier it will seem.

Of course, simply settling on a basic idea isn't enough: you must figure out a way of making your idea appeal to the reader. Perhaps you can devise a way of twisting some trite and commonplace concept into something a little off-center.

The writer always has the option of choosing to present a joke directly, peripherally, or sneak up on the reader from behind. For example: what if the idea of supposedly superior aliens was simultaneously very human?[114]

> A purple thing resembling a cow with poetic aspirations descended the ramp and trotted past. It was dragging a bluish angular creature with what appeared to be four or five heads, all of which were yipping excitedly, at the end of a silver leash.

RULE: TORTURED HUMOR ALMOST NEVER WORKS

Instead of forcing the characters into lock-step performance of their assigned roles, the writer should try to have fun with them and give them a life. The characters in a story, although they might be imaginary constructs, should also be shown to be human enough to extract a bit of joy from whatever dire straits the writer makes them face. Thumbing one's nose at adversity is always a trick that works.

RULE: EXAGGERATING OUTRAGEOUSLY MAKES IT FUNNIER

Exaggeration is a simple but effective way to put a humorous spin on the narrative and, coupled with an insight, can be made doubly funny. In the following example, Sam observes a snotty hotel clerk's reaction to news that the aliens are his new bosses.[115]

> [The clerk's]...face turned red, followed in quick progression by purple, and finally settled on a slightly rosy shade of white as he read the paper that emerged from one end of the container.

> "What the hell?" Sam asked as he admired the ability of the clerk to alter his coloration with such speed. It was a trait he'd not suspected any member of the human race of possessing.

RULE: DON'T PATRONIZE THE READER

Whenever the writer employs humor, they must always be aware of the fine line between amusement at their character's discomfort and making an assault on the reader's beliefs or opinions.

To be perfectly honest, much of what appeals to the reader's sense of humor will rely upon the banana peel syndrome—"better him than me!" At the same time, the writer must always leave enough truth in the humor to make the reader slightly, even subconsciously, uncomfortable—as if they can imagine themselves in this same situation, or being the butt of the joke. Of course, you need not pay any attention at all to any of the previous rules to artificially concoct a joke. In many cases, the situation itself will supply the material you need to develop the humor.

RULE: THE HUMOR MUST NEVER BE AIMED DIRECTLY AT THE READER, BUT SLIGHTLY OFF CENTER

Actions themselves can be amusing and often work well in this regard, such as when you describe a character slipping on a banana peel. The slipping of the action could be physical (missing a handhold or evoking a banana instead of a djinn) or virtual (failing to recognize the king, speaking the unspeakable word). In the latter case, the actions of the characters are the source of amusement.

RULE: THE WRITER SHOULD GRANT HIMSELF OR HERSELF PERMISSION TO PURSUE THE RIDICULOUS WHEN THE OPPORTUNITY PRESENTS ITSELF

Sometimes you have to be willing to put down in black and white something that would otherwise embarrass you. Dignity is for those people who get more than pennies per word, wear tweed, and have words like "insightful" appear on the flyleaf.

In order to be truly funny, the writer has to be less guarded in their thought processes. They shouldn't let their mental editor shut something out when it screams for admission. Whenever something humorous crosses your mind you should try to go with the flow and see where it takes you. Anything written this way will usually appear less stilted, more natural, and less contrived than otherwise.

One of the joys of being a writer is that you can always edit things out in your later drafts. No one will think you a clown for what you do in the privacy of your earlier drafts so have fun with it, act like a bozo, a clown, or the fool dancing before the king. If you have fun with what you are writing, then the chances are that the editor and readers will enjoy it as well.

Surprise is a strong part of humor and this can hold true for the writer as well as the reader. Writing humor sometimes means getting rid of mental limitations and letting your thoughts go where they may.

RULE: BE TRUE TO YOURSELF

Rather than be embarrassed by whatever creeps into their work, the writer should understand that no matter how much they might wish to disguise it, it is their own voice that makes their characters act as they do. A writer's words always come from their basic attitudes and beliefs, no matter how much they might torture them to seem otherwise. This is as true of their humor as it is of anything else they write.

RULE: HAVE FUN WITH YOUR WRITING

Regardless of the path to discovering your inner jester, the writer should always try to be true to himself or herself. They should let the forms their humor takes reflect their own attitudes, their own beliefs.

When used properly, humor can be an effective tool in the writer's arsenal, whether they are writing comedy or tragedy, fantasy, science fiction, crime, or even romance.

RULE: IGNORE ANY RULE THAT DRAINS THE HUMOR FROM YOUR WRITING

The worse part of writing humor is that nobody appreciates the hard work of the craft. The best part of writing humor is that everyone appreciates a bit of amusement now and then. Knowing this in advance frees you from any pretension that you are crafting undying prose, releases you from the mundane cares of the world, cures dandruff, acne, and improves one's sex life profoundly.

Despite the lack of critical acclaim, humorous fiction is very well accepted by editors and readers. Humorous stories are very much in demand in the magazine markets as well because they seem to have a broad appeal to readers. More importantly, humorous novels seem to stay on the shelf longer than more weighty tomes.

Stan Schmidt, editor of *Analog SF/F* for the past two decades, once advised that, although humor wouldn't bring either critical acclaim nor win awards, it is vitally necessary. "People always need to smile" were the words he used, which illustrates a very nice point, at least for us writers.

CHAPTER FIFTEEN

GOING WHERE OTHERS HAVE
GONE BEFORE...
AND WANT TO GO AGAIN
(FAN FICTION)

Carol Hightshoe

Storytelling is a tradition that goes back many centuries. It is one of the ways that we recount events, illustrate moral behavior, and entertain. We have been telling and retelling stories since verbal communication began.

Along with original stories, there is another form of storytelling—fan fiction, where the storyteller borrows the characters and world of another to tell their own stories.

As stories became more complex, storytellers began borrowing elements from each other. Some early examples of possible fan fiction include the Arthurian legends. Early tales of King Arthur did not include Lancelot, whom the Normans added when they began retelling the legends. In 1421, John Lydgate wrote *The Siege of Thebes* as a continuation of Chaucer's *Canterbury Tales*. In the mid 1800s to early 1900s, Lewis Carroll's works became the subject of parodies as well as fan fiction as fans rewrote them with alternate endings. It was the introduction of the mimeograph in 1887, which would eventually allow fans to produce and distribute their own magazines.

For our purposes, fan fiction will be defined as: The use of a particular universe and/or set of characters, by someone other than the original creator to tell their own stories. In many cases, this use occurs without the permission of the original creator. Note: this can sometimes even include authorized shared-world anthologies such as *Thieves World, Strange New Worlds*, the *Darkover Anthologies*, etc. even though they are written with a specific set of guidelines and under the direction of the rights-holder.

While fan fiction has been around almost as long as we have been telling and retelling stories, it was in the late 1960s and early 1970s when the story form erupted. The television show Star Trek created a phenomenon that continued to grow as the syndicated reruns drew in more and more fans. Eventually these fans gave birth to a subculture, which grew and soon embraced more than just the single series that helped to spawn it—modern fan fiction was born.

Distribution of fan fiction was originally limited to small fan produced magazines or fanzines. In recent years, the Internet has opened a new world for writers of fan fiction. Web sites like FanFiction.net provide places for you to post your work so others can read and comment on it. There are sections dedicated to anime, games, books, movies, cartoons, comics, and TV. If there are fans—there is probably fan fiction about it.

Even though fan fiction did not start blossoming until after the cancellation of *Star Trek* in 1969, fans began writing stories as early as 1967 in the first *Trek* fanzine: Spockanalia. Fans of the television show *Man From U.N.C.L.E.* also began writing and distributing their own stories in 1967. However, instead of publishing and distributing a regular fanzine, as the *Trek* fans were doing, they passed their stories along by hand.

Organization is what allowed Trek fans to move to the forefront of fan fiction. While some may argue whether *Star Trek* is the parent of modern fan fiction, its widespread growth and the diversity of its fans across the globe is why it is often associated with the beginnings of modern fan fiction.

Eventually, other television shows, movies, books, games, etc. began to see the same type of behavior in their fans. Today, if you do a quick Internet search for "fan fiction," you will get over three million sites listed. The popularity of fan fiction continues to grow, and has spread beyond the realm of science fiction.

Still, fan fiction seems firmly seated in the science fiction and fantasy genres as just a casual search turns up numerous sites dedicated to *Babylon Five, Star Trek, Star Wars, Dark Angel, Dr. Who* and a host of others. If you have a favorite world you like to visit, you can search for pages dedicated to it specifically—odds are you will find several.

I WANT TO PLAY TOO

The world of make-believe is a place most of us visit regularly as children. For some, we continue to visit as young adults and even as adults. Often things we are already familiar with inspire our imaginations. How many times when you were playing "cowboys and indians" or "cops and robbers" were you actually acting out scenes from books you had read, movies or TV shows you had watched?

From this simple stimulation of our imaginations, many of us eventually grow to love another person's imaginary world so much we want to play in it more directly. It is this desire that leads to writing fan fiction. You know the characters and the world, now you want a chance to tell your stories about them. This is probably the purist form of fan fiction. It is written in order to be able to share in that universe and to tell stories about the characters you love. Sometimes it is written so you can continue to visit a favorite place that is no longer accessible through other books or media. It is because this place and these characters are such dear friends that you return time and time again. You wonder what happened to them after they originally left and therefore you have decided to tell those stories.

Fan fiction also offers a way to learn and practice the craft of writing. You do not have to engage in the lengthy process of world building or character creation. You have a ready-made world with developed characters to write about. With the initial creative work done you can concentrate on telling the story.

There are those who say authors have a god complex—particularly those who write in the science fiction and fantasy realms. With their words, they create new worlds then populate them with various creatures and people. If those who create these universes can be compared to gods then those who write fan fiction might be considered demigods. Even though you do not create the worlds or the characters, you do play with them and put them into situations they must deal with. Those who are trying to achieve a little higher status are those who attempt to create within that universe—trying to leave their own personal stamp as it were: These are the writers of the Mary Sue, Slash, and Alternate Universe stories.

I WANT TO BE THE HERO (MARY SUE / GARY STU)

Just as there are different sub-genres in science fiction, there also are in fan fiction. For many of us the lure of fan fiction is indeed to tell the stories we would like to see or read. There are also those who want the chance to put themselves into the story. This has led to the sub-genre of fan fiction called Mary Sue stories.

Mary Sue stories, first identified by Paula Smith in 1973, primarily involve a character who is an idealized version of the author. This character is almost too perfect, everyone around him or her loves and respects them and they turn out to be the only person who can save the day. They will often have a romantic liaison with one or more of the other primary characters in the story. Their name is usually a play on, if not a copy of, the author's or they share other traits in common with the author.

The Mary Sue story is a definite carry-over from our childhood. If you are writing a Mary Sue story, you are saying you want to be the hero.

Most fan fiction that introduces a new character contains an element of wish fulfillment in it. Therefore, there is a bit of Mary Sue or her male counterpart Gary Stu in almost all fan fiction. Some would say there is a bit of them in all fiction. The problem with this sub-genre occurs when we have put so much of ourselves into the story that our character overshadows the ones who actually belong there. A Mary Sue character can easily become unbelievable to the reader if she is too perfect. To be believable, a character has to have flaws and make mistakes. A Mary Sue character does not normally, or if she does, she still turns out to be the only person who can fix the problem she created; not because fate demands she fix her mistake, but because she is the only one capable of doing so.

If you search for Mary Sue by name on the Internet, you will find sites devoted to explaining whom she is, ones that post author acknowledged Mary Sue stories, as well as the Mary Sue Society. In addition to running a webring for those who admit their characters are Mary Sues, the Mary Sue Society supports the idea that most fictional characters have Mary Sue roots.

According to their website <http://www.subreality.com/marysue.htm>:

> I've simply decided that there's no shame in admitting to having a Mary Sue (or, to use nicer term, an avatar), as long as you don't expect the world to hail his/her adventures with unbridled enthusiasm. Mary Sues serve a psychological need: they make their creators happy. And, sometimes, wonderful original characters have Mary Sue roots, way back in the misty morn of his/her writer's imagination.

HE LOVES HIM / SHE LOVES HER NOT (SLASH)

The sub-genre of slash fan fiction grew out of adult fan fiction. Called slash fiction for the use of a "/" to denote romantic relationships in the story, it was initially seen as being primarily homosexual in nature: i.e. K/S to denote a story involving Kirk and Spock in a romantic/sexual relationship. There are writers today who use the same shorthand to denote any pairings that take place within their story whether they are male/male, male/female, or female/female. Slash fiction is the sub-genre that perhaps creates the most controversy among fans.

Many fans want the characters to remain true to the restraints put upon them by their creators. They see fan fiction as a way of paying homage as well as a chance to play in a favorite imaginary world. These fans do not react well to seeing their favorite characters doing things that do not ring true with their perceptions of the characters' personalities.

Other fans enjoy using the characters and world setting to explore new ideas and themes. To them the speculative fiction idea of "what if" opens up new realms of possibility to explore. "What if" two of the main characters in the story were gay? How would that affect the relationship they had in the series? "What if" a love interest developed between characters? How far would it go?

In 1981, the Director of the Official *Star Wars* Fan Club sent several of the Star Wars fanzines letters giving them guidelines for publishing Star Wars fan fiction. Included in those letters was a restriction against pornography as well as a warning that they would take legal action if the guidelines were not followed. A few months after the original letters went out they sent another one, reminding fanzines about the guidelines. This time the letters also mentioned that Lucusfilms Ltd. would support fan fiction efforts of their fans, provided they followed the guidelines properly. While this tactic may have been effective with those fanzines hoping to gain recognition, it is doubtful it stopped the publication of all objectionable material. On Fanfiction.net there are over 16000 fan fiction stories written in the Star Wars Universe and on just a casual scan there is at least one story that lists itself as slash (almost non-consensual).

According to, <http://www.trickster.org/symposium/symp173.htm>, an online timeline of fan fiction in 1988 and 1989 actors and fans of *Blake's 7* began interacting at conventions. During this period, fans were able to pass some of their fan fiction to the actors. This included slash fiction. Having never seen their characters in this way, the actors were insulted; feeling the fans had betrayed them. Though ultimately unsuccessful, attempts were made to ban slash authors and slash fiction from *Blake's 7* fandom.

Slash fiction may also satisfy a personal need on the part of the author, much as the Mary Sue stories do. However, you would do well to remember you are not the only one who loves the characters and universes you are playing in. In addition, something you think you may be reading in a character's behavior may not be what the creator, writer, actors who bring that character to life (in the case of TV or movies), or even other fans see. While some creators do not mind fan fiction, most do care if it crosses certain boundaries that could damage their image and the image of their universe.

I WANT TO CHANGE HISTORY—BECAUSE YOU GOT IT WRONG (ALTERNATE UNIVERSES)

Often fans will complain about the death of a favorite character, or other things they wish the creator had not done with their universe. When this happens, fan fiction writers often turn to writing stories that ignore those events. In effect, they create an alternate universe.

The television series *War of the Worlds* was one where fans decided they did not like the way the series went in the second season and began writing their own stories. They followed the events in the first season and continued from there as if none of the subsequent episodes had ever existed, creating an alternate universe timeline.

The interesting thing about this type of fan fiction is the contradiction it sets up. Many who write fan fiction say they are fans of that universe and by extension fans of the creator. However, some seem to think they have a better idea of what should happen to the characters within that universe than the creator does. Many creators are insulted, instead of flattered by this. Since the fan fiction writer, who does this, is in essence standing up and saying, "You got it wrong, so I'm going to fix it for you." Perhaps they have a reason for feeling this way when confronted with this type of fan fiction written in their universe.

Another alternate universe "what if" fans enjoy is the "what if" the characters from one universe met the characters of another universe. This popular sub-genre has even led to official crossovers in comics such as the popular Marvel / DC crossovers and others.

SO YOU WANT TO PLAY TOO

Now that you've decided writing fan fiction is something you would like to try and you even have an idea of the type of story you will be writing what's next? The first question you have to ask yourself is why are you writing this? If all you want to do is play in a favorite universe and practice your writing skills, then you're probably off to a good start on a writing exercise. If this is something you want to publish, then you should visit the official website for the author, TV series or movie this universe belongs to and review their guidelines (if any).

For fans of *Star Trek,* Pocket Books sponsors an annual writing contest "Strange New Worlds". Those writers whose work is deemed worthy by the powers that be are published in an anthology each year and paid professional rates for their work. This is the way fan fiction and official tie-in fiction come together.

If you're not interested in "official" publication, but want to share your work with others, you can check out websites such as fanfiction.net or even do a search for online fanzines dedicated to the particular universe you are playing in. You may also find information on print fanzines that might be available and looking for stories to publish as well.

Different websites and fanzines cater to different types of fan fiction. While fanfiction.net is a large website that hosts stories from hundreds of different universes and accepts all styles, some other sites prefer to limit the stories to a particular style.

There are sites that cater to general fiction set in a particular universe, others that deal only with slash, and some that only want stories about particular characters. If you want to have your fiction appear on one of these smaller sites, you need to write the type of story they are looking for. Read their guidelines as well as the stories they have already published. Make sure your story is a good fit before sending it.

Your next step should be to familiarize yourself with that universe. Good fan fiction should, with limited exceptions (such as slash or alternate universe stories), weave itself into that universe seamlessly. Even in a Mary Sue story, the main characters from that universe should react in ways that are believable to the fans. So if you're writing in the universe of a media property such as *Firefly* or *Babylon Five*, watch the episodes, learn about the characters, consider picking up, if it is available, a copy of the show's "bible". This will give you information about the characters' backgrounds, and some of the ground rules that were established for the writers of the show.

If you are writing in a literary universe, be sure to read all of the available books and stories in that universe. Check out the author's official webpage and read what they have to say about the characters and that universe.

Writing fan fiction may sound easy when you realize that you don't have to worry about creating the universe and the characters. However, in some ways it can be harder than writing your own original fiction. The characters you are borrowing have their own voice and personalities and if you don't get them right, other fans will know.

However, once you know the characters and the universe, the sky can be the limit as far as fan fiction. You have a story to tell about these characters—so tell it, but be careful what you do with it once it is written.

DANGER, WILL ROBINSON, DANGER!

Legally, what risks do you face as a writer of fan fiction and what actions can rights holders take against you?

Copyright and trademark laws grant to the creator the right to control how their work is used and distributed—this includes derivative works. A derivative work is any work based primarily upon another work. Therefore, when you take the characters and setting from someone else's original creation and write a story you are creating a derivative work. You should be aware that this is prosecutable as a violation of copyright. In cases where the rights owner has substantial money invested in the development of the setting and/or characters, they may have registered trademarked the work. Lucusfilms Ltd.

has reportedly trademarked the names of all the planets used in the *Star Wars* movies as well as the alien creatures, not just the character names.

Over the years, the corporations behind some of the better-known universes have tried to stop fan fiction with mixed results. While some writers are willing to abide by rules established by the rights owner so they can continue playing in that universe, others are not. When large corporations start to crack down on fan fiction or other violations of their copyrights and trademarks they are often viewed as being greedy. We see them as trying to crush fans who have supported and helped them make the money and achieve the status they have. In truth, all the corporations are trying to do is protect what is legally their property.

Rumors have persisted among *Star Trek* fans for years that the lawyers for Paramount/Viacom had the audacity to send a Cease and Desist letter to the US Navy regarding the use of the name *U.S.S. Enterprise.* The U.S. Navy has denied that such a letter exists. Despite this, the rumor continues to circulate and serves to illustrate the fans' belief that crackdowns on copyrights and trademarks by rights owners sometimes go too far and are ridiculous.

Several members of the Science Fiction and Fantasy Writers (SFWA) were asked for their opinions on fan fiction. Most of the SFWA authors said they stayed as far away from fan fiction as they could in order to avoid potential problems.

Responding to the question of fan fiction, Elizabeth Bear wrote:

"Of my own work, I don't care what they write as long as they aren't charging for it, and I'm not expected to read it or comment on it. I would say that the ethical fan fiction writer, however, would respect the wishes of the property owner in this matter. It's one thing to borrow the lawn mower with the owner's consent, and another entirely to walk off with it."
<http://www.elizabethbear.com/>

In her response to the query, Susan Shwartz said the following:

"One of my first sales was a short story for the first Friends of Darkover anthology (Marion Zimmer Bradley) back in about 1978. There were several of those anthologies, but, as [others have pointed out], the project was spoiled by a fan who got litigious. I've written short stories in other people's universes a couple of times, an exercise I enjoy. I don't know whether professional Star Trek novels count. I do know, however, that one character in Josepha Sherman's and my series of Star Trek novels has proved quite popular among fans. There've been pictures (mercifully, fully dressed) and short stories in which this character has appeared. When the fiction has been moderately competent, it's kind of...well, my first thought is "this is funny. It's flattering that they like the character. Then, I start thinking of ways they've gotten him right or wrong. Sometimes, just to be evil-minded, I drop them a note.

And then there's the slash fiction. I feel as if the poor character's privacy has been invaded. Then I laugh like a mad thing. When I do get in touch with a fanfic writer, it's to tell her (so far, they've all been female) to write in her own universe because she stands a chance of selling that. I do that with the permission of my editor."

Writers make their living by creating worlds and universes for their fans to read about and enjoy. Creating derivative works and putting them out for others to read may cause fan fiction writers to be seen as depriving authors of their livelihood. After all, why pay to read the numerous tie-in novels being published in different universes (*Star Wars, Star Trek, Babylon Five*, etc.) when there are over ten thousand fan fiction stories set in the same universe at FanFiction.net? There is also a concern among some writers about the image fan fiction gives to their universe and their names.

How many times have you seen a movie adapted from a particular story or based on a particular universe? The writer who adapts the story into a screenplay, as well as the director of the movie, both have their own vision of that universe. How do you feel when they go off doing things with the characters that were never in the book? Many fans feel betrayed and angry about those types of changes. They went to the movie hoping to see the world they enjoyed visiting given life in a new medium and instead came away with the feeling that someone who did not understand what they were working with had ruined it.

The movie *I, Robot* is one such movie. While an entertaining movie, it bore only superficial resemblance to the stories written by Isaac Asimov. The movie did use characters and concepts from the robot stories—such as US Robot and Mechanical Men Corporation, Doctor Susan Calvin, and the Nestor series of robots. However, instead of being based on any particular story, it borrowed bits and pieces from the tapestry that made up Asimov's robot stories. By doing this, it meets our earlier definition of fan fiction: "The use of a particular universe and/or set of characters, by someone not connected in any way with their creation to tell their own stories."

Now, imagine you have never read or seen any of the *Harry Potter* books or movies. Still you have heard about them and you know, from friends who have talked about them, a little about the characters. One day you find an Internet site that has *Harry Potter* fan fiction on it. This particular site caters to slash fiction and you find stories that feature Harry and one his teachers, Professor Snape, involved in a romantic relationship. This type of story can color your perspective of the *Harry Potter* books as well as the author, J.K. Rowling.

At the other end of the debate are the fans. On a Klingon email list, fans who are involved in making Klingon videos and related works were asked if it bothered them that they were violating copyright laws in putting together derivative works based on someone else's universe? The responses received indicated some disregard and misunderstanding in reference to copyright.

Rick D. Day of Georgia responded:

"Not in this instance. ST is too universal to be blanketly copyright protected like a logo or song. You can not [sic] copyright the American flag. You can not [sic] copyright the term "earth" or copyright the Bible. ST is one of those entities that has transcended mere entertainment; it is now part of the very fabric of our society. If a profiteer blatantly knocks off, with no variation, another's product, that is one thing. But the fan universe is like a symbiotic parasite with the intellectual owners because each benefit from the existence of the other. Paramount is better off with us, than without us, indirect copyright infringement issues aside. Without the people who enjoy a product, that product is worthless (as a commercial vehicle for profit). If the intellectual owner decides to not pursue (with its own resources) new creative material that is indirectly based on old material, so be it. But the 2nd generation owner of intellectual property should be nothing but delighted that the product is being kept fresh by eager professionals with an affinity for the product. Why not let there be a Klingon series of films, if the product is treated equally in the creative process? Give them some basic moral guidelines (like no porn, etc) and sign off on the final product, with the proceeds going to a charity. Who is harmed by this approach?"

Who is harmed? It is an interesting question.

In 1980, *The Keepers Price* was published as a collection of stories set in the *Darkover* universe. Some of the stories contained in the anthology were stories taken from fanzines. Marion Zimmer Bradley, the creator of *Darkover*, was supportive of fans who wanted to play in her universe and encouraged them to submit to the anthology series. In many ways, *Darkover* fan fiction had evolved into sanctioned tie-in fiction. In 1992, a legal situation developed involving a *Darkover* story written by one of the fans and a new *Darkover* novel Ms. Bradley was working on. There are some conflicting stories on the exact details—some saying the woman tried to sue Ms. Bradley for stealing her idea and some that say Ms. Bradley contacted her for permission to use the idea, but was unwilling to negotiate any further than a small token payment and an acknowledgement in the front of the book. Because of the problems caused by the situation, the book was scraped and Ms. Bradley shut down the fanzine and the anthology series.

In this case, Ms. Bradley was harmed as the novel she had been working on was shelved and she never saw it in print or earned anything from it. Her time spent writing that story was lost. Moreover, the fans were hurt. They never had the chance to read that novel and a market that had been open to fan fiction closed. Another person possibly harmed was the fan fiction writer. In one online account of the situation, it is mentioned that a novel she submitted to DAW books was returned in an "incredibly short period of time." Whether this was a result of the book's quality or the fact it came from her (DAW was the publisher of the *Darkover* books) is not something that was established.

Some authors also believe fan fiction constitutes a form of identity theft. Fans associate certain characters and universes with a particular author or creator. When another writer preempts those characters and that universe, there is still an association with the original. Quick, what do you think of when someone mentions a robot named Marvin and a spaceship called the Heart of Gold?

If you are like most readers of science fiction, you probably thought of *The Hitchhiker's Guide to the Galaxy* series by Douglas Adams. Because of this type of association, whether intentional or not, the fan fiction writer is in essence assuming the original creator's identity in the mind of the reader, until they register that this particular work was not written by the person they are already familiar with.

In cases where both copyright and registered trademarks overlap, the damage can be more extensive. While the law says you do not have to defend a copyright to maintain it, the same is not true of trademarks. In order to protect a trademark, it must be defended. Many of the characters and unique names used in media fiction are trademarked and when rights owners feel those to be in jeopardy, they will send out warnings, also known as "Cease and Desist" letters.

It is doubtful fan fiction will ever go away because make believe is too much a part of human nature. The idea of being a part of something larger is part of what draws us into fandom. Once you are part of the community you want to be able to share your common love with others who understand it. For those of us who write fan fiction, we want to be able to leave our mark on that universe and say we were a part of it.

If you want to explore the world of fan fiction, you should familiarize yourself with copyright law as it applies to fair use and derivative works. One website that answers some of those questions in easy to understand language is "*10 Big Myths about Copyright Explained*" by Brad Templeton <http://www.templetons.com/brad/copymyths.html>. There he answers questions about copyright notices, whether not charging for something constitutes a violation of copyright or not, what "fair use" was designed to protect, as well as others.

Simply put: Once an original idea is put on paper or other media, it is considered protected by copyright unless specifically stated otherwise. While there are provisions for fair use in copyright law, those were designed to allow short excerpts to be used for commentary, news reporting, research, and education. When used in this manner, you must attribute where the excerpt came from. Fair use also allows the creation of parody works. Of course, the area most affected by fan fiction is derivative works. As Mr. Templeton states:

> "U.S. Copyright law is quite explicit that the making of what are called "derivative works"—works based or derived from another copyrighted work— is the exclusive province of the owner of the original work."

The existence of websites such Fanfiction.net are a testament to the number of writers who want to play in other people's universes. The fact these websites continue to exist also shows that many of the rights-holders are willing to let you play as along as you stay in the appropriate playground.

During April of 2006, a fan fiction writer managed to get a book titled *Another Hope* published and listed on both Amazon.com and Barnes&Noble.com. This book was a fan fiction novel set in the *Star Wars* universe. The book was listed during the week of April 16th and created a flurry of discussion across the Internet. By April 21st a notice had been posted on the author's website that the book would be removed from distribution and by April 22nd her website was no longer accessible.

Not only were professional writers upset with the publication and commercial sale of this book, but a large percentage of fan fiction writers were also. Many of whom feared this blatant violation of copyright by a fan fiction writer might eventually backlash on the fan fiction community as a whole.

If you are a fan of a particular universe and want to try your hand at writing something, Laura J. Underwood offers the following advice:

> "But if you Must Sin and commit Fanfic based on someone else's work—and assuming said author is alive and well and still writing their own stuff—get the author's permission... And if the author says Nay—show enough respect for their work to accept the refusal and abide by their wishes."

Beginning writers can use fan fiction as an exercise to develop their writing skills. By not having to worry about the complex details of character or world creation, you are free to concentrate on plot and telling the story. Again, it is not recommended that you post or publish these writing exercises. Like other skills, you must exercise your writing skills regularly to keep them sharp. You can use fan fiction as one of those exercises. There is also the self-gratification you can receive by writing a story in which you project yourself into a particular universe or the satisfaction of "righting" a "wrong" the creator of the universe made.

Still we should tread lightly in another's universe, and leave it in the same state we found it.

Another important point to remember: If a writer has written something that appears to be an opening for another story at the end of one story, or scatters hints throughout one story that could lead to another, odds are they are already working on that sequel or secondary story. Just because you can also see the logical path the story should take, then write your own fan fiction based on that opening, does not mean the author stole your idea. Chances are they have already been working on that idea.

Remember, these characters and worlds belong to someone else. Treat them with respect; you are only borrowing them.

CHAPTER SIXTEEN

WRITING GRAPHIC NOVELS AND OTHER FORMS OF SEQUENTIAL ART

Dave A. Law

INTRODUCTION

There are two standard misconceptions that people have about sequential art, or, the more common term, comic books. The first is that anyone can write a comic book. What is it beyond a collection of pictures? The artist does all the work and the illustrations are the reason why most people buy a comic. This couldn't be further from the truth. A good comic book story requires all the aspects you have read about elsewhere in this guide, just written in a different format. Without the writer to provide the plot, the dialog, and characters the comic is simply pretty pictures. Writing comics, like any other creative endeavor, takes time for the author to become proficient and skillful.

The second misconception is that comic books are juvenile and only about superheroes. You may have seen the latest big screen blockbuster about one of these action heroes. Isn't that all there is to it? If you enter a good comic book store, you will realize this isn't the case. Publishers now produce many comic books geared towards a more mature audience and there are comic books written in virtually every genre, some of which are made into films. Did you realize that *Men in Black* was originally a comic book?

Graphic novels are a type of comic book. These are currently more of a hot commodity that traditional agents are now considering handling them. As such, the focus of this chapter is on graphic novels, but everything stated within it applies to all forms of comic books. While this chapter cannot hope to cover every aspect of writing graphic novels, it will give you the basis of how to begin.

HISTORY

Pictorial tales have existed since prehistoric times with tales painted on cave walls. However, comic books in the form we are accustomed to today, began in 1933 with the publication of *Funnies on Parade*. This lead to the introduction of such comic strips as Alex Raymond's *Flash Gordon* and other action adventures. The late 30s saw the introduction of superhero comics with Superman in *Action Comics #1* in June 1938 and Batman in *Detective Comics #39* in May 1939. The 40s were flooded with superhero comics, mostly based upon the Superman model. Superhero comics have been a primary part of comic books ever since.

Though the term 'graphic novel' has been used to describe other titles, it wasn't until 1978 when Will Eisner popularized the term to describe his work of *A Contract with God*, a slice-of-life drama about living in the 30s, that the phrase started to be used to describe long comic works. Though graphic novels have had their share of superhero stories, there is a greater variety of genres represented within this format. British publications of such titles as *Judge Dredd, 2000 AD*, and others well represent the SF genre.

MEMBERS OF THE TEAM

Unlike writing novels or short stories, writing a graphic novel is a team effort and in this sense, it is more like scriptwriting for the screen. With a screenplay, any number of people including actors and directors may change parts of the story. However, with a graphic novel, due to the smaller size of the team, the writer has more control over the final product. Some consider this as a good medium between novels and film, maintaining the literary level of a novel while adding in the visual aspect of film. Though some talented people can complete the whole process themselves, most of us require working with at least one other person to create our comic stories.

Let's go over the various tasks involved in creating a graphic novel:

WRITER: This is you, the person who initially creates and writes the story, detailing to some degree what the visual representation of this story will be.

PENCILER: This person takes your comic script, and in pencil lays out the visuals of the story. How rough these pencils are depends upon whether or not the penciler will ink the story himself or not.

LETTERER: The next person to take part, and this may in fact be the same person as either of the above, is the letterer. This person draws the balloons, captions and letters the words in ink, based upon placement by usually either the editor or writer.

INKER: This person, who sometimes is the same person as the penciler, now puts into ink all the penciled artwork, making whatever corrections are necessary. By way of textures, shading, and shadows, the inker adds form and substance to the illustrations. How much texture is included depends on whether or not colored artwork is required.

COLORIST: If the artwork is to be colored, the inked pages are copied. Nowadays, the colorist works from pages scanned into computer, adding the required color, tones, and shades within an illustration software application. If anyone is of the illusion that this is simply coloring a book when you were a child, it isn't. It takes all the artistic ability of any other of artist working on this comic. A skilled colorist can improve the look of the book.

EDITOR: Lest we forget, overseeing the entire process, is an editor. The editor ensures the quality of production at each step of the process, particularly at the earlier stages, when revisions are easier.

ELEMENTS OF A COMIC PAGE

A variety of elements makes up the story page of a graphic novel. It is necessary to understand these elements to write the script.

The first element is the story page itself. The page can take on a variety of forms.

REGULAR STORY PAGE: This is series of panels of sequential artwork. A panel is simply a picture or shot from the story. Each panel contains a bit of the action within a story. It is a common beginner mistake to ask an artist to draw two or more actions within a panel. A panel can contain only one action. Typically, a story page has around six panels to it. The more panels, the quicker the action. The fewer the panels, the slower or more dynamic the imagery. Each panel is the sequential telling of the story one frame at a time.

SPLASH PAGE: This is a special type of story page that has one or two images. It is normally the first page of the graphic novel containing the title and credits. You can think of it as a second cover to the story.

FULL-PAGE SPREAD: This is a story page, which contains a single panel and picture. You can think of it as a dramatic pause in the action.

TWO-PAGE SPREAD: This is the same as a full-page spread, but across two pages, with a large scene. You must carefully plan a two-page spread and insert it the correct place; otherwise, this risks forcing the reader to turn the page to see the second half of the picture. It is not commonly necessary to have such an image.

Besides the images, the text on the page tells the story to the reader. This text takes the form of speech and thought balloons, as well as captions.

SPEECH BALLOON: This is the dialog of a character. The tail of the balloon shows who is talking. The balloon can have multiple tails, if more than one character is saying the same thing.

THOUGHT BALLOON: This contains the thoughts of a single character. Again, it is possible that more than one character is thinking the same thoughts, and the small circles linking the characters to the balloon would reflect this.

CAPTION: Used in a variety of ways, this rectangular dialog box can allow for a level of storytelling otherwise not easily obtained with either fiction written for the page or the screen. A writer uses captions to indicate a shift in time and/or place, a character's inner thoughts, or as a vehicle of the author's omniscient comments or footnotes.

SCRIPT FORMATS

There are two common ways of writing a script: full script and plot first (Marvel style). Every writer and publisher has his own preference. Each script format has its advantages and disadvantages.

FULL SCRIPT:

It is most similar to a TV or movie screenplay in that it describes in detail the visual contents of each panel on a page, as well as lays out the dialog and captions on the page. Once this script is complete, edited, and revised, your work is complete as far as the creation of the story goes, and you can move onto other projects while the rest of the team completes the graphic novel.

Full script is the usual format for most small publishers. If you have a choice, you would use this format when you are not comfortable with the artist you are working with or wish to have more control over the story.

While publishers aren't as strict on the actual format of the script as movie producers are with screenplays, you should be consistent in how you write your script. A common format goes something like this:

PAGE ONE: (5 PANELS)

Panel 1: Pages are capitalized with the number of panels on the page noted with it. Each panel has the description of the action shown within it, with enough detail so that the artist illustrating it knows exactly what is happening.

CHARACTER #1: DIALOG FROM ANY CHARACTER STARTS WITH THE CHARACTER NAME AND THEN THE WORDS SPOKEN IN CAPS.

CAP: CAPTIONS AND SOUND EFFECTS ARE DONE SIMILARLY UNDER HEADING OF 'CAP' OR 'SOUND' SO THE LETTERER KNOWS WHAT IS REQUIRED HERE.

ADVANTAGES:

You have full control over the story and ensure that your vision of the story is more truly interpreted, plus the story is completely developed, and you are not relying on anyone else to meet your deadlines.

DISADVANTAGES:

Once written, it is more difficult to make changes, it's slower to write than plot first, and it can restrict creativity

PLOT FIRST (MARVEL STYLE):

This style was originally created by Stan Lee for Marvel Comics when he started writing and evolving their superhero universe in the early 60s. In this style of script, you outline the plot as a detailed summary of the action, including all the important details. It is often broken down into pages, and sometimes even into panels; however, most of the dialog and text are not yet included. The penciler then takes this script and creates the penciled pages. From these penciled pages, you then write out all the dialog and related text for these pages. In essence, this type of scripting is a two-step process.

In most cases, you are only able to use this format if you are working with a larger publisher. When given a choice, you would use this format when you are comfortable with the artist you work with and wish to create a truly collaborative story.

The format of this type of script is similar to a short story manuscript you would send to a publisher.

ADVANTAGES:

You can correct omissions from the original plot. You can be inspired by the artwork, and the artist does some of the work for you and has a freer hand with interpretation, making this is more of a team effort.

DISADVANTAGES:

Artwork may have scenes longer or shorter than you originally had planned, and artwork may vastly diverge from your original concept, plus you may not even like the artwork, and it may dissuade you.

TYPE OF STORIES

A variety of formats can be used to create illustrated stories. Here are the most common:

GRAPHIC NOVELS

Strictly speaking, a graphic novel is an original long, completely told, comic story. It is essentially a novel told with sequential artwork. Sometimes you will see collected versions of stories written in another comic format listed as a graphic novel, but these really are trade paperback collections of those stories rather than a true graphic novel. Though used to describe works as short as 48 pages, graphic novels are at least from 96 pages long, and most tend to be around 150 pages.

ONGOING SERIES

These are the standard comics. You see these within a comic book store, or on comic racks elsewhere. The story is a continuous serial dealing with the same characters and/or situation. A regular comic book may include a single-issue story - a short story, or a story told over multi-issues called a story arc. Large companies may also publish 'Mega Series', where a storyline is told over a number of different comic titles. A regular story usually runs around 24 pages, allowing for editorials, letters to the editor, and ads to fill out the rest of the comic.

MINI SERIES

This is a complete story told in a predetermined number of issues, typically four or six, and published in a regular comic book format. Within each issue, there must be some major change, development, or reversal, and the issue must end with a cliffhanger to get the reader to come back for the next installment. Similarly, each issue should incorporate a brief summary of what has happened before, as there is no guarantee that a reader has read the other issues and/or remembers what happened previously.

MAXI SERIES

Similar to a mini series the predetermined length of the story is longer and is usually twelve installments. These types of stories are rare due to the difficulty in maintaining sales over the entire series.

COMIC STRIP

This is either a single panel, or a strip of three or four panels, published in newspapers, magazines, or online. Nowadays these tend to be humorous with perhaps a slight storyline between strips. Most currently published adventure comic strips are reprints of serials created in the 30s and 40s.

WORKING WITH ARTISTS

While on occasion, you may be able to land a comic writing job without initially having an artist involved, generally, especially if you are writing a graphic novel, you first need to find an artist to work with. Perhaps you have artistic ability yourself. However, assess those abilities honestly and see if they are up to the standard of the market you are considering approaching. If they are, you can completely ignore this section and move on to the next. For the majority of us, this isn't an option.

Fortunately, finding an artist to work with isn't as daunting a task as you might think. Ten years ago, you might have been restricted to talking to local comic shop owners, as well as posting notices there and at local art colleges. While both still are good avenues, especially if you want to work with a local artist, the Internet offers a much easier way. There is a variety of notice boards, where comic talent can post ads. The reference section of this guide lists a few.

When talking to a prospective artist, you need to make certain that the two of you can work together, and you both understand what you are looking for, as well as where and how you plan to market your title. It's easy enough just to select the first artist who answers your ad. Making certain the artwork and style matches your project, as well as whether or not it is likely the two of you can work together, will save you many hassles in the long run and, hopefully, avoid your having to find another artist. This, of course, assumes you find an artist that "does it all". Fortunately, if you find an artist that simply pencils, typically he will know someone who inks, etc.

This leads to the question of whether you should pay an artist for work done on speculation. Yes, you can find artists who are willing to work with the hope that a story will sell, and some of them are very talented. However, you are more likely to find a higher quality artist if you are willing and able to pay the artist for the pages required to create a proposal package for a publisher. While you can find publishers who will accept writing samples without artwork, having the right artist illustrate the stories, even if these are samples stories, can make all the difference in the world.

After you have found an artist, you will begin working with this artist. Generally, with a longer storyline, such as a graphic novel, there will be the need to create character sketches of the main characters. This serves a few purposes. First, it allows you to get a feel for what information the artist needs, and ensures that you are both in accord. You have to realize that this is a collaboration, and while the story is yours, the artwork that will bring the story to life is the artist's. You could easily send an artist a whole volume about a specific character, or a few lines, but in neither case are you likely to get what you want. A character description, as well as any description of an important setting in a story, should be a few paragraphs.

You should not detail just the physical description, but also points about the character's personality and mannerisms, as the artist will reflect these in how the character is illustrated. The description should be enough for the artist to get a good feel of the character, but without overloading the artist with information that isn't required nor hamstringing the artist's creativity. Again, this goes back to the fact that the work is a collaboration.

FINDING A PUBLISHER

While you can start writing a graphic novel, and obtain an artist for it before even considering a publisher, you may find that there isn't a market for it, or that the market for it is limited. The marketplace is always changing, and what applies today may no longer be relevant by the time you read this chapter. Start reading comic book trade publications as well as comic book news sites. The resource section of this book lists some of them. This will give you an idea of who may be interested in the type of story you hope to have published.

SELF-PUBLISHING

There is also another option, which is self-publishing. While other fiction industries still frown upon this, the comic book industry has a long history of successful self-publishers. This doesn't mean that this is a shortcut to any comic writing success, as you still require a professionally done graphic novel with a good story and quality artwork. Many first time self-publishers believe they can get away without hiring an outside editor, but such work is usually full of grammatical errors and obvious spelling mistakes. Regardless of how well you may be able to write, the importance of having someone else look over the work can't be emphasized enough. It is the difference between something looking professional and polished, and something looking amateur and unreadable.

One common mistake about self-publishing is that people don't realize is that it is a business, and you have to treat it as such. Besides creating the work, you have to be able to successfully market and promote your product. Not everyone has the business sense to make this successful. Self-publishing, like any other small business, takes a lot of work just to break even, let alone make a few pennies for yourself. It is not something recommended, unless you know what you are doing and are willing to throw a few thousand dollars away without any hope of return.

CREATOR-OWNED PROJECTS

Assuming you have taken the advice, and have decided to find a publisher, you will need to create a submission package. Each publisher's guidelines ask for something a little different, but the idea is generally similar. However, it is always best to check a publisher's guidelines before submitting anything to them, even if you have read the guidelines previously, as these might have changed in the meantime. The package you are looking to create is similar to what you would send to an agent. However, in this case, typically, you are skipping the initial one-page query, and jumping right in with the story package. There needs to be a cover letter, a summary page of your story, and in this case, instead of chapters, you need to include some pages of sequential artwork. In place of artwork, you may include pages from your script, if you are certain the publisher will accept a proposal without an artist attached to the project. Many, particularly smaller publishers, will not.

In the cover letter, you need to, briefly, within a page give a blurb about the project and those involved. This letter has to convince the publisher that the graphic novel, or other comic project that you are proposing, is of interest enough for them to look at the other pages. In the summary page, you need to give the complete overview of the entire story, including the beginning, middle, and ending. If you were proposing a continuing series, this would be an outline of the first several issues. This outline should be one page, and no more than two. The last item you need to include is sample pages from your story. This sample should be between three and five pages, and should be consecutive pages. These need not be the first pages of the story, but rather those that give the best representation of the story.

You can be more creative in the submission package by including such things as character sketches. However, it is best that you keep this package to a minimum, unless the publisher asks for more. Editors have a limited amount of time to go over submissions, and unless you can capture their attentions quickly, it really doesn't matter what you send. More recently, there has been the option to submit to agents as well; but in these cases, you have to follow their standard guidelines for submitting novels, with initial query letters before submitting a package.

WORK-FOR-HIRE PROJECTS

There are other ways of gaining a comic writing position other than a creator-owned project. Many publishers, particularly large ones, have work-for-hire positions open. These positions differ in that the company owns the property that you wrote. They pay you a fee for your writing and take ownership of the story. While this may not seem favorable, it has the advantages that the pay, particularly with a large company, will be higher than for a creator-owned product from a small publisher, and you get to play in someone else's world that you may have enjoyed. In a sense, this is licensed fan fiction for pay.

To gain such a position, you will have to send a submission package as well, but here, instead of proposing your own project, you will include samples of your writing in the style and genre the publisher specified. Sometimes the publisher may not want to see a full script but rather plot outlines of possible one-issue filler stories. Again, publishers routinely change their guidelines, so it is always best to check before you submit anything.

Unfortunately, publishers do not advertise all work-for-hire positions. There are, however, other ways of breaking into the industry.

BEING AN ARTIST

Artists have an easier time due to the visual aspect of the work, such that a publisher can quickly tell whether an artist is appropriate for a project. First obtaining a position as an artist gives you an inside track for any writing assignments.

Get employed by the publisher.

The position doesn't matter. Simply working for the publisher allows you the ability to network with those managing the company, and can sometimes lead to a writing assignment or at least inside considerations.

WORK AS AN EDITOR

Similar to the above two.

SELF-PUBLISH, OR GET PUBLISHED BY A SMALLER COMPANY

In either case, you are building up a portfolio and experience to show to a larger publisher. In rare cases, your creation might be successful enough that you could transfer it to a larger publisher; just don't count on it.

Half the trouble sometimes is simply finding the jobs available. As with many industries, publishers will not necessarily advertise the best opportunities well or at all. This is why it is important to network. This means to not only to go to conferences and conventions to meet and talk with others, but also to get involved and be active with online organizations. The more people you talk to, not only the more you learn about the industry, but also the better prospect you have to hear about opportunities you wouldn't have heard about otherwise.

SIGNING THE CONTRACT

Once you do sell your graphic novel or land a comic position, you will be given a contract. Be certain you read over the contract, and if there are any clauses that you are uncomfortable about, do not sign. If you don't understand any part of the contract, feel free to ask, or get professional advice. Don't be afraid to negotiate, regardless of the size of the company. Just don't expect the pay rate to change, but you might be able to change any clauses you are uncomfortable or uncertain about.

CONCLUSION

While this chapter has not covered every aspect of graphic novel writing, it should provide you with enough information to pursue any comic writing venture you intend to undertake.

CHAPTER SEVENTEEN

SCIENCE FICTION FOR YOUNGER READERS AGED EIGHT TO TWELVE

Simon Rose

One of the best things about writing science fiction is that more or less anything you can imagine is possible. Your novel can involve time travel into the past or future, alien worlds, parallel universes, other dimensions and so much more.

Writers are often told to 'write what they know' and while this is also true for children's literature, it takes on a whole new meaning when writing for younger readers. To be successful, you have to be able to see through a child's eyes. You need to try and recall your own childhood, remember how things felt when you were seven, ten, or twelve years old. Who were your friends when you were that age? What experiences, books, or movies shaped your formative years? Are there memories from that time that will stay with you for the rest of your life? You may even find yourself remembering things you thought you'd forgotten forever. One of the best things about writing for children is that it allows you to write about the kinds of things that used to fascinate you when you were young. For most of us, our childhood is a lost, magical time before we grew up. Even if we have children of our own, it's difficult to remember just how things felt to us when we were young. And of course, stories for young children can be very imaginative, which makes writing them so much fun.

The best writers of science fiction specialize in suspending our disbelief, transforming the impossible into the possible, or at least into the believable. Even if super powers, magical abilities, out of this world technology, or the supernatural are a key element, if it's going to work at all, a science fiction story has to be well grounded in reality. In The Alchemist's Portrait, my first novel for young readers, Matthew travels back in time to seventeenth century Amsterdam by means of a magical painting, which acts as a time portal. A simple idea perhaps, but how does it exactly work? You need to have a plausible method of traveling back in time. Too many so-called time travel stories neglect to do this. More often than not, especially in stories for younger readers, the main character journey back in time in the first chapter or two, and then spends the entire adventure in the past, before returning safely home. While these types of stories are set in a particular time period, they would perhaps be more accurately classified as historical fiction.

If you are intending to write science fiction, your science, even if it's the product of your imagination, has to appear authentic. For example, you must describe exactly how a time machine works or how dinosaurs can be recreated, as Michael Crichton does so well in Timeline and Jurassic Park. Unlike adults, children are less likely to question what they see in print. Yet even though young readers may not be all that interested in delving into the facts of a story, editors and reviewers will scrutinize the technical details. Consequently, the fictional machinery has to work. In The Clone Conspiracy, the technology and cloning techniques depicted in the novel are pure invention, but still have to be explained, even if not in intricate detail. Children have usually seen enough movies and read enough books about cloning, experiments, and laboratories to comfortably accept what they are reading as entirely possible. For the most part, children have fabulous ideas for time machines, devices, or methods, but have difficulty explaining how they actually function. They are also usually very clear on the means to travel back in time, but have given little thought to their return trip. While time travel remains fiction, the methods by which it takes place still have to seem believable. If readers consider the method in a story to be completely ridiculous or it raises more questions that it answers, they will be turned off by the story altogether. Just as the scientific equipment has to be in working order, so the historical details have to be well researched for the story to remain credible.

'Writing older' is generally recommended when composing novels for young readers. As a rule, children do not want to read about lead characters their own age or younger, but prefer them to be slightly older. If your story is designed for readers eight to twelve, your heroes and heroines should usually be around twelve or thirteen, but no older than that. Age also has to be taken into account in not talking down to the reader. Although you are writing for children, you shouldn't oversimplify the writing or change your style and definitely don't preach to the reader. Children dislike being hit over the head with the point of a story. If you feel you really have to convey a message, make sure it actually fits in with the text, integrate it into the dialogue, or make it help solve the problem of the story in some way. However, if the story is too preachy, children usually dismiss it altogether, much preferring a good adventure instead.

When you first begin writing, you may be discouraged by what are supposedly popular books for children. In recent years, young readers were being steered toward books focusing on such areas as divorce, drug addicts, abuse, and incurable diseases, usually by helpful teachers, librarians, and family. However, the things children were supposed to like reading about were actually topics that adults, whether publishers or educators, thought they should like. This changed with the advent of Harry Potter and its subsequent phenomenal popularity. While you may have no desire to write fantasy about wizards, witches, dragons, or goblins, it is refreshing to discover that children still have a taste for classic tales of adventure and for most of them; this is epitomized by fantasy and science fiction.

While there are no hard and fast rules about the length, word count or number of chapters in children's literature, the story has to be tight and very fast paced. As with most stories, it's important to hook the reader right at the start with a great beginning. This is even more imperative with children's literature, where the reader's attention span may sometimes be considerably shorter. Your novels should contain exciting, fast-paced action, each chapter having a cliff hanger ending, encouraging the reader to turn the page and not put the book down. The children's story has to move quickly, but also flow evenly. The pace of an adult story can slow down at various points, with no distraction for the reader. A linear plot is needed for the younger reader, but it doesn't need to be so simple that it detracts from the story you are trying to tell. Even a straightforward plot can have several interesting and intriguing subplots. However, lengthy sections of dialogue should be cut unless they are essential, such as important pieces of exposition. Many writers for children also waste a lot of time describing the book's main character, either through their physical appearance, personality, or environment. If the story is sufficiently well written, the reader should be able to picture the main character in only a few sentences or at least within the first chapter in which they appear. You also don't want to overload the story with details that will bore readers and tempt them to close the book. The more you can blend the necessary information into the narrative, the better the story.

Even if the adventure takes place in an alien dimension or another time, children will enjoy the story far more if it somehow relates to their own experiences. At first, this seems hard to achieve. After all, it isn't every day that someone gets transported to the edge of the universe, meets someone from another world, or travels into the deadly arenas of ancient Rome. However, the problems the hero might encounter can be universal and the reader will identify with his or her struggle much more easily. The lead character in a story can be a regular boy or girl, complete with homework, parents, friends, a busy school life, annoying siblings, pets, and all the rest, but he or she can also have incredible adventures. If the character is someone they can easily relate to, the reader will have a much deeper interest in the story.

No matter where or when the adventure takes place, the children in the story have to solve their own problems and overcome the enemy themselves. There can certainly be adult characters in the book, but the main character has to be successful as a result of their own efforts, skill, or strategy. In The Alchemist's Portrait, Matthew receives a great deal of information from Tess, who works at the museum where the infamous portrait is being painstakingly restored. He is however, ultimately responsible for finding a solution and winning the day. In The Clone Conspiracy, Lisa Mackenzie is able to set Luke and Emma along the right path to uncovering a nefarious international scheme, but again the young protagonists are the ones who solve the riddle. In The Emerald Curse, Sam's grandfather, Charles Kelly, plays a major role in the story. However, it is Sam who has all the ideas, formulates strategies, and resolves the conflict.

Just as the lead character has to be someone the young reader can identify with, the supporting cast members have to seem real too. They may be weird looking aliens or misshapen subterranean beasts, but if they are going to play anything more than a passing role in the tale, they need to have depth as characters, even if they aren't human beings. Well-drawn characters, in whatever setting they appear, are always popular and rarely forgotten. Some character types have been depicted in stories countless times, such as malevolent witches or magicians, the wise counselor, the reluctant hero, the evil advisor, the noble king, the scatterbrained scientist, among many others. Yet characters can't just be replicas of those seen so often in the past. Neither should the writer attempt to duplicate characters that have been successful in recent years, such as those from Harry Potter, for example. Just as in adult writing, one of the author's main challenges is to make their characters more than empty cardboard cutouts and make them truly come alive for the reader. This can be even more of a challenge if the character in question isn't even human. However, they still have to be just as realistic as any other person created for a work of fiction. The character needs a personality, things we can sympathize and identify with, mannerisms, quirks, likes and dislikes, in short anything that makes them unique as an individual, even if that individual isn't human.

The settings of stories are also very important and have to be realistic. Any novelist must invent a complete imagined world, but the one created by a writer of science fiction must rest on very solid foundations, even though it may be vastly different to the world we live in every day. The time travel methods employed in The Alchemist's Portrait and The Sorcerer's Letterbox have to appear to be able to work in a feasible way. The laboratories and labyrinthine underground complex has to be sufficiently well drawn in The Clone Conspiracy to capture the reader's imagination. Similarly, if the action takes place on board a space ship or on an alien planet, we need to get a clear picture of that environment, including working technology and how the characters interact, not only with each other, but also with their surroundings.

Let's assume that you've decided that you really want to write for children. Your family, friends, and working colleagues are all suitably impressed and tell you that you have real talent. However, it's still advisable to take some kind of writing course to hone your skills and learn the ropes from a professional instructor. This can take the form of creative writing classes in the evenings at a local college or one via correspondence through the Internet. As with any other venture, it's a good idea to do your homework before investing any money, but there are many quality courses out there. Not only will you further develop your skills as a writer, you will also learn how to submit your work to prospective publishers. A submission that is well put together can make all the difference between attracting someone's attention or swiftly receiving a standard rejection letter in the mail.

No matter what genre you decide to concentrate on, you need to do your research thoroughly. Find out what kinds of books are currently being published in your chosen area of interest. Take a trip to your local bookstore and examine what is on the shelves and what appears to be popular. Also, you should take note of which companies are publishing these books. This will give you a good idea of where you should submit your work, once it's ready to be sent out. Some publishers, especially those of adult books, specialize in science fiction or fantasy. However, in children's literature, fantasy and science fiction show no signs of waning in popularity and many of the major and smaller houses publish books in these genres.

In contrast to those who write for adults, children's authors have far more opportunities to secure speaking engagements. Unlike adult writers, children's authors are always being invited to speak at schools, particularly elementary schools. And depending on the age range of your books, you may be invited to junior and senior high schools. Teachers and librarians are always looking to bring artists into the school each academic year, so it's very important to keep them informed of your latest work, any award nominations and so on, in order for you to remain on their radar screen. The visit of an author to a school can be invaluable, inviting children to unlock their own creative potential, whatever form that may take. As a published author, you are able to inspire the children and thus help encourage them in their own writing. You should always offer to work with the teachers or librarians before each visit and to meet with them prior to your appearance at the school. Teachers often present an author with specific requirements, to compliment their own programs, so you may need to discuss ways to adapt your presentations to suit their needs. If you put in the effort, word of your expertise will soon spread. Your visits to schools will be greatly anticipated and extremely well received by both the students and the staff. Consequently, teachers will have no hesitation in recommending you to their colleagues. Children are also always thrilled, even sometimes in awe, to meet a published author, especially if they have read and enjoyed your books. Meeting your readers can be one of the most rewarding aspects of school visits.

It's important to remember that while some schools may simply be looking for an author to come to the school and merely read to the students, this is mostly not the case. Teachers want you to not only inspire their students, but also to conduct writing exercises designed to help them be more creative in their own work. If you are intending to make a long-term career out of school visits, you need to have a well thought out series of presentations, workshops, and other material. Your sessions also shouldn't only relate to your own books. They should deal with areas such as editing and revision, where writers get ideas from, character development and story structure, among others. Some schools prefer to hire an Artist in Residence and this can often be for a full week, a term or even for the entire duration of the school year. School visits represent a wonderful opportunity for children's authors. You are able to talk about your own work, sell some autographed books, market yourself to a wider audience, as well as making a real difference in the lives of your readers.

Writing for children, in whatever genre you are passionate about, can be very rewarding. But science fiction can be so much fun simply because your story can be about virtually anything you can imagine. Science fiction books for younger readers can certainly be simpler than those for adults, yet still need to adhere to the same principles, rules and guidelines associated with good writing. The story needs a credible setting, well researched science and technology, convincing characters the reader can identify with and be fast paced enough to keep the reader engrossed in the story until the very end. Like books for any other genre or age group, if a science fiction tale aimed at younger readers is any good, people will enjoy it and tell others. A well told story will always stand the test of time.

PART V
PUBLISHING AND BEYOND

CHAPTER EIGHTEEN

SO YOU'VE FINISHED YOUR SHORT STORY/NOVEL, NOW WHAT?

Michele Acker

INTRODUCTION

So, you've finished your short story or novel. You've spent hours, months, perhaps even years on your baby and now you're done. You've written The End and everything. Now you're ready to submit. You're ready to have editors and/or agents fall all over themselves to sign you up and offer you lots of money for your wonderful, exciting piece of fiction. Right?

Wrong! Unless of course you happen to be Stephen King, or Orson Scott Card or Piers Anthony—and I'm assuming you aren't—you have a long way to go before you reach that point, if ever.

This chapter isn't aimed at those of you who've acquired an agent, been published and are making a living writing, it's for those of you just starting out. You've written your first novel, your first short story and you need to know where to go from here. What do I do next?

The sad truth is that most budding novelists don't sell their first book, or their second book or even their third. Even most of those 'overnight success cases' you see in the news, took years to accomplish. They might have made it big on their first published novel, but most wrote two, three, four, even five previous books that were either never submitted, or rejected without being published.

If you have that passion, if you want to be the best novelist or short story writer you can be no matter how long it takes, then this chapter will help you with the next step and give you some insight on how to find an editor or agent for your work.

Assuming you write or want to write Science Fiction, I'm going to give you as much genre related information as I can. Though in some cases, I'll give you more general information when I feel it applies.

BEFORE SUBMITTING

Since critique groups, writing classes, and other forms of preparing your work for submission are covered in another chapter, I'll just talk a little bit about Conferences and Conventions, and how they can help advance your career.

CONFERENCES, CONVENTIONS & WORKSHOPS

What's the difference between the three you ask? Aren't they the same thing? No, they are manifestly not the same thing. Though all three can be helpful to a writer's career, they're helpful in entirely different ways.

Take Conferences for instance. Conferences are first and foremost for writers. You wouldn't see a fan at a conference unless they had a desire to write their own books. Conferences are for networking and meeting other writers. Conferences are for attending panels and discussion groups and workshops about the craft of writing and the process of getting published. Conferences are for meeting editors and agents and pitching your novel once you're ready.

Conferences are held all over the country and for every genre you can imagine. Most last from one to three days. But no two are the same. If you're thinking about attending one, make sure to do some research to find the right one for you. How do you find them? There are several resources. There's a section listing conferences by area of the country in the back of the Novel & Short Story Writer's Market, and there are numerous online sources as well. By far the best online resource is Shaw Guides http://writing.shawguides.com/. They list every conference imaginable. The database is free to use and searchable in several categories, month of the year, state, country and genre.

But from the dozens of conferences available, how do you choose the right one for you? One of the first things you need to consider is genre. Does the conference cater to the genre you write? For instance, you probably don't want to pay good money to attend a conference for romance writers when you write science fiction or fantasy (or maybe you do, there are whole sub-genres of science fiction romance and fantasy romance, but you get the idea). Or you don't want to attend a non-fiction writer's conference when you write fiction.

Then take a look at who's attending, who the speakers are. Are they writers you admire? Do the editors and agents represent the genre you write? And if so, does the conference offer you pitch sessions with the editor or agent of your choice? Do they charge extra for the privilege or is it included in your registration fee? Is it on a first come first serve basis, or are there other criteria you have to meet? If you have a finished novel and you have the opportunity to pitch at a conference, go for it. Conferences are one of the best ways to meet prospective agents and editors. But go even if you aren't going to pitch. The chance to network with other writers isn't something to be dismissed.

Another thing you want to look at is cost and location. How much is the conference fee? Is it close enough to drive or do you have to buy airline tickets too? If it's not close to home, do you have family and friends you can stay overnight with, or do you have to pay extra for a hotel room? Can you find someone to room with?

Conventions on the other hand are all about the readers. There are a wide range of conventions with an even wider range of focuses. Some focus on a theme or a certain show, like *Star Trek* or *Star Wars*. Some focus on graphic novels (novels told in a comic book type format). Some focus on a particular author like Butchercon for fantasy novelist Jim Butcher. And some are more general, focusing instead on a whole genre such as The World Fantasy Convention or the World Science Fiction convention.

Unless you're attending as a fan, the real benefit from attending a convention (also called cons) comes after you're published. They can be a great way to attract new readers. Conventions usually have small tables for artists and authors to rent to showcase their work or autograph novels. The bigger cons have panels where authors can talk about their novels, answer questions, or read excerpts.

And conventions are easy to find. A lot of major cities have at least one a year, sometimes more, though most aren't well advertised. The nice thing is you don't have to travel across country to attend one. Check your newspaper, your local libraries, and the internet for a convention near you.

Workshops are more like conferences than conventions, but they usually last longer, anywhere from three days to six weeks. And they're all about the author and the writing process and improving your work.

The main difference between a conference and a workshop isn't so much the length, it's the activities. Unlike conferences where you go to panels or discussion groups or classes to listen to experts in their fields, in a workshop, you go to work. At a workshop, you're expected to write, not just notes, but really write. To work on your novel or short story in progress. There are lectures and classes, yes, but there's also homework and writing assignments and one on one instruction in some cases. Workshops aren't so much about networking, though that's an added benefit; they're about work, lots of hard, stretch your brain kind of work.

Workshops are usually smaller and more intimate and they almost always cost a lot more than a conference. If you're looking to attend one, make sure you research them ahead of time. They aren't cheap and you want to make sure you spend your money wisely. Also, be prepared to work and work hard. You'll be mentally exhausted by the end, but if you put everything you can into improving your writing, you'll find the time and energy you've spent is worth every penny.

A few workshops you might consider:

THE BREAKOUT NOVEL INTENSIVE WORKSHOPS <http://www.free-expressions.com>. Run by agent Donald Maass and the staff at Free Expressions, the workshops are based on his best-selling book, *Writing the Breakout Novel.* They offer invaluable advice and hands-on instruction on how to take your writing to the next level. There are three week long workshops a year, one on the West coast, one on the East coast and one in the central United States. Class sizes are limited to only thirty-five people, so if you're interested, sign up early. Unlike some workshops, this one doesn't require a writing sample to get in.

CLARION: One of the most prestigious workshops for Science Fiction and Fantasy writers is Clarion (Michigan), Clarion West (Washington), and Clarion South (Australia). All three are six week long workshops and are run both by visiting writer/instructors and resident writer/instructors. To apply, you must submit a sample of your writing. And unlike the Breakout Novel Workshop which focuses on novels, the Clarion workshops are for short story writing only.

ODYSSEY WORKSHOP: Similar to Clarion, but not as prestigious, is the Odyssey Workshop. This also is six weeks long, but unlike the others, you can work on either short stories or a novel while you're there. And while Clarion only accepts fantasy and science-fiction writers, Odyssey accepts all speculative fiction writers including those who write horror and magical realism. Each week there is a different writer/instructor and every student has the chance to have work read and critiqued by them as well as attending their classes. You must submit a sample of your work to get accepted.

SUBMITTING YOUR SHORT STORY—RESOURCES

Once you feel your short story is ready to submit, how do you go about finding the right market for your work? And while you're looking, don't rule out anthologies. They can be great places to showcase your work, but be careful. The pay varies wildly, anywhere from copies to a share of the royalties to professional rates of five cents a word or more.

There are many places to look for markets, some in print, and some on the internet. Probably the most widely used print source is Writer's Market. There are several different ones, depending on what you're looking for. The two I use most often are the Novel and Short Story Writer's Market and the bigger, more general Writer's Market. If all you write is fiction, the Novel and Short Story Writer's Market is fine. But if you want to write articles or book reviews, etc, you'll want the bigger book, which includes magazines, publishers, and agents who accept non-fiction. But keep in mind that the two books, while they may have a lot of the same information, are separate databases and some fiction markets found in one, might not be found in the other. You'd do best to choose the Writer's Market best suited to what you're writing, whether it be fiction or non-fiction.

But remember, while these books are great resources, they become obsolete the minute they come off the press. So use them to find a market you're interested in, then follow up with further research to make sure the market is still in business, they haven't moved, and that the person you're supposed to submit to still works there. Sending your submission with wrong information brands you an amateur. It only takes a little more effort to make sure the information you have is correct.

Writer's Market also has an online database that's updated on a daily basis. The cost is very reasonable for a year, or a monthly plan is available.

Online markets are more prevalent, especially for speculative fiction writers (science fiction, fantasy, and horror).

FICTION FACTOR, <http://www.fictionfactor.com>, not only provides market listings, but articles on the craft of writing fiction as well.

SPECFICME NEWSLETTER, <http://www.specficworld.com/sfme.html>, a bi-monthly newsletter listing new markets. The yearly cost includes six issues.

SPECULATIONS, <http://www.speculations.com/>, on online newsletter/market list. There's a charge to join, but what you get is pure information, no ads taking up space. The information is updated regularly and new market information is sent directly to you by email. They also have a question and answer type forum that's free.

RALAN.COM In my opinion, by far the best market for speculative fiction writers is Ralan Conley's website, <http://www.ralan.com>. The site is updated every couple of days and has the most extensive listing of speculative fiction markets I've seen anywhere. He has listings for anthologies, book publishers, pro markets (3 cents a word or more), paying markets (anything up to 2.9 cents a word), and 4 The Love markets (markets that don't pay anything). Best of all, it's free.

In your search for a market, you'll want to check several things to make sure your story fits their guidelines. Is it the right genre? Don't send psychological science fiction stories to magazines that only accept hard science fiction for instance. What's the suggested word count? Does your story fall within the correct parameters? Take a look at the pay. Is whatever they're offering something you can live with? You wouldn't want to submit your story to a non-paying market if your goal is to make money, however, if your goal is to get exposure and writing experience, submitting to a non-paying market might be perfectly acceptable. Do they accept email submissions, or only snail mail? Simultaneous submissions (the same story to more than one market at a time, which is frowned upon by most publishers whether stated or not)? Multiple submissions (more than one story to the same market)? Where are they located? If you live in the states, you might think twice about submitting to an overseas market. If you have to snail mail the submission, the cost of postage might be more than you'd make if you sold the story.

Once you find a market that looks promising, before you pop your submission in the mail (or send it by email), take another look at your writing. One of the marks of a professional is to always be realistic about your writing. Ask yourself the hard questions. Is it at a level that would be accepted by this publication? Have you done enough research? Have you read back issues of this particular market? Sure, you can shoot for the moon, but realize that where you are now may be less than what you thought.

MARKET RESEARCH

This may sound like same thing I addressed above in Resources, but it's not. Once you've figured out which markets you're interested in submitting to, your next step is to do the research. What this means is to buy, borrow, or otherwise secure as many back copies of the target market as you can. Read them from cover to cover. Get an idea of the kinds of things they like. Does your story fit their vision? Is it like the other stories, but different? Is it too similar or too different? Either one will likely get you rejected.

What this research does too is let you see what others are writing and how they're writing. Not only can you learn to improve your work by reading the mistakes others make, but you can learn by reading published authors in your genre. Look how they put a story together, how they open the story, how they resolve things at the end. Analyze what you've read, look at what works and figure out how they did it, then look at your own work and see if their technique is something you could use.

Read until you think you've read enough, then read some more. And even after you're published, keep reading. Keeping abreast of the current market will help you continue to be published.

COVER LETTERS AND FORMATTING

What is a cover letter and when do you use it? A cover letter is the letter you enclose with your short story when you submit it, either by snail mail or e-mail. It's very simple and straightforward. All you need to do is say the title of your story, a short bio about yourself, and whether or not your manuscript is disposable. If you met someone at a conference, you might mention that as well, but that's it. Plain and simple. Unlike a query letter for a novel, you don't need to outline your story. No editor will judge you on what you don't put in a cover letter, but they might judge you on what you do put.

Following is a sample of the one I normally use.

Date

No Name Anthology
Joe Smith, Editor
Address
City, State, Zip
(I always include name and address even if I'm submitting by e-mail)
Dear Mr. Editor:

I herewith enclose my short story, titled The Story, for consideration in your No Name Anthology.

Short publishing history/bio if you have one. If you don't, leave this part blank. Never, never, never invent things to put in this space. Believe me, if you make things up, editors will know.

Thank you for your time and consideration. An E-mail address has been included for your ease in responding. (If I'm sending by snail mail, I say something like, 'Enclosed is an SASE, consider the manuscript disposable) Thank you.

Best Wishes,
Michele Acker
Address
City, State Zip
Home phone
Cell phone (optional)
e-mail address

See? Simple. All you need to do is give just enough information to whet the editor's appetite and get him to read your story. But perhaps this is your first submission and you don't have any previous publishing credits, what then? Simple, just leave out the bio paragraph. Whatever you do though, don't tell the editor you've never been published or this is your first short story. Not only will they be able to figure that out for themselves when you don't include a bio, but it marks you as an amateur. Writing and getting published is all about professionalism. If you want people to take you seriously, be as professional and polite as you can possibly be. Which leads to my next subject.

MANUSCRIPT FORMATTING

I'm addressing the subject of manuscript formatting in the short story section, but the same rules apply to novels as well.

I'll give you some of the basic rules for proper formatting, but first and foremost, always follow a market's guidelines. If they tell you to change the font color of every italicized word to red, do it. If they tell you to single space your manuscript with a double space between paragraphs, do it. Why? Because that's the way they want it and submitting your work is all about following directions. Some places may tell you not to follow directions, to stand out so they'll notice you. And you might be tempted. But I warn you right now, don't do it. Be professional. Follow the rules. Stand out not because you can't follow directions, but because you can. Editors get so many submissions a year they look for ways to reject you, to make their job easier. Why give them an excuse? Why shoot yourself in the foot when your goal is to get published?

If your chosen market's guidelines say 'use standard manuscript formatting,' this is what it means:

Font and font size. Some editors prefer Courier because it more closely resembles a typewriter and all the letters take up the same amount of space. Proportional fonts like Times New Roman are a little harder to read, but most editors don't mind it. So unless they specify, go ahead and use either Courier or Times New Roman in a 12 pt font. Don't use fancy fonts that are hard to read.

Line spacing and indenting. Unless they say otherwise, always double space your manuscript and don't put extra lines between paragraphs. Use # to indicate a space between paragraphs, if for instance, you want to break from one place to another, or one point of view to another. Indent the first line of every paragraph. Use your tab key.

Margins and underlining. Use 1" margins all around. Justify the left margin and leave the right margin ragged. Make sure you only use one side of the page, whether you use a typewriter or print off from your computer. Underline words that should be italicized (Italics are easily missed).

Contact information and page numbering. In the upper left corner of your first page put your name, address, phone number and email address. In the upper right corner put your word count. While the easiest way to determine word count is by using the word count feature in your word processing program, you shouldn't use this number unless the guidelines specifically tell you to. Instead, round your word count based on the length of your manuscript. Here are some basic guidelines taken from an article titled, "What is a Word?" written by Chuck Rothman for SFWA (Science Fiction & Fantasy Writers of America). Go here to read the entire article <http://www.sfwa.org/writing/wordcount.htm>. In the end, the last thing you need to stress about is the word count, at least until you finish the manuscript. Obsess instead about doing the best writing you're capable of.

- Count the number of characters in an average, mid-paragraph line (BTW, this all assumes a monospaced font, such as Courier. If you're using a proportional font, such as Times New Roman, the number of characters can vary immensely, throwing off the numbers and word count).
- Divide by six. This is the number of words per line.
- Count the number of lines on a page. (This includes blank lines.)
- Multiply #2 by #3 to get the number of words per page.
- Multiply by the number of full pages (plus any fractional pages), to get the total number of words.
- Round the number to the nearest hundred. This is the number you put on the front page of the manuscript.

In the header put your name and page number in the upper right corner. Alternately, you can put your name in the upper left corner and the page number in the upper right. Either way, make sure to leave the first page header blank. Again, follow instructions if there are any.

Story title. Go down about a third of the page and type the name of the story, preferably in all caps, and center justify. Below the title type, By and Your Name, also center justified. If you use a pen name here's the place to put it, as long as your contact information has your real name and address. At the end of the story, type End or The End and center justify.

In the end, you should always follow the guidelines of the market you're submitting to. Most state how they'd like to see their submissions formatted, but if you're unsure, or if the market doesn't say, use standard formatting. There are all kinds of articles on the internet about proper manuscript formatting, use the resources if you need them.

SUBMITTING YOUR NOVEL: DO I NEED AN AGENT?

Must you have an agent to sell your novel? No. Should you have an agent? It's a good idea. Here's why:

Agents have contacts. They know which editor at which house is looking for what kind of manuscript. They can get your work in front of the right person at the right time. They can contact editors ahead of time and pitch your novel to them, get them excited about seeing your work.

Editors trust agents. They know that if an agent submits to them, the work is at least worth reading because the agent has already filtered out unsuitable manuscripts or those that aren't yet ready for publication.

Agents know contracts. Unless you sell to Harlequin or Silhouette[116] you'll need someone to negotiate your contract for you. Of course, you can always hire a literary lawyer, but they can only make sure your contract is on the up and up or suggest things you might want to change. They can't negotiate a higher advance for you, or get you selling bonuses or a bigger advertising budget. Agents can do that for you.

Agents can submit to places you can't. Because of the large number of people submitting work, many of the big houses won't take unagented manuscripts anymore. There are always exceptions of course; you might meet an editor at a conference who asks you to submit to them, or maybe you final in a contest where one of the judges is an editor. But for the most part, you need an agent to get your work in front of the right people

Agents help you make your work the best it can be before they submit it, giving you the best possible chance of selling. It's in their own best interest to do this as it means a bigger profit for both the agent and the author. Of course, not all agents edit their client's manuscripts and not all authors want them to. If that's what you want, make sure the agents you query provide that service.

If you absolutely don't want to have an agent, you can try to sell your work yourself. Many people have done so and quite successfully, but expect the process to be more difficult and take longer. If you do decide to go the agent route, be careful about whom you choose. A bad agent is worse than no agent at all. Make a list of agents you want to query, then thoroughly check them out through every resource you can find.

RESOURCES

How do you find an agent? Or maybe the question should read, how do you find the right agent for you?

First of all, you want to make sure the agents you're querying represent the genre you write. For instance, you don't want to submit science fiction to an agent who handles romance and you don't want to submit fiction to an agent that only handles non-fiction or screenplays.

Then make sure the agents on your list are reputable. Are they a member of AAR (Association of Author's Representatives) and if not, do they follow AAR's canon of ethics? An agent doesn't have to belong to AAR to be reputable. Some big agencies, like Trident Media for example, don't belong because they have no desire to, even though they qualify. And other agencies, like Firebrand Literary, don't belong because they deal with book packagers, which AAR frowns upon. Book packagers, in case you're unfamiliar with the term, usually come up with concepts or story ideas themselves, then find an author or authors to write the book. Examples of this would be the Sweet Valley High YA books, or the once popular Goosebumbs books. Then you have book packagers like Wizards of the Coast, who hire writers to write in a specific world they've created. Other examples of this would be Star Trek and Star Wars books. Some authors make a very good living writing these kinds of books. Others don't like them because it takes away some of the creativity of writing fiction, such as building your own fictional world, or creating your own characters.

Other agents haven't been in business long enough to join AAR or don't have enough sales to qualify yet. That doesn't make them bad agents. Many sources will tell you to only query agents that belong to AAR, but as long as they follow AAR's code of ethics and don't charge up front reading fees, I don't think it's all that important. But keep this in mind, never, never, never pay an agent out of your own pocket for anything. Remember this mantra, "The money flows to the author." Once your book is sold, the checks will come to the agent, she/he will take their share plus any costs for postage, photocopying, etc (which expenses will have been discussed with you when you signed the author/agent contract), then pass the rest on to you. The only time it might be acceptable to pay an agent out of your pocket is if you severed the relationship before the agent sold any of your work. In that case, some agents might expect you to reimburse them for expenses, while most agents will just write it off as part of the costs of being in business. These are all things you should discuss upfront before signing with any agent.

But how do you find the perfect agent? Where do you search? There are many resources for finding agents, the most obvious being *Writer's Market* or

The Novel and Short Story Writer's Market. But by no means are they the only source you should use. They don't list even half of the available agents. Right now there are hundreds if not thousands of literary agents representing everything from screenplays to non-fiction to textbooks to fiction in any genre you can imagine. No one source lists them all, so your best bet is to use several.

Another good written resource is *Jeff Herman's Guide to Literary Agents.* Their list is more extensive than *Writer's Market,* but still only a drop in the ocean. And like *Writer's Market,* some of the information it contains has changed by the time you buy it in the store.

There are several good online markets as well. All agents who are members of AAR are listed on their website, <http://www.aar-online.org/mc/page.do>. You can search by name of the agent, name of the agency, or by keywords including genre. You can be assured that everyone listed is a member of AAR, but there are many good agents who don't belong for whatever reason.

The best online market I've found so far is Agent Query, <http://www.agentquery.com>. They only list reputable, non-fee charging agents whether or not they are members of AAR. This is also a searchable database and each agent's profile provides you with the agency name, contact information, what genres they represent, and how they prefer to be queried. For more well established agents, it also lists some of their previous sales.

Another good resource is Publishers Marketplace, <http://www.publishersmar-ketplace.com/>. On their website you can read about recent deals, including first books sold, foreign rights sold, and movie deals. You can look up agents who represent your genre and you can find the agent of any published author listed in their database. It's not free, the cost is $20.00 a month, but it is an invaluable resource for anyone who wants to keep updated on what's selling, who's buying, and what kind of advances are being paid. Everyone in the publishing industry reads and keeps track of this information. If you're serious about your career, it's a small enough investment to make.

It's always good to be referred to an agent by one of their current clients. That's one of the reasons it pays to network. If there's an author you know and admire perhaps they'd be willing to give you a referral to their agent. Or maybe you met an agent or editor at a conference, they like what you've written but it's not something they represent. Perhaps they'll refer you to a colleague or another agent they know that's looking for your kind of work. It doesn't happen often, but it does happen.

By far the best resource to meeting and networking with agents and editors is to attend conferences, if you can afford it. Not only do conferences allow you to network with other authors who might be of benefit to you in the future (and visa-versa), you get to meet editors and agents face to face. There's nothing like meeting someone in person to give you a sense of who they are, to see them as real people and not some amorphous, out of reach entity. If you see one in a bar, offer to buy them a drink. Chat about things, books you've read, things you've enjoyed about the conference, classes you've attended (especially if it was one of theirs) and above all, be polite, professional and never pushy. If they like you and enjoy talking to you, they will ask you what you write and that's your chance to pitch to them. But only if they ask. And then follow up. If they request a partial from you, send it! As soon as you get home. You have no idea how often I've heard agents say they've asked for things at a conference and never received them.

QUERY LETTERS

As stated in the interviews below, a good query letter is essential in finding an agent. Why? Because it's the first thing an agent sees of your work. You want it to be as professional as possible, meaning no typos, no misspellings, one page preferably (single spaced is standard), no weird fonts, etc. Make it as nice and clean and easy to read as possible. A query letter is like meeting someone in person for the first time, you only have one chance to make a good impression.

Query letters, good ones anyway, are hard to write. I know. The last one I wrote ended up being revised at least a dozen times before I was satisfied with it. How important are they? A good query letter can be vital in getting someone to consider your work. First impressions are everything. In most cases, it's the only contact you may have with an agent or editor, which is a good reason why you should always enclose the first few pages of your novel with your query (unless of course they ask for more). If you've written an unexciting query, you still have a brief chance to impress the agent enough to get them to request more.

To write a good query, one that draws an agent's attention, you need to do more than just give a brief outline of your novel. While most agents want several basic things in your letter, such as genre, word count, novel title, bio, and a short description, you don't need to be boring. You can keep it short and simple, and still make it intriguing enough for them to ask for more. Start with a good hook, one that will keep them reading, but make sure the hook makes sense. Don't put something down just because it sounds exciting if it has nothing to do with the novel itself. And don't just list what happens (this happens, then this happens, then this happens), show the plot, especially the internal and external conflict.

Good stories are all about conflict, without it, you don't have a novel any agent would want to represent. Think about the plot. What makes it different from other science fiction novels? Highlight those differences. If you can do all that, you have the makings of a good query letter.

If you've never written a query letter before and you want to see samples that worked or didn't work, there are tons of resources both online and written, such as the Writer's Market books. One of the better online resources is a blog written by an editor who calls himself Evil Editor, <http://www.evileditor.blogspot.com/>. He not only posts and critiques query letters (all genres) that have been emailed to him by his readers, he also posts openings to unpublished novels (also emailed to him) and previously published work, enabling you to see what works and what doesn't. Miss Snark (an agent), http://misssnark.blogspot.com/, runs a twice a year 'crap-o-meter' where she critiques either query letters or the first page of your novel, depending on her mood at the time. The rest of the year she answers reader's questions and gives out professional advice for those looking for representation. Even when she isn't running the crapometer, you can read past entries along with her comments in the archives. Seeing the mistakes others make can help you improve your own work. One of Miss Snark's blog readers started her own crap-o-meter, <http://www.crapometer.blogspot.com/>, where you can submit query letters, synopsis, or beginning pages for critiquing. She isn't an industry professional, but her comments and those of her readers can be helpful nonetheless.

The Writer's Market books always include articles about writing query letters in the front of the book, usually giving both good and bad examples, and explaining what the agent liked or didn't like about each one. There are also plenty of books on how to write not only query letters, but synopsis as well. Just go to Amazon.com, or Borders.com, or Barnsandnobel.com and do a search. There's quite a few to choose from. There are also find plenty of online articles on the subject as well. You can also get recommendations from your writer contacts, and if you have a critique group, let them help you perfect your letter. Sometimes additional eyes catch things you've missed, or they can give you suggestions on how to improve your query.

BEYOND THE QUERY

While some agents might request a full from just a query letter, most will ask for a partial first, then if they like it, they'll ask for a full. Some agents will ask you to submit the first three chapters with your query letter and synopsis, allowing you to bypass the partial process. This is good for both of you. It allows you to wow the agent with your writing even if you haven't written a good query letter, and it allows the agent to get a feel for your voice right up front. Because agents and editors are so inundated with slush they look for anything that will allow them to reject your submission. Don't give them that chance. Good queries are hard to write so if you can, give yourself a second chance not to get rejected. One New York Times best-selling author, James Rollins (who also writes Fantasy under the pseudonym James Clemens), once advised me to send a partial to every agent, even if all they request is a query letter. Whether you choose to do this or not is up to you. You might upset an agent or two, but most won't reject you just because you sent too much material. They may not read everything you sent, but they'll at least take a look at the first few pages. Then too, you have to consider the cost of postage for all those partials. A better option might be to send the query letter and the first five pages of your manuscript. It accomplishes the same objectives and saves money on postage.

Say you have a request for a full from a particular agent and they ask for an exclusive. Do you grant them one? To understand this question, you need to know what an exclusive is. Granting an agent an exclusive means that you promise not to show your manuscript to anyone else until she/he has a chance to read it and get back to you. So do you grant an exclusive? That's up to you. If this is an agent you'd really like to have and you don't already have fulls out with anyone else, you should consider it. But put a time limit on it. Anywhere from two to six weeks is pretty standard and it depends on what you're comfortable with. Certainly don't grant an open ended exclusive because it might be months before the agent gets back to you. But not all agents ask for exclusives and sometimes knowing that other agents have your work gets them to read it faster (but don't count on it, that's not always the case).

Once an agent offers you representation, one of the first things you should do is ask to see a copy of their agent-client contract. While not all agents offer one, most do. And some agents who don't normally offer written contracts will probably write one up for you if you feel uncomfortable about not having one. Once you get the contract, look it over carefully. There are several things you want to check out before you sign. First of all, you want to see what kind of Terms they require. When you want to terminate your relationship, how much notice do you need to give? Thirty to sixty days written notice is normal. Never sign with an agent that holds you to a specific term, like two years for instance. If things go wrong between the two of you, or you feel the agent isn't doing his job, you don't want to be locked into a contract you can't get out of.

Secondly, you should look at their fee structure. Some agents charge for copying, postage, long distance phone calls, etc, but many don't. Some put a cap on a particular work, paying all fees up to say $100, then charging for everything beyond that. Some agents only charge for unusual expenses. All are legitimate, but should be worked out beforehand with the author as part of the contract.

Most everything else spelled out in the contract you should know already because if you were smart, you'd have already thoroughly researched the agent. But certainly read over the contract and make sure nothing has changed. Do they still charge 15% commission for instance? But be wary, some agencies have begun the practice of trying to tie up an author's work for the length of copyright instead of length of contract. The following is quoted from an article appearing on the RWA National website:

> "The prevailing practice in the past has been for authors to assign rights in their publisher/author contracts to their agent for the life of the publisher/author contract. In other words, as long as the publisher with whom the agent negotiated the contract kept the book in print, the agent would receive a commission on advances and royalties. This approach makes sense. The agent negotiated the contract and should receive the fruit of his or her efforts.
>
> In the past, if the author's association with the agent that negotiated a contract ended, then if the publisher reverted rights of the properties in the negotiated contract back to the author, all rights would return to the author. The author could enter into an arrangement with another agent to resell the returned properties, or to sell foreign rights, or the author could resell the book on his or her own.
>
> Now a few agencies are trying to change the rules. They are requiring their authors to sign contracts that give the agency (not necessarily the individual agent selected by the author) representation rights for the length of the copyright (which is the life of the author plus seventy years) even if the agency does nothing to effect a new sale."

If you see this clause on the contract, and this is an agent you really want, talk to them, see if they'd be willing to remove this clause or change it to read 'until the book goes out of print'. Some might be willing. If they aren't, don't sign, or if you do, make sure you're fully aware of what you're doing. Don't go into anything blind.

You can also have a literary Lawyer look over the contract, for a fee, to make sure you aren't signing something you'll later regret.

If everything looks on the up and up and you feel comfortable with that agent, go ahead and sign the contract. But if anything jumps out at you, or you don't understand something, ask. Any reputable agent will be more than happy to answer any questions or concerns you might have. That's part of their job.

To get some insider information on submitting to agents and editors, I've interviewed Agent Donald Maass with The Donald Maass Agency, Agent Nadia Cornier with Firebrand Literary Agency and Editor Liz Scheier with Roc. Their answers are as follows:

DONALD MAASS, AGENT

Donald Maass is president of the Donald Maass Literary Agency in New York, which he founded in 1980. He represents more than 100 fiction writers and sells more than 100 novels per year to top publishers in America and overseas. He is himself the author of fourteen pseudonymous novels and of the books *The Career Novelist* (Heineman, 1996), *Writing the Breakout Novel* (Writers Digest Press, 2001) and *Writing the Breakout Novel Workbook* (Writers Digest Press 2004). He is a past president of the Association of Authors' Representatives, Inc. (AAR).

NADIA CORNIER, AGENT

Nadia Cornier has been an agent since 2004. She formed Firebrand Literary in September 2005 after leaving the Creative Media Agency. Firebrand represents an eclectic mixture of romance, young adult, mainstream, and non-fiction projects. Prior to working as an agent, she began Cornier & Associates, LLC a small marketing firm specializing in author services that still runs in conjunction with her agency. Her experience with marketing has led her to develop "campaigns" to market her authors' projects to publishers and beyond instead of simply selling them. Nadia is also the co-author of *How to Write and Sell the Young Adult Novel*, Writer's Digest December 2006.

LIZ SCHEIER, EDITOR

Liz Scheier started her career as an editor in 2000. She spent four years at the Bantam Dell Publishing group, leaving in early 2004 to join the New American Library, a division of the Penguin Group USA. She acquires mainly science fiction, fantasy, and horror for the Roc imprint, but is also interested in biography, humor, popular culture, and works of GLBT interest. She is a graduate of Bryn Mawr College, where she studied English literature and therefore rendered herself blissfully unemployable in any other field.

> What do you see as the market for Science Fiction? All things being equal (the novels equally as well written), do you have an easier time selling a Fantasy novel or a Science Fiction novel? How about cross-genre novels (for instance, Science Fiction and Mystery)? Do you see this trend changing in the near future?

DONALD: Fantasy is much easier to sell than Science Fiction. It's not that there isn't good stuff being written, it's just that consumers aren't buying it. Fantasy is easier for people to understand, where Science Fiction, especially hard Science Fiction, is more difficult. In Fantasy, anything with vampires is doing well right now, as well as werewolves, dark elves, goblins, etc. in our world. Fantasy Romance does very well and is very durable. Time Travel isn't much in demand anymore unless it's in a Romance novel.

NADIA: Because the majority of the books I represent are young adult works, I'm going to answer in terms of those (and hopefully that's ok). The YA/Children's market seems to hold a wider appeal for fantasy authors - perhaps because of the recent success of books like *Harry Potter* or *Eragon*, or perhaps (more telling) the number of young female editors who claim not to enjoy science fiction. I find this odd, personally, because many of the same editors will agree that they enjoyed movies like the *Matrix* or *I, Robot* (well, who wouldn't like a Will Smith flick?) - these movies *are* science fiction! I think many people just say they don't enjoy science fiction because of what science fiction used to be... it has become more and more appealing to the wider market of readers who aren't into hard-science fiction. There are more sub-genres (and cross-genres!) within the SF market that now allow readers who would never have thought themselves SF readers to become fans of the market. But, just like people who automatically answer "I like all kinds of music except Rap and Country" there are still people who will respond, "I like all kinds of books except SF and Fantasy!" when really that just might mean they don't really know what they are reading. I think the more "mainstream" and accessible to the every day reader this genre gets the more the SF fan base will grow.

LIZ: It does tend to be a bit easier to sell fantasy than science fiction. This can be chalked up to any number of factors; fantasy tends to be written in series, so that readers can follow along with characters they've grown to love over multiple books; SF, particularly hard SF, can be daunting to readers who aren't science-minded. We've seen a lot of great crossover in the fantasy world, particularly what I tend to think of as the Buffyesque category—urban fantasy, which is, at face value, fantasy mixed with contemporary suspense. I do see this trend continuing, as authors feel freer to try their hands at new fields—or to invent their own.

> In today's market, is it better to get an agent to represent me as opposed to submitting directly to publishers? Why? What can an agent do for me that I can't do for myself?

DONALD: The fields of Science Fiction and Fantasy tend to be more open to accepting unagented submissions, so you don't have to have an agent to sell. However, a good agent can do things for you that you can't do for yourself. A good agent keeps abreast of the changing markets, can negotiate better offers and can help with career counseling.

NADIA: If we're talking about the adult SF market, it's easier to get an agent once you have a book deal. Well, it's always easier to get an agent once you have a book deal...

but, in this case there is a limited number of publishers and editors that you can send your project to and perhaps because of this, it makes more sense to "go it alone" if you must. That said, working with an agent at any point in your career (pre- or post-sale) is helpful. An agent might be able to get you a better deal than initially offered. Your agent will negotiate your contracts, help you with any conflict resolution, and work towards building and guiding your career. That said, there is nothing an agent can do for you that you can't do for yourself with enough time, energy and resources—but wouldn't you rather be writing?

LIZ: It is absolutely better to have an agent to represent you. For instance, my schedule doesn't permit me to read unsolicited queries or manuscripts, so the only way submissions reach my desk is if I've met someone at a conference at editor appointments, or through an agent. Agents are experts at their markets; they'll know which editors would be the best match for a project, and will know how best to present and pitch your work. Once an offer is made, they can help negotiate the contract, and act as your advocate in all aspects of your career.

> What do you think of authors who have self-published? Is it a career breaker or does it depend on the number of books they've sold? How about any who've been e-published?

DONALD: Self publishing or e-publishing is a negative only because in most cases the quality of that writing is very low. 999 times out of 1,000, self published and e-published books cannot be resold to New York publishers. It does happen, but it's a rare occurrence. One area where e-publishing seems to work is erotica. Publishers like Ellora's Cave have shown that writers can make money with e-publishing, but I think that's a special case.

NADIA: Unfortunately, unless an author has sold 5,000 copies or more of their self-published novel—I simply don't count it. It doesn't count against you or for you, it simply doesn't count. Why? Well, I have no idea what the author's objectives were when deciding to self-publish—but I do know that without a professional editor, copy-editor, marketing department, art department, sales department, publicity... you get the idea—without all these people a book simply won't be the best it can be. The publishing process can take up to two years (more if you count the time the author needs to write the book) to get to the shelves... self-publishing and e-books skip a lot of these steps and you have to be careful regarding which ones they are skipping and the end results. That said, there are quite a few very respectable e-publisher and small presses that do put out great projects that just don't fit into the lines that the corporate presses have. But, do your research and never pay to have anyone read or publish your project!

LIZ: Self-publishing is often a very good option for certain types of nonfiction. For fiction, self-publication or e-publication wouldn't affect my decision one way or the other, unless they've sold an extraordinary number of copies.

> If an agent rejects my submission, is it okay to submit to a different agent at the same agency? Under the same situation, is it okay to submit to a different editor at the same publishing house?

DONALD: Yes & Yes

NADIA: Iffy - but I'd err on the safe side with no. To both questions. Why? If I read a project that I think is great, but not right for me - I'll pass it along. Most agents will. If an agent passed on the project, it probably meant it wasn't right for the agent and the agent didn't feel it was right to pass along. I feel the same way about editors. I can't resubmit a client's project to another editor if one passes... It just doesn't work if there wasn't a mega-amount of editing done to the manuscript. But once the editor leaves, feel free to resubmit to that house.

LIZ: I can't speak for agencies; since agents work more independently within agencies than editors do within houses, they may work differently. It would be unprofessional to submit to more than one editor within the same imprint, even if the two submissions aren't simultaneous.

> How important is formatting when submitting to an agent or an editor? Following guidelines? What formatting errors would cause you to reject a manuscript?

DONALD: Formatting by itself isn't the main issue. It's just that we so often find that manuscripts improperly formatted are also written poorly. I think it's a matter of inexperience.

NADIA: Proper formatting is a sign of respect. Respect that you are showing your own project and respect for the editor and agent's time. No one will reject your project (well...most won't) based purely on a lapse in formatting, but if you don't show them respect by following the proper guidelines for submissions, they will respond in kind by not showing you the same respect in considering your submission.

LIZ: It's absolutely essential to present the manuscript in neat, easy-to-read format. I read at least a thousand pages a day, usually more - my eyes just wouldn't be able to handle a tiny font or single spacing! It shows courtesy and professionalism to follow guidelines. This isn't a matter of being compulsive or needlessly picky; it's simply not physically possible for me to read more than a few pages of hard-to-read type. And when I buy a book from an author, I'm hoping to begin a long, productive relationship with that author; if s/he is already behaving unprofessionally, it doesn't give me much hope for how things will go in the future.

> I've been offered a contract with a particular agent. What are the five most important questions I should ask?

DONALD: Are you a member of AAR? Does the contract allow for termination by the author/what is the termination clause? Is there a perpetuity clause? What are the rights of succession in your contract/what happens if my agent dies, who takes over? What's your plan for my novel? What's the best plan for my career?

NADIA: Does this project need to be edited before submitting/Do you do editing with your clients? Do you do career planning with your clients? Can I see a copy of your contract? What type of support do you offer your clients after a deal is done? What do I need to know about you, your agency, and your working style?

> How important is it for an agent to be located in New York?

DONALD: It's less important than it once was. Now the most important thing to consider is how well your agent keeps up with the market.

NADIA: These days? It's a toss up. A good agent is no longer judged solely on his/her location - but his/her connections. If your prospective agent isn't in NYC (or even if he is) check out what kinds of deals he has done, who he has worked with, what he did prior to becoming an agent. These details are more important than what city he calls your editor from.

LIZ: Not terribly. There are many extremely talented and well-connected agents who have worked with very well-respected agencies, and who then strike off on their own all over the country. However, agents who live in NY do have better opportunities to network with editors, so they may be more likely to be aware of changes in the industry.

> I've heard that having a bad agent is worse than having no agent at all, so what distinguishes a bad agent from a good agent, and how do you tell the difference? How do you tell if an agent has experience? What kind of experience is the most valuable?

DONALD: A bad agent can be a good agent who happens to be the wrong agent for you. How do you tell? If they don't communicate with you. If they push you to write solely for the market when you have no feeling for that type of story. If they keep your money. Unfortunately, there's no easy way to know that stuff ahead of time. I'd listen to what they say about your writing. Is it specific? Is it insightful? What is the quality of the conversation? Is there listening or just telling? Does the agent have experience with your kind of story? Ask.

NADIA: The second deal I ever did was for a client who left a really huge agency to work with me—she took a huge risk but it was a calculated risk that turned out to be a great choice (yay!)—A new agent isn't necessarily a bad agent—so let's cross that off the list of distinguishing features of a bad agent. A bad agent (aside from the handle bar moustache and the greased back hair) may ask you for a fee to read your manuscript, may not have worked with any respected agencies prior to starting his/her own, may not have any sales, may make "unfair demands" upon your representation-rights in his agency contract. But—worst of all—a bad agent doesn't care. Has no great love for your project, no passion. This is the person you must run away from...nothing will kill your project faster than someone who doesn't care about it.

> Does an author sign with the agent or the agency? Does an agent represent the writer or the ms?

DONALD: As far as my agency is concerned, you sign with the agency. We represent the writer.

NADIA: Check the contract. You sign with the agency - and the agent of record is the one who signs you...the contract will detail whether or not the agent represents all works by the writer or a particular project. Check this carefully!

> What are your five biggest turnoffs when it comes to reading query letters? What distinguishes a good query letter from a bad one?

DONALD: Turnoffs: A query that's too long, one page is more than enough. Over summarizing, just tell me the basics of the story. Too much hype, saying things like, "This is the best novel you're every going to read." Queries that tell you nonsense facts about nonsense, like, "There are 5 million mothers in American today and all would benefit from reading my novel, (title)." Test readers that aren't publishing professionals, "5 independent test readers read my novel and loved it." Comparisons work, but only if they're accurate. Good ones are rare.

NADIA: Turnoffs: Calling me "sir" or "editor"; cutting & pasting a writing sample when I expressly ask authors not to do so; telling me that their mother/daughter/neighborhood children love their book (unless your mother/daughter/neighborhood children are editors at a NY Publishing House—I don't care); Forgetting to tell me their name, the title, the word count - or simply not telling me anything about the book at all; people who insult their own book, their own genre, or one of my clients. A good query is professional, succinct, and tells me everything I need to know about the project.

LIZ: I don't really ever read query letters (most editors don't—an agent would be able to give you a better answer here) but I can boil my query letter turnoffs down to a single word: unprofessionalism. Seeing my name spelled wrong, having a letter addressed to "Dear Gentlemen" (in a 90% female industry!), receiving a letter that tells me nothing about the plot, is unspecific, or is printed on stationery with kittens cavorting around the borders—these are all really good ways to make sure the letter goes in the trash! A query letter is a business proposal and should be approached as such.

PUBLISHERS

MAJOR PRESSES

Having a major press (such as Roc, Ace, Bantam) publish your work is the dream of every writer. For a few it's a dream come true, a dream that involves lots of hard work and perseverance, but for many, many others, it's an unobtainable goal. Why? Most major presses for instance don't take unagented submissions, so you have to either meet the editor (and impress her) at a conference, or else you need an agent. And sometimes it's harder to find an agent than it is to sell your book. Still, it's definitely worth the time and effort to look.

The same markets you used to find an agent you can use to find an editor, especially Writer's Market. By far the best way to meet an editor (and agent for that matter) is at a conference. Editors who don't take unsolicited, or unagented manuscripts will often take one from someone they've met at a conference, either in a social situation or during a pitch session.

The value, of course, of being published by a big press is the power they have, not only to get your book out there, but to get behind your book, to give it the boost it needs to help it be successful. They can do larger print runs, pay more for publicity, etc. Keep in mind though that large presses can only do so much and they will put more money into a novel they know will be a best seller (for instance a novel written by a previous New York Times best selling author), than they will behind a new, unknown author. Still, being published by the 'big guys' is its own reward, an acceptance into the big leagues of major publishing as it were.

Large presses also pay the biggest advances, though you have to 'earn out' your advance before you see any royalty money. Earning out means you have to make enough in royalties to pay back the publisher for the advance. It's sort of like a loan and is also known as an 'advance against royalties'. The size of the advance you get depends on a lot of things, your publishing history, how well your last book sold, if you have an agent (agents can usually negotiate a higher advance and better terms for an author than an author can do for themselves), and the publishing house. Some publishers can afford to pay higher advances than others. Once you've earned out your advance, you start making royalties, which are generally paid once or twice a year. The amount of royalties you receive depends not only on the number of books sold, but also on the royalty percentage stated in your contract. Most publishers pay 6%-8%, but can go as low as 2% or as high as 12%. Usually you start out at the lower rate (6%), then it increases after you sell a certain number of books (after the first 50,000 copies, for example). But again, this all depends on your contract, which is another good reason to have an agent.

If you decide to submit directly to editors instead of finding an agent first, you can find publishers who accept Science Fiction and Fantasy in one of several Writer's Market books, or go online to <http://www.ralan.com> and look under the section of book publishers.

SMALL PRESSES

Small presses are usually known as Indy Publishers (Independent Publishers). Sometimes they are run by a university, sometime just by a small staff of editors under a single publisher. They can be good places to try, especially if you have a novel or non-fiction book that doesn't fit a specific market or genre. Indy presses will often take a chance on a book a New York house won't touch. Why? Because they can afford to. Most Indy Presses don't pay advances and when they do it's usually minimal. The good thing is, since you don't have to pay back an advance, you start earning royalties right away. Because small presses don't have a high overhead, they can usually afford to start at a slightly higher percentage rate than big publishers, say 10% instead of 6%. And they don't do large print runs, usually employing POD (Print on Demand) technology, allowing them to keep their print runs small so they don't have to put out the cost to warehouse books they can't sell.

Indy presses can be easy to work with—for instance, you don't need an agent to submit to them—but they aren't as well known as the big presses. Even if the press has distribution through Ingram's or Baker & Taylor, that doesn't mean bookstores will buy or stock their books. Usually you have to go to the store buyer, give them a copy of the book, and ask them to consider carrying it in their store. And that's only one branch. If you want your book in more than one branch, you have to approach them separately.

Because Indy presses have very small budgets, they can't do much to help market your book. They just don't have the funds. Which means that you spend a large portion of your time marketing the book yourself with only minor help from the publisher. That said, they can still be a good, viable alternative for getting your book published.

If you write Science Fiction or Fantasy, there are several good Independent Presses you might want to consider such as Edge Science Fiction and Fantasy Publishing <http://www.edgewebsite.com/authors.html>, or Mundania Press <http://www.mundania.com/> (check <http://www.ralan.com> for more small press listings. They list large press and e-book publishers as well).

E-PUBLISHING

E-publishing is becoming more and more common, especially in the field of erotic romance. There are several very successful e-publishers in this field, including Ellora's Cave and Loose ID (pronounced 'lucid'). There are many other e-publishers including those that handle Science Fiction, Fantasy, and Horror, such as Double Dragon Publishing <http://www.double-dragon-ebooks.com>. If for whatever reason you don't want to go the traditional route, you might want to consider this growing trend. Following are some facts about e-publishing from authors who have chosen to go that route.

E-publishing contracts are author friendly. They allow you to cancel with 60 days notice by either party. But remember, normal publishing houses have been in business for a long time. They have their publishing procedures down pat. Not so for a lot of e-publishers, especially ones that are just starting out. Mix ups with royalty statements and late payments have and do occur quite often.

E-publishers pay a higher royalty for every book sold, which can be an attractive alternative to traditional publishing. Most e-publishers pay 35-50% royalties on the sale price of the book to the author, while some may pay as much as 60%. Some of them also pay their authors monthly, rather than quarterly. However, most e-publishers don't pay advances. While this is changing at some houses, no one yet has gotten a big advance. It might happen though, just don't expect it to happen any time soon. That they're paying advances at all is new. Remember too, that unless you're writing erotica, you shouldn't expect to make thousands of dollars with e-books. You may only make a couple hundred. The royalty rate is higher, but they are often against the discounted price that eReader or Fictionwise demands rather than the cover price. And because many readers want an actual book they can hold, the market for e-books is smaller. Smaller market, fewer books bought, fewer royalties.

One of the best things about e-books is that you can download ten or more into your reader. For traveling, it's great. When you're through, you can upload them into the computer, then download other stories. E-books don't take up much hard drive space and hard drives today are so large that one could store hundreds of books in a computer and still have plenty of room for writing tools, software, games, whatever you like. In order to store hundreds of print books, you'd have to have an awful lot of bookshelves and plenty of storage in your house. Many books are less expensive as a download, too.

And e-books offer instant gratification. If someone is intrigued by a blurb or excerpt of your book on your website or publisher's site, they can purchase it right then, in their pajamas, without needing to wait for Amazon or Barnes and Noble or Borders to deliver a package to the door. Or getting dressed to go shopping. Impulse buys can be good.

Electronic publishing is still an evolving medium. New technologies are being developed, new markets are cropping up. E-books are gaining in acceptance and popularity. Several major publishers now publish their books in electronic format, so it's not quite as odd as it once was. Electronic publishers themselves are getting better and better recognition too (Ellora's Cave, for instance, has RWA recognition).

From the perspective of the reader who enjoys reading on a PDA or computer, e-books are fantastic. They can carry multiple books around with them in a small device and read them just about anywhere. Most of the publishers have gotten a clue and now charge a mass market price for them so they're very affordable. You can print them out and have them signed by your favorite author, just like a traditional book if you like.

From the author's perspective, e-publishing can be an excellent choice either for a book that doesn't fit a traditional publisher's niche, or for a book that's out of print that the author wants available for purchase. The good e-pubs like Hard Shell Word Factory <http://www.hardshell.com>, do everything they can to get their books into as many online outlets as possible, including Amazon. Hard Shell, in particular, does a very nice job with their cover art, but that's not the case with every e-publisher. If cover art is important to you, as it is to most authors, you might want to check a publisher's current titles before you decide to sign with them. Most e-publishers just don't have the same high quality cover art as print publishers.

There's a faster turnaround on seeing your book delivered. Edits can be exchanged online through email so there is no need to wait for the mail to deliver paper. Cover art is delivered the same way. It's very speedy.

But the majority of people are turned off by e-books for the sole reason that there's no physical book in their hands, on shelves, in stores. Many e-publishing houses now have options to go to a trade paperback print-on-demand format, so there's a growing possibility that going with an e-publisher means that you will still get a print book. It just may be six months down the line. The downside is that while most of them do release trade paperback versions after the e-book has come out, some of the e-pubs (not Hard Shell) price them exorbitantly. Plus, they can be hard to buy anywhere but on-line, where the reader has to pay for shipping. Some bookstores won't order them because they either can't get them through Ingrams or Baker & Taylor or else the discounts aren't sufficient.

Then there's the problem of selling the books. You can't use normal promotion methods like giving out bookmarks. They'd be useless for an electronic book. And a lot of people don't recognize the names of e-publishers or don't know about e-books in general. This means the response to news of a sale or series or what have you can be underwhelming.

So do think about e-book publishing as a viable alternative, but be aware of all the facts before you make a final decision.

SELF PUBLISHING

The terms Vanity Press, Self-Publishing and POD Presses are confusing. In some ways they're similar, they allow you to publish a book that for various reasons might not be acceptable to larger commercial publishers, but in the end they're different enough that you need to know what you want to accomplish in order to choose the right option for you. See <http://www.sfwa.org> for some good articles on the subject.

VANITY PRESSES

Basically, a vanity press prints and binds a book at the author's sole expense. Because costs include the publisher's profit and overhead, vanity publishing can be quite expensive. You have to pay for each book produced and there's usually a minimum number of books you have to order. In order to insure a profit, vanity presses charge far more than the actual production cost of the book. And because they make all their profit from the author, they have no economic incentive to market their author's books, offering them only through you (the author) or the publisher's website. Unlike commercial publishers, vanity presses don't screen for quality, they publish anyone who can pay, therefore the quality is often not very good.

On the good side though, all books are the property of the author so any money made from the sale of those books goes directly to the author (though most books don't sell enough to cover the cost of printing). If your goal is to publish a family history or genealogy, or maybe a personal memoir that only your family and friends would be interested in, a vanity press might be a good alternative.

SELF-PUBLISHING

While self publishing also requires the author to pay for publishing, the costs are often quite a bit less. The author can control every aspect of the process since they don't have to buy a pre-set package of services. It can also result in a higher-quality book. As in vanity publishing, completed books are owned by the author and he keeps all profits from the sales.

Some services like Publish America or IUniverse call themselves commercial publishers, but really they are nothing more than vanity presses. They require upfront fees that are pretty steep. Publish America does pay an advance of $1, but it's mainly just a marketing ploy designed to give them the appearance of legitimacy. Whatever you might like to think, they are not real markets. These presses will publish anyone's work, no matter how good or bad it is. Also, they are listed as the publisher and pay their authors in royalties, which are usually quite low. And most books they publish sell few if any copies. For example, according to IUniverse's fact sheet, the company reports it published 22,265 titles through 2005 with sales of 3.7 million. That sounds like a lot, but if you break it down, that's only an average of 166 sales per title and most titles don't even sell that many.

POD PRESSES

POD (or Print on Demand) is simply a term for a kind of printing technology and doesn't refer to particular publishers at all. For instance, while quite a few independent presses use POD technology to lower their business costs, they are a commercial publisher in every other way. POD technology allows a small publisher to produce a few books at a time instead of larger print runs of several hundred or several thousand. However, over the past few years, POD has taken on a specific meaning and has tainted the print on demand technology in general, mainly thanks to the ease of the technology allowing unqualified or unscrupulous people to set themselves up as publishers.

POD-based publishing service providers aren't publishers in the traditional sense, but provide publishing services to writers. Like vanity presses and self-publishing, they charge a fee for publication (usually less than a vanity press), they don't screen submissions and they don't provide editing, proofreading or book marketing (though some, like Lulu, offer these options for an additional cost). Unlike vanity and self-publishing, title to the books belongs to the publisher (sometimes exclusively) and income to the author comes in the form of royalties. Also, you have less control over the final product, since you're limited to the package of services the publisher offers. Royalties can be less than you think. POD services are likely to base their royalties not on the book's retail price, but on its net price (retail price minus discounts and the publishers overhead), so you don't always know how much will be deducted.

The good thing about POD technology in general is that each book can be produced at the time that it's ordered, which means you don't have to store unsold books. If you're an established author, POD technology is a good way to bring your out-of-print books back into circulation. It can also be a good option to a non-fiction author with a niche market who has the time and the ability to self-promote or who tours and speaks extensively and can sell their books on those occasions. POD books can be almost indistinguishable from traditionally-printed books, but they're usually more expensive, which can make them harder to sell. Most readers don't want to pay $25 or $30 for a trade paperback.

If you decide to go this route, it's better to go with someone like Lulu.com. They don't charge any upfront fees and they use POD technology to produce their books. This means you don't have to buy a lot of books then store them in your home until they get sold. People can go online to Lulu.com and order them whenever they want. Lulu also has additional services, for a fee and done by an outside company, that gets your book listed on Amazon.com and Books in Print, which allows other booksellers to carry the title (although there's no guarantee they will of course).

Self published books are hard to get into reader's hands and almost impossible to get reviewed. Sure, there have been success stories, but they are few and far between. Don't count on it happening with your book. The best advice I can give you if you decide to self-publish is to make sure you get your manuscript professional edited. One of the big reasons self-published books don't do well is because most of them are neither well written, nor well edited. Then prepare yourself to market your book as hard as you can. It's the only possible way you can be successful with a self-published book.

But if you want to sell your book to the general public, try somewhere else. And if you do decide to go this route with one book then write another you want published the traditional way, don't mention the self publishing on your query letter. Most agents don't consider publishing with Publish America or IUniverse as viable publishing credits. In fact it may turn them off altogether.

SCAMS

Publishing scams are everywhere. You as an author need to be aware of what constitutes a scam and how to avoid them. Remember, money always flows to the author. Anyone who requires you to pay upfront fees, whether they're an agent or a publisher, is trying to scam you. Don't do it. It will only cause you heartache and an endless amount of trouble. Why do people try to scam writers and why are we so vulnerable? Because we want to be published. For most of us it's a dream, sometimes an obsession. We want to go into the bookstore and see our name on the cover of a book; we want people to read the things we've written. None of us want to be told the road to getting published is long and hard. We want to believe it's easy and the unscrupulous want us to believe it can be. They feed on those desires and offer us our dreams. But remember the old saying, 'If it looks to good to be true, it probably is.' Still, many people don't believe it or don't pay attention to what's going on around them.

As long as there are victims to scam, scammers will continue to exist. You need to learn how to spot them. The best way to do that is to stay informed. Search the web. Check up on anyone you query, and especially on anyone who either offers you a publishing contract or offers to represent you. Search online for sources of scammer agents and editors. There are quite a few Writer Beware Websites you can check for information.

While there are many good sites, two of the best are Preditors & Editors, <http://www.anotherealm.com/prededitors/> and the writer's beware section on the SFWA (Science Fiction & Fantasy Writer's of America) website, <http://www.sfwa.org/beware/>. You should check out prospective agents or editors on AAR's website to see if they're a member (though don't immediately rule out anyone who's not. A lot of good, reputable agents and agencies don't belong, such as the Trident Media Group for instance). Also, you should check them out on the Publisher's Marketplace website <http://www.publishersmarketplace.com/> to see if they have any deals/sales listed (again, if you don't find anything, don't automatically rule them out. Some newer agents might not have made their first sale yet, and a lot of agents and editors don't post all of their sales, and some don't post any, but that doesn't mean they don't have any, only that they chose not to post it).

Be diligent, do your research and you'll avoid months, even years of heartache and regrets.

NEVER GIVE UP

The hard truth of the matter is that most writers will never get published. Why, you ask? Why do some writers succeed, when others, maybe even those with more talent, don't? Mostly it comes down to attitude. Writers who succeed have several things in common that have nothing to do with inherent talent. They don't mind hard work, they're willing and able to improve themselves, and above all, they never give up. If you want to succeed in this business, never give up.

WHAT HAPPENS NEXT

Once you perfect your novel or short story, you need to research, research, research to find the right place to send your work. If you've written a novel, submit to the editor or agent of your choice. In fact, ideally, submit your query letter (and possibly sample pages) to several editors or agents so you're not pinning your hopes on any one submission. However, if you've written a short story, keep in mind that submitting the same story to multiple markets is frowned upon and marks you as an amateur. You will have to submit one story at a time to one market at a time. It's just part of what you need to know in order to be successful in the publishing business.

So, now you've done everything you can, you've followed all the guidelines, researched all the markets and you've sent your baby out to be poked and prodded and judged and maybe, hopefully, loved. What do you do next?

You get started on your next book or short story and you wait. That's it. You wait. Good luck.

CHAPTER NINETEEN

THE ART & SCIENCE OF BOOK PROMOTION

Ian Irvine

Writing fiction is very hard and the world couldn't care less whether you succeed or fail. No one, not even your publisher, editor, or agent, cares about your books the way you do. They have other books and other authors, and know that every year some will fail (sometimes unexpectedly) and others succeed (equally unexpectedly). But for you, the success of your books is everything, and an early failure may doom your career.

To succeed as a writer you have to be focused, motivated and capable of getting things done to tight deadlines. You must also understand the business of writing, the promotion of your books by your publisher and yourself, and the long-term development and maintenance of your career. The key to success is managing your career like any other business, and that means not only writing great books that your readers want more of, but also investing in your writing name by promoting it for the long term.

But how do you promote your novels? An awful lot has been written about book promotion but most is directed at non-fiction. Fiction is much harder to promote, and why should you have to anyway?

SURELY PROMOTION IS THE PUBLISHER'S JOB?

Competition for the book buyer's dollar is ferocious, for there are more books published, and more imported, every year. More than a quarter of a million new titles are published in English-speaking countries every year and this number has doubled in the past twenty years. Nationally, bookshops stock hundreds of thousands of titles, the majority of which sell less than a few thousand copies a year. The big online retailers such as Amazon.com list several million titles. Locus lists more than 2,000 SF titles published in English each year and the number is increasing every year.

Fiction is only a small part of the total, but most fiction titles (including SF) sell less than 10,000 copies in the US, less than 5,000 in the UK and less than 2,000 in smaller countries such as Australia. On such books the publisher makes little profit or, commonly, a loss. Clearly, publishers can't afford to promote the majority of their books. Neither do they want to spend a fortune developing new authors who may move to another publisher once they become successful. Only new authors who are likely to sell a lot of copies in the near future will get significant promotion.

So don't expect a big campaign for your first book. With rare exceptions, bestselling authors aren't created overnight. Even if your publisher did spend big money promoting you, it could fail because the media won't cover you until it's convinced that you're newsworthy, and unless booksellers love your novel they won't sell it effectively. Most authors only get big promotion after years of building their following with a series of novels, then finally writing a breakout book that also reaches the market at the right time.

If your book isn't going to be promoted, you must either promote it yourself or take the significant risk that it'll fail. Fortunately, there's no better person to promote your work, for no one knows it the way you do, and as a new author lots of people will be willing to give you a chance.

For your first book to have a chance of selling well, you've got to reach a critical mass of readers who like your work enough to recommend it to others. Most beginners' books that succeed do so because of personal recommendations (i.e. readers who love the book and tell others about it), while failure to gain word-of-mouth referrals is the main reason why other books fail. The chief aim of first-novel promotion, therefore, is to build awareness about your book to ensure you get that critical mass of initial readers. Even then, your book can fail if readers don't like it enough, but at least you will have given it a chance. Huge amounts of promotion can make almost any book sell well for a while, but that would cost far more than it would earn back. And if readers don't like your first book, no amount of promotion will induce them to buy the second.

But you've got to do your promotion quickly and effectively, starting months before your novel comes out and continuing for at least three months after it appears. By that time, if it's not selling, bookshops will return it and it's almost certainly doomed.

Even if your first book sells well, you can't stop promoting. It's easier for your second and subsequent books because some readers have heard of you, but writing careers are built over a long time and many books. For every four days you spend on writing, you should allocate one day for promotion. Promotion is cumulative—sooner or later it will build up to the point where the media and the public becomes interested in you.

Overnight success does happen, but it's rare and unpredictable. If your first book hasn't sold well your task will be much harder, because the trade will see you as a loser. However, assuming you can still get your books published, you may be able to turn your career around by clever and persistent promotion.

But you have to be realistic. Unless you're a marketing genius with money to burn, your own efforts can't turn a flop into a bestseller. How do I know? Because I've tried every single promotional idea I could think of, then done my best to determine which of them were effective. Most had little impact on their own, though the cumulative effect was a modest increase in sales.

If that's the case, what's the point of going through all the agony of self-promotion (and for many writers, it is agony)? Because you've got to attain that critical mass of readers early on, to give word-of-mouth a chance to get going, and the extra sales you bring in can be all important.

Unfortunately, most readers aren't influential, so even if they like your book they may not tell many people about it, nor be persuasive. However, a few readers who are both persuasive and natural communicators may influence dozens or even, through their networks, hundreds of readers to buy your book. Such people can turn an ordinary seller into a bestseller. Unfortunately, you don't know who they are or how to find them, so you've got to try and reach as many readers as possible and hope that enough of them are influential.

What is that critical mass of readers? No one knows, and it undoubtedly varies from book to book. If readers love your book, it may only take a few thousand sales to get the buzz going, whereas if they only like it a lot, it may take 10,000 sales or much more. I suspect the buzz about kids' books spreads more quickly than in the more diverse adult market.

Say the critical mass figure for your book is 10,000 sales. If it has a decent cover, the sales team gets a good sell-in to the bookshops (say, 12,000 copies) and does a modest amount of promotion, they might expect to sell 7,000 copies. If you were paid a small advance, your publisher is making a profit at this point and may not do any more. Unfortunately for you, even if readers really liked your book, you didn't achieve critical mass to get the buzz going, so your sales quickly die off. Your book is likely to go out of print in a year or two and you might find it hard to get the next one published.

But if, by your own clever promotion, you can get that sales figure up towards 10,000 copies, you've given your book a chance of getting the buzz going, where more sales lead to more word-of-mouth and sometimes a genuine bestseller.

Whatever country you're from, think beyond your local market. Even the US market only represents half of the world market for books in English. SF is a global literature. There are people in every country who could be interested in your books, and the internet gives you the power to reach them.

THE FACTS OF BOOK PROMOTION

This is what you need to know about book sales and marketing before you start:

1) Sales and marketing are both very expensive, and most books aren't going to sell enough copies to justify much more than the minimum expenditure (i.e. an entry in the publisher's sales catalogue).

2) Promotion doesn't increase the size of the market—all it can do is influence people to spend their money on your book rather than someone else's.

3) For fiction, the most effective form of promotion is generally in-bookshop, so the first aim is to get as many of your books as possible into the shops, prominently and enticingly displayed. If your publisher can't get bookshops to stock them, the chances of the public buying many are low.

4) It takes a lot of work (and money) behind the scenes to get bookshops to stock a new author's book in quantities—this includes good book design, an attention-grabbing cover and blurb, quotes from relevant authors, reviewers or celebrities and, if you're lucky, a well-thought-out marketing and promotional campaign.

5) Fiction is much harder to promote than non-fiction, and for every author whose name has been successfully promoted, there are several for whom promotion (sometimes heaps of it) has failed.

6) Advertising will help if it's properly targeted, but it's very expensive and needs to be repeated a lot to make much difference. Word-of-mouth is king. That's why, when a new movie comes out, by Saturday night everyone in the country knows whether it's a hit or a dog. With books, it can take months to get word-of-mouth going. More often it's years and a number of books.

7) It's difficult to promote an author that no one has ever heard of and even if you do get some free publicity, it won't sell many books. For a new author, a feature article in a capital city newspaper would be lucky to sell a hundred books. The same-sized article about a big-name author might sell a thousand copies plus a heap of backlist. Ditto with radio interviews—it's important to do them, but even if you do twenty or thirty they may only sell a few hundred books. Do them anyway—those sales could be the difference between

success and failure, and it all helps in the long-term task of building awareness about your writing.

8) To become a successful author, you have to establish your name as a brand that the reading public can trust. If they spend twenty dollars on your book, they expect to get their money's worth of entertainment. If they don't, readers will feel ripped off and that will undo your hard work.

9) It's hard to know what's going to work and what isn't, and therefore the secret of successful promotion is to do a lot of different things in the hope that some of them will be effective, though they all cost money and often serious amounts of it.

DOING IT YOURSELF

If your publisher can't afford to promote your book, you must. You can't sell to bookshops and you probably can't afford advertising, but you can promote effectively. After all, no one knows more about your work than you do, and your main requirement is talk enthusiastically about it to people who love books.

Since you weren't expecting publication, treat your advance as a windfall and spend it promoting your book. Spend it wisely, but quickly. To have a chance of succeeding, your book has to sell that critical mass of copies in the first two months, to ensure that:

- bookshops will be re-ordering and there'll be a positive buzz in the industry, rather than returning it with negative feelings; and

- hopefully, word-of-mouth from satisfied readers will keep your sales going long after the initial sales period.

Don't leave it too late. You've got to start, at the very latest, two months before the books come out and be ready for your biggest push as soon as they're in the bookshops. And whatever you're planning to do, be sure to keep your editor, publisher, agent, and publicist informed. They need to know so your efforts won't duplicate or interfere with theirs. It's also an important part of promoting yourself as an energetic author who really wants to push the books they've invested so much in.

You've got to spend money to give your writing career the best chance of success, though in the beginning you'll be spending more than you earn back. Hold your nerve and keep spending. You've always got to be thinking of the long term, not just your next book. Once you've got a backlist, promotion sells all your books.

Promotion is cumulative. Though it may not seem to be working at the time, it all goes towards building your profile in the eyes of readers, booksellers and the media. One day, as long as you hang in there, it'll pay off. Hone your public appearance skills, but don't keep pushing your books, or yourself. Push the story.

What if you don't have the money for self-promotion? Cut some of your discretionary spending (e.g. give up smoking, drinking, gambling, or non-essential shopping or travel) for a year, and use the money saved. Can't give up any of those things, even to succeed as a writer? Maybe you don't want it badly enough.

YOUR PROMOTIONAL PLAN

The first thing to do is to prepare a promotional plan which sets out all the things you plan to do, how you're going to do them, when they have to be done by, and what they'll cost in money and your own time. It's also helpful to summarize what your publisher's promotional plan is, so you can dovetail your work with theirs and avoid duplication. If your publisher hasn't told you what their plan is, ask.

Different kinds of books require different forms of promotion. A major author with a topical new novel may be best served by a traditional author tour focusing on national TV, radio and print media, while an unknown author of general interest SF may be better served by a grassroots campaign in their local region, and expanding outwards if that succeeds. An author writing in a specialized subgenre of SF might concentrate on the genre magazines, bookshops, conventions and websites, nationally or globally. For children's SF or fantasy fiction, it can be better to focus on print media, such as children's magazines, educational supplements and parents' magazines, plus the Internet.

Your promotional plan should contain the following elements:

WHAT YOUR PUBLISHER IS DOING, E.G. SOME OR RARELY ALL OF:

- Sales (to get your books into the shops)
- Advertising
- Publicity and public relations (interviews, media and public appearances)
- Give-aways in print media and radio; prizes or competitions
- Review copies, reading copies and copies submitted for awards
- Inclusion in bookseller's catalogues
- Point-of-sale promotion (posters, dump bins etc)
- Price promotions, e.g. '3-for-2'
- Author tour, etc.

WHAT YOU'RE PLANNING TO DO, E.G. SOME OR ALL OF:
- Promoting the book to your publisher's sales and marketing teams
- Design and printing of promotional materials
- Distributing these to friends/family/personal and business contacts
- Doing bookshop visits, signings and launches

ORGANIZING PERSONAL APPEARANCES, READINGS ETC.
- At festivals and conventions
- Giving talks to community & business groups, libraries etc
- Doing school visits (if appropriate for your books)
- Teaching workshops and seminars, or more formal writing courses

DIRECT MARKETING
- Targeted mail-outs
- Leafleting outside bookshops etc.
- Notice board poster campaigns

INTERNET MARKETING
- Communicating with your fans
- Great website
- Using email lists; etc

GETTING PUBLICITY
- Advertising;
- Author tour;

NETWORKING;
- Promoting yourself to your publisher as a model author.

CREATE PROMOTIONAL MATERIALS AND DISTRIBUTE WIDELY

Your first and most important task is to get your bookmarks, postcards and/or other promotional materials designed and printed. Publishers are rarely innovative but you can be. For example, my son is experienced in 3D media and for the first book of my children's fantasy quintet, Runcible Jones: The Gate to Nowhere, I paid him to create four high resolution captioned teaser images, each representing an arresting scene from the book, which I had reproduced at all sizes from postcard up to large poster size. I circulated thousands of copies to friends, contacts, bookshops, schools, libraries, and the media. The images were of such high quality that they attracted attention everywhere, as did his 3D animations and the presentation on my website.

If you lack design skills, have someone design your materials for you. Get your handouts printed on card or thick glossy paper so they look good and people will be inclined to keep them for a while. Cheap flyers will be thrown away within minutes and you'll have wasted your money.

You can get thousands of handouts printed for a few hundred dollars at any instant print shop. Many of the printing chains have cost calculators on the net—simply select your options and they'll tell you what the cost will be. The unit cost goes down dramatically between a few hundred and a few thousand copies, so always order the maximum number you can afford.

They must be in color and show the front cover of your book. The rest is up to you, but make sure they're well designed (your publisher's design department might do this for you). Many print shops offer an inexpensive design service.

Hand your bookmarks or postcards out around the office, on the train, whenever you give a talk, and give one to everybody who tries to sell something to you, including shop assistants and the taxi driver on your way to the airport. Always carry some in your bag. If you only give out a few a day, that's a thousand contacts in a year, and people who've met you are far more likely to try your book than strangers.

Give bookmarks to your friends and relatives, who'll generally be happy to distribute them at work or socially. Many people will go out of their way to promote your books because they know you. Have some flyers or book covers blown up to A4/letter or A3/tabloid size (in color) and ask friends and relatives to put them up on work, community, school and university notice boards. Thousands of people will see them before they're taken down.

Distributing good quality handouts to the public can also be effective, though you need to target them carefully, e.g. at conventions or talks, or to customers going into or coming out of large bookshops. Handing out cheap leaflets to people walking down the street, however, is a waste of time and money.

Whatever you do to promote your books, work out how to assess its effectiveness and change whatever isn't working.

VISIT BOOKSHOPS

It's important to contact all the SF outlets, but remember that they have a small and declining share of the SF market, so you need to reach mainstream bookshops too. Write to a few hundred key bookshops, enclosing a one-page letter that tells what kind of a book yours is and sets out, enticingly, why people would want to read it. If you've had good reviews, include copies plus some of your handouts. You can download bookshop addresses from the Yellow Pages, clean them up, and do a mail merge in your word processor, though if you want to do a big mailing it may be easier to buy a mailing list.

Whenever you travel, drop into every bookshop you can find, say hello and talk about your latest book and how it's selling. Give them copies of any great reviews, or a single page of quotes, tell them about award short-listings, overseas sales or any other worthwhile news, and talk about your next book. Once you've got a few books in print, customers are always asking booksellers when the next one is coming out, and staff love to be able to say they've met you. You'll often meet management and genre sales staff. Sometimes they'll take your picture with them, or get you to autograph their personal copies of your books. Take the time to talk to them. It's great to meet people who love books as much as you do. They also know what books are selling, they're in charge of re-ordering, and customers often ask them for reading recommendations. Hand-selling in bookshops is a vital part of spreading the buzz.

Offer to sign books. Some bookshops may not be interested, especially if it's your first book, though once you have a recognizable name they'll generally be pleased for you to sign some (or occasionally all) of their stock. Signed copies increase sales by 20-30%, staff will put 'signed' stickers on them, and sometimes make a special display. Leave a stack of your handouts for staff to slip into the shopping bags of customers who've bought similar books, or to be kept on the counter near the cash register.

MAKE PERSONAL APPEARANCES
HOLD LAUNCHES AND SIGNINGS

Book launches and signings can be scarifying for the author, and if they're not well publicized it's common for only a handful of people to come. Even when they are well promoted, it's hard to get a lot of people to attend a fiction signing. You'll generally do better in suburbs or country towns than in city bookshops, where customers are used to seeing big names. Your local bookshop may be enthusiastic but one in the city centre won't be unless you're famous, and could want a big fee for hosting a launch as well as a contribution from yourself or your publisher to offset advertising costs.

Make sure you ask all your friends, relatives, and acquaintances to turn up. Don't be too upset if you don't get a lot of people on the night—the shop window and in-store displays will sell books for the week or two they're there, and the bookshop will make a special effort to sell all the books you've signed. I've often done signings where the bookshop has only sold a dozen books at the time, but has subsequently sold another fifty or more.

Always have a pile of handouts to give to passers-by. Consider getting a lapel badge made up with your name and 'author' on it, or a similarly labeled hat, or T-shirt showing your book cover. Bring a small display with copies of great reviews or articles about you, mounted posters or any other appropriate props you have. Whenever someone comes up to you, hand them a copy of your book as you talk, make eye contact, and be friendly.

GIVE READINGS

Select your readings carefully. Make sure they're short (5-10 minutes max), dramatic, about an engaging character that the audience can identify with, and end leaving them wondering what will happen next. And of course, that they're suited to the audience you're reading to—explicit sex, graphic violence or more than the occasional swear word will rarely go down well, and are never appropriate for school audiences.

Rehearse each reading beforehand, several times if you're not a fluent reader. Tell your audience how long each reading is going to be, or else reluctant listeners may feel as though they're in prison with an indefinite sentence. Read dramatically, make eye contact with people in the audience, and use their reactions to focus your delivery.

GIVE TALKS

Give talks to Rotary and other community groups, at old people's homes, to libraries and businesses. Thousands of organizations are looking for interesting, different or motivational speakers, but whenever you're talking to a general (i.e. non-SF) audience, focus on aspects of your book that they can relate to.

Not everyone can be an inspirational speaker, but everyone can become a competent and interesting one. If you're afraid or inexperienced, join Toastmasters or some other public speaking group and speak regularly on a variety of topics. Consider paying for professional instruction if you're going to be speaking to large, demanding audiences.

Never wing a talk or panel session, no matter how experienced you are. You'll often get away with it, though you won't be at your best, but occasionally you'll freeze up embarrassingly, or talk in clichés rather than making a relevant and thoughtful contribution, or drone on without making your points.

Always prepare and, if you're giving a talk, always rehearse it. But don't read your talk unless you're so paralyzed by stage fright that you can't do it any other way. A read-out talk is boring, and some people will be irritated that they're getting a speech rather than a conversation with the author.

Prepare the following, at least:

- A series of talking points about the book or books you're there to publicize;
- A couple of relevant anecdotes, preferably light-hearted (not dirty jokes);
- One or two brief excerpts you can read in an emergency (e.g. if you lose the thread of your talk, or the previous speaker has just made all the points you planned to);
- One or more props you can show to break the ice (e.g. copies of your book, maps, posters, book covers, etc)
- Give-away copies for the audience at the end of the talk;
- Have plenty of your handouts available for your talks, and make sure everyone gets one.

ORGANIZE SCHOOL VISITS

Register with school speaker's agencies. School visits can be a terrific way to promote children's or YA books, because the buzz about a good one spreads quickly. School visits can also be a nightmare if they're badly organized, especially if you end up with a huge audience but no teacher there to maintain order. Once you're put in that situation, it's difficult to maintain rapport.

You have to expect a certain amount of misbehavior and develop a strategy to deal with it. The best way is to be an interesting and entertaining speaker. Don't drone on. After twenty minutes of a speech, even the best behaved kids will have turned off. You have to give them variety: e.g. show them interesting stuff, read a brief, dramatic story, put on a performance (if you can do that kind of thing), tell anecdotes (especially embarrassing ones), ask students to perform a short piece of your writing, and allow plenty of time for questions.

ATTEND WRITERS' FESTIVALS/BOOK FAIRS AND CONVENTIONS

If you're writing popular fiction, and especially genre fiction, it can be hard to get an invitation for the big writers' festivals, though your publisher can facilitate invitations. Your own networking helps too, as does developing a reputation for being prepared, speaking well, and always having something to say.

It's not hard to get on a discussion panel at an SF convention. Simply fill in the membership form, pay the money then contact the organizers with an idea for a talk or panel, or indicate which of their panel topics (on the convention website) are of interest to you. Speaking at SF conventions is a valuable part of promoting yourself, but don't spend all your budget on it. You need to broaden your reader base, as the same small group of people tend to go to conventions and they'll soon know about you. But by all means go for social reasons, or to further your contacts.

TEACHING

Teaching is a valuable way to promote yourself. Imparting your accumulated wisdom to others can also be very rewarding, and you'll find that you learn as much about your own writing in a week-long workshop as you would in months of analyzing it.

DIRECT MARKETING

Whatever you're writing, there'll be a group of people interested in it. If your heroine does cross-stitch, market to all the shops and clubs that are into needlework. If the book is about dolphins, promote to fishing, diving, boating, marine, environmental, and conservation groups. Whatever the organization or business, you can download all the relevant addresses in Yellow Pages.

For children's' or YA books, it can be useful to market directly to public and school libraries, especially if you've got dramatic handouts or a relevant media release.

Never throw away a mailing list or a business card; anyone who knows you is a potential book buyer.

INTERNET MARKETING

Get yourself a good website. If you can't do the design and web mastering yourself, find a friend or relative who can. Don't spend a fortune. Plenty of people can do the job cheaply. It's not hard to design a good site and you don't need gorgeous graphics. All you need is great content (i.e. useful information, not advertising) that is clearly and simply organized, and quick to download.

Steer clear of graphics that take forever to download; they're a big turnoff and most people will click past to another site. Assume that many readers don't have high speed access. People go to your site for content (i.e. information), so make sure there's lots of interesting material on it, and that it's changed or updated regularly.

Write some informative, general interest articles for your site (i.e. not ones that are just about yourself). They'll attract traffic to your site and other sites will link to it. Accelerate the process by letting key interest groups know that your article is up. If they like it they'll tell others and the Internet will do the rest. One article on my site, The Truth about Publishing, attracts as much traffic as the rest of the site put together.

Other items that will attract visitors back to your site:

- First chapters or samplers from your published books, as well as teasers for what you have coming up next;

- An opt-in newsletter and/or blog (an opt-in newsletter tells you how many people are really interested in your work, and you can contact them directly whenever you have a new book coming out);

- Include a page of reader's reviews (but ask permission first and don't use readers' full names);

- 'How-to' articles on any aspect of writing or publishing.

- Hosting a forum.

- Prizes, competitions, and give-aways.

Once your site is up, register it with Google. It'll be indexed within a few weeks and picked up in Google searches ever after. There's no need to register with other search engines and don't pay to be registered with any. Make sure your site contains lots of links and exchange links with other writers—that way your site will come near the top of the list in a Google search.

Promote your site. Have its address printed in your books, at the bottom of your emails, on your business cards, flyers, bookmarks, letterhead, posters, and anything else that you or your publisher produce.

Join relevant internet groups (e.g. genre writers, special interest groups). Lots of people there will be interested in your work and you can help to promote each other. Put your email address in your book and on your website. You'll end up getting more junk mail, but spam filters can take care of most of it, and at least you'll be available to your fans. It's a great boost to start the writing day with a letter from someone who's appreciated your work. And then, reply to every email. I often get mail from fans saying that I'm the first writer who's ever replied to them, yet fans are the people who do most to spread the word about your writing. Communicate with them; tell them about your new books, answer all their questions and provide special information for their fan websites.

Monitor the stats for your site regularly. See what content attracts extra visitors and what makes little difference.

NETWORK, NETWORK, NETWORK

Networking is vital, not just because it can help to gain reviews, awards, grants, invitations to festivals, new book contracts and a myriad of other opportunities, but also because you need to understand the system, what's happening now and how the industry is changing. And not least because writing is a solitary profession and it's great to hang out with other people in the industry.

Get to as many conventions, writers' festivals, and book fairs as you can, and meet people. Don't hide because you're shy. Keep a running list of contacts in various categories, such as fans, other people or groups who could be interested in your work, other writers, other people in the industry (editors, publishers, agents, booksellers), publicists, media contacts, etc.

If you've got a book coming out in the UK or US and the publisher is doing some promotion, go there. They won't pay your travel expenses unless they're planning a huge campaign, which is most unlikely, but they'll organize promotional activities for you. Meet key people at your publishers, agree to every promotional activity they suggest and take every opportunity to help get your book off to a good start there. It does make a difference.

GIVE STUFF AWAY

Order as many giveaway copies as you can from your publisher. You'll often get a special discount if they're not for resale. Even better, negotiate extra free copies in your next book contract.

Give away copies of your books to influential people and send them off to other writers whose work you like. It all helps to get the word out about yourself. Give reading copies to bookshop staff; donate copies to local schools, colleges, and libraries. When you give talks, always take a few spare copies, and hand them out to people in the audience afterwards.

AUTHOR TOURS

A five-city author tour can cost tens of thousands of dollars. A 15-20 city tour in the US could cost up to $100,000. These are fantastic sums of money, requiring phenomenal additional sales to pay for them, and are only worth it if major media coverage (i.e. print feature articles and national TV and radio appearances) can be obtained. This will rarely be the case unless the author is already famous. For beginning writers, no matter how well hyped, book tours are likely to be exercises in public humiliation, with few people turning up for signings, readings and talks, and many of those being budding writers looking for the key to their own success.

Some authors have done their own author tours by organizing bookshop appearances and talks in a selection of cities, then going on the road for weeks. This is much less costly, but also less effective because of your lack of profile and advertising of the events. It may not be an effective use of your time and money.

ADVERTISING

Print advertising doesn't do much to attract buyers unless you're already a big name (though it helps to get bookshops to stock your books). People are so deluged with advertising that they turn off, which is why the really big advertisers hammer us unceasingly. It's also expensive so, unless you can afford to spend tens of thousands of dollars on advertising, it's not worth you doing it (except, possibly, in genre magazines).

PROMOTE YOURSELF TO YOUR PUBLISHER

Even if you do everything listed above, and use the media effectively, it's most unlikely to propel you onto the bestseller lists. The problem is, no matter how hard you promote, you're an amateur trying to do a professional's job without either the contacts or the inside knowledge to do so effectively. Most books that become bestsellers have had major promotion from their publishers beforehand, or as soon as they began to sell well. Publishers have the knowledge and resources to do it professionally. And most bestsellers are by writers who already have a big name, or are a celebrity in another field.

So how can you, a novice, or even an author with a few books published, convince your publisher to make a big promotional effort for your next book?

- It has to have some kind of mass appeal, whether it's literary fiction or SF. Niche books, those that are wacky or far from the mainstream, and category (i.e. pulp) fiction are never going to get major promotion.

- You have to write the best book you can. Your editor will be irritated if you miss your delivery deadline, but it's better to produce a great book late than a second-rate one on time.

- Give your publisher everything she needs. This includes working cooperatively with your editor on revisions, but also providing useful, timely input to the designer and cover artist, copy for the blurb, cover quotes, catalogue copy, and by filling in the author questionnaire.

- By having done everything you could to assist your publisher in promoting your previous books.

- By enthusing your publisher's staff about your book. The best start for any book is to have key people at your publisher abuzz with excitement about it. Whenever you visit your publisher, take the opportunity to see as many people as you can. Not just your editor, but also design, production and sales and marketing staff. They're all busy people but if you can talk enthusiastically about your book, and what's great about it, they're more likely to take the time to read it.

- Try to organize a brief meeting with the sales reps. They're great people who love books and, unless this is your first book, they've been selling yours for some time, know lots about you and would love to meet you. They're frantically busy though, so don't waste their time. Tell them briefly and clearly what's so different and great about your book, and why it'll appeal to a big audience.

- If you've got a new series coming out, or a different line of books, ask if you can give a presentation at the annual sales conference. This may be hard to arrange, but if they agree, make yours a knockout presentation that they won't forget.

- Above all, be a model author, because it really helps when your publisher is deciding where to spend their promotional dollars. The reliable author who works hard promoting their books gets the money, not the one who constantly misses deadlines, whines and expects people to do everything for him. And make sure you keep your editor and publicist informed of all that you're doing to promote your books—they need to know.

If you do all this, and your sales grow steadily to the point where you're becoming an important author, one day your publisher will decide to spend big money on you and put together a promotional team with the contacts and media savvy to lift you into the big league. It may not work, of course—there are no guarantees in publishing—but you'll have done all you can.

WORKING WITH THE MEDIA

If you energetically do everything in the previous section, it'll probably save your books from failing, but it's unlikely to make them bestsellers. You simply can't contact enough people with your talks, handouts, signings, web site etc, and only a fraction of those you do contact will buy your book. To make a big difference to your sales you've got to leverage your efforts, by using the media to get publicity.

GETTING PUBLICITY

'Publicity is like a trustworthy third party saying good things about you,'

(Jessica Hatchigan) and that's why corporations with mega-advertising budgets also spend a fortune to get good publicity. In a typical newspaper or magazine, half the articles are likely to have been initiated or influenced by publicists, and most of those outside the news pages.

Unfortunately, everyone with a product to sell is trying to get publicity for it. It's hard to get the media's attention and they aren't particularly interested in writers anyway, and especially not genre writers. So to get media coverage you must learn to think like a publicist—they make their living by knowing what media people want and how to present it to them.

What do the media want? The news media are only interested in news, and as an SF writer you're unlikely to be newsworthy unless you've done something controversial, or to do with a celebrity, or there's lots of money involved (a million dollar advance, a movie deal). However, other sections of the media are looking for items involving real people doing interesting things or having noteworthy experiences, so to get publicity all you have to do is find a new angle about yourself or your writing.

When your publisher is promoting your book, any media appearances will be organized by a hired or staff publicist, who will write and distribute a media release, send out reading copies of your book to reviewers and key media, and organize interviews and appearances.

HIRE YOUR OWN PUBLICIST

If you can afford it, you should consider hiring your own publicist to supplement what your publisher's is doing. Half the authors on the New York Times bestseller list at any time will have their own publicists, and virtually all of the big name authors. And a lot of big name authors are only big because they invested heavily in their careers at an early stage.

BEING YOUR OWN PUBLICIST

If your publisher isn't using a publicist for your book, and you can't afford to hire one, you'll have to do it yourself.

Here are the Five Golden Rules for getting publicity (after Kat Smith).

1) Put yourself in the media's position. What is it about you or your book that would interest the audience of the newspaper, magazine, radio program, or TV show you're approaching?

2) No one interviews a book. You have to be an informative, entertaining, articulate, or controversial guest.

3) Get hold of the media guides required to identify and understand

the media that could be interested in you.

4) Never give up. Promotion is cumulative and even if the media knock you back for the first few books, if you stick at it, eventually you'll get their attention.

5) If you give the media the interesting story they're looking for, they'll give you the publicity you need to sell your books.

MEDIA KITS AND MEDIA RELEASES

The first step to getting reviews, feature articles, interviews, or guest appearances is to prepare your media kit. If the editors or producers you've approached don't see an entertaining, relevant story or intriguing guest there, they'll immediately lose interest in you. Your media kit promotes you as a writer and everything you've written.

The full kit will only be sent to selected, key media. Present it in a pocket folder with your name and the book's name and publication date on the front. Stick a color copy of the book jacket there. Each page should contain your contact details and your publicist's. Your media kit should be printed in a standard, easy-to-read font, preferably black on white paper, and contain the following items:

- Your pitch letter addressed to the editor or producer of the show you're targeting, setting out who you are and what you're seeking (review, interview, guest appearance, etc). Below that, put a headline (why your idea will interest the show's audience), then brief points on: what your book's about; why it's unique; why it's perfect for this audience; how it ties in with some important current event or issue; and why you're the best person to talk about it.

- Table of contents.

- Media release for the book (see below).

- Author bio (written in third person). In a hundred words or less, it says who you are, what you've done (professional and otherwise), and gives brief details about your writing, including bestsellers, major awards, international success; what your skills, abilities or special talents are; and where you live. Mention TV and radio experience if you have it.

- Author photos, color and black and white, professionally taken.

- Book info, including title and subtitle, author, publisher's name and contact details, distributor, book's ISBN, number of pages, format, publication date, and price.

- Copy of book jacket or cover flat (or color copy of it).
- FAQ—questions you'd like the media to ask you, so you can explain what the book is about and why someone would want to buy it. Or better, a Q&A session with yourself.
- Critical praise. Quotes from great reviews (and photocopies of key ones), praise from famous authors, prizes and awards or short-listings.
- Previous promotion, in reverse chronological order, including a list of reviews, interviews, and media appearances. Availability of radio and/or TV demo tapes.
- The interview schedule for this book to date.

Next, prepare an enticing media release for the book you're promoting now. The media release goes to all targeted media and sets out everything the media need to know about your book in a single page, including:

- Release date.
- Attention-grabbing headline, followed by two or three brief, direct paragraphs that bring out the key features of your book. Pretend you're writing a three-paragraph news story about the book, in the third person. Tailor it to the interests of the target media. What will the media find newsworthy about it? Or what will entertain their readers, viewers, or listeners?
- One-paragraph bio of the author, highlighting previous bestsellers, awards, special expertise etc
- Publicist's contact details.
- Book details, including title, series title (if relevant), publisher, price, number of pages and ISBN;

On a second page, provide a list of questions you'd like to be asked (so in your answers you can get across your key message points). Reviewer's quotes and award details can be put on a third page, but don't go beyond that.

For more on how to get good press (after Robert J Sawyer):

1) Define yourself as an important or interesting writer in some way, e.g. as the nation's most awarded or bestselling SF writer, or an expert in the field you're writing about.

2) Find something about your books that's newsworthy or topical.

3) Make your work transcend genre boundaries, so it's relevant to a general audience.

4) Write a great media release that highlights these points.

5) Find a way to overcome the media's prejudices about SF (by showing your book's general relevance, awards you've received, important reviews, big sales, etc).

Consider including a Press Room page on your web site, containing the key elements from your media kit, including a recent color photo, a generic interview, the media release for your current book, author bio, book info, great reviews, and a list of key previous appearances.

IDENTIFYING RELEVANT MEDIA

Contact the SF trade publications such as Locus and the specialty SF magazines, and send them information and review copies where appropriate. Also contact the key fanzines and websites that review and list books, but don't stop there. You also need to contact the mainstream media.

You can find out the contact details, circulation figures, etc for US media in Bacon's Media Directories, for the UK in Hollis Media Guide, and Australia in Margaret Gee's Australian Media Guide. These are expensive for an individual but large libraries should have them.

From these references, you can identify media and people who could be interested in you or your book. These will include book and magazine literary editors, specialist magazines that your story is relevant to (e.g. diving magazines if, say, there's a scuba diving theme), and the electronic media. Working without a publicist, you probably won't have much success with the major newspapers, magazines, and radio stations unless you write a great media release, but it's worth trying.

The chances of any TV station being interested in a novice or genre writer are remote, though you may be lucky with a local station, especially if you're well known in your community. People in your area will be interested in you because you're local, so contact all the media at every place you've ever lived. Providing a few copies of your book as prizes in competitions and giveaways also helps.

It's much easier to get publicity for non-fiction, because the target audience is readily identifiable. The major media outlets are reluctant to interview novelists because they're rarely interesting enough. Only a minority of people read fiction regularly and most of them read only one genre, therefore few people in the audience will be interested in your book. On the other hand, thousands of radio stations have to fill up their 24 hours each day with a regular supply of guests, and newspapers have pages to fill daily, so as long as you have an interesting story to tell, or can talk about topical issues, they'll often give you an opportunity. And once you do a few good interviews, your publicist can use the vibe to get you others.

APPROACHING THE MEDIA

Your publicist will normally send you a copy of the draft media release for your book, for comment. You'll generally be able to improve it because of your knowledge of your book and its intended audience, but remember that the media get dozens of media releases every day. You've only got half a minute to attract their attention.

The media release provides attention-grabbing information about you and the book. By all means use any special attributes you have (e.g. extreme beauty, unusual experience, interests, or job), but don't over-hype or you'll be seen as flaky, in which case the publicity you'll get is unlikely to be worth it.

The media release will be distributed at the same time as reading copies are sent to reviewers, i.e. a month or two before the official publication date for mass market editions. If you're published in hardcover this can occur up to six months earlier, because coverage in key media is booked months in advance, and bound galleys are sent out rather than finished books. If the publisher isn't producing galleys, it can be worthwhile having them made yourself. If you wait until finished books are available, by the time reviews appear there may not be many copies of your books left in the bookshops.

In a good promotional program, your publisher will send the media release to between 50 and 150 media outlets. It'll generally be faxed or emailed, though in some campaigns it'll be posted, perhaps along with some relevant attention-grabbing gimmick. For my eco-thriller Terminator Gene, set in a grim near future of dramatic climate change, we created a newspaper of the 2030's set with articles about rising seas flooding the Sydney Opera House, England finally winning a cricket series against Australia, etc. But if you do use a gimmick, make sure it's original and well done. Anything cheap, tacky or in bad taste is worse than having none. The same applies to cheap give-aways like embossed pens, key rings, and fridge magnets.

Your media release serves a number of functions. Local and regional newspapers, especially from your area, may quote from it with or without interviewing you. Occasionally the literary editor of a newspaper or magazine may commission a review of your book because of it. Mostly, however, your media release is the tool that gains you interviews.

WHAT YOU CAN EXPECT FROM THE MEDIA

You'll get local interviews purely on the basis of your media release, though for major media you'll need to send the full media kit. For national radio and TV you may also need to supply a demo tape, if you have one, but don't send it unless requested.

The mainstay of book promotion is the radio interview. If your press release strikes a chord with the media you might gain a handful of articles in the entertainment/giveaways sections of suburban or regional city papers, none or one or two reviews in important regional papers or magazines, no TV interviews, but dozens of radio interviews. Therefore, most of your energy should go into preparing for radio.

For genre fiction where there is no obvious hook to the real world, however you'll be lucky to get many interviews outside your local area, apart from specialist SF programs. The media isn't interested.

In most cases, the media will simply book interviews with your publicist. However, for major radio interviews, or most TV appearances, your publicist will have to convince the producer that you're a reliable performer. She'll do this by citing your appearance history on other relevant programs, and ideally by providing a demo tape compiled from previous interviews. The producer may also want to interview you before accepting you as a guest. It helps to have video footage of you in action (giving a talk or doing something interesting in the real world) but it has to be at least semi-professional quality (not home video).

YOUR MEDIA SCHEDULE

Your publicist will prepare a media schedule once most of your interviews have been booked, and update it when new ones are added or existing ones rescheduled. If you're being your own publicist, you must do your own schedule. It includes your name, the book title, your phone, fax, email and mobile contact details (plus hotel or office contacts if you're traveling), and the publicist's contact details, then lists each interview, starting with the first, its date and time in your local time, the interviewer's and program's name and contact details, the location if a studio interview, and whether it's live or a pre-record. The schedule should also show the local time of the program if in a different time zone. You must double-check every detail of the itinerary, even if it's done by a professional publicist, and confirm anything that doesn't look right. Mistakes in date or time are common, and very embarrassing.

Your media schedule should also list all the media that are still being chased, and those which haven't made up their minds yet.

PRINT ARTICLES AND REVIEWS

Beginners don't get many reviews. Ten times as many books are published each week as there is space to review them, and most reviews go to well-known authors or celebrities. Furthermore, hardcovers and trade paperbacks get most of the reviews because the media sees these as significant books. In the UK, mass-market paperbacks are rarely reviewed in important newspapers or magazines; in the US, almost never. I have eight fantasy novels published in the UK, all selling well and reprinting regularly, yet I've never had a review in any newspaper there.

If you're newsworthy (i.e. won a major award, gained a huge advance or, after a number of books your sales are taking off) there's a good chance of getting a feature article in a newspaper or magazine. Sometimes this will come about because a freelance journalist pitches the idea to an editor. More often, the editor will decide that your profile is now sufficient to do an article about you. You can facilitate this by circulating a press release each time you've done something noteworthy, or if something in one of your books resonates with an important public issue. Don't pester them. Several times a year is enough.

PREPARING FOR INTERVIEWS

First, prepare five or six message points that encapsulate your book. This is the minimum that you want to get across in every interview. Then distil a sound bite from each point.

Think of some anecdotes about yourself or your writing, e.g. where you got an unusual idea from, or several interesting, funny or embarrassing things that have happened to you. Anecdotes help the public to identify with you. Practice your delivery in front of family or friends, and tailor it to the program you'll be appearing on.

Always take a copy of the media release to the interview, as well as a copy of the book. The interviewer will often read from the media release in introducing you, or from the blurb on the back of the book. Most interviewers won't read the book but many will ask the questions you provided with your media release (or after the interview was booked).

Make a list of the typical questions that interviewers ask, and prepare answers to them. Here are some questions writers are frequently asked:

- Where do you get your ideas from?
- Why did you write this book?
- What point are you trying to get across?
- When did you start writing, and why?
- What's your professional background?

- What do you read?

- Have you won any awards? Or had any movie offers?

- What advice would you give to beginning writers?

- Are the events or characters based on people you know?

- Do you write every day or just when you feel like it?

- Tell us about your book.

- What, or whom, are your main influences?

DOING RADIO INTERVIEWS

Most radio interviews will be done over the phone, so make sure you have a quiet place to do them where you won't be interrupted. Mobile phones are unreliable and few radio stations will agree to do interviews on one. Major radio programs will do the interview in-studio if you're in the same city.

Most interviewers will be more interested in you than your book. They'll want to focus on aspects of your work, unusual life experiences, exotic or quirky hobbies, dangerous pursuits, or something topical or controversial about your book. These details must be in your media kit; without them your publicist will find it hard to secure interviews.

Give the interviewer (or your publicist) a brief list of topics that you'd like to talk about, or questions you'd like to be asked, in advance. Many interviewers will use them.

Prepare answers that will enable you to get across your message points and sound bites. Keep them in front of you in case you freeze and can't remember them. If the interviewer is wandering off topic, bring the discussion back to the points you want to make about your book. Make sure your talking points are interesting, intriguing, dramatic, humorous, or thought provoking, according to the kind of book yours is. Ideally they'll raise questions in the reader or listener's mind, and therefore concern about their outcome, which can only be satisfied by reading your book.

Write down the interviewer's name (it's easy to forget it when stressed, and embarrassing when you do) and use it at least at the beginning or the end of the program. Don't use it all the time—you don't want to sound like the host of a shopping channel.

Many interviewers will tell you their questions in advance. If they don't, ask. Also ask how long the interview is going to be, otherwise you can find it ending abruptly before you've got your key points across. If a lot of your interviews are short or ending abruptly, it may mean that you're not coming across in a way your audience can relate to (i.e., you're boring or worse, offensive). Find out and get help.

On major stations, interviews will generally run for 5-10 minutes, though you may get longer on a late night talk show. On smaller city stations, as well as community or local radio, or specialist SF programs, you may get half an hour or more, especially if you've established a rapport with the announcer through previous interviews. If you're getting a lot of long interviews, they like you.

Work out plans for 5-minute, 10-minute, and longer interviews, setting out the points you must get across. Make your best or most important points first, in case you don't get a chance later on. Otherwise, you're likely to find that the interview is over and you've said nothing that would arouse the audience's interest in your book.

After you've done a few interviews, you'll notice that questions fall into a familiar pattern. Note down the questions you get asked all the time and try to think of a number of interesting ways to answer them, so you don't come across as bored. Be cheerful and animated, rather than flat, opinionated, or cranky.

HOW TO GET ON TV

To get TV interviews you have to learn to think like a producer. Remember, it's not his job to sell books, but to make interesting TV, and you have to find a way to present yourself as a guest whose story will be interesting to the audience. Get experience on smaller TV programs before you try out for the big ones, and ask for a tape of the show before you go on. You'll need it for your media kit.

The following points, modified after 'How to get on Oprah', by Susan Harrow, are relevant to getting on most major TV programs.

1) Know the show you're approaching, what its audience likes and who to approach to get on it (you can identify relevant producers from the credits).

2) Don't pitch your book, or yourself, unless you have a great story about yourself. Pitch a controversial topic, national issue, or problem your book sheds light on. An issue that's relevant to the audience.

3) Sell your idea in one page, in a great media release.

4) Create six dynamic sound bites, of 10-20 seconds each, encapsulating your essential message. Practice with a timer. Use these when you talk to the producer. They should be what you want the audience to remember. And have some visual props for the show.

5) Practice the 5-second promo (i.e. just like the promo used to sell next week's show).

HANDLING TV INTERVIEWS

Even if you're used to doing radio and print interviews, TV interviews can be confronting. It's not easy to stay calm and focused, and present your story well, when you're staring down the barrel of a camera under the glare of the studio lights. If you hope to do a lot of TV appearances, hire a media trainer. She'll interview you in a range of situations then play them back, showing you where you're going wrong and coaching you to fix those problems.

Before you go to the studio, rehearse your message points and sound bites until you have them fluently. Take a copy of your book, the media release, and your list of topics or questions.

At the studio, ask the producer what the focus of the interview will be and what questions will be asked. Prepare brief answers to them in ways that will allow you to get across your key points.

Write down the interviewer's name and anything else you have to remember. Practice relaxation and transferring the stress or nervousness to a part of you that's off camera, e.g. your foot.

In the studio:

- Ignore the cameras, just focus on the interviewer. Maintain eye contact—it's supposed to look like a chat. Be enthusiastic.

- Be clear about your objectives. You want people to remember: your name, the book's title, and enough about it to know that they'll find it interesting or enjoyable—your message points and sound bites.

- Know when to be quiet. Just answer the question clearly, simply and briefly, then stop. If you're starting to ramble, end it as smoothly as possible then wait for the next question.

- If you don't want to answer a question, or the interview becomes confrontational, stay calm. Change the subject to one of your message points.

- Remember that the interview isn't over until you've left the studio. Talk afterwards isn't off the record and what you say may be used in the introduction to your interview.

ENDNOTE

If you do all this, you'll be well on the way to making your books a success, but always remember that successful fiction begins and ends with great storytelling. Or as Donald Maass puts it, 'The secret of success is simple—please your readers on a regular basis.'

CHAPTER TWENTY

THE WRITING LIFE

Piers Anthony

This is a volume of information and advice for science fiction writers. I'm sure there is a great deal of useful information in it, but since I am contributing to it as it forms, I haven't read it. I am going to try to address matters that concern writers that may not be covered elsewhere, especially those that relate to the ordinary life of the average writer of whatever genre. National celebrity author tours and million dollar sales may make headlines; I've been there, but they are not part of the existence of ordinary writers. "Celebrity Writer" is a virtual oxymoron. If you get to autograph your books at your local bookstore, be grateful; this is about as far as you are likely to get. Your life is apt to be considerably more mundane. Even—dare I say it?—dull. Join me now for an advance taste of that dullness, spiced by a whole lot of attitude and gratuitous advice. This is my nature; it's what I do, in and out of fiction.

So you want to be a writer. Specifically, a science fiction writer. Congratulations; you have just signed up to be the neighborhood oddball. Your neighbors will wonder why you stay home all day instead of taking a real job, and may become suspicious because you have no visible source of support other than your hard-working spouse. Visible? There may be no writing income, period. Did you know that fewer than one in a hundred aspiring writers will ever sell material for money, and fewer yet will ever earn even a marginal living by it? That's why my first rule of writing is to have a working spouse. And yes, that is how I did it: my wife worked for years to sustain us while I was that damned fool who thought he could write. Later things changed, and I became a national bestseller. I was lucky. You probably won't be.

You won't necessarily have much support from your family, either. Say you're a typical family man—aspiring female writers may reverse the genders with impunity—with a wife, two children, a dog, and a cat. They all will have better things for you to do than sit mooning at your keyboard all day. I have been the route. I'm of retirement age now, in my 70s, but I went through the whole of it. My writing efficiency was cut in half when our first surviving child was born. (We lost three stillborn in the first decade of our marriage; that was why my wife was free to go to work, and I could afford to take the risk of writing: no family to support, then.) Yes, I learned how to feed a baby and how to change a diaper; the two sort of go together.

The experts will tell you to set a writing schedule and stick to it. Forget that; experts aren't real people. They have secretaries and things to handle the niggling details of existence. You won't be able to have a secretary or a schedule. My own example shows why.

I was the one staying home, doing nothing visible; I took care of my little girl. She was hyperactive, always in motion, even when asleep; I could not leave her for an instant, as I learned the hard way. One example will do: when she was learning to stand and walk, I turned away from her for a few seconds to change the station on the radio. When I turned back, she opened her mouth, and blood welled out. In those few seconds she had fallen against the couch and split her lip.

So when she was a baby, I put her in the bassinette on my lap and typed my novel. She liked the vibration and motion of the keys; they lulled her to sleep. But the moment I paused to think of my next sentence, she would wake and fuss. I had to keep typing, even if it was gibberish. (I see my critics nodding; now they have the explanation for my ineptitude. If you're lucky enough to make it big, they will disparage you too. It's a mark of success.) Actually, that's not the best way to write, unless you're batting out a novel in a month for Chris Baty's *No Plot, No Problem* contest, where word count is the only thing that counts. That didn't exist way back then.

So I learned a different way, and you may have to also. I starting writing my first drafts in pencil, on a clipboard. Then I was able to follow my toddler around, inside and outside, and drop the clipboard in time to catch her before she stepped onto the anthill or out onto the city street. This proved to be so versatile that I was able to write when waiting in doctor's offices—doctor's place no value on your time, only on their own, so you can wait anywhere from minutes to hours—or when traveling. Then I would type my second drafts efficiently when I had typing time. That would be when my daughter was sleeping, or when my wife was home to watch her. After 17 years of that, I realized that my daughter had gone off to college, so I no longer needed the clipboard, and I switched to the computer. But this system will work for you too; pencil is versatile, and can give you much extra working time you would otherwise lack. Keep it in mind. A computer is wonderful, but don't be chained to it beyond reason.

Even when the children are grown and gone, this does not mean you can set and keep a writing schedule. In the past year my wife came down with a slow, mysterious, debilitating illness. She lost strength in her legs, and took several falls, which did more damage. She couldn't use crutches because she lost strength in her arms too. In fact she couldn't move the wheelchair around herself; I had to heave her into and out of it, and push her around. I took over all the household chores: meals, dishes, laundry, shopping, whatever. My writing efficiency had returned to 100% with the departure of our children; now it plummeted to 25%. Schedule, schmedule; I wrote when I could. For example, I would take her to the hospital for a day-long treatment, drive home, fix my lunch, digest the mail (which could take time, without her help on the email/spam), type like mad for two hours, then drive to the hospital to pick her up. That was my writing day. Yes, I made pencil notes in the off-times. In due course they diagnosed her with CIDP, or Chronic Inflammatory Demyelinating Polyneuropathy. In plain terms, the fatty insulation around her nerves was getting eaten away, shorting out the nerves so that the signals could not get through to her muscles. Expensive treatments covered by Medicare had miraculous effect, and slowly she recovered the use of her body. Today she is free of the wheelchair, but I still do chores and accompany her to town, just in case. So the distractions of children can be replaced by those of age; there may be no free lunch here.

So how are you going to make it, if you can't make and keep a schedule? Because you do have to write, or be judged as a failure of talent or application. Apart from the clipboard, there are tricks or organization that should help. Say you're at the computer, and you can't focus immediately—a sick child or spouse can have that effect, if you are human—so you take a break by playing one of those nifty computer games. And suddenly your working time is gone and you have written nothing. It does happen. This brings into play an inexorable concept: discipline.

Yes, you have to have it. The difference between writing and a real job is that there is no boss breathing down the back of your neck to keep your nose to the grindstone. If you aren't self-motivated, you're lost. In that respect I never had much of a problem: I love writing, and I start suffering oxygen starvation when I don't write for too long a period. If you discover that you want to have written a book more than you enjoy the actual process of writing it, you have to recognize that and either have the discipline to write anyway, or to give up the dream.

Probably it's an in-between state. You may want to write, but somehow the time you have for it is not when your muse is speaking. It's called Writer's Block. If only you could get perfectly aligned, oh what a storm of writing you'd be doing! I'm not disparaging this; I've been there too. I learned in due course to summon the muse to come when I had the time, solving that problem. But the muse still visits me in her time too, such as when I'm in the shower or on a shopping trip with my wife. What to do?

Pencil and paper to the rescue! Just a little pocket-sized notepad will do, or even a folded sheet of blank paper. Scribble a note, then record the idea more fully when you have typing time. I have an Ideas file where I have several hundred notions summarized, and I go to it when I need one. You have more imagination than you think, if you could just capture every notion as it passes, and this is how. Don't trust to your memory for those notes; when you're at the machine, you may discover that you have no idea what that genius notion was. I've been there too. It's frustrating as hell. Use the damn pencil, followed by the file.

Perhaps the most frequent question I get is where do I get my ideas? Yes, capture them when they occur randomly, but what about when you have a novel to write, you're out of notions, and your muse is picking flowers in some other writer's garden? There are several things. You have to be alert for notions, so as to recognize them when they pass. For example, I was writing a children's novel, with a boy walking a long magic path. Then I had to go somewhere on our long forest drive, so I used my adult scooter, with large wheels instead of those dinky casters on children's scooters. I coasted downhill, but on my return had to keep pushing uphill. And I thought, how about a scooter than always coasts downhill, regardless of the terrain? And I went back inside and wrote a scene where the boy finds a magic scooter like that. My mind was attuned to the novel, and my mundane routine translated to a good notion. Okay, so this is fantasy; if I had been writing a science fiction novel, the scooter would have had an anti-gravity field. Same principle.

It works when you're reading, too. As a general rule, you should read nonfiction to get ideas, rather than fiction. I read science magazines galore, and they are busting out all over with new things. But even when reading fiction, you can find notions. Back when I was first getting into fantasy, having been a science fiction writer, I did some research by reading several fantasy novels. One of them was Terry Brooks' The Sword of Shanarra. At one point, as I vaguely recall more than a quarter century later, they were in a mundane setting when there was a sort of wavering, like an invisible curtain, and then there was magic. That was all, but the notion of a curtain lingered in my cranium. I would have done it differently. So in due course I did: in Split Infinity I had an invisible curtain between the high-science world of Proton and the classical-fantasy world of Phaze. Now you know. Don't copy other folks' ideas, but it is fair to do your own distinct take on them.

But mainly I don't depend on the muse at all. I work out my ideas in logical fashion, defining what I need and crafting something that meets the specs. One of the hoary amateur notions is that you have to have ideas come to you out of a clear sky, gifts of the mysterious muse. The hell you do. Grab that snake by the tail and wrestle it into the shape you need. In fact, the whole business of writing is a lot more down-to-nitty-gritty-earth than most folk realize. I think of it as being like highway construction. You need to get from here to there, and you can mark them on the map. But in between there may be a mountain, a river, a village, and an unfathomable bog. So you have to get legal access to the route you need, pay off the balky villagers, bridge the river, tunnel through the mountain, and fill in the bog after you win the environmental impact lawsuit brought by the property owner. (It turns out that he confused "bog" with "blog" and you're not trashing his web site. I'm an environmentalist myself; I wouldn't fill in a real bog.) Only then can you build your highway. So with your novel, figuratively; once all the sweat and frustration is done, critics will fault you for lacking imagination in its routing. Imagination has nothing to do with it. The sneaky truth is that your readers will not know the difference between flashes from the muse and days of misbegotten sweat: it all reads just exactly like fiction. That saw about genius being 10% inspiration, 90% perspiration is true.

I mentioned files. There's another file that relates. I keep a record of what I do each day. Not just how many words I wrote on my current novel, or how many pages I read in the current book. I note how much time I spent in town, how many letters I wrote, what video I watched, what computer game I played, and so on. I abbreviate things so they can fit on one line per day, but I do record them. Not only does that enable me to identify what I did on any past day—sometimes I need to pinpoint the date of something—it is an ox-goad of an incentive. I don't like to look back and discover I was goofing off instead of writing. You won't either. It's like that boss looking over your shoulder.

Now this is not something you have to do; you don't have to do anything I recommend here. But I never suffer writer's block, and I am constantly turning out fiction. I'm explaining my system, and it should work for you too. One of the things I have discovered is that when I crank up my computer in the morning, I am distractible. Things are racing through my mind, so that it can be hard to focus on my text. So I record my thoughts in my "Piers" file, and when I do that, they lose their power to distract me, and then I can focus on business. What thoughts? Anything at all that interests me, that isn't my actual fiction writing. How fast I ran my exercise run that morning, or how many times I hit or missed the target in my archery practice. I try to keep physically fit; I exercise seriously. That helps keep my mind fit, as I inexorably age. I note how I'm doing in my writing. I recall incidental dialogues. It's a diary; anything goes into it, and it's not for publication or reading by anyone else. Okay, today some folk have online diaries or blogs; you can do that too, if you wish. Mine is more private.

For example, one day when I went to the post office I was surprised, because it was noon Saturday and no cars were in its parking lot. Was it closed? No, it was open, so I went in to fetch my mail. Then another car came up, and a woman followed me in, and passed me, going to her box. I saw her only glimpsingly, but she was a bombshell. I wondered what a creature like that was doing out here in the hinterlands. That was all there was to it; I never saw her again. But I recorded it in my Piers file. Not that I had any ideas; I'm an old man, married 49 years, and what would such a creature ever want with me anyway? So as with bird watching, I look and appreciate without any further expectations.

And I wondered: suppose she had caught me looking? Suppose she challenged me: "What are you looking at?" What could I say? Well, maybe "I think I died, but I'm not sure where I wound up. Are you an angel or a devil?" Maybe she'd laugh. Thus my secret flight of fancy, that I would never want anyone else to read. It is safely locked in my Piers file. Just as your secret thoughts can be locked in your personal file, as you clear your mind of distractions.

Still, what about writer's block for those who can't so readily shake it? I have remarked that it's a failure of the real desire to write. That put me in danger of getting killed by other writers. They do want to write, but sometimes just can't. As with sleeping: maybe you have an important deal tomorrow and you need a good night's sleep, and can't sleep, and the more that bothers you, the wider awake you become. It can be frustrating as hell.

I realized at the outset that I could not afford writer's block. So I worked out a way around it. I call it my [bracket] system. In my early days, writing in pencil or on a manual typewriter, I had nowhere in particular to go when I stalled. So I went into [brackets] to mark off that section of my text, and discussed what the problem was. [My hero has just taken the girl he loves into his arms, and opened his mouth—and I have no idea what he says.] So then I considered various options, and finally, after much struggle, came up with a really new line: "I love you."

Okay, maybe that's a bit simplistic. But it illustrates the technique. When you stall, discuss it with yourself. Ask questions, suggest answers. You are having a dialogue with someone who is just as smart as you are. If something satisfactory doesn't occur quickly, keep discussing it, whether for a minute, an hour, or a day. Sometimes I have spent several days in brackets. Whatever it takes. The point is, you are still writing. It's not text, but it's working on it. Actually I don't use brackets any more; I use a separate file on the computer. But the principle is the same, and it still works.

One thing about the assorted files I use: I like to color code them. If your word processor will do it, make one with a yellow background, another with a light blue background, and so on. That way you'll know immediately which file you're in, and won't start typing text in your notes file or otherwise fouling up. I feel comfortable with my familiar colors, and that helps. My computer screen feels like home; everything is my way.

One question I get is about naming my characters. Over the decades I have named thousands of characters, and I try (without perfect success, memory being what it is) to avoid repetitions. So I need a constant source of new names. Well, I buy name-the-baby books and use them to name my characters. It's amazing how many different names there are, with variants. I also make notes of interesting names I encounter; that's how I came by Exene for a girl. I also note words that can be adapted as names, like Finesse, Nuance, or Chlorine. But be wary of borrowing the names of your friends, because you will lose those friends the moment your character does something they don't like.

I am paranoid about losing material, having done it on occasion. One slip with a computer can wipe out a novel. So I have several safety devices. When I write a novel, I write it one chapter at a time: that is, each chapter is a separate file. That reduces the risk; I can't wipe out more than a chapter. I also back up my material every day. And I print it out every day. So even if my computer completely wipes out, like maybe a hard disk crash—I've been there too—and the backup disk is bad, I'll still have those daily printouts.

One thing about writing: you need a space of your own. Otherwise you'll be interacting with other folk and not getting down to it. In fact my wife and I not only have space, we have computers of our own: "mine," "hers," and "ours." I write my novels on mine; she keeps our accounts on hers; we handle email on ours, which machine has no connection to the important stuff. And wouldn't you know it, we run into time conflicts on "ours." Mine is set up with all my defaults, including my Dvorak keyboard; hers is Querty. We can't even type on each other's systems, and have to change "ours" constantly from one keyboard to the other.

Something else a writer must face: rejections. The fact is you get them by the bushel, and every one hurts, even after decades of success. So what is the proper response to a rejection? "That @#$%&!! idiot wouldn't know a good piece if it hit him in the face! Because it just did." Then send it out to the next market. With luck, somewhere down the line, it will be eagerly snapped up, published, and will win awards and make you famous. Then you will have proved the rejecting editors were idiots. Meanwhile, don't let them get to you, because if they do, the idiots win.

And reviews: I read of an interview with the wife of a writer, who complained that if he got a good review, it washed out the rest of the day, and if he got a bad review, it washed out the rest of the week. So? Don't marry a writer if you don't like the attitude. Reviewers are a different and inferior species; expect the worst of them, and you may still be disappointed.

So what of the classic writer's lifestyle portrayed in movies? Where he seems to spend no time at the keyboard, instead dating lovely women, meeting servile publishers, and flying his own airplane? Forget it; no real writer lives like that. A real writer writes.

However, just so you know: there are problems for the successful writer too. You will discover that you are near the bottom of the totem when it comes to attention by your publisher. Author's copies may be late or absent, checks ditto, and your editor may be chronically absent when you call. All your publisher wants from you is what it calls content: you're a content-provider, nothing more. Not all publishers are honest, so you have to watch carefully. When I caught a publisher cheating me, near the beginning of my career, I sent a stiff query, got stonewalled, got a lawyer, got some of the money owed, and also got blacklisted for six years by that publisher and any others it could persuade. The publisher was dishonest and I had the rights of the case throughout, but others might believe the lies, and many did, including it seems an organization for writers. Today I survive, while almost all the blacklisters are out of business, but that was a matter of grit and survival rather than justice. There is a saying in the US Army: "There ain't no justice." That's sometimes true in publishing, too. This is one of the ugly sides of the business: justice can be secondary to power, and publishers have the power. I am a singularly ornery writer when it comes to dishonesty; today I don't hesitate to take legal action when it is required, and I have always won my case. It is also why I maintain a listing of electronic publishers at my <http://www.hipiers.com> site, and don't mince words when they foul up: I want other writers to have more options than I had, and to be able to protest wrongdoing without suffering retaliation. So if you get wronged, be cautious; if you protest, you may be punished rather than the bad publisher, as I was.

Another problem is fan mail. Oh, sure, it's fun to receive letters and emails praising your work. But if you answer them, as I do, it can take time. For several decades, one third of my working time has gone to answering my fan mail. That's because I do it responsively, myself. If you choose to do the same—and most writers don't—you will have to allow for that loss of time. It's not wasted; there are many intelligent and worthwhile readers out there, with valid questions and comments. But it does take time.

You will also receive solicitations. Others feel that if you are successful, they deserve what you have. Especially, they want autographs, pictures, and free books. It got so that half my fan mail consisted of sending out autographs, though I kept a list and did not honor repeat requests from the same people. There are autograph hounds out there who solicit from any name they find. When my free autographs started showing up on sale on eBay, I called a halt, and that helped bring the volume of my mail down to about half what it had been.

What else? Writing is a sedentary occupation. If you sit on your butt all day you may get a lot of text done, but you'll also get fat. I exercise seriously, with dumbbells, running, cycling, and archery. No, I'm no great shakes in any of these; that's not the point. The point is to maintain my physical health, because, would you believe, that can also have significant impact on mental health. I value my mind beyond all else; I use it to earn my living. I'm not a teetotaler, but I don't drink and write, for the same reason I don't drink and drive: it can be dangerous to my welfare. Sure there are stories about the writer with his beer chronically on his desk. But I'll bet he's not as good a writer as he would be with his mind clear. That goes double for you.

My time always seems to be at a premium, maybe because any extra time I have goes to writing. So I look for ways to save time. That's why I wear a beard: I don't have to shave every day. More recently I have grown my hair long, and I wear it in a ponytail: no more haircuts. I normally wear T-shirts and blue jeans: low upkeep. The fact is, I seldom meet anyone who is anyone, so what's the point? Actors make their living from their appearance and manner, and so do politicians. Writers don't. A writer should be largely invisible. His words may range the universe, but he is almost by definition a homebody. Writing is a solitary occupation. However, I do put on halfway respectable clothing when speaking at a local library, addressing a writer's group, or high school class, or when attending a fan convention.

Welcome to the writing life. It isn't exotic or fancy. I mow my own lawn, wash the dishes, clean up dog poop, and try to keep up with other chores. So will you. But at least you're writing. That's what counts.

APPENDIXES

CONTRIBUTORS

MICHELE ACKER
YOU'VE FINISHED YOUR SHORT STORY/NOVEL, NOW WHAT?

Michele Acker articles and short stories have been published in various online zines and newsletters. Her stories also appeared in the anthologies, *A Time To...*, *The Stygian Soul*, *Chimeraworld #2* and *F/SF*, and will be in the forthcoming *A Firestorm of Dragons*, which she also helped edit. She was a contributing author for *The Complete Guide to Writing Fantasy*.

JEANNE ALLEN
SEARCHING FOR THE DEFINITIVE DEFINITION OF SCIENCE FICTION

NAVIGATING YOUR WAY THROUGH OUTER SPACE: FACTS, THEORIES, AND CONJECTURES

Jeanne Allen is the author of the science fiction romance novel *Orphilion Dreams* and the novellas "*Isadora*" and "*Treasure of Arvalis*," both published in the critically acclaimed *Twilight Crossing*s anthologies of speculative fiction. Jeanne teaches science in the secondary school and physics and chemistry at the college freshman level. She lives in the North Woods of Minnesota.

PIERS ANTHONY
THE WRITING LIFE

Website: http://www.hipiers.com/
Piers Anthony is one of the world's most popular SF/Fantasy authors having written 131 novels at last count. His books are read and loved by millions of readers around the world, and he daily receives letters and e-mails from his devoted fans. Piers Anthony lives in Inverness, Florida.

MILENA BENINI
I DON'T KNOW THAT BUG-EYED MONSTER FROM ADAM: CLICHÉS IN SF

ATTACK OF THE MONSTER PLOT: IDEAS, SETTINGS, AND PLOTS

Website: http://www.sff.net/people/Milena/
Milena Benini is a writer, translator and editor of speculative fiction from Croatia, with a B.Litt. from St. George University, Oxford. She has written six novels. She has twice won the SFera award (Croatian national SF award), in 1998 for *Kaos (Chaos)* and in 2006 for her latest novel

McGuffin Link. She has also written numerous short stories, a number of which were published in English as well, and has taught at several writing workshops, some for genre writers and some more general. For several years, she was a member of the Critters online workshop, as well as The Horse Latitudes workshop. She edits Croatia's only SF magazine *Futura*.

ORSON SCOTT CARD
SCIENCE FICTION AS WESTERN UNION

Website: http://www.hatrack.com/

Orson Scott Card is an internationally published and award winning author. His numerous awards include being the first author to win both a Hugo and a Nebula for Best Novel in consecutive years and won a Hugo for his nonfiction book *How to Write SF & Fantasy*. He is currently a professor of writing and literature at Southern Virginia University and lives in Greensboro, North Carolina.

CAROL HIGHTSHOE
GOING WHERE OTHERS HAVE GONE BEFORE AND WANT TO GO AGAIN (FAN FICTION)

Website: http://www.carolhightshoe.com

Carol Hightshoe has been published in various anthologies and magazines including *Creature Fantastic, Illuminated Manuscripts, PanGaia Magazine, Stories of Strength, The Stygian Soul, Baen's Universe*, and *Tales of the Talisman*. In addition to her own writing, she is the editor of the online e-zines: *The Lorelei Signal* <www.loreleisignal.com> and *Sorcerous Signals* <www.sorceroussignals.com>. She is also a member of SFWA, SCBWI, Broad Universe, and Pikes Peak Writers.

IAN IRVINE
THE ART & SCIENCE OF BOOK PROMOTION

Website: http://www.ian-irvine.com

Ian Irvine is an author of nine bestselling fantasy novels, a trilogy of SF eco-thrillers and various fantasy novels for children; his books have been published in eleven countries. Ian is also a marine scientist and has developed some of Australia's national guidelines for the protection of the oceanic environment. Ian lives with his family in the mountains of northern NSW Australia.

DAVE A. LAW (Editor)
WRITING GRAPHIC NOVELS...

Dave A. Law is a published writer and editor whose short stories, poetry, articles, and comic books have seen print in various publications over the last two decades. He has a BSc in Computer Information Systems with highest honors and works as a software developer. He currently runs a software company for writers, Intellectus Enterprises <http://www.intellectusenterprises.com>, is chairman of an e-publisher, Virtual Tales <http://www.virtualtales.com>, and sits on the editorial board of *Flash Me* Magazine. He lives in Calgary, Canada with wife and two daughters.

WIL MCCARTHY
TECHNOLOGY IN SCIENCE FICTION

Website: http://www.wilmccarthy.com/

Engineer/Novelist/Journalist Wil McCarthy is a former contributing editor for *WIRED* magazine and the science columnist for the SciFi channel, where his popular "Lab Notes" column has been running since 1999. A lifetime member of the Science Fiction and Fantasy Writers of America, he has been nominated for the Nebula, Locus, AnLab, Colorado Book, Theodore Sturgeon and Philip K. Dick awards, and shares partial credit for a Webbie and a Game Developers' Choice Award. His short fiction has appeared in magazines like *Analog, Asimov's, WIRED, Aboriginal SF* and *SF Age*, and his novels include the New York Times Notable *Bloom*, Amazon.com "Best of Y2K" *The Collapsium* (a national bestseller) and, most recently, *To Crush The Moon*. He has also written for TV.

MICHAEL MCRAE
ALIEN CREATION

Michael McRae has a rather diverse background in medical science and science communication, having worked in the past as a medical scientist and more recently as a science communicator traveling around Australia, encouraging the public to see the benefits of scientific literacy and critical thinking. He has taught science in London and currently teaches secondary school in Australia. He was a contributing author to *The Complete Guide to Writing Fantasy*.

TINA MORGAN
BRINGING CHARACTERS TO LIFE

SLASH & BURN: WHEN TO MAKE YOUR MANUSCRIPT BLEED

Tina Morgan is the Managing Editor for *Fiction Factor* <http://www.fictionfactor.com/> e-zine, an online magazine for fiction writers, and publisher of *The Fractured Publisher* <http://www.fracturedpublisher.com/>, a humorous e-zine that promotes small press and e-books. Her stories, *"Soulmate"* and *"Transcendence"* appear in *The Stygian Soul* published by Double Dragon. She was a contributing author for *The Complete Guide to Writing Fantasy* and *The Fantasy Writer's Companion*.

BOB NAILOR
SCIENCE FIRST, FICTION SECOND

Bob Nailor is a science fiction and fantasy author, poet, and columnist. He was the production manager for *The Emporium Gazette*, an online writer's newspaper. Bob contributed to *The Fantasy Writer's Companion*. His stories have been included in the anthologies *13 Nights of Blood: Legends of the Vampire, Spirits of Blue and Grey: Ghosts of the Civil War*, and *The Archives of Arrissia*. He is currently the vice president of the Northwest Ohio Writer's Forum, Toledo, OH and is the coordinator for the NW Ohio Writers' Conference.

DARIN PARK (Co-Editor)
TIME LINE: A HISTORY OF SCIENCE FICTION

Darin Park was born in Newfoundland, Canada, and he has worked largely as a courtroom recorder and transcriptionist. He fell in love with Science Fiction at an early age. His favorite authors include Isaac Asimov, Robert Heinlein, and Spider Robinson. He has published eight short stories, and his humorous short, "*The Devil, You Say?*" won the Publisher's Choice Award in *Futures Magazine* in 2001. He originated the book concept and edited *The Complete Guide to Writing Fantasy* published by Dragon Moon Press.

KIM RICHARDS
THE MANY FACES OF SCIENCE FICTION: SUB-GENRES

WORLD BUILDING

Website: www.kim-richards.com

Kim Richards writes Horror, Science Fiction and Fantasy, as well as children's fiction. She wrote "*Beauty Is*" for *Surreal Magazine #4*, and has fiction to be published in the forthcoming *A Firestorm of Dragons* and *Mindscaps* anthologies. Currently, she produces a monthly newsletter for Pretty-Scary.net and a quarterly newsletter for the Santa Rosa Junior College Neighborhood Association. She lives in Santa Rosa, California.

SIMON ROSE
SCIENCE FICTION FOR YOUNGER READERS

Website: http://www.simon-rose.com/

Simon Rose has won critical acclaim and a growing and devoted fan base among children, parents, and teachers for his novels about medieval history, strange dimensions, science, and magic. His books spring from an avid interest in everything from history to science fiction to comic books. His début novel *The Alchemist's Portrait* was ranked by reviewers with the best fantasy of its kind, and the follow up, *The Sorcerer's Letterbox*, was short-listed for the Silver Birch and Diamond Willow Awards in 2005. His third novel, *The Clone Conspiracy* was described as a 'fast paced medical science mystery', and *The Emerald Curse*, published in 2006, as 'his strongest middle-grade novel yet'. Simon lives and writes in Calgary, where he is in constant demand as a presenter for youth audiences. Details on his presentations, plus interviews, readings, reviews, teacher and reader comments may be found on his website.

BUD SPARHAWK
LAUGH LINES

Website: http://www.sff.net/people/bud_sparhawk/

Bud Sparhawk has appeared frequently in SF magazines and anthologies and has been a three-time finalist for the Nebula. He has a degree in Mathematics from the University of Maryland, an MBA in Finance from Oklahoma City University and is the vice president of a small company. He lives with his wife in Annapolis, Maryland.

APPENDIX B

REFERNCES

The following is a listing of books and articles referred to throughout this guide, as well as related future readings. Although not intended to be exhaustive, this listing is a start point if you would like to read further about writing science fiction.

Unfortunately, many of the books listed are out of print. However, most are available in large libraries and used copies are typically available through your favorite online bookseller. You should also note that the Internet is volatile and sites that once existed sometimes disappear. Fortunately, if one of these links doesn't work you usually can find it on the Wayback Machine <http://www.archive.org>, an historical archive of the Internet and the pages on it.

GENERAL BOOKS

Analog and Isaac Asimov's Science Fiction Magazine. *Writing Science Fiction & Fantasy*. St. Martin's Griffin, 1993

Bova, Ben. *The Craft of Writing Science Fiction that Sells*. Cincinnati: Writer's Digest Books, 1994

Card, Orson Scott. *How to Write Science Fiction and Fantasy*. Cincinnati: Writer's Digest Books, 1990

Doctorow, Cory and Karl Schroeder. *The Complete Idiot's Guide to Publishing Science Fiction*. Alpha, 2000.

Dullemond, Tom and Darin Park, ed. *The Complete Guide to Writing Fantasy*. Calgary: Dragon Moon Press, 2003

Gerrold, David. *Worlds of Wonder. How to Write Science Fiction & Fantasy*. Cincinnati: Writer's Digest Books, 2001

Gunn, James. *The Science of Science Fiction Writing*. Lanham, Maryland: Scarecrow Press, 2000

Kilian, Crawford. *Writing Science Fiction and Fantasy*. Self-Counsel Press, 1998.

Longyear, Barry B. *Science Fiction Writer's Workshop 1. An Introduction to Fiction Mechanics*. Backinprint.com, 2002

Tuttle, Lisa. *Writing Fantasy and Science Fiction*. A&C Black, 2005

Williamson, J.N., ed. *How to Write Tales of Horror, Fantasy & Science*. Cincinnati: Writer's Digest Books, 1987.

MARKETS (SELECT)

MAJOR MARKETS

Analog Science Fiction and Fact Magazine
 <http://www.analogsf.com/information/submissions.shtml>
Asimov's Science Fiction Magazine
 <http://www.asimovs.com/info/guidelines.shtml>

Baen Books. <http://www.baen.com/FAQS.htm>
Tor Books. <http://www.tor.com/torfaq.html>

SMALL PRESS
Dragon Moon Press <http://www.dragonmoonpress.com/>
Mundania Press. <http://www.mundania.com/>

ELECTRONIC PUBLISHERS
Double Dragon Publishing. <http://www.double-dragon-ebooks.com>
Hardshell Word Factory. <http://www.hardshell.com>

MARKET SEARCH
Duotrope's Digest (Market for Writers).
 <http://www.duotrope.com/digest/index.aspx>
The Market List—The Writers Market Resource. <http://www.marketlist.com/>
Pier's Anthony's Internet Publishing. <http://www.hipiers.com/publishing.html>
Quintamid Market Database. <http://www.quintamid.com/q/mdb/list/>
Ralan's Webstravaganza. <http://www.ralan.com/>
Spicy Green Iguana. Advanced Magazine Search.
 <http://www.spicygreeniguana.com/search/index.asp>
StoryPilot's Science Fiction & Fantasy Market Search Engine. <http://storypilot.com/>
Writer's Guidelines Database. <http://www.writerswrite.com/guidelines/>
Writer's Market—Where & How to Sell What You Write.
 <http://www.writersmarket.com/index_ns.asp>

REASEARCH

ENCYCLOPEDIAS
Encyclopaedia Britannica Online. <http://www.britannica.com/>
Highbeam Reasearch. <http://www.encyclopedia.com/>
Encyclopedia Smithsonian. <http://www.si.edu/resource/faq/start.htm>
Wikipedia. <http://www.wikipedia.org/>
The Physics factbook. <www.hypertextbook.com/facts>
Ask the Experts. Scientific America.
 <http://www.sciam.com/askexpert_directory.cfm>

GENERAL
Intellectus Enterprises—Reference Links for Writers,
    http://www.intellectusenterprises.com/ref_links.html

SOFTWARE

AutoRealm—Mapmaking < http://autorealm.sourceforge.net/index.php>
Campaign Cartographer —Mapmaking. *ProFantasy*.
< http://www.profantasy.com/products/cc2.asp>
Idea Tracker—Organizing Plots/Ideas. *Intellectus Enterprises*.

< http://www.intellectusenterprises.com >
It's Full of Stars —Star Charts. Claus Bornich.
<http://www.geocities.com/CapeCanaveral/7472/ifosweb/index.htm>
Newnovelist—Novel Writing Software. *Creativity Software Ltd.*
<http://www.newnovelist.com/?source=ie>
Write Again!—Submission Tracking. *Asmoday Enterprises.* <http://www.write-again.com>

TIME LINE: A HISTORY OF SCIENCE FICTION

Raymond, Eric Steven "A Political History of SF". *Eric S. Raymond's Home Page.*
<http://www.catb.org/~esr/writings/sf-history.html> November 28, 2006
"Science Fiction". *Wikipedia.* <http://en.wikipedia.org/wiki/Science_fiction>
"A Brief History of Science Fiction & Pulp Magazines". *PULPDOM Magazine.*
    <http://www.stationlink.com/pulpdom/pulphist.html>
Taormina, Agatha. The History of Science Fiction. a Chronological Survey.
<http://www.nvcc.edu/home/ataormina/scifi/history/default.htm> November 5, 2003
"Timeline". *Ultimate Science Fiction Web Guide.*
<http://www.magicdragon.com/UltimateSF/timeline.html>

SEARCHING FOR THE DEFINITIVE DEFINITION OF SCIENCE FICTION

Bain, Darrell. "Fantasy vs. Science Fiction" December, 2002.
Douglas, Deron. Double Dragon Publishing. <http://www.double-dragon-ebooks.com>
Franklin, H. Bruce. *Preface to The St. James Guide to Science Fiction Writers.* 4th edition. Jay
    P. Pederson, Ed. Detroit: St. James Press, 1996.
Heinlein, Robert. *Expanded Universe.* "Ray Guns and Spaceships." Ace Books, 1981.
Runté, Robert, ed. "Definition of Science Fiction." *The NCF Guide to Canadian Science
    Fiction and Fandom*, 2003 Edition.
    <http://www.uleth.ca/edu/runte/ncfguide/sfdef.htm> 2000.
Science Fiction Contemporary Mythologies. New York: Longman, 1978. Introduction by
    Frederik Pohl.

THE MANY FACES OF SCIENCE FICTION: SUB-GENRES

Braunbeck, Gary A. "'Forget Genre'. Look What I Found In My Brain".
    <http://www.sff.net/people/lucy-snyder/brain/2006/03/forget-genre.html> March 13, 2006
Chilson, Rob. "Science Fiction & Fantasy. Describing Our Field". *Locus Online.*
    <http://www.locusmag.com/1998/Issues/11/Commentary_Chilson.html> November 1998.
Genreflecting. <http://www.genreflecting.com>. 2004
Gilks, Marg and Moira Allen. "The Sub-genres of Science Fiction". *Writing World.*
    <http://www.writing-world.com/sf/genres.shtml> 2003
"Glossary". *The Christian Guide to Fantasy*
    <http://www.christianfantasy.net/glossary.html>. 2000
Goldschlager, Amy. "Science Fiction & Fantasy. A Genre With Many Faces". *The SF Site.*
    <http://www.sfsite.com/columns/amy26.htm>. 1997
Louise, Anna. "Genre". *Anna Louise's Journal.*

<http://alg.livejournal.com/77377.html>. March 17, 2006

Masterson, Lee. "Science Fiction Sub-genres". *Fiction Factor*.
    <http://www.fictionfactor.com/articles/sfsubgenre.html>

Mone, Gregory. "Is Science Fiction About to Go Blind?". *Popular Science*.
    <http://www.popsci.com/popsci/science/e9fb0b4511b84010vgnvcm1000004eecbccdrcr
    d.html >. August 2004

WORLD BUILDING

BOOKS

Bank, Michael. *Understanding Science Fiction*. Morristown, N.J.: Silver Burdett Co, 1982

Gillett, Stephen L. *World Building*. Cincinnati: Writer's Digest Books, 1996

Ochoa, George and Jeffrey Osier. T*he Writer's Guide to Creating A Science Fiction Universe*.
    Cincinnati: Writer's Digest Books, 1993

ARTICLES/SITES

Baxter, Stephen. "Building New Worlds Construction and Influences". *The SFWA Bulletin*,
    <www.sfwa.org/bulletin/articles/Baxter.htm>

Lisle, Holly. "Worldbuilding—Rollicking Rules of Ecosystems". *Official Holly Lisle Author
    Website*. <http://www.hollylisle.com/fm/Articles/rules-of-ecosystems.html>

Lisle, Holly. "Questions About World Building". *Official Holly Lisle Author Website*.
    <http://hollylisle.com/fm/Articles/faqs8.html>

Masterson, Lee. "World Building 101". *Fiction Factor*.
    <http://www.fictionfactor.com/articles/worldbuilding.html>

Morgan, Tina. "Research, Research, Research". *Fiction Factor*.
    <http://www.fictionfactor.com/articles/island.html>

Morgan, Tina. "The Ethics of World Building". *Fiction Factor*.
    <http://www.fictionfactor.com/articles/ethics.html>

Morgan, Tina. "World Building for Science Fiction or Fantasy". *Fiction Factor*.
<http://fantasy.fictionfactor.com/articles/worldbuildingsf.html>

Savage, Steven. A Way With Worlds. <http://vs24.cedant.com/www/>

Strauss, Victoria. "An Impatient Writer's Approach to World Building". *The Fantasy Novels of
    Victoria Strauss*. <www.sff.net/people/victoriastrauss/impatient.html>

Swann, S. A. "Worldbuilding. Constructing a SF Universe". *S Andrew Swann's Home Page*.
    <www.sff.net/people/SASwann/text/wb.htm>

World Building. <http://users.tkk.fi/~vesanto/world.build.html>

"Worldbuilding From The Ground Up". *Writer's Write*.
    <www.writerswrite.com/journal/apr00/eoscon.htm>

World Builder Projects. <http://hiddenway.tripod.com/world/>

Wrede, Patricia C. "Fantasy Worldbuilding Questions". *SFWA*.
    <http://www.sfwa.org/writing/worldbuilding1.htm> 1996

ALIEN CREATION

Barlowe, Wayne Douglas. *Barlowe's Guide to Extraterrestrials: Great Aliens from Science
Fiction Literature*. Workman Publishing Company, 1987

Pickover, Clifford A. *The Science of Aliens.* Basic Books, 1999

Schmidt, Stanley. *Aliens and Alien Societies.* Cincinnati: Writer's Digest Books, 1996

Webb, Stephen. *If the Universe Is Teeming with Aliens... Where Is Everybody? Fifty Solutions to Fermi's Paradox and the Problem of Extraterrestrial Life.* Springer, 2002

NAVIGATING YOUR WAY THROUGH OUTER SPACE. FACTS, THEORIES, AND CONJECTURES

MULTIPLE TOPICS

Hartmann, William K. and Chris Impey. *Astronomy. The Cosmic Journey.* Pacific Grove, CA: Brooks/Cole, 2002.

Hawking, Stephen. *A Brief History of Time.* New York: Bantam Books, 1988.

Hawking, Stephen. *The Universe in a Nutshell.* New York: Bantam Books, 2001.

"The History and Future of Space Exploration." *TheSpaceSite.com.* <http://www.thespacesite.com/space_contents.html> Series of articles.

Rees, Martin, Editor. *Universe, the Definitive Visual Guide.* Dorling Kindersley, 2005.

Scientific American Quarterly Issue. The Future of Space Travel. 11 May 1999. Series of articles.

SPACE IS A MIGHTY BIG PLACE...

Brown, Dwayne, et al. "*NASA's Pluto Mission Launched Toward New Horizons.*" Kennedy News. <http://www.nasa.gov/mission_pages/newhorizons/news/release-20060119.html> 19 Jan. 2006.

"Interstellar Mission." Voyager. The Interstellar Mission. *NASA Jet Propulsion Laboratory.* <http://voyager.jpl.nasa.gov/mission/interstellar.html> 25 Aug. 2005.

Powell, Corey S. "Field Guide to the Entire Universe." *Discover.* Dec. 2005. 28-35.

THE COLD, COLD VACUUM OF SPACE

Landis, Geoffrey A. "*Human Exposure to Vacuum.*" <http://www.sff.net/people/Geoffrey.Landis/vacuum.html> Revised, 8 Jan. 2001.

GRAVITY, ANYONE? AND PSYCHOLOGICAL EFFECTS OF SPACE TRAVEL

Graham, John F. "*Chapter 31. The Human Body in Outer Space.*" Space Exploration. From Talisman of the Past to Gateway for the Future. <http://www.space.edu/projects/book/chapter31.html> 1995.

Hall, Theodore W. "*Artificial Gravity and the Architecture of Orbital Habitats.*" Space Future. <http://www.spacefuture.com/archive/artificial_gravity_and_the_architecture_of_orbital_habitats.shtml> 20 Mar. 1997.

HAZARDS OF RADIATION

Parker, Eugene N. "Shielding Space Travelers." *Scientific American.* Mar. 2006. 40-47.

Semeniuk, Ivan. "Showered in Mystery." *Astronomy.* Jan. 2001. 43-47.

Suplee, Curt. "The Sun. Living With a Stormy Star." *National Geographic.* July 2004. 4-33.

REDESIGNING HUMANS TO WITHSTAND THE TRIP

Kurzweil, Ray. *The Age of Spiritual Machines*. New York: Penguin Books. 1999.

"Nanotechnology. Drexler and Smalley make the case for and against 'molecular assemblers.'" *Chemical & Engineering News*. <http://pubs.acs.org/cen/coverstory/8148/print/8148counterpoint.html> 1 Dec. 2003.

Popular Science. Cover. *Here Comes the Super Human*. Sept. 2005. Series of articles.

Siegfried, Tom. "Exodus from Earth." *Astronomy*. Jan. 2000. 51-55.

RELATIVISTIC EFFECTS AND TIME TRAVEL

Davies, Paul. "How to Build a Time Machine." *Scientific American*. September, 2002. 50-55.

Hawking, Stephen. "A Brief History of Relativity." *Time*. Dec. 1999. 67-81.

FUTURE SPACECRAFT

Aldrin, Buzz. "Roadmap to Mars." *Popular Mechanics*. Dec. 2005. 65-71.

Collins, Graham P. "Antimatter Propulsion. What Would It Take?" *Scientific American*. June 2005. 85.

Ford, Lawrence H. and Thomas A. Roman. "Negative Energy, Wormholes and Warp Drive." *Scientific American*. Jan. 2000. 46-53.

Hoversten, Paul. "Deep Space 1 sets record with ion propulsion system." Space.com. <http://www.space.com/scienceastronomy/solarsystem/deepspace_propulsion_000816.html> 17 Aug. 2000.

"Hyperspace (science fiction)." Wikipedia. <http://en.wikipedia.org/wiki/Hyperspace_%28science_fiction%29>. Page last modified. 11 Oct. 2006.

Lepre, Lyn, and Dr. Tony Phillips. "Setting Sail for the Stars." *Science@NASA Headline News*. <http://science.nasa.gov/headlines/y2000/ast28jun_1m.htm> 28 June 2000.

McCarthy, Will. "Faster Than Light, Part II. The Quantum Connection." SciFi.com Lab Notes. <http://www.scifi.com/sfw/issue199/labnotes.html>.

Millis, Mark G. "Prospects for Breakthrough Propulsion from Physics." NASA Breakthrough Propulsion Physics (BPP) Project. <http://gltrs.grc.nasa.gov/reports/2004/TM-2004-213082.pdf> May 2004.

Odenwald, Dr. Sten. "Hyperspace in Science Fiction." *The Astronomy Cafe*. <http://www.astronomycafe.net/anthol/scifi2.html> 1995.

Overbye, Dennis. "On Gravity, Oreos and a Theory of Everything." *The New York Times*. 1 Nov. 2005.

"Tachyon." Wikipedia. <http://en.wikipedia.org/wiki/Tachyon> Page last modified. 29 Sept. 2006.

Zeilinger, Anton. "Quantum Teleportation." *Scientific American*. Apr. 2000. 50-59.

Zona, Kathleen, Editor, Warp Drive, When? NASA. Glenn Research Center. Last updated. March 17, 2006. <http://www.nasa.gov/centers/glenn/research/warp/warp.html> Series of articles.

MIGRATION FROM EARTH

"Long-term space travel (Generation Ships)." *Astrobiology. The Living Universe*. <http://library.thinkquest.org/C003763/index.php?page=future02> 2001.

SEARCHING FOR ALIENS

"The Drake Equation." *Nova Origins*. PBS. (Link to interactive.)
<http://www.pbs.org/wgbh/nova/origins/drake.html> July 2004.
SETI Institute, Search for Extraterrestrial Intelligence.
<http://www.seti.org/site/pp.asp?c=ktJ2J9MMIsE&b=178025>

CONCLUSION

Ferris, Timothy, "Interstellar Spaceflight. Can We Travel to the Stars?" *Scientific American Quarterly Issue*. The Future of Space Travel. 11 May 1999. 88-91.

I DON'T KNOW THAT BUG-EYED MONSTER FROM ADAM. CLICHÉS IN SF

Cherryh, C. J. "Writerisms and other Sins. A Writer's Shortcut to Stronger Writing". *SFWA*.
<http://www.sfwa.org/writing/chadvce.htm> 1995
Freedman, Terry and David, eds. *The Wordsworth Dictionary of Cliché*. Wordsworth, 1996.
McIntyre, Vonda N. "Pitfalls of Writing Science Fiction & Fantasy".
<http://www.sff.net/people/Vonda/Pitfalls.html> September 8, 2003
Sterling, Bruce. "Turkey City Lexicon". *SFWA*.
<http://www.sfwa.org/writing/turkeycity.html>

ATTACK OF THE MONSTER PLOT. IDEAS, SETTINGS, AND PLOTS

GENERAL

Allen, William Rodney, ed. *Conversations with Kurt Vonnegut*. University Press of Mississippi, 2003.
Booth, Wayne C. *The Rhetoric of Fiction*. University of Chicago Press, 1961.
Eco, Umberto. *Faith in Fakes—Travels in Hyperreality*. Random House, 1986.
Forster, E.M. *Aspects of the Novel*. Penguin, 1970.
Miller , James E., jr., ed. *Myth and Method*. University of Nebraska Press, 1960.
Mukarovsky, Jan. *Literary Structures, Norms and Values*. MH, 1999.
Vipond, Dianne L., ed. *Conversations with John Fowles*. University Press of Mississippi, 2003.

SCIENCE-FICTION SPECIFIC : BOOKS

Aldiss, Brian and Wingrove, David. *Trillion Year Spree. The History of Science Fiction*. Gollancz, 1986.
Alkon, Paul K. *Science Fiction before 1900*. Routledge, 2002.
Freedman, Carl. *Critical Theory and Science Fiction*. Wesleyan University Press, 2000.
LeGuin, Ursula K. and Attebery, Brian, eds. *Teacher's Guide to Accompany the Norton Book of Science Fiction*. W.W.Norton, 1993.
LeGuin, Ursula K. *The Language of the Night. Essays on Fantasy and Science Fiction* (revised edition). HarperPerennial, 1992.
London, Brooks. *Science Fiction after 1900*. Routledge, 2002.
Mann, George, ed. *The Mammoth Encyclopaedia of Science Fiction*. Robinson, 2001.
Roberts, Alan. *Science Fiction*. Routledge, 2000.
Suvin, Darko. *Metamorphoses of Science Fiction*. Yale University Press, 1979.

ARTICLES/SITES

"Clarke's three laws". Wikipedia. <http://en.wikipedia.org/wiki/Clarke's three laws>
The Dream Café <http://www.dreamcafe.com/main.cgi>
Making Light. <http://www.nielsenhayden.com/makinglight/>
Preditors and Editors. <http://invirtuo.cc/prededitors/>
"SF and Genre". *The Internet Review of Science Fiction.*
   <http://www.irosf.com/forum/thread.qsml?thid=10091>
SF Site. <http://www.sfsite.com/>
Stephen Hunt's SF Crowsnest. <http://www.computercrowsnest.com/>
Treitel, Richard. "Science versus Magic". What is Science Fiction.
   <http://www.treitel.org/Richard/sf/magic.html>

CRAFT OF WRITING

BOOKS

Kress, Nancy. *Beginnings, Middles & Ends.* Cincinnati: Writer's Digest Books, 1999
Lukeman, Noah. *The First Five Pages.* Fireside, 2000.

ARTICLES

Allen, Roger MacBride. "The Standard Deviations of Writing". *SFWA.*
   <http://www.sfwa.org/writing/mistakes_allen.htm> January 4, 2005
Bradley, Marion Zimmer. "What is a Short Story?" *Marion Zimmer Bradley Literary Works Trust.* <http://mzbworks.home.att.net/what.htm> 1996
Bradley, Marion Zimmer. "Why Did my Story Get Rejected?" *Marion Zimmer Bradley Literary Works Trust.* <http://mzbworks.home.att.net/why.htm> 1997
Collins, Ron. "The Purpose and Structure of a Story". *Typoshere.*
   <http://www.typosphere.com/essays/purpose_of_structure.htm> 1996
Lisle, Holly. "One-Pass Manuscript Revision". *Holly Lisle Official Author Website.*
   <http://www.hollylisle.com/fm/Workshops/one-pass-revision.html> June 2002
Smith. David. "Being a Glossary of Terms Useful in Critiquing Science Fiction". *SFWA.*
   <http://www.sfwa.org/writing/glossary.html> January 4, 2005
Watt Evans, Lawrence. "Watt-Evans' Laws of Fantasy (& More)". *The Misenchanged Page.*
   <http://www.watt-evans.com/lawsoffantasy.html> May 28, 1997

PLOTTING

"Character Arc". Wikipedia. <http://en.wikipedia.org/wiki/Character_arc>
Cannell, Stephen J. "What is the Three Act Structure?" Writer's Write. <http://www.writerswrite.com/screenwriting/lecture4.htm> 2003
Hayden, Teresa Nielson. "The Evil Overlord Devised a Plot". Viable Paradise.
   <http://www.sff.net/paradise/plottricks.htm> 2000
"Story Arc". Wikipedia. <http://en.wikipedia.org/wiki/Story_arc>
Swann, S. Andrew. "On Plot". S. Andrew Swann's Home Page.
   <http://www.sff.net/people/SASwann/text/plot.htm> July 1, 2006
Rossio, Terry. "The Storyteller Cut". Wordplay
   <http://www.wordplayer.com/columns/wp45.The.Storyteller.Cut.html> 2003

GOING WHERE OTHERS HAVE GONE BEFORE AND WANT TO GO AGAIN (FAN FICTION)

Bunnell, John C. "About Fanfic". <http://www.sff.net/people/jcbunnell/aboutfic.htm>
The Fanfic Symposium. <http://www.trickster.org/symposium/symp173.htm>
Fanfiction.net. <http://www.fanfiction.net/>
The Official Mary Sue Society Avatar Appreciation Site.
   <http://www.subreality.com/marysue.htm>
Templeton, Brad. "10 Big Myths about Copyright Explained". Brad Templeton's Home Page.
   <http://www.templetons.com/brad/copymyths.html> October 2004

WRITING GRAPHIC NOVELS AND OTHER FORMS OF SEQUENTIAL ART

BOOKS

Eisner, Will. *Comics and Sequential Art*. Poorhouse Press, 1985
Eisner, Will. *Graphic Storytelling*. Poorhouse Press, 1996
Haines, Lurene. *Writer's Guide to Business of Comics*. Watson-Guptill,1998
McCloud, Scott. *Understanding Comics*. Harper Paperbacks, 1994
McCloud, Scott. *Reinventing Comics*. Harper Paperbacks, 2000
Moore, Alan. *Alan Moore's Writing for Comics*. Avatar Press, 2003
O'Neil, Dennis. *DC Comics Guide to Writing Comics*. Watson-Guptill, 2001
Panel One. *Comic Book Scripts by Top Writers*. About Comics, 2002
Panel Two. *More Comic Book Scripts by Top Writers*. About Comics, 2003
Salisbury, Mark. *Writers On Comics Scriptwriting*. Titan Books Ltd, 2002

SITES

Creating Comics. <http://www.members.shaw.ca/creatingcomics/books.html>

SO YOU'VE FINISHED YOUR SHORT STORY / NOVEL, NOW WHAT?

WORKSHOPS

Clarion Science Fiction and Fantasy Writers' Workshop. <http://clarion.ucsd.edu/>
Odyssey: The Fantasy Writing Workshop. <http://www.sff.net/odyssey/>
Writing the Break out Novel. <http://www.free-expressions.com/success.htm>

CONFERENCES

The Guide to Writer's Conferences and Workshops. <http://writing.shawguides.com/>

NEWSLETTERS

Fiction Factor. <www.fictionfactor.com>
Speculations. <http://www.speculations.com/>
SpecFicMe Newsletter. <http://www.specficworld.com/sfme.html>

ARTICLES

Rothman, Chuck. "What is a Word?" SFWA. <http://www.sfwa.org/writing/wordcount.htm> January 4, 2005

AGENTS

AgentQuery: Find the Agent Who Will Find You a Publisher
<http://www.agentquery.com/>
The Association of Authors' Representatives (AAR). <http://www.aar-online.org/mc/page.do>
Publishers Marketplace. <http://www.publishersmarketplace.com/>

EDITOR BLOGS

Evil Editor. <http://www.evileditor.blogspot.com/>
Crapometer. <http://www.crapometer.blogspot.com/>

SCAMS

Preditors & Editors. <http://www.anotherealm.com/prededitors/>
Writer Beware. <http://www.sfwa.org/beware/>

THE ART & SCIENCE OF BOOK PROMOTION

BOOKS

Blanco, Jodee. *The Complete Guide to Book Publicity*. Allworth Press, 2004
Gladwell, Malcolm. *The Tipping Point. Little*, Brown & Co. 2002
Harrow, Susan. *The Ultimate Guide to Getting Booked on Oprah*. Harrow Communications, 2004
Hatchigan, Jessica. *Be your own Publicist*. McGraw Hill. 2002
Levinson, J C, R Frishman and M Larsen. *Guerilla Marketing for Writers*. Cincinnati: Writer's Digest Books, 2001
Raab, Susan. *An Author's Guide to Children's Book Promotion*. Two Lives Publishing, 2005
Robertson, Robin ed. *Mortification. Writer's Stories of their Public Shame*. Harper Perennial, 2003

ARTICLES/SITES

Bennett, Steve. "Ten Essential Tips for Succesful Interviews". Media Mentor. <http://www.mediamentor.com/authors/tentips.html> 2004
The Official Web Site of Orson Scott Card <http://www.hatrack.com>
Irvine, Ian. "The Truth about Publishing". <http://members.ozemail.com.au/~irvinei/publishing.html> January 2005
Holly Lisle Official Author Website. <http://www.hollylisle.com/>
Robert J Sawyer. <http://www.sfwriter.com/>
Smith, Katherine. "The Five Golden Rules of Publicity For Authors". Writers Write. <http://www.writerswrite.com/journal/oct02/ksmith.htm> November 2002

ENDNOTES

[1] Gerrold, David. *Worlds of Wonder. How to Write Science Fiction & Fantasy*. Cincinnati: Writer's

Digest Books, 2001. Quote used with the permissions of the author and publisher.

[2] Bova, Ben. *The Craft of Writing Science Fiction that Sells.* Cincinnati: Writer's Digest Books, 1994. Quote used with the permissions of the author and publisher.

[3] Heinlein, Robert. *Expanded Universe.* "Ray Guns and Spaceships." Ace Books, 1981. Quote used with the permission of The Heinlein Prize Trust and Spectrum Literary Agency.

[4] *Science Fiction Contemporary Mythologies.* New York: Longman, 1978. Introduction by Frederik Pohl. Quote used with the permission of the author.

[5] Franklin, H. Bruce. Preface to *The St. James Guide to Science Fiction Writers.* 4th edition. Jay P. Pederson, Ed. Detroit: St. James Press, 1996. Quote used with the permission of the author.

[6] Douglas, Deron. Double Dragon Publishing. <http://www.double-dragon-ebooks.com> Quote used permission.

[7] Runté, Robert, ed. "Definition of Science Fiction." *The NCF Guide to Canadian Science Fiction and Fandom, 2003 Edition.* <http://www.uleth.ca/edu/runte/ncfguide/sfdef.htm> 2000. Quote used with the permission of the editor.

[8] Card, Orson Scott. *How to Write Science Fiction and Fantasy.* Cincinnati: Writer's Digest Books, 1990. Quote used with the permissions of the author and publisher.

[9] Gunn, James. *The Science of Science Fiction Writing.* Lanham, Maryland: Scarecrow Press, 2000. Quote used with the permissions of the author and publisher.

[10] Bain, Darrell. "Fantasy vs. Science Fiction" December, 2002. Quote used with the permission of the author.

[11] Elkins, Thomas. "Oblate Spheroid". *Regents Exam Prep Center.* <http://regentsprep.org/Regents/earthsci/units/introduction/oblate.cfm>

[12] Hamilton, Rosanna L. "The Moon". *Views of the Solar System.* <http://solarviews.com/eng/moon.htm>

[13] Barrett, Paul. "Re: Why is Venus the hottest planet, and Mercury is more near the sun?". *MadSci Network.* <http://www.madsci.org/cgi-bin/cgiwrap/www/circR?/posts/archives/2000-12/976245331.As.r.html>

[14] Berger, Dan. "Re: Do you think that there is any possibility to the 'hollow earth theory' ?" *MadSci Network.* <http://www.madsci.org/cgi-bin/cgiwrap/www/circR?/posts/archives/1997-12/873378252.Es.r.html>

[15] Carter, Lynn and Dave Kornreich. "Can you hear sounds in space?" *Ask an Astronomer.* <http://curious.astro.cornell.edu/question.php?number=8>

[16] "Hadron". *Wikipedia.* <http://en.wikipedia.org/wiki/Hadron>

[17] "Pluto". *Wikipedia.* <http://en.wikipedia.org/wiki/Pluto>

[18] Bellis, Mary. "The Saga of the Submarine". *About.com.* <http://inventors.about.com/library/inventors/blsubmarine5.htm>

[19] Crisafulli, Michael & Karen. "Jules Verne's Nautilus". *Gallifrey.* <http://home.att.net/~karen.crisafulli/nautilus.html>

[20] Pérez, Ariel, Garmt de Vries and Jean-Michel Margot. "Jules Verne FAQ". *Zvi Har'El's Jules Verne Collection.* <http://jv.gilead.org.il/FAQ/#C1>

[21] "A Princess of Mars". *Wikipedia.* <http://en.wikipedia.org/wiki/A_Princess_of_Mars>

[22] "USS Nautilus (SSN-571)". *Wikipedia.*

<http://en.wikipedia.org/wiki/USS_Nautilus_%28SSN-571%29>

[23] "A Gravity Assist Primer". *NASA Jet Propulsion Laboratory.*
<http://www2.jpl.nasa.gov/basics/grav/primer.html>

[24] "Is zero-G hazardous to your cells?", *MSNBC,*
http://www.msnbc.com/news/434229.asp?cp1=1

[25] Malik, Tariq. "Red Planet Calling: How Mars Probes Phone Home". *SPACE.Com.*
<http://www.space.com/businesstechnology/technology/calling_mars_031008.html>

[26] "Understanding life in extreme environments". *USA Today.*
<http://www.usatoday.com/news/science/biology/life-extreme-envior.htm>

[27] Angelo, Carlos. "Heinlein". *Carlos Angelo.* <http://www.wegrokit.com/bio.htm>

[28] "Catherine Asaro". *Wikipedia.* <http://en.wikipedia.org/wiki/Catherine_Asaro>

[29] "Isaac Asimov". *Wikipedia.* <http://en.wikipedia.org/wiki/Isaac_Asimov>

[30] Bianchi, Reinaldo A. C. "Arthur C. Clarke Biography". *Arthur C. Clarke Unauthorized Homepage.* <http://www.lsi.usp.br/~rbianchi/clarke/ACC.Biography.html>

[31] "Edgar Rice Burroughs". *Wikipedia.*
<http://en.wikipedia.org/wiki/Edgar_Rice_Burroughs>

[32] "Average Annual Earrings Per Full-Time Employee, By Industry: 1900—1960". *Smart Fun.*
<http://www.hfmgv.org/education/smartfun/modelt/carowners/earnings.html>

[33] "Roger Zelazny". *Wikipedia.* <http://en.wikipedia.org/wiki/Roger_Zelazny>

[34] "Frank Herbert". *Wikipedia.* <http://en.wikipedia.org/wiki/Frank_Herbert>

[35] "Fiction Submission Guidelines". *Strange Horizons*
http://www.strangehorizons.com/guidelines/fiction.shtml>

[36] Masterson, Lee. "Science Fiction Sub-genres". *Fiction Factor.*
<http://www.fictionfactor.com/articles/sfsubgenre.html>

[37] Gilks, Marg and Moira Allen. "The Sub-genres of Science Fiction". *Writing World.*
<http://www.writing-world.com/sf/genres.shtml>

[38] Masterson, Lee. "Science Fiction Sub-genres". *Fiction Factor.*
<http://www.fictionfactor.com/articles/sfsubgenre.html>

[39] Goldschlager, Amy. "Science Fiction & Fantasy: A Genre With Many Faces". *The SF Site.*
<http://www.sfsite.com/columns/amy26.htm>

[40] Mielville, China. <http://www.darkecho.com/darkecho/workshop/terms.html>

[41] Philbin, Mike. Personal email. March 6, 2006

[42] Mone, Gregory. "Is Science Fiction About to Go Blind?" *Popular Science*, August 2004

[43] Lisle, Holly. "Questions About World building". *Official Holly Lisle Author Website.*
<http://hollylisle.com/fm/Articles/faqs8.html>

[44] Strauss, Victoria. "An Impatient Writer's Approach to World building". *The Fantasy Novels of Victoria Strauss.* <www.sff.net/people/victoriastrauss/impatient.html>

[45] Strauss, Victoria. "An Impatient Writer's Approach to World building". *The Fantasy Novels of Victoria Strauss.* <www.sff.net/people/victoriastrauss/impatient.html>

[46] Savage, Steven. "It is the little things that count". *A Way With Worlds.*
<http://www.seventhsanctum.com/www/column/WayWorld2.html>

[47] Savage, Steven. "Your Main Character". *A Way With Worlds.* <http://www.seventh-sanctum.com/www/column/WayWorld1.html>

[48] Card, Orson Scott. *How to Write Science Fiction and Fantasy.* Cincinnati: Writer's Digest Books, 1990.

[49] Baxter, Stephen. "Building New Worlds Construction and Influences". *The SFWA Bulletin,*
<www.sfwa.org/bulletin/articles/Baxter.htm>

[50] Bova, Ben. *The Craft of Writing Science Fiction that Sells*. Cincinnati: Writer's Digest Books, 1994

[51] Ibid

[52] Card, Orson Scott. *How to Write Science Fiction and Fantasy*. Cincinnati: Writer's Digest Books, 1990

[53] Savage, Steven. "Pyramids of Power". *A Way With Worlds*.
<http://www.seventhsanctum.com/www/column/WayWorld6.html>

[54] Savage, Steven. "Getting a Vision". *A Way With Worlds*.
<http://www.seventhsanctum.com/www/column/WayWorld7.html>

[55] Morgan, Tina. "Research, Research, Research". *Fiction Factor*.
<http://www.fictionfactor.com/articles/island.html>

[56] Morgan, Tina. "The Ethics of World Building". *Fiction Factor*.
<http://www.fictionfactor.com/articles/ethics.html>

[57] Morgan, Tina. "World Building for Science Fiction or Fantasy". *Fiction Factor*.
<http://fantasy.fictionfactor.com/articles/worldbuildingsf.html>

[58] Bank, Michael. *Understanding Science Fiction*. Morristown, N.J.: Silver Burdett Co, 1982

[59] Morgan, Tina. "The Ethics of World Building". *Fiction Factor*.
<http://www.fictionfactor.com/articles/ethics.html>

[60] Baxter, Stephen. "Building New Worlds Construction and Influences". *The SFWA Bulletin*,
<www.sfwa.org/bulletin/articles/Baxter.htm>

[61] Bank, Michael. *Understanding Science Fiction*. Morristown, N.J.: Silver Burdett Co, 1982

[62] Bova, Ben. *The Craft of Writing Science Fiction that Sells*. Cincinnati: Writer's Digest Books, 1994

[63] Savage, Steven. "It is the little things that count". *A Way With Worlds*.
<http://www.seventhsanctum.com/www/column/WayWorld2.html>

64 Strauss, Victoria. "An Impatient Writer's Approach to World building". *The Fantasy Novels of Victoria Strauss*. <www.sff.net/people/victoriastrauss/impatient.html>

[65] Savage, Steven. "Your Main Character". *A Way With Worlds*. <http://www.seventhsanctum.com/www/column/WayWorld1.html>

[66] Swann, S. A. "Worldbuilding. Constructing a SF Universe". *S Andrew Swann's Home Page*.
<www.sff.net/people/SASwann/text/wb.htm>

[67] "Worldbuilding From The Ground Up". *Writer's Write*.
<www.writerswrite.com/journal/apr00/eoscon.htm>

[68] "Worldbuilding From The Ground Up". *Writer's Write*.
<www.writerswrite.com/journal/apr00/eoscon.htm>

[69] Bova, Ben. *The Craft of Writing Science Fiction that Sells*. Cincinnati: Writer's Digest Books, 1994

[70] Savage, Steven. "Your Main Character". *A Way With Worlds*. <http://www.seventhsanctum.com/www/column/WayWorld1.html>

[71] Bova, Ben. *The Craft of Writing Science Fiction that Sells*. Cincinnati: Writer's Digest Books, 1994

[72] Banks, Michael. *Understanding Science Fiction*. Morristown, N.J.: Silver Burdett Co, 1982

[73] Morgan, Tina. "World Building for Science Fiction or Fantasy". *Fiction Factor*.
<http://fantasy.fictionfactor.com/articles/worldbuildingsf.html>

[74] "Worldbuilding From The Ground Up". *Writer's Write*.
<www.writerswrite.com/journal/apr00/eoscon.htm>

[75] Baxter, Stephen. "Building New Worlds Construction and Influences". *The SFWA Bulletin*,
<www.sfwa.org/bulletin/articles/Baxter.htm>

[76] Masterson, Lee. "World Building 101". *Fiction Factor*.
<http://www.fictionfactor.com/articles/worldbuilding.html>

[77] Baxter, Stephen. "Building New Worlds Construction and Influences". *The SFWA Bulletin*, <www.sfwa.org/bulletin/articles/Baxter.htm>

[78] Ibid

[79] Bova, Ben. *The Craft of Writing Science Fiction that Sells.* Cincinnati: Writer's Digest Books, 1994

[80] Swann, S. A. "Worldbuilding. Constructing a SF Universe". *S Andrew Swann's Home Page.* <www.sff.net/people/SASwann/text/wb.htm>

[81] Savage, Steven. "Magic and Technology". *A Way With Worlds.* <http://www.seventh-sanctum.com/www/column/WayWorld5.html>

[82] Morgan, Tina. "Research, Research, Research". *Fiction Factor.* <http://www.fictionfactor.com/articles/island.html>

[83] Swann, S. A. "Worldbuilding. Constructing a SF Universe". *S Andrew Swann's Home Page.* <www.sff.net/people/SASwann/text/wb.htm>

[84] Savage, Steven. "Magic and Technology". *A Way With Worlds.* <http://www.seventh-sanctum.com/www/column/WayWorld5.html>

[85] Savage, Steven. "Intelligent Life and Culture". *A Way With Worlds.* <http://www.seventh-sanctum.com/www/column/WayWorld4.html>

[86] Savage, Steven. "Intelligent Life and Culture". *A Way With Worlds.* <http://www.seventh-sanctum.com/www/column/WayWorld4.html>

[87] Savage, Steven. "In the Beginning... there is a lot of planning". *A Way With Worlds.* <http://www.seventhsanctum.com/www/column/WayWorld3.html>

[88] Lisle, Holly. "Worldbuilding—Rollicking Rules of Ecosystems". *Official Holly Lisle Author Website.* <http://www.hollylisle.com/fm/Articles/rules-of-ecosystems.html>

[89] Card, Orson Scott. *How to Write Science Fiction and Fantasy.* Cincinnati: Writer's Digest Books, 1990

[90] Bova, Ben. *The Craft of Writing Science Fiction that Sells.* Cincinnati: Writer's Digest Books, 1994

[91] Savage, Steven. "Retcon as Continuity". *A Way With Worlds.* <http://www.seventh-sanctum.com/www/column/WayWorld9.html>

[92] Swann, S. A. "Worldbuilding. Constructing a SF Universe". *S A. Swann's Home Page.* <www.sff.net/people/SASwann/text/wb.htm>

[93] NASA Institute for Advanced Concepts <http://www.niac.usra.edu/index.html> Quote by Robert A. Cassanova and Sharon M. Garrison, used with permission.

[94] This is not strictly true, of course: particularly lately, a school of thought has emerged that defines genre fiction through the readers' perception, and not its' content, but this is irrelevant as far as this book is concerned. For those who are interested, however, see, for example, the discussion at IROSF (Internet Review of Science Fiction) forum, <http://www.irosf.com/forum/thread.qsml?thid=10091>.

[95] *Sky High,* feature film. USA: Disney Studios, 2005

[96] McCaffrey, Anne. *The Ship Who Sang.* New York: Ballantine Books, 1970

[97] Bujold, Lois McMaster. *Cetaganda.* New York: Baen Books, 1996

[98] Card, Orson Scott. "Interview with Orson Scott Card". *Fiction Factor.* <http://www.fictionfactor.com/interviews/orsonscottcard.html> 2000

[99] How careful Clarke was can best be illustrated by the following anecdote: in the making of the movie, the background of one scene required instructions for the use of toilette in a space station. Even though it was just background for a short scene, Clarke wrote the

INDEX

A

T

U

V

W

X

CPSIA information can be obtained at www.ICGtesting.com
Printed in the USA
BVOW03s1600280714

360752BV00002B/59/P